DATE DUE			
OC 14 '97			

The Natural History of Puget Sound Country

The Natural History of

A Weyerhaeuser Environmental Book

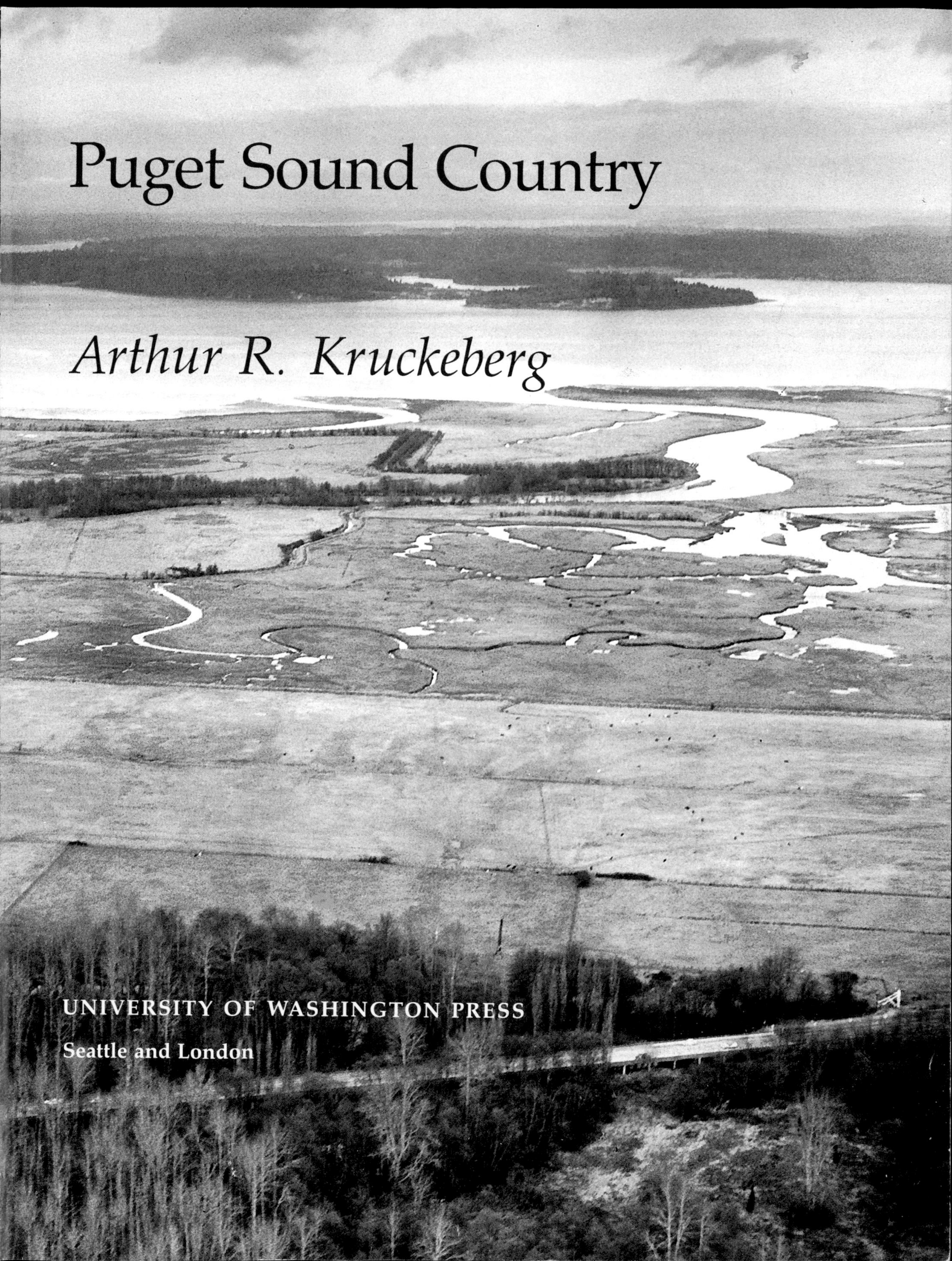

Puget Sound Country

Arthur R. Kruckeberg

UNIVERSITY OF WASHINGTON PRESS

Seattle and London

The Natural History of Puget Sound Country has been published with the assistance of a grant from the Weyerhaeuser Environmental Books Endowment, established by the Weyerhaeuser Company Foundation, members of the Weyerhaeuser family, and Janet and John Creighton.

Library of Congress Cataloging-in-Publication Data
Kruckeberg, Arthur R.
  The natural history of Puget Sound country / Arthur R. Kruckeberg.
    p. cm.
  Includes bibliographical references and index.
  ISBN 0-295-97019-7 (alk. paper)
    1. Natural history—Washington (State)—Puget Sound Region.
  2. Man—Influence on nature—Washington (State)—Puget Sound Region. I. Title.
  QH105.W2K78   1991
  508.797'7—dc20   90-12368
                                                            CIP

*Title-page photo: Nisqually Delta
(Courtesy of the Washington State
Department of Wildlife.)*

*Puget country—that westernmost
piece of the Pacific Northwest, so
lavishly endowed by Nature—is a
natural drainage basin (defined by the
heavy line), its waters running into
the grand inland sea, Puget Sound.
(Map by Nancy Eberle.)*

To Ruth Kirk, Frank Richardson, and Victor Scheffer,
sensitive and articulate interpreters of our region's
natural history

Contents

*Puget country is rich in aquatic habitats,
with lush hardwood vegetation at their
borders. Nisqually Wildlife Refuge,
Pierce County. (Photo by Mary
Randlett.)*

Maps

*Rock and subalpine forest form the
high eastern rim of Puget country.
Stevens Canyon, Mount Rainier
National Park. (Photo by Ruth and
Louis Kirk.)*

Preface

The chief aim of this book is to give its readers a measure of understanding about the workings of natural systems in the Puget Sound basin. Ecological understanding is a cultural imperative for each of us as we live out the last years of the twentieth century. And what better place to begin that deeper appreciation than in the place we live? From such appreciation can come wise decisions and actions to preserve and protect what is left of the Puget Sound basin's natural beauty and wild, self-sustaining life in variety.

All life is part of a regional and global fabric. Each organism draws upon finite resources and energy. Each interacts competitively or cooperatively with a neighbor. Some interactions are direct and close-knit, like the preying of sea gulls on fishes. Others are more indirect, often so remote that only when the intervening links of the chain of interaction are broken, can the connections be detected. For example, it is hard to link the decomposing activity of bacteria in the Skagit Bay mud flats with the subalpine forest-and-meadow communities on the slopes of Mount Baker. But it is inevitable that human interventions, or a natural but catastrophic change on the slopes of the mountain, will agitate the web of relationships in the mud-flat ecosystem. The vast accumulation of mud-flow material that poured into the Cowlitz and Columbia rivers immediately following the 1980 eruption of Mount St. Helens is a dramatic case in point.

From the arrival of North American Indians on the scene to the ever-burgeoning populations of the twentieth century, the human impact on other life has been profound. The overwhelming magnitude of human interventions on natural ecosystems is in itself an obvious reason for including humans in an account of Puget Sound biology. Another reason is more subtle. All of our awareness of Puget Sound natural history is a product of people's observations. No other organism but humankind—Northwest Indian, fur trader, early settler, and twentieth-century citizen—has the ability to record impressions of the natural world in its surroundings. So, our view of Puget Sound life is a product of communication, a fact to be taken as both a miracle and a warning. A miracle in that we can record and communicate our versions of the real world; a warning in that what we get as the communicated accounts from observation will be inevitably imperfect in quality and completeness.

Libraries and voluminous card files of references are testimonials to the steady inventorying of plants, animals, and microorganisms in our local surroundings. From the first exploration of Puget Sound in 1792 to the most recent Ph.D. thesis filed, the cataloguing has gone on. To be sure, there are great gaps. Some groups of organisms are poorly known, and for various reasons (lack of interest, inaccessibility, no commercial value, the fashions of science, etc.). Assuredly there will be discoveries of more, mostly obscure, kinds of life. But the checklists and handbooks for identifying the living world of the Northwest are mostly done.

My task simply could be one of packing all this into one volume and calling it the natural history of life in and around Puget Sound. But the living world is more than a catalogue of all its organisms. As the linguist might choose to tell of language's interconnectedness, its roots, its drama, rather than compile a dictionary, I choose to tell of the quality and variety of life, its interdependencies, its singular as well as common attributes. For any particular organism's place in the encyclopedia of nature, let the reader find the proper handbook. Identifying organisms is a fascinating game in its own right. My account of Puget Sound life may entice the reader to try a hand at old-fashioned trial-and-error identification. The list of handbooks in the "Further Reading" section of the bibliography can open the door to that delightful study.

Puget Sound was "discovered" by Europeans two centuries ago. Yet, a few thousand years before that sighting by Captain George Vancouver in 1792, Puget Sound was first seen and its nearby land lightly settled by coastal Indians whose origins are still something of a mystery. To them this was a new land. New, indeed, for those first inhabitants did not know that this piece of the planet was only a few centuries past a time of crisis—Ice Age oblivion and rebirth.

The land and water that occupy much of the Puget Sound trough were given a fresh start only 13,000 years ago. During the last great continental glaciation, the massive Puget lobe of a Canadian ice sheet had covered the country, obliterating most of the lowland Puget landscape, chilling its borders, and destroying much of its life. The Puget Sound basin emerged from its icy sleep when the great glacial tongue receded northward, and soon plant and animal life returned to reclaim the barren terrain, newly free of ice.

The ice had radically altered life and land. Today, a second catastrophic epoch is in full swing, one hardly less destructive than the great erasures wrought by ice. A human invasion now rolls over the land—a self-centered enterprise that leaves little untouched.

Europeans are now altering the living historic monument of towering forest and vital inland sea that existed only for 13,000 years, between the last Ice Age and their arrival.

One by one the natural assets of Puget country suffer at the hand of western man. Primeval forest is all but gone in the lowland Puget basin. The unique and delightful wooded prairies throughout the southern end of the basin are rapidly yielding to development. Even samples of the remarkable mounded prairies (Mima mounds) are being bulldozed to oblivion. Lakes and streams, the hallmarks of the "wet" west side of the Cascades, have been tainted by the pollutants of a citizenry unmindful of the consequences of its life style. But the crowning insult has been the progressive deterioration of water purity in that inland maritime jewel of our region, Puget Sound itself. Toxic chemicals have accumulated to dangerous levels in the more urbanized reaches of the Sound.

Unlike the relentless flow of ice, the human wave has the capacity to judge the effects of its actions on its surroundings. This ability to weigh consequences, to predict outcomes, and to take alternative steps can lead to the wise husbandry of nature. Central to the matter of choosing alternatives is *understanding;* that is the mission of this book.

This we know,
The earth does not belong to man;
man belongs to the earth.
All things are connected,
like the blood which unites
one family.
Whatever befalls the earth
befalls the sons of earth.
Man did not weave the web of life.
He is merely a strand in it.
Whatever he does to the web
he does to himself.

Chief Seattle

In southern Puget country, Garry oak woodlands are adorned in spring with balsamroot and other wildflowers. (Photo by Mark Sheehan.)

Acknowledgments

No one can be expected to be an expert on all facets of the physical and biological environments of a place on our planet, and thus many individuals have been consulted on particular aspects of Puget Sound natural history. I accosted old friends and casual acquaintances with questions that bothered me. I usually got what I wanted, and I offer my thanks to all those itinerant respondents.

Special thanks go to colleagues who read the manuscript. Ruth Kirk, Jerry Franklin, and Victor Scheffer critically read the entire work and made valuable suggestions. Dennis Paulson kindly updated the status of Puget Sound bird life. Robert Dunnell, Eugene Hunn, and Nancy Turner read the section on Indians; Alan Duxbery on marine habitats; Frank Badgley on climate; Donn Charnley, Steve Porter, Linc Washburn, and John Whetten on geology; and W. T. Edmondson on Lake Washington. Their good advice is reflected in the book, although I of course am accountable for the result.

Sources of illustrations are cited in Credits (page 454). The names of photographers and artists contributing to the book are given in the captions. To all those whose talents are displayed throughout the book, I offer my sincerest appreciation. To Michael Emerson, who did not live to see his artistry in print, I pay special tribute.

Robert Monroe, former curator of special collections, and Richard Engeman, at the University of Washington's Suzzallo Library, were most helpful in locating illustrations, especially of early human activity in Puget Sound. April Ryan and Stanley Shockey (Graphics and Photography, University of Washington) contributed to several illustrations, and Robert Hutchins put the finishing touches on many others. Anna Shawver and Kay Suiter cheerfully and skillfully typed various drafts of the book and Kay put the index on the computer; for their patience, tenacity, and skill I am most grateful.

Staff members of the University of Washington Press have been a joy to work with. To Marilyn Trueblood, whose fine editorial judgment I usually followed; to Veronica Seyd, whose impressive talents for book design are evident in the "look" of the book, and to Naomi Pascal, who persistently kept the Press and the author on track, my deepest thanks.

The book was supported in its pre-publication phases by Sylvia Duryee, Noreen Frink, Linda C. Helsell, Gretchen Hull, and Douglas and Nancy Morningstar, as well as by the University of Washington Graduate School Research Fund. I acknowledge with gratitude this timely generosity.

And, finally, I thank my wife, Mareen, who witnessed with understanding and patience the birthing of the book. Mareen also was the first to read an early draft and offered helpful comments.

Introduction

"When we try to pick out anything by itself, we find it hitched to everything else in the universe."—John Muir

Satellite image of the Puget Sound region, as well as adjacent Olympic Peninsula and the Cascade Range.

Approach Puget Sound from any direction and its grand design—a sinuous union of land and inland sea—is revealed. Two towering north-south mountain ranges flank a fiordlike arm of the Pacific. Islands stud these waters and a lowland forest of evergreens borders them. For other parts of the globe, the lay of the land, whether desert, prairie, tundra, or forest, may stretch without variety as far as the eye can see. But here in a seaward corner of Washington State, the picture is dazzlingly different. Mountains, lowland terrain, and water provide the ingredients for spectacular landscapes.

The ten thousand square miles of earth's surface occupied by Puget Sound country are a geographer's delight. Nearly all the landmarks of any mapmaker's visual aids are there in quantity. The Olympic and Cascade mountains border the Sound with towering summits and countless ridges, slopes, and valleys. In turn, the mountainous terrain has created drainages of all sizes, from rivulets and creeks to great rivers. The lowland terrain has its own share of topographic variety: hills, valleys, streams and rivers, lakes, bogs, prairies, and forested flats and slopes. And where the land meets the pulsing tidal waters of the inland sea, still other landforms emerge: rocky headlands, steep bluffs, and wooded slopes. At water's edge come the deltas, estuaries, salt marshes, and beaches of rock, pebble, and sand. To complete the geographer's lexicon of the place, there is the diversity of landforms within and beneath the waters of Puget Sound: bays, inlets, submarine canyons with sills and trenches, and the mosaic of bottoms patterned by mud, silt, sand, and rock.

The tapestry of land and water takes on greater richness when generously stocked with plant and animal life. On nearly every inch of land surface and throughout the fertile waters, life in varied form and function endows the Puget Sound scene with color, texture, and animation.

As each of us explores the fabric of land, water, and life, the urge to satisfy a curiosity begins. How did this great north-to-south trough of land and sea come into being? What sort of life flourished in ancient times, sustained by different climates and landforms? Once the past is revealed, there is a need to understand the contemporary scene. How does our place on the planet affect the workings of Puget Sound country through tides and climate? How do the shapes of the land affect the life within the Puget Sound basin? Then, at a far less grandiose level, curiosity about the simpler bits and pieces of the Puget Sound ecosystem call for answers, as straightforward as the reply to What is that tree? or What is that insect?

Today's naturalist is not content with mere catalogues of what is to be found in the natural world. Lists of rocks, butterflies, plants, or snakes simply stimulate a more penetrating search. The imaginative naturalist has an insatiable curiosity about the interrelatedness of the animate and the inanimate in his or her surroundings.

In probing the natural world, what kinds of questions do we ask? Easiest are the "what" and "how" questions. What is it? and How does it work? usually can be given direct answers. The unknown tree or insect gets a name and a place in its family tree to satisfy the What is it? question. Though more demanding of observation and thought, the How does it work? question also has ready answers. The literature of how things function in the world of life is the product of patient experiment and observation by plant and animal biologists. It is only when curiosity persists to the How come? stage that science reveals its tentative and ever-probing qualities. The answers to What for? questions asked of the color of a flower, the hair on an insect's body, or the slime of a slippery slug, are within the domains of ecology and the study of adaptations.

The How come? questions are the most difficult. They seek to know how particular plants or animals evolved, what their ancestors were, and how their modern versions came into being. Answers to all these questions about natural phenomena make up the substance of this book. What best gives cohesiveness to this substance will be answers to the "What for?" (ecological and adaptational) and the "How come?" (evolutionary) questions.

Visualize Puget Sound country from an imaginary platform twenty thousand feet in the air. The picture is a vast land-water-air basin bounded on the east by the crest of the Cascade Range, on the west by the lofty east flank of the Olympic Mountains, on the south by low hills just south of Chehalis, and on the north by the delta of the Fraser River in Canada. From this imaginary vantage point in space, one would see a roughly oblong basin of gigantic proportions (see map of drainage basin, p. 359). The basin's rim, spectacularly etched by its mountainous perimeter, intercepts and channels the bountiful supplies of water in moisture-laden air from the Pacific Ocean. Descend now to a most characteristic piece of this land-and-water basin: the dynamic border between land and water on Puget Sound itself.

Two hundred years ago, on a point of land just back from the beach, there was nearly continuous forest, towering upward and

The topographic bonanza of mountains, lowland terrain, and water multiplies habitat types for all kinds of life in Puget country. The bold, sinuous line defines the common drainage of the Puget basin. (Map by Nancy Eberle.)

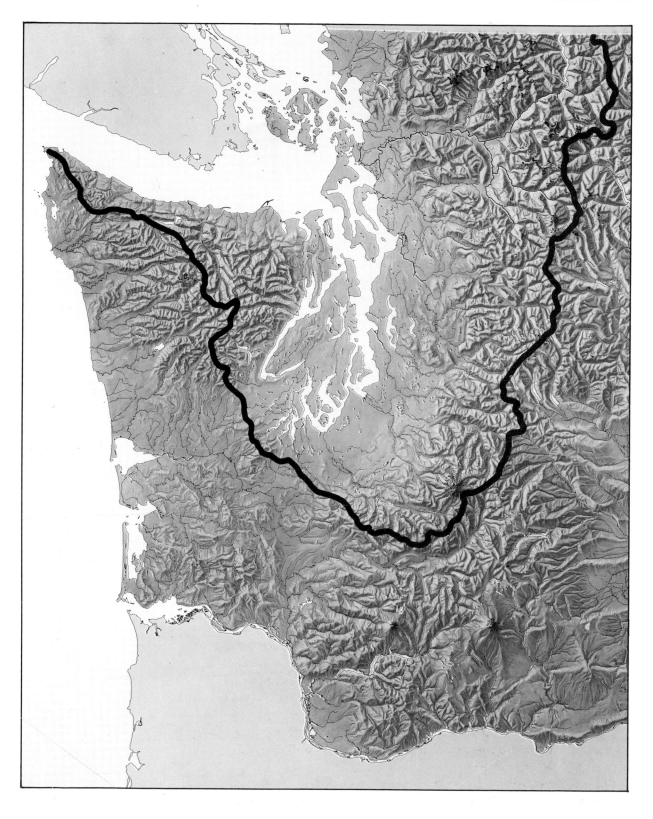

spreading landward as far as the eye could see. The dark greens of fir, hemlock, and cedar, the bright greens of maple and alder, blended with a mosaic of greys, browns, and greens, the massive trunks of forest trees copiously clothed with mosses and lichens. The forest floor where light could penetrate was a carpet of subdued color from the variety of shrubs and herbs at home there in the forest understory. With only the light touch of aboriginal man, mature *coniferous* forest had been since glacial times the all-encompassing living fabric. From the evergreen landscape around Puget Sound we can "read" the most reliable of all environmental recorders: the forest has been the thermometer, rain gauge, and soil analyzer, a sensor of present and past events.

The even-tempered maritime climate defines life in the basin. Conifer forest thrives on thirty-five to fifty inches of rain a year, distributed from mid-September to late June. The Pacific Ocean and Puget Sound act as thermostats to keep temperatures mild, usually avoiding extremes. The forest needs only a fraction of the

Land meets water nearly everywhere in Puget country. Lowland forest and meadow face Puget Sound, Whidbey Island. (Photo by Mary Randlett.)

full intensity of the sun's energy, highest in summer and lowest in winter. Luxuriant vegetation occurs paradoxically on acid soils of rather low fertility, but the annual recapture of recycled nutrients is self-restoring. The forest is a living testimonial to particular and dependable cycles of seasonal change within a regional climate, events that run their course on a terrain sculptured by geologic events of recent and ancient past. Other terrestrial life accommodates to the dominance of the forest landscape. Animals, from deer and bear to tiny insects burrowing in the soil, are largely tuned to a forest habitat. In Puget Sound country, nearly all life on land is the life of the forest; it is the crucial key for revealing the workings of this life-support system.

Surrounded by forest, Puget Sound, the long inland arm of the Pacific Ocean, reaches its way east through the Strait of Juan de Fuca and south down between the Cascades and the Olympics. It is a life-support system of its own, yet it promotes response in its forest neighbors on all sides. The daily surge of the tides unceasingly restores the waters of the gigantic aquarium that is Puget Sound. Here is another living world, dramatically unlike that of the nearby forested land.

At that same imaginary spot of shoreline where we looked landward to forest, turn the mind's eye toward a great inland sea. Sandy or rocky coastline, or crumbling bluff, everywhere waterward some sea life clings to the uppermost splash zone of salt water. At low tide, we see a few limp fragments of sea lettuce or rockweed kelp, and a hardy colony of snail-like limpets or barnacles. Then down the tidal incline we meet an increasing richness of marine life. First, beyond the splash zone, is the stressful intertidal, where exposure to dryness alternates with inundation by water. Here grows a plant life utterly alien to forest or meadow of dry land. Algae—kelps, rockweeds, and their kin, in hues of green, brown, and red—live here. They cling to rocks, or to each other, or they float, gently undulating in the tidal flow. Marine animals of the intertidal, no less alien to land than are marine plants, live sedentary, floating, crawling, and swimming existences, in sizes, shapes, and colors related to the daily changes in their environment.

Below the intertidal, the real undersea garden begins: a new kind of "forest." The eye sees at the surface a brown, massive tangle of gently pulsating ribbons. This is the floating canopy that covers a forest of thin, brown, tubular stems, reaching many feet from submarine bottom to the water surface. Such luxuriant displays of the gigantic bull kelp dominate the underwater landscape in many a subtidal habitat along the borders of Puget Sound. Here in bull-kelp forests or other deep-water underseascapes, where

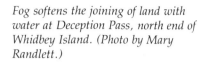

Fog softens the joining of land with water at Deception Pass, north end of Whidbey Island. (Photo by Mary Randlett.)

Rocky promontory and beach, one of many shoreline landscapes along Puget Sound. (Photo by Asahel Curtis.)

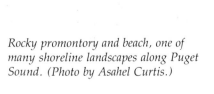

water is eternal, the eaters and the eaten of the marine world of animals dwell. Fishes of all sizes and shapes, from tiny sticklebacks to salmon and sharks, exact their room and board down here. Seagoing mammals, such as harbor seals, porpoises, and killer whales, occasionally cast their shadows on the dimly lit submarine landscape.

Environment, Ecology, Ecosystem: A Search for a Framework

The perceptive resident in Puget Sound country comes to have an intuitive grasp of the interconnectedness of the natural and manufactured strands of the fabric that envelops the region. Each of us is comfortable with the notion that land, air, water, and living things all interact. Poet, artist, philosopher, commonsense person, and scientist sketches her or his own view of the planetary unity. Of all these modes of expression, the scientific has been the latest to synthesize the elemental pieces into an interactive whole. Only in the present century has there emerged a science of environment. And only in the most recent times has this synthesis been recognized as a scheme for viewing the interlacings of all the disciplines of science that probe the mysteries of the world. The three sciences most directly engaged in environmental studies are geology, climatology, and biology. The synthesis of each discipline's store of knowledge goes by various names, one shading into the other in meaning. Ecology, environment, ecosphere, ecosystem—each addresses the structure and function of the living world. Today, concern for the plight of twentieth-century men and women in a finite world has taken ecology out of the textbook into the mainstream of mass communication. Television and newspapers, magazines, and paperback books by the ton use the environmental vocabulary in shades of interpretation from rigorous and reliable to harmfully misleading.

In the rush to save the earth from human misadventures, some communicators have seized upon the word ecology as an instrument for making miracles. "Apply a liberal pinch of 'ecology' to business, industry, agriculture, lifestyle, urban thrombosis, etc," they seem to be saying, "and Lo! man's affronts to Nature are healed." Actually, of course, ecology is not packaged goods for sale over the counters of human commerce. Its value, despite its limited span of the known-to-unknown, resides in the commerce between the mind and the natural world. More than simply an intellectual pastime, coming to know ecology in principle and discovering the ways of specific ecological systems become guides for planetary survival.

Particular environments have particular ecologies. The frame of reference for any one living environment is the *ecosystem* at that place. Wherever organisms (plants, animals, and microbes) interact with each other and with their physical surroundings, look for an ecosystem in action. No one sample ecosystem, whether it be a Douglas fir forest, a tide pool, or a bog, is self-contained. Solar energy and regional climate are among the external influences that reach into an ecosystem from beyond its borders. Conversely, each local ecosystem is part of a larger ecosystem. An acre of forest or a piece of Puget Sound coastline is but part of a continuous system. At any place along that continuum, we may put an arbitrary boundary around a specific area and look at it as an ecosystem. Still larger ecosystems are within our grasp. The earth-as-spaceship is the most inclusive ecosystem. Somewhere along the scale of increasing size and complexity from the minimal life-support system at a point on the planet to the global ecosphere, Puget Sound as an ecosystem can be logically accommodated. Is it well enough known, however, to be comprehended as an interacting system?

There is much that *is* known about the Puget Sound basin, but it has yet to be synthesized into a working model of a total regional ecosystem. The present account of the basin's natural history draws upon diverse scientific disciplines. A listing of some of them previews all we want to survey: geology (topography and landscape-forming processes, structural and historical), hydrology (groundwater, surface runoff, water impoundments), climatology (regional, local, and microscale), oceanography (physical, geological, and biological), limnology (biology of lakes, ponds, and streams), fisheries (freshwater and marine fish and shellfish), forestry (forest ecology, management), zoology (invertebrate and vertebrate animals and their ecologies), botany (freshwater and marine algae, fungi, lichens, mosses and ferns, and seed plants).

Furthermore, the history of human life in the Puget Sound basin—both prehistoric and for the recorded past—draws upon anthropology, archaeology, social and economic history, the arts, and so forth. Each will play a part in an account of the region's natural history.

The Natural History of Puget Sound Country

Flat terrain and low hills prevail near sea level, but with Mount Rainier and the Cascade Range forming a high eastern rim to the basin. View of Lake Washington and the Mercer Island bridge with Mount Rainier and pre-eruption Mount St. Helens in the background. (Photo by Josef Scaylea.)

1 The Lay of the Land

Landforms and Geology of the Puget Sound Basin

"Civilization exists by geological consent—subject to change without notice."
—*Will Durant*

Nature has played intricate games with the earth's surface here in the coastal Pacific Northwest. Imagine a pliant rubber pad twisted in such a way as to create a richly textured, aesthetically pleasing surface of ridges, valleys, and plains. Now, keep the pad slowly but inexorably changing—and you have a model for the sequence of Puget Sound landforms. The topographic magnificence we see today is actually a dynamically unstable and ongoing product of landforming processes acting over vast spans of time. The seeming stability in configuration of the land is deceptive. Ice, water, and wind, as well as earthquakes and periodic volcanic rumblings, join in the continual process of "making" Puget Sound and its basin. Mountains, valleys, river bottoms, lakes, ponds, canyons, flats, and the Sound itself create habitats and thus define the character and diversity of life.

Present-day landscapes provoke the question, "How come?" Processes and events in the course of the earth's history can account for the creation of the contemporary landscape; historical geology also helps explain the origins of the living landscape: the plants, animals, and humans.

Landforms in the Puget Sound Basin

The Puget Sound trough as a north-south lowland basin is bounded on the east by the Cascade Range and on the west by the Olympic Mountains. Its northern part reaches the artificial boundary between the United States and Canada, and it ends at the base of the low hills of the Coast Range near Olympia. Perhaps the most natural definition of the basin's borders comes from the flow of its rivers. The land from alpine summits to sea-level tideflats forms a gigantic drainage system, reaching the salt water of the inland sea. The scope of this account of regional natural history comfortably conforms to that drainage basin.

Maps of the region (pp. v, xix, 359) avoid a boundary along the northwestern sector of the Puget Sound province. The lowland

3

basin here reaches out to embrace the San Juan Archipelago and the dissected coastlines of Whidbey Island, Kitsap Peninsula, and the eastern base of the Olympic Mountains, as well as the western perimeters of mainland Snohomish, Skagit, and Whatcom counties. The topography of the land takes its prime character from the meeting of land and water, the sinuous coastline of Puget Sound. Its many irregularly shaped islands, embayments, and river deltas demand an explanation in the time dimension of the geologist. The lowlands in and around Puget Sound proper have the appearance of a partially drowned landscape. But, as we will see later in reconstructing the genesis of the trough, the drowning turns out not to be simple inundation caused by a rise in level of the Pacific Ocean during the post-glacial epoch.

Everywhere, except for the few modest peaks in the San Juan Islands and the nearby mainland (Chuckanut Range), the relief in the basin is low, with elevations largely below five hundred feet above sea level. Yet, low hills and terraces intrude everywhere. Two major land-shaping processes finish off the basin's contemporary look. Most dramatic was the action of the latest continental glaciation, a massive sheet of ice that reached south from the Fraser River valley in British Columbia to just south of Olympia and west to near Shelton. Great loads of glacially bulldozed rock, gravel, and finer materials were dumped or washed into irregular beds, piles, mounds, and hilly stripes to cover the underlying bedrock. Then, following the retreat of the glacier, a second process—stream-cutting—began scouring channels that entered either Puget Sound, Hood Canal, or Grays Harbor. Ice and water thus account for the most recent and the ongoing feats of modeling the lowland terrain.

South of Olympia, below the terminus of the last glacial ice sheet, the country developed its own runoff system of erosional meltwater channels directly from the retreating perimeter of prehistoric ice. The present patterning of the land is thus traceable to ice-age events of the recent past, reaching a climax about 18,000 to 13,000 years ago.

Most of the land-forming materials in Puget Sound country are the rocky, gravelly, sandy, and silty sediments of present workings of water and past actions of ice and water. Nearly every river bank, road cut, borrow pit, or other excavation exposes the loose, unconsolidated, water-worn materials, mapped by geologists as "Qal" (alluvium of the Quaternary, the period from nearly two million

Low profile topography of the San Juan Islands in the Strait of Juan de Fuca: the Sucia Island group.

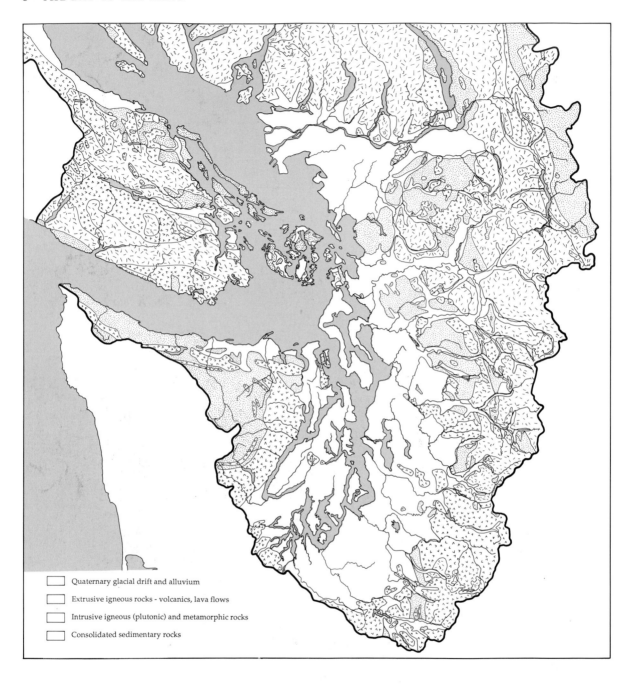

Quaternary glacial drift and alluvium

Extrusive igneous rocks - volcanics, lava flows

Intrusive igneous (plutonic) and metamorphic rocks

Consolidated sedimentary rocks

Geological map of the entire Puget Sound drainage basin. (Map by Nancy Eberle.)

Major rock types in the Puget lowland:

Glacial till, a sedimentary deposit of late glacial origins, along Interstate 5, south of Mount Vernon. (Photo by Stephen Porter.)

Exposure of igneous (volcanic) rock along Interstate 90, just west of North Bend. (Photo by Mary Randlett.)

years ago to the present). But not all relief has been created by piles and drifts of Qal. While touring Puget country, one often passes through road cuts where the materials are truly bedrock. The quarries just south of Boeing Field, which have furnished the huge angular stones for urban rockeries and rock walls, the occasional exposures of bedrock seen along Interstate 90 between Bellevue and North Bend, and the massive outcrop of bedrock along both Chuckanut Drive and Interstate 5 just south of Bellingham, reveal a geology ancestral to the surface (Qal) materials.

Geological History of the Puget Basin

How does the geologist reconstruct events of the past? Materials of the earth's crust, as well as the particular textures and forms they assume, can be read as history. No matter how complex or chaotic the present configurations of the land may appear, the patient earth scientist can unravel the probable sequence of events that formed the landscape. The guiding principle is simply that the present is the key to the past. Given enough time the same processes that presently effect crustal change (erosion; deposition of sediments; and weathering of rock by wind, water, glacial ice; the continual movement of the earth's massive plates, which cause earthquakes, volcanic eruptions, and other earth-deforming mechanics) can account for the crustal changes of the past. These universal earth-changing processes require sufficient spans of time to allow for the grand events of the past to run their course. Using classical and modern timing devices (fossils in comparable stratas, or radioactivity of elements with short and long half-life periods), students of the earth's history have constructed a time-bounded model of the critical stages in the development of the earth's outer layers.

To talk of spans of time measured in tens of thousands and millions of years is to put the human time frame of four-score-and-ten to a mind-stretching test. A device for understanding the long reach into the ancient past is to let a twenty-four-hour day stand for all of the 4.5 billion years since the earth began. The "seconds" hand of the geological clock cannot reveal the millisecond of geological time that is one person's life. And the time span for the existence of *Homo sapiens* is barely more than the tiny arc of time from three minutes before the twenty-fourth hour!

Geologic Events Before the Ice Age

The record of Puget Sound's history through eons of time has several chapter headings, each a signpost for the beginning of some major shift of the earth's crust. These chapter headings are the key points on the well-known Geological Time Scale (Table 1).

For our reconstruction of geologic change in Puget Sound basin landforms, we begin with the last 100 million years, near the end of the Mesozoic Era. Of course, over the last one billion years, global and regional plate-tectonic events have been preparing Northwest landforms, events including many collisions, where the growing North American plate time and again overrode the various "Pacific" plates which in turn plunged below (subducted) the lighter continental plate, causing repeated episodes of plutonic and vol-

Table 1. The Geological Time Scale

Approximate Age (millions of years)	Era
(.01)	
2.0	
5.3	
24.	Cenozoic
37.	
58.	
67.	
144.	
208.	Mesozoic
245.	
286.	
320.	
360.	
408.	Paleozoic
438.	
505.	
570.	
	Precambrian
2500.	
4600.	

Period	Epoch	Some Important Global Biological Events		
Quaternary	(Recent)			Man
	Pleistocene			
	Pliocene			Mammals and birds numerous
	Miocene			
	Oligocene		Flowering plants	
	Eocene		Conifers	
	Paleocene			
Cretaceous				Reptiles numerous
Jurassic				
Triassic		First Seed Plants		
Permian			Amphibians numerous	
Pennsylvanian		Extensive coal formation		
Mississippian			Spore-bearing plants numerous	Insects appear
Devonian		First land animals / First land plants		
Silurian			Vertebrates appear / Algae numerous	
Ordovician		Fossils first abundant		All basic invertebrate types appear
Cambrian				
		Fossils rare and uncertain	Calcareous algae	"Worms" / Other invertebrates?
		Oldest sedimentary rocks	Single-celled life forms / "Origin of life"	
		Chemical Evolution		
		Origin of Planet Earth		

canic igneous activity. Other smaller-scale events were the "arrival" of microcontinents called terranes (small fragments of continental or oceanic lithosphere) which became attached to the North American plate. More than fifty such events characterize the pre-Cenozoic history of the Pacific Northwest.

The latest Mesozoic event was the arrival and docking of the "Okanogan" terrane against the older North American continent, about 100 million years ago. This relatively small mass of granitic and sedimentary rocks probably resembled today's "island continents" such as Borneo or New Zealand. Volcanoes, produced by the heat generated from the collision, left their deposits of ash and lavas on the surface of the newest part of North America. This event also moved the northwestern shoreline of North America more than fifty miles to the west (from its old position about at today's Idaho-Washington border).

A long, quiet period followed, during which the higher portions of the old and new northwestern North America were eroded to a low plain, with large amounts of sediment deposited into the Pacific to the west. The plant life of this early age (Eocene epoch of the Cenozoic era) is now fossilized as beds of coal, and was unlike anything growing here now.

The next terrane to be added was that of the "North Cascades," about 50 million years ago. This caused considerable deformation (folding and faulting) of the older Okanogan and western sedimentary deposits, producing a series of folded rocks which trended roughly northwest to southeast. These folds created a deep fabric in the rocks which persists today, as seen in the many rivers that flow away obliquely from the major north-to-south-trending crest of the present Cascades. The Pacific shoreline was once more moved westward, to about a line running from Bellingham to North Bend and through Enumclaw. Renewed volcanic activity along the center of the North Cascades terrane(s) added to the rocks already there, and literally buried the southern portion of this region.

A period of vast volcanic activity followed, between 14 and 7 million years ago, in and onto the lowlands of what is now southeastern Washington and northeastern Oregon. This vulcanism was dominated by immense outpourings of lavas, which had their source in the earth's mantle, at least 30 to 60 miles deep. These fluid lavas produced extensive flows (in area greater than 60 by 185 miles, and 330 to 660 feet thick). These lavas were extruded from many fissures in the general area of today's Blue Mountains.

The total outpouring of lavas exceeded 7,600 feet in thickness and some flows extended from Spokane and Omak to the north down to northern California and Nevada to the south. Some of the

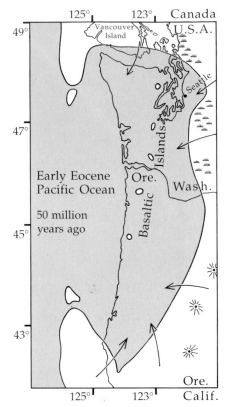

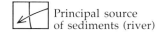
Approximate paleocoastline superimposed on present one

Principal source of sediments (river)

Volcano

Coal swamp

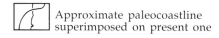
Miles   50   100

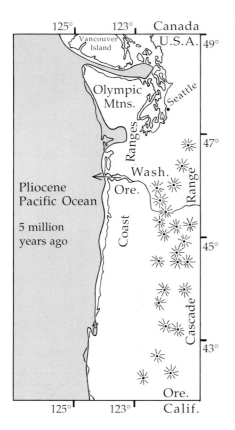

Two Northwest landscapes of the geologic past: early and late Tertiary.

Left: During early Eocene, 50 to 60 million years ago, the Puget basin was mostly under water, with isolated volcanic islands just west of Puget Sound; lowlying coal swamps bordered ancient sea to the east.
Right: By Pliocene times, 10 to 15 million years ago, western Washington was mostly above the sea. (Maps adapted by Michael Emerson.)

Fossil palm leaf from early Tertiary times when plant life was subtropical. The Chuckanut Formation south of Bellingham contains fossils like this one. (Photo by the author).

earliest flows reached the Pacific, before the rising Cascade Range prevented movement in that direction. The flows piled up on one another in a very irregular schedule. At times fewer than 100 years would pass between two successive events, lasting only four to eight weeks. At other times more than 10,000 to 20,000 years would elapse between events. The longer times between flows allowed deep soils to develop, and vegetation and animals to thrive on the flat, moist landscapes. This explains the existence of the Ginkgo Petrified Forest at Vantage. This rich plant life developed about

Table 2. Geologic and Biological Events in the Pacific Northwest Since Early Cenozoic (the last 67 million years)

Geologic Epoch	Age Before Present (B.P.)	Geologic Events	Climatic and Biological Events
Holocene (Late Glacial to Recent)	10,000 yrs.	Post-glacial rise of sea levels; intrusion by sea into Trough, gouged out by last glacial events. Modern landforms left by glacial activity, rivers, and humans following retreat of ice.	Climate cool temperate (11,000–8,500 B.P.), then warm temperate interval (8,500–3,000 B.P.), then return to cool temperate to present. First humans in Puget Trough, 10,000 B.P.
Pleistocene	ca. 2.0 million yrs.	Latest vulcanism forms present Cascades astride volcanics and exposed older rocks. Alpine glaciers form on highest peaks. Continental glaciation advances into Puget Trough between Olympic and Cascade mountains; several advances and retreats, the latest reaching south of Olympia, then retreating between 12,000 B.P. and 10,000 B.P. Sea level lowers about 120 meters during glacial maxima.	Modern vegetation bordered glaciers. Large Ice Age mammals present.
Pliocene	5.3 million yrs.	Marine encroachment limited to Strait of Juan de Fuca and Grays Harbor. Continued uplift of Coast Ranges, Olympic Mountains and Cascade Range to present elevations. Continued sporadic vulcanism.	Cool temperate conifer forests prevailed.

7 million years ago, only to be overwhelmed by the next flow.

Contemporaneous events, beginning about 15 million years ago, were the arrival of a number of microcontinents (terranes) of significantly different character. Vancouver Island and other areas to its east and north represent an oceanic melange of pillow basalts and sediments which was literally "smeared" against North America. These sporadically attached masses are known collectively today as "Wrangellia." Others, such as seen today in the San Juan Islands, were similarly transported in and "jammed" against North America.

A late arrival in this procession was a large mass of pillow basalts and interbedded marine sediments which were "crunched" into the angle formed by Wrangellia and the San Juan terranes to the north and North American (Cascade) terrane(s) to the east. This

Table 2. (continued)

Geologic Epoch	Age Before Present (B.P.)	Geologic Events	Climatic and Biological Events
Miocene	24 million yrs.	Massive flows of Columbia River basalt, from vents in Blue Mts. area. Continued collision of N. American and Pacific plates causes ongoing uplift of Cascades; further events of vulcanism in Cascades. Collision of Olympics terrane onto N. America. Further events of early Cascade vulcanism.	Shift to cooler, drier climates, change from broad-leaved deciduous to mixed coniferous forest.
Oligocene	37 million yrs.	Continuing tectonic compression events (nw-se–trending folds) which will define future drainages. First of many n.-s.–trending Cascadian volcanic events.	Coal-producing swamps extensive east of Pacific shoreline; warm temperate forests of sequoia, oak, sweet gum, sycamore.
Eocene, Late	58 million yrs.	Arrival of North Cascades terrane(s); extensive vulcanism. Pacific Ocean shoreline moved to just east of Seattle.	Humid coal swamps with volcanically produced sediments on coastal plains.
Paleocene and Early to Middle Eocene	67–58 million yrs.	Pacific Ocean shoreline along a line from Republic to Walla Walla. Oceanic vulcanism produced "island arc" volcanic chain similar to present Aleutians.	Low, flattish lands bordered seacoast to east, supporting subtropical forests of palms, broad-leafed trees and conifers, and small primitive mammals.
(End of Mesozoic)	68–70 million yrs.		

collision caused the new arrival to be literally stood up and slivered against itself like a deck of cards being pushed against a wall, with slices of repeated units of rock sliding up past each other. Thus, the Olympic Mountains were created.

Another important event during this hectic time was the development of a major transverse fault (like the San Andreas fault of California) in the North Cascades. Called the Straight Creek fault, this major tectonic structure caused at least 93 miles of off-set of the core rocks of the Cascade terrane(s). Though it ceased movement about 4–5 million years ago, it is indicative of the major scale of tectonic events which have been acted out in the region.

As the Pliocene epoch closed, about 2.2 million years ago, the Cascades were raised to their maximum height, blocking the movement of most of the moist Pacific air into the area to the east, and

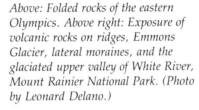

Above: Folded rocks of the eastern Olympics. Above right: Exposure of volcanic rocks on ridges, Emmons Glacier, lateral moraines, and the glaciated upper valley of White River, Mount Rainier National Park. (Photo by Leonard Delano.)

changing the climate there into the semi-arid one we see today. The future Puget Sound basin was formed due to the subduction of the Pacific plate which was carrying the Olympic terrane eastward toward its collision with North America. Sediments rapidly filled this narrowing trough, and isostatic rebound (uplift) kept it at least at or near sea level for much of the past 4 million years.

East of this feature, the continuing slow, shallow subduction of the Pacific plate beneath North America provided the energy and substance to feed the vulcanism which has long been a powerful way of life around the Pacific Ocean's rim. By the mid-Pleistocene, all but one of the Cascade's major volcanoes had appeared. The

Above: Complex array of metamorphic
rocks in the upper South Fork of the
Stillaguamish River drainage, North
Cascades. (Photo by the author.) Below
left: Massive exposure of columnar
lava (welded tuff) formed on cooling,
in Mount Rainier National Park.
(Photo by Ruth and Louis Kirk.)

youngest, St. Helens, came on the scene 4,500 years ago.

All of these past events have produced a remarkably complex
fabric for us to study today. The North Cascades (north of Snoqualmie Pass) are a jumble of highly deformed, intensively meta-
morphosed sedimentary, plutonic, and metamorphic rocks, the
products of the North Cascade terrane(s). Rocks like granites, di-
orites, schists, and gneisses seen here are as spectacular as any in
the world. The Washington Cascades to the south of the pass, on
the other hand, are a "slag pile" of volcanics thousands of meters
thick, which effectively mask the older rocks and structures from
our view.

Left: Volcanic rock outcrop of Table Mountain, northeast of Mount Baker. (Photo by the author.)
Below: Mount Rainier, the volcano that towers 14,410 feet over the Puget Sound lowland; glaciers on the upper slopes and ice-sculpted ridges and glaciated valleys below.

Opposite top: Glacier Peak, a 10,568-foot-high Cascade volcano astride older North Cascade metamorphic rock. (Photo by Bob and Ira Spring.)
Below: Spectacular glaciated valley in the North Cascades, east of Bellingham. Rocks are mostly igneous and sedimentary, highly deformed by metamorphism.

Earthquakes in the Puget Trough

Geologists are fond of quoting historian Will Durant that "civilization exists by geological consent—subject to change without notice." Geologic events give their consent to human occupancy of the land mostly in slow, measured actions. But when earthquakes strike, the effects are sudden, dramatic, and often catastrophic. Puget Sound *is* earthquake country, even though the frequency and intensity of quakes is usually less than at other more turbulent places on the planet. Two major quakes in the Puget lowland stand out in recent history: the 1949 Olympia quake of 7.1 magnitude (cited as major) and the 1965 Tacoma-Seattle quake of 6.5 magnitude (large). Damage to buildings and other human fabrications was substantial and significant alterations of landforms occurred, mostly in the form of landslides. But earthquakes of lesser magnitude occur in the Puget lowland with greater frequency. Only quakes of large to major magnitude make the headlines.

Earthquakes in western Washington are intimately associated with the dynamics of plate tectonics. Just to the west of the Pacific Coast two massive plates of earth's mantle persistently converge. The oceanic Juan de Fuca plate dives under the continental North American plate to its east at the rate of three to four centimeters per year. The convergence of the two plates then becomes the stage on which seismic activity is displayed. Besides these deep earthquakes associated with subduction, other symptoms of plate convergence are present: the chain of Cascadian volcanoes from Mount Shasta in the south to Mount Garibaldi in British Columbia, and the highly deformed rocks of the Olympic peninsula.

Can we expect more major quakes like the ones of 1949 and 1965? A report on Washington earthquakes issued by the Division of Geology and Earth Resources, Washington State Department of Natural Resources, by Noson et al. (1988) estimates quakes of magnitude 6 (large) every 10 years, and return times of 35 to 110 years for quakes of greater magnitude. This report and a companion work (Thorson 1986) contain a wealth of detail on local seismicity and the geology of earth movements; they will remind us that our place on the planet is restless!

Ice, the Dominant Sculptor: Pleistocene Glaciers in Puget Sound

By the end of the Tertiary, a lowland sedimentary trough, defined by two north-south mountain ranges, had been made ready for its next major shaping. Ice was to be the sculptor. Repeated advances and retreats of continental ice sheets from Canada descended into

A massive earth slide disrupted the rail line near Olympia during the Seattle-Tacoma earthquake. (Photo by G. W. Thorsen.)

The glacier that once covered Puget Sound was 3,000 feet thick. Some idea of its depth is shown in this drawing of the glacier as it might have looked towering over the Seattle skyline. (Drawing by Pamela Harlow.)

Puget Sound. It was the action of ice and its later meltwaters that gave shape to the landscapes of today.

Though often called the "Ice Age," the Pleistocene was not one period during which the land was continuously covered with ice. Many advances and retreats of continental glaciers are recorded by the repeated scourings and deposits of rock-laden glaciers.

The Fraser Glaciation was the latest of the major advances of northern ice into western Washington. Yet Washington and the Pacific Northwest were not alone in having endured repeated interludes of icy inundation. It was a time of repeated ice advances and retreats on the northern continents of our restless planet. The Pleistocene epoch, beginning about 2.2 million years ago, made a telling impression worldwide but especially on the northern parts of North America and Eurasia. Massive continental glaciers spread out over northern lands until a confluent mass of ice, two to seven thousand feet thick, covered vast landscapes.

Each glacial advance and retreat (a stade) was followed by a warmer interglacial period. During interglacials, montane glaciers, which were much reduced during continental ice maxima, extended themselves, often overriding continental ice deposits as

Glaciers in southeastern Alaska today simulate the icy scene for Puget Sound at the height of the Vashon glaciation. The Malaspina Glacier bordering Yakutat Bay in Alaska is the choice of glaciologists for a close contemporary match to the Puget Sound Ice Age environment. Shown here is the nearby Brady Ice Field at Glacier Bay. (Photo by Ruth and Louis Kirk.)

Opposite page, far right: Extent of latest (Vashon) glaciation in Puget Sound. The continental ice sheet reached its maximum advance about 14, 000 years ago. (Map by Michael Emerson.)

they moved into the Puget Sound basin. Since each successive glacier acts like a gigantic but imperfect bulldozer, obscuring some of the topographic signs of the previous ice age, the most recent glaciation leaves the clearest imprint of its presence. The latest in Puget Sound, the Fraser Glaciation, began to put the finishing touches on our land about 20,000 years ago. Glacial geologists, so fascinated with their slice of geo-time as to call themselves "Friends of the Pleistocene," see the Fraser Glaciation as having three phases or "stades." It is only the last, or Vashon, stade that need claim our attention here.

Named for glacial deposits left on Vashon Island in central Puget Sound, the ice of the Vashon phase at its maximum covered all of Puget Sound and the adjacent lowlands down to its southern terminus near Tenino, just south of Olympia. At the present-day Canada-United States border, the Vashon ice sheet was nearly six

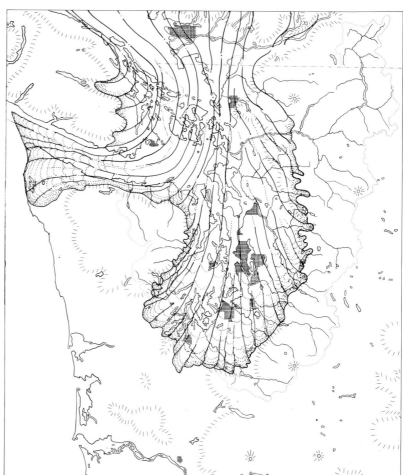

Top: A huge glacial erratic deposited in lowland Thurston County near Lawrence Lake. (Photo by Stephen Porter.)
Bottom: Glacial erratic from Canada, deposited on country rock (dunite), nearly 5,000 feet high on the Twin Sisters Mountain east of Bellingham. (Photo by the author.)

thousand feet thick. Huge boulders left resting at that elevation in the northern Cascades prove the thickness of the ice. Called "erratics," they are not rocks like those in the immediate vicinity, but are traceable to Canadian origins and were beyond question brought here by glacial ice. These boulders occur everywhere in the Puget Sound basin.

Late Pleistocene events in and around Seattle have been bracketed in time by radiocarbon dating. The great Puget lobe of the Vashon glacier passed over the vicinity of Seattle about 15,000 years ago, covering the land with an ice sheet three thousand feet thick. The nearest vantage point on ice-free land for an ancient citizen of Seattle would have been on Tiger Mountain or some other westerly promontory fringing the Cascades. And looking westward, that person would have seen a vast sea of ice stretching without interruption to the eastern flank of the Olympic Mountains. The great glacier, on the average advancing between two hundred and five hundred feet per year, reached its southern limit a few miles south of Olympia.

This last surge of continental ice remained in Puget Sound for no more than 1,500 years. But during that time, following the previous interglacial period and its more temperate environment, the glacier's impact was immense. The Vashon glacier gouged out new landscape features in some areas and, on retreating, left awesome loads of rock debris of all sizes in other areas.

From causes still obscure, the frigid times of the late Pleistocene yielded gradually to a worldwide warming trend. About 14,000 years ago, the massive Vashon glacier began to retreat at its southern terminus, and by roughly 11,000 years ago the glacier persisted only from the Canadian border northward. Everywhere along the Puget Sound trough the retreating ice sheet left rock debris as evidence of its presence. It carved the massive ice-rounded low hills that now dot our landscape. Its scourings, called drumlins, rasped out during its advance, were left behind and exposed. Lake Tapps, Lake Sammamish, and Lake Washington, as well as Puget Sound and Hood Canal, are the spectacular products of this glacial energy. Piles of gravel and finer deposits left by the glacier are seen everywhere today, especially where man or nature excavates the land. The retreating glacier was also producing torrents of milky meltwater that created new channels, running largely in southerly and westerly directions. Today's rivers, creeks, ravines, and even valleys now dry, as well as the hundreds of lowland lakes and ponds, are the remains of that vanished glacier.

The impact of the Vashon glacier and its turbulent retreat can be seen in variety around Puget country. An example of these effects now gets closer attention.

Glacial Deposits at Possession Point, Whidbey Island. Though early explorers like Captain Vancouver would find the present day shoreline of Whidbey Island altered in many places, the high bluff at the southern tip would have changed but little. Strata that tell the most complete story of Pleistocene times are boldly exhibited here at Possession Point. On the top of this steep three-hundred-foot promontory rests the deposit of the last glaciation, the unsorted boulder-clay layer called Vashon till. Successive and distinct layers downward to the base of the cliff from the topmost Vashon till are the evidences of previous glacial and interglacial times. At the bottom lies a sedimentary stratum that tells of the next older advance of Pleistocene ice into Puget Sound; however, it is too old to provide a radiocarbon date for its duration. The vertical sequence of materials at Possession Point tell of the action of water and ice: water-deposited (cross-bedded) sediments are relics of the inter-

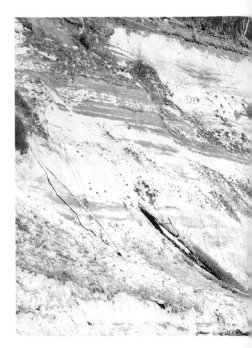

Top: Vertical section through glacial till at Possession Point, southernmost tip of Whidbey Island. This exposure is the most complete record of Ice Age deposits in northern Puget Sound. (Photo by Stephen Porter.)

Bottom: A layer of peat in the Whidbey Formation, at Double Bluff, Whidbey Island. Although beyond the range of carbon-14 dating, other methods indicate this layer to be about 100,000 years old. (Photo by Stephen Porter.)

Table 3. Geologic Events in the Puget Trough Following Last Glacial Maximum

14,000 B.P.	Deglaciation begins and proglacial Lake Russell forms between the retreating ice margin and the Black Hills area
13,500	Continental ice leaves Seattle area clear
13,200	Lake Russell replaced by marine waters in Puget Sound as ice clears Straits of Juan de Fuca
13,000	Glacial-marine sediments deposited on northern lowlands
11,000	Ice retreats to southern British Columbia somewhere around Vancouver
11,400	Minor readvance of ice to just north of Sumas, northern Washington. Rapid deglaciation from then on

B.P. = Before present

glacial periods, and the non-bedded massive deposits are those left during glacial times. Some of the younger deposits contain organic matter, often identifiable and datable, that yields a history of such plant and animal life as could come and go, or endure, through the Pleistocene.

Life in Puget Sound During Pleistocene Times

As in the present, animal life in the past was dependent on green plants and on the environmental conditions that plants could tolerate. Marine and terrestrial green plants existed then, at times luxuriantly and at other times precariously. Throughout the Pleistocene, the green world retreated and advanced as the position of nearby ice shifted, and each renewed glaciation largely obliterated evidence of its predecessor. Though we have hardly any record of marine plant life during the ebb and flow of the glaciers, the story of plant life on land is substantial. The evidence for the kinds and quantities of terrestrial vegetation of the Pleistocene Epoch is of a remarkable sort. Since both glacial and interglacial times were not particularly placid, plant remains are usually badly fragmented. Fortunately, the botanical specialty of palynology can reconstruct the past from bits and fragments. Pollen, spores, and other bits of plant detritus of glacial deposits or in the sediments of ancient lake bottoms can be identified. For instance, at Possession Point on Whidbey Island, the organic remains are decipherable. Henry P. Hansen, pioneer palynologist of the Pacific Northwest, was able to tell much about the succession of climates at Possession Point by

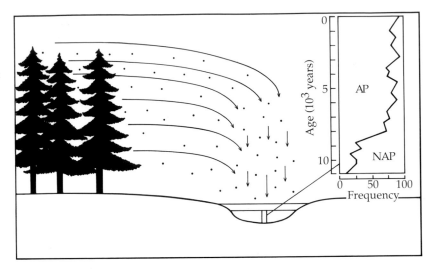

How pollen grains from trees that get into lake or bog sediments can be used to determine past climates and vegetation. AP = arboreal pollen; NAP = non-arboreal pollen. (Stephen Porter diagram, adapted by Michael Emerson.)

the sequence of plant fragments, especially pollen, from vegetation of a colder period (lodgepole pine) that persisted during an early interglacial to vegetation of a warmer period during the full interglacial when fir and hemlock dominated. Since all lowland lakes in western Washington are postglacial in origin, the "pollen in lake sediment" method of detecting vegetation change works only for postglacial times.

Did plants and animals living at the southern border of the Vashon ice sheet have a stressful existence? The environment at the glacial border probably was not unlike the local bare and frigid zones that we find around contemporary glaciers in southeastern Alaska. As a first premise, the Vashon ice sheet, like the continuous ice sheet of eastern North America, might have produced a frigid impact that could be felt many miles away from the ice front. In eastern North America, when continental ice prevailed in Pleistocene times, immense climatic disturbances called glacial anticyclones formed over the ice mass. Such storms developed severe, drying frost winds that moved out over the ice-free land, creating permafrost or frozen ground—hardly a place for a vigorous vegetation cover. Was this the austere scene for life in Puget Sound during the glacials? Later glacial times here were severe, but not nearly so inhospitable to the nearby plant life as they were for eastern North America.

The abundance and variety of animal life in Puget Sound during the Pleistocene surely changed, as did the vegetation, in response to successive continental glaciations. Migrations of animals in and out of the basin were effectively controlled by the availability of ice-free environments. Although animal life had thousands of years to

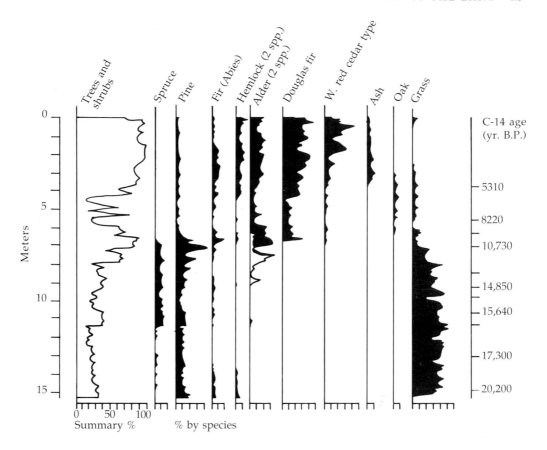

0

Meters

5

10

15

Trees and shrubs

Spruce

Pine

Fir (Abies)

Hemlock (2 spp.)

Alder (2 spp.)

Douglas fir

W. red cedar type

Ash

Oak

Grass

C-14 age (yr. B.P.)

5310

8220

10,730

14,850

15,640

17,300

20,200

0   50   100
Summary %

% by species

Changes in past climates and vegetation gleaned from analyzing changes in types of tree/shrub/herb pollen deposited in bogs though time (ca. 10,000-year-long record). Decrease in pine pollen (and increase in other tree species) means a warming trend. (Cathy Barnowsky diagram, adapted by Michael Emerson.)

develop, it is disappointing to find that fossil evidence of animals enduring the Pleistocene is scanty. The fossil record that does exist shows the usual bias in fossilization. Fossils of marine invertebrate animals with hard parts and the larger vertebrates predominate. Within older interglacial beds are evidences of a marine interlude, when clams and other shelled mollusks were present. Modern counterparts of these animals now inhabit the colder, more northerly, Pacific Ocean waters; yet in Pleistocene interglacial times they flourished in the expanded reaches of Puget Sound.

The record of vertebrate inhabitants of Puget Sound during the Pleistocene interglacials is even more scanty. A dearth of careful field studies of interglacial strata and natural destruction of the potential fossils can account for the lean record. Most museum collections of Pleistocene mammals are the contributions of casual collectors who found only the larger bones. Moreover, either the animals fled before the advancing ice or, if they died in its path, their remains would have been mauled by the glacial "machine." Yet despite these deficiencies, some rewarding fossil surprises do occur. The horse, bison, caribou, woolly mammoth, and mastodon roamed Puget Sound in interglacial and early postglacial times. A small mastodon skeleton has been found near Port Angeles, and numerous teeth and tusks of both mastodon and mammoth have turned up in scattered localities in western Washington. In addition to the animals now extinct in Puget Sound, present-day vertebrate species like deer, squirrels, foxes, and many species of rodents and birds would have been a part of the interglacial scene. But to date no fossils of these animals have been found.

Confrontation: The Continental Ice Sheet Enters Montane Valleys

As the lobe of continental ice grew, glaciers in the Cascades and Olympics shrank in size. Evidence of the work of mountain glaciers is recorded in the spectacular U-shaped upper montane valleys, gouged out to their gently curved trough-shaped contours by moving ice. Any of the rivers that flow toward Puget Sound show this classic effect of glacial engineering. Striations on the bedrock flanking the valleys provide evidence of glacial etching as the ice descended the valleys. The Skykomish, the Stillaguamish, and the Snoqualmie rivers in their upper reaches clearly reveal the dual effects of glaciation: high jagged ridges and U-shaped troughs. Were it not for this degradation of mountains by glacial ice, the Cascades and Olympics would be no great challenge to the rock-climbing mountaineer; only modest sloping terrain would have persisted today.

During the growth of continental ice, reduced water supply caused most montane glaciers to shrink considerably. The tongues of continental ice that slowly ascended into the mouths of the montane valleys soon blocked these valleys with massive deposits called moraines. The result was the formation of large glacial lakes, fringed with ice from above and from below. The contemporary evidence for these pondings of meltwater from the receding montane glaciers upstream is dramatically displayed some five miles east of North Bend. Here the Puget lobe of the Vashon glacier created three massive moraines, damming all three valleys now called the south and middle forks of the Snoqualmie River and the Cedar River. The low ridge across which Interstate 90 begins its first ascent to Snoqualmie Pass from North Bend is a delta moraine, a gigantic mound of glacial tailings dumped there by the Vashon glacier and coarse sediment accumulated in a lake dammed by continental ice. Eastward beyond the morainal rampart and traveling up the river gorge itself, one can find the fine-textured sediments that rim the canyon and that were deposited in the prehistoric "South Fork Lake." As you drive over Snoqualmie Pass highway, between the second and third crossing of the South Fork stream (Interstate 90), look for these ancient glacial lake sediments; where

Right: The U-shaped Elwha Valley in the Olympics was once occupied by glacial ice; the glacier is gone but its impress on the landscape remains. (Photo by Mary Randlett.)

Opposite, below: Just below glacial ice on Mount Rainier are the earth-shaping products of the glacier: a broad valley devoid of trees, and one or more lateral moraines. (Photo by Mary Randlett.)

Below: Proglacial lakes formed between continental and montane valleys anywhere on the western slope of the central part of the Cascade Range. (Diagram by Michael Emerson and Sandra Noel.)

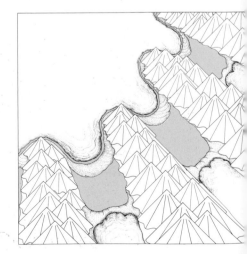

A glacier made these etch marks on the rock. These glacial striae are easily seen at Box Canyon, Mount Rainier National Park. (Photo by Ruth and Louis Kirk.)

they are exposed, their many-layered horizontal bedding is obvious. The opportunities to see clearly defined postglacial geology along this heavily used highway and mountain corridor are diminishing year by year. The new Interstate 90 highway has taken some bites out of the great moraine east of North Bend. And farther to the east, highway construction has removed some of the prehistoric lake sediments.

Interpretation of the glacial geology at the interface between continental and montane glaciers may appear to be merely a game of academic interest only to geologists and those fascinated with the origin and history of landscapes. But here in the upper Snoqualmie Valley, where three ancient lakes once existed, the consequences of correctly interpreting this kind of glacial confrontation are startlingly evident. Just to the south of the great North Bend moraine and the south fork of the Snoqualmie River lies the Cedar River drainage. Like the Snoqualmie, it had its Ice Age lake, complete with delta moraine and bedded lake sediments. The scene was then set for a new kind of confrontation a few thousand years later: people, the earth movers, decided to reshape the land.

In the early 1900s the city of Seattle built a reservoir on the old lake bed, later building a ninety-foot-high concrete dam between the bedrock to the west and the glacial moraine on the east. In December 1918, the Cedar Reservoir failed—not at the dam but

These horizontal beds of clay (fine lake sediment) are telltale evidence of a Pleistocene proglacial lake where continental ice blocked the montane runoff and ice in the valley of the South Fork Snoqualmie River. (Photo by Mary Randlett.)

through the moraine. Between midnight and 2 A.M. of December 23, a great outburst occurred in the eastern part of the north face of the morainal embankment approximately 6,000 feet from the dam. Between 800,000 and 2,000,000 cubic yards of detritus were washed out in a period estimated at between twenty minutes and two hours, "producing a great amphitheatre-shaped crater" in the embankment face. Discharge of water at the time of the initial outburst was estimated at between 3,000 and 20,000 second-feet. "The flood passed down the valley of Boxley Creek to the Snoqualmie River," destroying the tracks of the Milwaukee Railroad, the small town of Edgewick, and the sawmills and other property of the North Bend Lumber Company (see Mackin 1941:468–69).

The account of the break in the morainal embankment and the flood by geologist Hoover Mackin did more than just record the events of the disaster. Mackin was concerned about the causes for the failure of the Cedar Reservoir. The geological key to the solution of the breakthrough rests with the interpretation of the nature and source of the moraine at the dam site. If the natural embankment had been the moraine of a mountain glacier, then the moraine slope facing the impounded dam would not have failed. But if, as was the true situation, the moraine had been built into the valley by delta deposits from an advancing Vashon glacier, then using the moraine as a reservoir embankment would be disastrous. The crucial evidence for the "up-from-below" source of morainal material is the quality of these coarse sediments themselves. Mackin found no materials in the moraine that could have come from the Cedar River drainage basin. Rather, these materials were the scourings from elsewhere made by the Puget lobe of the Vashon glacier. The up-ice face of any moraine will have a thick *clay* deposit on it from the inevitable lake which forms as the glacier retreats from its moraine. In this situation, the clay face was on the opposite face from the impounding reservoir and was quickly flushed away! Had geological advice been sought before the site was selected, a catastrophe could have been avoided.

The Outwash Plains of Southern Puget Sound Country

With the retreat of the Vashon ice sheet, its overloaded meltwater fanned out south of it and deposited massive stream deposits in the outwash plains. Later runoff carved channels in this surface, and occasional floating slabs of detached ice with loads of rock were released downstream. The drama of the "great melting," and its attendant meltwater debris, was nowhere more strongly played out than in the area commonly called the Tacoma prairies. Most of the gravelly outwash plains or "prairies" include that sector of the

Puget trough bordered on the north and west by Tacoma, on the east by the Puyallup River near Kapowsin, by the Black River on the southwest, and on the south by Chehalis. Nearly all of Thurston County and the western sector of Pierce County have patches of prairie, created by deglaciation. There still remain today evidences of this great erosional force that surged down the Chehalis River to the sea. Terraced channels, often connected now with lakes or dry kettlelike depressions, are the landforms that still boldly record the impact of meltwater, ice, and rock debris.

Follow any drainage system in the area from Spanaway, just below Tacoma, south through the east borders of Fort Lewis to Roy, Yelm, Rainier, then west to Little Rock, and finally south to Tenino, and you are following a course once set by Vashon glacial runoff. A tour south and west from Kapowsin all the way to Little Rock can give the traveler firsthand views of the glacier's southern border and a traverse of several of these late Pleistocene drainage ways. Even without seeing the characteristic landforms, you will know you are in prairie country the moment forest gives way to grassland. Expansive stretches of grassy plains intrude upon forest everywhere down here, and even the forest takes on a distinctive character—open, parklike stands of pure Douglas fir. Plant and animal life of the prairies receive a more detailed accounting later.

Here and there in the gravelly outwash prairies, the traveler is sure to encounter the remarkable mounded topography that interrupts the usually flat terrain. Classics of their kind, these haystack-like mounds have been variously described as "hogwallow" microrelief, as pimpled plains, or as the Mima mounds. The latter name commemorates Mima Prairie, a pimpled plain just southwest of the village of Little Rock; it is the type locality of Mima topography, and nearly the last local example of high-quality mounded terrain. The mounds here are evenly spaced at about eight to ten per acre and cover more than a thousand acres. A person standing in the trough below the mounds is dwarfed by the rounded hillocks that measure up to seven feet in height and as much as forty feet in diameter.

In cross section, the grass-, moss-, and flower-covered mound has a curved surface layer of blackish soil, reminiscent of the rich prairie soils of the Midwest. But looks are deceiving; mound soil is rather infertile. Unlike Midwest prairie soils made of more fertile wind-deposited materials, the Mima mound and Tacoma prairie soils have weathered only slightly from the rock and gravels of the glacial outwash. Whether one examines soil profiles of the open prairies nearby or those of the mounded prairies, the story is always the same: a thin mantle of black sandy loam of low fertility overlies the sorted, gravelly workings of the Vashon glacier. Con-

Distribution of gravelly outwash plains (prairies) in the Tacoma-Olympia-Yelm prairie triangle. Prairies with Mima-type mounds include Mima Prairie, Mound Prairie, Rock Prairie, Rocky Prairie, and Violet Prairie.

A typical gravelly outwash prairie in the Fort Lewis area. The forest-prairie border, formerly very abrupt, is now blurred by the reinvasion of Douglas fir. (Photo by Frank Lang.)

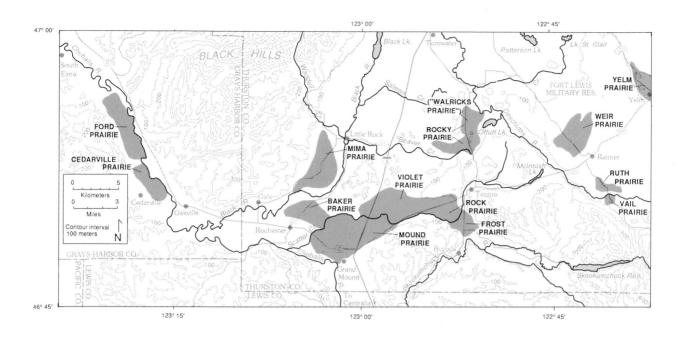

troversy and mystery over their origin as well as conflict over their preservation continue to keep the Mima mounds in the limelight. Chapter 7 contains a detailed account of the mounds and the gravelly prairies. See also Appendix 5.

Recent Vulcanism

Though glacial action left its bold mark on the land, volcanic "fire" competed with ice during late glacial and recent times. The last major volcanic outbursts in the Puget Sound region's segment of the great "Pacific Ring of Fire" occurred repeatedly from the Pleistocene and at times recorded in human history to the present. Pleistocene vulcanism finalized the north-south alignment of the present Cascade Range by adding massive substance to the five towering volcanic peaks. The volcanic superstructure of the Washington Cascades begins in the north with Mount Baker (10,750 feet), followed southward by Glacier Peak (10,430 feet), Mount Rainier (14,410 feet), Mount St. Helens (8,365 feet as of 1980), and Mount Adams (12,307 feet). The recent explosive "subtraction" of 1,312 feet from the 9,677-foot pre-1980 summit of Mount St. Helens (the youngest—4,500 years old—and the westernmost volcano) is a bold reminder of the unsteady state of our volcanic Cascades. Dramatic volcanic displays like the May 18, 1980, eruption of Mount St. Helens, and milder demonstrations like the steam venting on Mount Baker in the late 1970s are telling exhibits of nature's restlessness.

Beginning on the surface of the ancient Weaver Plain of Eocene times, with increment on increment and by flow and eruption, vulcanism has persisted as a dominant geomorphic force for ages here. The present volcanoes, though, do not date back to more than one-half million years ago. Most volcanic activity within historic times has been the innocuous venting of steam and ash. But more violent exhibitions occurred from late prehistoric times, some less than a thousand years ago, to the present. A clever technology has been developed to probe that stretch of time and environment loosely called the post-Pleistocene (Holocene), which links the last Ice Age advance into the beginning of early human and historical times.

Palynologists, it will be recalled, can reconstruct past environments from pollen in sediments of bogs and lakes. They first make the assumption that the organic remains in a particular stratum of water-borne sediments accurately mirror the kind of life that existed nearby. Thus, pollen grains, other vegetable fragments, and the shells of tiny aquatic plants and animals all become ingredients for reconstructing a particular post-Pleistocene span of time.

But this method by itself lacks the definition of calendar time. The palynological method cannot disclose with great accuracy when a particular forest type prevailed. Another scientist, the geochronologist, using geologic data, can accurately date Pleistocene events by the radiocarbon dating of organic fragments. The chronology now has a tell-tale marker throughout the Northwest, one provided by an ancient Cascadian volcano. Nearly all the postglacial lakes of Puget Sound contain a layer of ash in the vertical sequences of their otherwise predominantly organic sediments. This ash layer drifted into every pond and lake in the region from a massive eruption of Mount Mazama in Oregon. The radiocarbon age of the peat directly beneath the ash is 6600 years, and the deposits above the ash are younger. By combining rates of sedimentation with radiocarbon dating of dead plant and animal remains, scientists can reconstruct the time course of life since the retreat of the Vashon ice. Ash from repeated eruptions of Glacier Peak, Mount Rainier, Mount Adams, Mount Baker, and Mount St. Helens, also identified in the profiles of lake sediments, helps in dating post-Pleistocene life and events.

The sediments of a typical Puget Sound lake profile reveal a postglacial story of changing, fluctuating climates—first cool, then warm, and then back to cool again. The profile is really a pollen profile, for the dominant deposit in the sequence comes from the rain of pollen, shed by surrounding vegetation, season after season. Another bonus from the pollen record is the confident translation of past vegetation into past climate; spruce and pine signify a cool climate, while grass and Douglas fir tell of a warmer epoch.

One cannot read a pollen profile, a Pleistocene sequence of glaciation to deglaciation or any other chain of events through geologic time without asking inevitably, Is there no status quo? Surely, incessant change is the theme of planetary existence. The two centuries of European occupancy of the Pacific Northwest are too brief an interval to detect any significant change in geology or climate. Yet we can be certain that change is ongoing. It is no wonder that we find the geologist often interpreting the Age of Humankind simply as another interglacial period of the Pleistocene, rather than as the end of the Ice Age and dawn of a new geological revolution.

Seattle viewed through rain on a ferry window. (Photo by Mary Randlett.)

2 Climate and Weather

"Our climate is delightful when framed and glazed, that is, beautiful through a window."—Horace Walpole, 1771

Throughout geological time, a gaseous atmosphere has sustained life on our planet, sometimes precariously, other times abundantly. For as long as there has been life, the dependence of most living things on an atmosphere has been absolute. Thus, regional climate and weather are crucial nonliving components governing all life in the Puget Sound basin.

Human inhabitants of Puget Sound can scarcely evade the weather. Though in modern times they circulate indoors in a "cell" of artificial climate much of the time, the real world of sunshine, clouds, wind, rain, snow, or chilling temperatures continually stimulates the senses. Unless our indoor environment has no windows, we see and therefore react to the weather out there.

Weather is our day-to-day encounter with the regularities and caprices of the local and regional blanket of atmosphere. Some humans are more patient and curious than others, enough so to record daily weather over years, decades, and centuries. When cumulated and averaged (or normalized), weather becomes climate, and a weather forecaster prefers to be called a climatologist. The difference between weather and climate can be dramatized by example. For Puget Sounders, the daily weather in mid-July of some years can be uncomfortably hot, with daily maximum temperatures in the eighties. Yet any climatologist would describe summers in Puget Sound as cool. Over the years, the average July maximum temperature for this region of the Northwest is close to 73 degrees Fahrenheit. Weather is for day-to-day living; climate is for charts, textbooks, and patient observers.

Climatic Controls

Weather and climate need the perspectives of time and space and the expanses of land and sea for a fuller comprehension. Three dominating climatic controls bring the region a particular brew of daily weather. They are (1) the Pacific Ocean, acting as the region's thermostat and generator of moisture-laden air, (2) the semi-permanent high and low pressure cells that hover over the North Pacific Ocean and that propel the maritime air in the direction of the Sound, and (3) the mountains bordering Puget Sound, which regulate the flow of regional atmosphere.

The combined effect of these controls is a predictable general climate, described as maritime: mild and wet. Since each control operates over a range of landforms, astonishingly different weathers occur within short distances. Witness the differences illustrated in Table 4, for example, between Sequim's fifteen inches of rain on the northeast and leeward end of the Olympic Peninsula and the eighty inches received at Aberdeen in the Grays Harbor area at the opposite and windward, southwestern end of the Olympic axis. The southern flank of the Olympics receives the full impact of the ocean's bounty of rain, while to the north the mountains act to bar precipitation over lands in their lee, to create a "rain-shadow."

Constantly living with weather, humans have acquired an intuitive sense of what kind of weather to expect at any given season. Yet our sense perception of weather is not infallible. How reliable, for instance, is memory of what a typical January or July should be? Past weather, patiently tallied as climatic data, jogs the memory and corrects misconceptions. Some chart and graph study will make our claims for and against Puget Sound weather a bit more accurate.

Start with that stock in trade of the meteorologist, the climatological normals for our region. Table 4 portrays an annual progression of averages for temperature and precipitation, but it reveals only long-term normals. The drier-than-normal year of 1987 dramatically contrasts with the average Seattle climate. Another way to portray Puget Sound climate combines temperature and precipitation in a way that highlights the summer drought period (see diagram, p. 38); Seattle and Olympia have only a modest summer drought period in contrast with that in Yakima, east of the Cascades.

To emphasize the well-buffered, equable climate of lowland western Washington, compare in Table 5 the pertinent statistics for Seattle with those for St. John's, Newfoundland, a maritime city lying on our same latitudinal band (47°N). For Seattle and environs, normal temperature maxima progress from around 45 degrees F in the winter to 78 degrees F in late July and early August. The progression is gradual and the range from winter to summer is small. The average temperature minima through the year show the same moderating pattern, though at a level approximately ten degrees lower than the maxima. The winter minima hover well above freezing while summer minima (nighttime temperatures) reach down to the comfortable mid-fifties range. But across the continent, St. John's has a climate more demanding on humans. From December through March, temperatures are below freezing; snow comes in November and in every month thereafter until May.

Nineteen eighty-seven was a year of drought. The graph compares normal rainfall with 1987's actual precipitation.

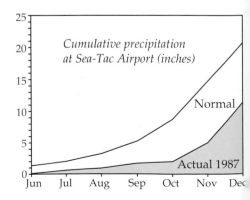

Table 4. Average Monthly and Annual Climatic Data for Selected Localities in Washington

	Jan	Feb	Mar	Apr	May	Jun	Jul	Aug	Sep	Oct	Nov	Dec	Annual
	Temperature (°F)												
Aberdeen	39.7	41.8	44.1	48.7	53.3	57.1	60.1	60.6	58.7	52.7	45.2	41.9	50.3
Olympia	38.1	40.9	44.2	50.0	55.1	59.1	63.9	63.4	58.5	51.4	43.8	40.7	50.8
Seattle City	41.2	43.6	46.4	51.8	57.4	61.4	65.6	65.0	61.2	54.4	46.9	43.8	53.2
Sea-Tac													
Airport	38.3	40.8	43.8	49.2	55.5	59.8	64.9	64.1	59.9	52.4	43.9	40.8	51.1
Everett	38.6	41.0	44.6	49.6	54.7	58.9	62.4	61.8	57.9	51.8	44.4	41.2	50.6
Bellingham	36.8	39.5	43.0	48.0	53.2	57.8	61.0	60.6	56.7	50.1	43.1	39.6	49.1
Monroe	38.0	40.9	44.7	50.3	55.9	60.2	64.1	63.6	59.2	52.2	44.2	40.7	51.2
Stampede													
Pass	23.5	26.6	30.0	36.5	43.9	48.9	56.2	55.6	51.9	42.4	31.4	27.0	39.5
Sequim	37.9	40.1	42.8	47.8	53.1	57.2	60.4	60.8	57.4	50.6	43.6	40.2	49.3
Wenatchee	26.2	31.5	42.3	52.2	60.5	66.5	73.4	71.5	63.5	51.1	37.7	31.1	50.6
Spokane	25.3	30.0	38.1	47.3	56.2	61.9	70.5	68.0	60.9	49.1	35.7	30.1	47.8
	Precipitation (in.)												
Aberdeen	12.70	10.23	9.19	5.56	3.43	.70	1.51	1.79	3.71	8.13	11.09	14.50	84.54
Olympia	7.85	6.62	5.40	2.96	2.01	1.79	.76	.89	2.09	5.28	7.67	9.05	52.37
Seattle City	5.19	3.90	3.32	1.97	1.59	1.41	.63	.74	1.65	3.28	5.00	5.42	34.10
Sea-Tac													
Airport	5.73	4.24	3.79	2.40	1.73	1.58	.81	.95	2.05	4.02	5.35	6.29	38.94
Everett	4.45	3.58	3.33	2.39	2.26	2.25	.93	1.12	1.98	3.54	4.55	4.86	35.24
Bellingham	4.14	3.22	3.11	2.26	1.82	1.93	.99	1.10	1.98	3.64	4.51	4.89	33.59
Monroe	6.03	5.01	4.59	3.21	3.01	2.53	1.04	1.34	2.49	4.65	6.32	6.54	46.76
Stampede													
Pass	12.03	10.15	10.60	5.60	4.25	4.09	1.46	2.04	4.39	8.81	12.58	16.19	92.19
Sequim	2.18	1.73	1.30	.93	.97	1.15	.47	.59	.95	1.57	2.31	2.66	16.81
Wenatchee	1.16	.98	.67	.47	.65	.91	.11	.37	.47	.73	1.14	1.34	9.00
Spokane	2.44	1.86	1.50	.91	1.21	1.49	.38	.41	.75	1.57	2.24	2.43	17.19

From E. L. Phillips, "Climate of Washington," Weather Bureau, U.S. Dept. of Commerce, 1965.

How can the two coastal regions, Newfoundland and Puget Sound, have such different climatic regimes and yet be on the same latitude? Classifying the Sound's climate as Western Maritime and that of coastal Newfoundland as Continental begs for further explanation. For Newfoundland, the behavior of winds from the Atlantic controls the frigid climate. The cold winds and cold waters, moving from the north and subject to forces constantly tending to deflect them to the right of their path, favor a cold climate at all seasons. Moreover, warm waters and winds from the south Atlantic are deflected to the right toward western Europe, bypassing eastern Canada. Add to this the fact that the westerly winds from

Table 5. Annual Progression of Temperature and Precipitation for Seattle, WA, and St. John's, Newfoundland

	Jan	Feb	Mar	Apr	May	Jun	Jul	Aug	Sep	Oct	Nov	Dec	Annual
Seattle													
Mean Temp.	41	44	46	52	57	61	66	65	61	54	47	44	53
Mean Precip. (inches)	5	4	3	2	2	1	1	1	2	3	5	5	34
St. John's													
Mean Temp.	24	23	28	35	43	51	59	60	54	45	44	29	41
Mean Precip. (inches)	5	5	5	4	4	4	4	4	4	5	6	5	54

Figures are rounded off to the nearest whole number.

Below: Annual progression of norms and extremes of temperature and precipitation. (Rendering by Michael Emerson and Robert Hutchins.)

Temperature: Solid lines are for normals of high and low temperatures; jagged lines show extremes of high and low temperatures during 1987.

Precipitation: For each month, left bar is 1987 record and right bar is normal.

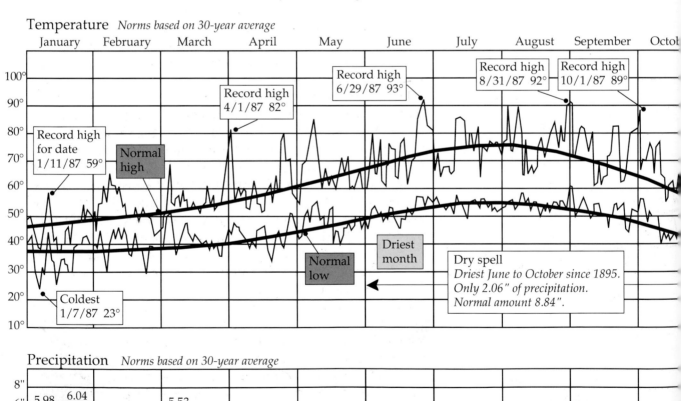

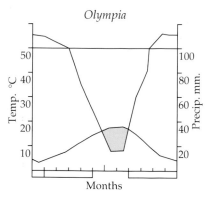

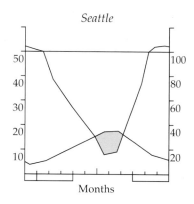

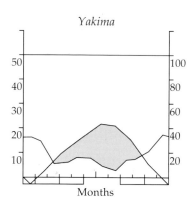

Above: Annual cycles of temperature and precipitation joined in a single graph. Note the differences in temperature and precipitation in the summer months for the three localities, Seattle and Olympia contrasted *with Yakima, east of the Cascade Range. Drought periods are visibly distinguished by high temperatures and minimal rainfall. (Chart adapted by Michael Emerson.)*

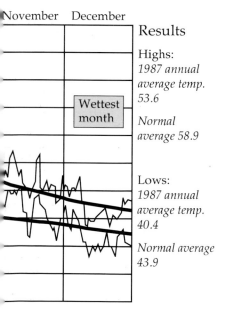

November December

Results

Highs:
1987 annual average temp.
53.6

Normal average 58.9

Lows:
1987 annual average temp.
40.4

Normal average 43.9

Wettest month

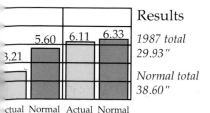

Results

1987 total 29.93"

Normal total 38.60"

| 3.21 | 5.60 | 6.11 | 6.33 |

ctual Normal Actual Normal

off the North American continent are cold and dry, then it is clear why the Newfoundlander is a victim of subarctic climates. Indeed, latitude plays second fiddle to intercontinental forces of wind and water movements.

Precipitation comes mainly as rain to Puget Sound; over 75 percent of it falls between the beginning of October and the end of March. Snowfall in the lowlands is not more than 5 percent of total precipitation. As elevation increases, the percent of precipitation falling as snow markedly increases. In the heart of the Olympics (at Blue Glacier on Mount Olympus) about 80 percent of total precipitation comes as snow. Annual precipitation for the Puget Sound basin ranges from 33 inches at Bellingham and 36 inches for Seattle, up to 52 inches at Olympia. A grand average of 40.39 inches has been struck for all of Puget Sound lowland. Every month brings some precipitation, though minimal amounts fall from June to September.

Humidity follows the temperature and precipitation patterns of gradual change over the year. High humidity dominates from October to March, with a significant decreasing trend from late spring to early fall. When high summer temperatures do come to Puget Sound, the humidity obligingly falls, a blessed contrast with areas east of the Rockies where high humidity and high temperatures test the fortitude of man and beast.

"Considerable cloudiness with increasing showers. High 58, low 46. Chance of rain: 20 percent tonight; 30 percent tomorrow." That prediction, so frequently heard during a Puget Sound year, is an

immediate consequence of cloud cover. Clouds deflect the sun's input, to reduce the on-the-ground warmth for the period. The result is a drop in temperature. Western Washington, where the sun just skirts the southern horizon in winter, has the lowest heat budget of any place in the United States, outside Alaska. Add to an already meager solar input, the dominating cloud cover, and the heat reaching the land is even less. The close relationship between temperature and cloud cover (and usually rain) reveals a good deal about regional weather. The effects of latitude and cloud cover on the annual heat budget are crucial in regulating the activities and qualities of terrestrial life within our Puget Sound ecosystem. Table 6 tells the heat budget story as a function of latitude and cloudiness for an average year.

The climatic controls of the Pacific Ocean, the oceanic pressure cells, and the terrain interact to make local weather. All major bodies of water—fresh or marine—prevent temperatures on adjacent land masses from taking headlong flights up or down the Fahrenheit scale. The Pacific Ocean and Puget Sound, as well as

Above: Map of average annual precipitation in inches. Contour lines (isohyets) define zones of equal rainfall for western Washington and southwestern British Columbia. Thus, rainfall in the vicinity of Seattle is between the 30- and 40-inch isohyet.

Opposite: Dramatic cloud formation shows weather in the making over Puget Sound. (Photo by Mary Randlett.)

Table 6. Solar Radiation (in Langleys)

Hourly, Seattle (SeaTac Airport)

AM	1	2	3	4	5	6	7	8	9	10	11	Noon
January							.2	2.8	5.3	8.3	10.0	14.6
June				1.2	6.8	15.4	25.6	36.8	47.2	55.9	61.0	62.7

PM	1	2	3	4	5	6	7	8	9	10	11	Midnight
January	12.3	8.5	3.5	.4								
June	60.5	52.9	43.1	30.8	19.0	8.4	1.5					

Average Daily Solar Radiation, Seattle vs. Phoenix, Arizona, 1968

	Jan	Feb	Mar	Apr	May	Jun	Jul	Aug	Sep	Oct	Nov	Dec	Annual
Seattle	79	143	261	389	503	514	558	455	331	192	103	66	300
Phoenix	300	405	524	631	709	721	648	599	546	441	330	274	511

Note: Langley is the heat unit used to denote one gram calorie per square centimeter (data from U.S. Weather Bureau).

the many lakes in the region, form a great atmospheric heat reservoir; their waters have tremendous capacity for storing heat and for releasing it only slowly. Adjacent land masses capture far less heat although they may reach a higher temperature than the water in the process. When the land cools, the heat reservoirs of ocean, Sound, and lakes release their stored warmth to the circulating masses of air. We are thus enveloped by a thermostatically controlled blanket of air, cooled in the summer and warmed in the winter.

Besides its buffering effect on temperature, the Pacific Ocean exerts other profound influences on the lowland climate. From mid-October on into early spring, the prevailing winds come eastward from the ocean, bringing moisture from the North Pacific. As this moist air moves over the cooler land, it condenses to bring the predictable rainy season to the Pacific Northwest coastal region.

Now if the land were monotonously flat, the Pacific air would lose its moisture gradually along an east-trending path. But mountains exert a profound effect on the wet air borne by the prevailing westerlies. Both the coastal rampart of the Olympics and the windward face of the Cascades deflect the eastward-moving air. When caused to rise by a topographic barrier (orographic lifting), the moist Pacific Ocean air comes to saturation, and precipitation results.

The Pacific Ocean and the mountain ramparts of Puget Sound are but passive props on the regional weather stage. The real driving force is a complex integration of solar heat flow and planetary movements. These two global engines drive the atmosphere in more or less predictable directions. The result for Puget Sound and the Pacific Northwest is the development of two major pressure cells over the North Pacific Ocean. Pressure here is the force exerted by a given column of the atmosphere upon objects below it; that is, the weight of air per unit area.

The two pressure cells are born of the worldwide circulation which carries warm air poleward from the tropics and returns cooled air to the tropics. The results in the Northern Hemisphere are vast swirls of cyclonic (counterclockwise) and anticyclonic (clockwise) winds around areas of low atmospheric pressure and high pressure, respectively.

Earl L. Phillips, former climatologist for the Washington State office of the Weather Bureau, described the essential influences of the two oceanic pressure systems:

> The location and intensity of the semi-permanent high and low pressure areas over the north Pacific Ocean have a definite influence on the climate. Air circulates in a clockwise direction around the semi-permanent high pressure cell and in a counter clockwise direction around the semi-permanent low pressure cell. During the spring and summer, the low pressure cell becomes weak and moves north of the

Aleutian Islands. At the same time, the high pressure area spreads over most of the north Pacific Ocean. A circulation of air around the high pressure center brings a prevailing westerly and northwesterly flow of comparatively dry, cool and stable air into the Pacific Northwest. As the air moves inland, it becomes warmer and drier which results in a dry season beginning in the late spring and reaching a peak in mid-summer. (1965:2)

He went on to explain the winter low pressure system:

In the fall and winter, the Aleutian low pressure center intensifies and moves southward, reaching a maximum intensity in mid-winter. At the same time, the high pressure area becomes weaker and moves southward. A circulation of air around these two pressure centers over the ocean brings a prevailing southwesterly and westerly flow of air into the Pacific Northwest. This air from over the ocean is moist and near the temperature of the water. Condensation occurs as the air moves inland over the cooler land and rises along the windward slopes of the mountains. This results in a wet season beginning in October, reaching a peak in winter, then gradually decreasing in the spring.

Dominant Pressure Systems

These gigantic heat and wind engines—the semipermanent low and high pressure systems of the North Pacific—deserve closer attention. The Aleutian Low, a trough of low pressure that occupies the Gulf of Alaska from October to February, comes into being at the same time that cold and dry air is being produced in continental Asia and North America. This cold air, most often from Asia but sometimes from Alaska and northern Canada, flows around the low and meets the relatively warm oceanic current, known as the North Pacific Drift. This warms and moistens the air, mixing it through deep layers, converting it into a Polar Pacific air mass. As this hybrid airstream moves eastward it continues to gain moisture that condenses as precipitation, especially when it reaches the coastal land mass. As the air advances inland, still more moisture falls on the land when the air encounters the Cascade and Olympic mountains.

Frequently in winter, the joint effect of the mountain barriers and the prevailing high pressures over the inland areas of Oregon, Washington, and British Columbia may cause the eastbound storms to stagnate for days over the Gulf of Alaska. More rarely in winter, Polar Continental air breaks out of the interior of Canada to reach the coastal area without having made the detour around the low pressure cell and across the warmer ocean. The severe freezes of November 11, 1955, and February 1–10, 1989, are two examples of

Winter weather in the Pacific Northwest. A typical, mild but rainy day (March 5, 1989) west of the Cascades, while snow is predicted east of the mountains. (Rendering by Robert Hutchins.)

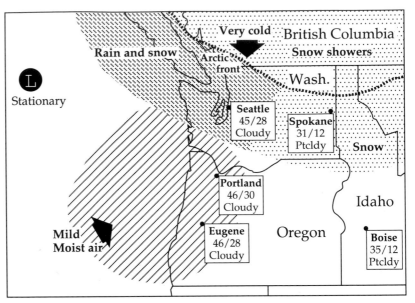

Key

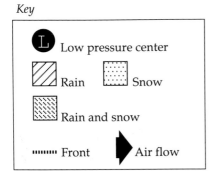

polar eccentrics that got deflected down the Fraser River to congeal Puget country with below-freezing weather. More about the historic 1955 freeze shortly.

In summer, the Aleutian Low weakens and retreats northward while the North Pacific High, which was in subtropical latitudes during the winter, moves northward. Cool North Pacific air descends into Puget Sound from the north, a direction dictated by the relatively low pressure of the now-warmed land mass. Moreover, in the summer, cold Pacific Ocean waters upwell to create the conditions for the familiar fogs and low stratus clouds on the open coast. Such an overcast quickly dissipates as the oceanic air moves east over inland areas that are heated during the day.

The "patient climatologist's" view of predictable maritime weather year in and year out may seem a bit unreal to Puget Sounders who often bear witness to devilish capriciousness in day-to-day weather. What accounts for an unusually wet period in June and early July? Or, how can we explain the unexpected change in August from hot dry days to gusty wet ones? How does it happen that several clear but cold days often follow one after the other in winter? The daily users of the commodity called weather are as much affected by the course and causes of inconsistencies in weather as by the more predictable displays.

Above: Low fog and mist rising off the inland sea in the San Juan Islands. (Photo by Mary Randlett.)

Left: Water vapor rises from the surface of the Nisqually River near Elbe, to join the fog enveloping the forest. (Photo by Mary Randlett.)

Eccentricities of Weather

Two or three samples of eccentric weather should suffice to show that the great climate-making machinery of sun, winds, and tides does not run with perfect predictability. First, look at the causes of those occasional summer rains that dampen a garden party, cause backpackers to huddle for shelter, and upset a host of other plans for outdoor human pleasures. In summer, the general flow of surface air is from the north and northwest, heading east through the Strait of Juan de Fuca and down the Sound. This air has come from the huge Pacific High Pressure Cell, which may be centered west or southwest of Puget Sound but which extends well to the north. As it reaches the coast, it is kept cool by the North Pacific Ocean, but does not usually form a cloud cover because it is simultaneously sinking or subsiding very slowly. If the wind shifts from the northwest to the south and southwest, the temperature drops, and cloudiness increases. With the shift in prevailing winds, comes some rain. This quick change is brought about by one of the traveling low pressure cells that occasionally come as far south as Seattle's latitude in midsummer. When they do come, they bring thunder showers or two or three days of rain. Just such a shift can happen any time in summer. It can be warm and dry for several days all over the Puget Trough up to mid-August. Then, overnight, the rains will come, steadily or with intermittent drizzle and overcast for several days following. The migrant low has interrupted the flow of warm, dry air from the dependable summer North Pacific High.

In winter, Puget Sounders resign themselves to a predictable cloud cover, drizzle, rain, and a nearly stabilized temperature regime of 36 degrees F at night and 45 degrees F by midafternoon. But every so often in the winter, the protective cloud buffer and the narrow range of temperatures well above freezing give way to an abrupt cold spell. At such times, the Sound is blanketed by cold polar air that has spilled out of the Great Plains, passing over the Rockies and eventually over the Cascades. By the time this air reaches Puget Sound it will have gained some heat but still be able to chill life in the basin, at temperatures near the freezing point. Although the mountains take some of the bite out of the polar air, western Washington can get a good chill. As the polar air is dry and clear of clouds, nighttime cooling may push the temperature to 20 degrees F or lower. Often a snow cover may precede a cold spell. The clear, cold weather may last a week or more, until altocumulus clouds reappear, bringing precipitation again, first as snow then as rain. The warmer maritime air with its rain, called a "chinook," dissipates the snow. Then, back to normal.

Above: A storm brewing over Seattle is watched by strollers on Harbor Avenue in West Seattle near Duwamish Head. (Photo by Betty Udesen.)

Below: Dramatic cloud formation. (Photo by Mary Randlett.)

Most often the visitations of polar air to the Sound are short-lived and not too severe. But late fall of 1955 proved to be an untimely and near catastrophic exception. Earlier than most polar thrusts, the freeze of 11–17 November caught native vegetation, gardens, and crops totally unprepared. Up to the eleventh, minimum temperatures had remained well above freezing so that the hardening process for plants had not begun. Then,

> . . . on the 10th, colder air overspread Canada, though minimum temperatures south of the border were in the 40's. On the morning of the 11th, very cold air accompanied by strong northerly winds moved into Washington, and on the morning of the 12th, temperatures west of the Cascades ranged from 10° to 15° and from 0° to 10° east of the Cascades. The temperature continued to fall until the morning of the 15th when readings ranged from 0° to 15° in western Washington and 0° to −19° in eastern Washington. The cold air extended across Idaho, Oregon, and into northern California. New record low minimum temperatures for November were established in most areas. Several thousand boxes of apples were frozen and unharvested vegetable crops were a complete loss. (Phillips 1962).

The local Internal Revenue Service office was flooded with calls from homeowners wanting to write off as tax losses the devastation wreaked on their gardens. The record of the tree rings and branch growth in forest trees still marks with precision the coming of the unforgettable November 1955 freeze.

Snow in lowland Puget Sound is expected each winter but in modest amounts. Our average snowfall for over seventy years is 11.1 inches,[1] ranging from a trace to a remarkable 61 inches. Heavy snowfalls make history and 61 inches is one such historic snow. Even before the fleecy white deluge of the winter of 1916, more than the usual depths of snow had come to Seattle. January of that year was a particularly snowy month with 23.3 inches falling, and 4 inches remaining on the ground on the thirtieth. Then,

> . . . snow began falling before noon on 31 January and 11 inches had fallen by 1700 on February 1st. Street car traffic was delayed on some of the hills, but the worst was yet to come. From 5:00 PM on the 1st of February to 5:00 PM on the next day, 21.5 inches of snow fell and had accumulated to a depth of 26 inches. The maximum depth of snow on the ground in the downtown area was 29 inches measured at 10:00 PM on the 2nd of February. By the previous noon, trees had begun breaking under the weight of the snow and street car traffic was suspended on nearly all lines. . . . The dome of St. James Cathedral collapsed under the weight of the snow. . . . The old Alki Natatorium and the West Seattle Christian Church were damaged and a section of the grandstand at Denny Field on the University of Washington campus fell. (Phillips 1962)

1. An inch of rain equals ten inches of snow, approximately.

Above: Rhododendron leaves droop during a spell of below-freezing temperatures in a Puget Sound garden. (Photo by the author.)

Above right: A heavy snowfall in rural Puget lowlands.

Right: Downtown Seattle at First Avenue and Pike Street was nearly immobilized by the exceptionally heavy snowfall of 1916. Record snowfalls are rare in lowland Puget country. (Photo by C. F. Todd.)

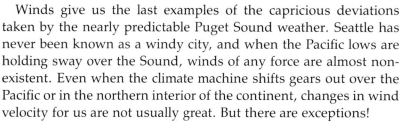

Left: Occasional severe winds lay waste to lowland forests. This "blowdown" of 1921 was in Clallam County just landward of the Strait of Juan de Fuca. (Photo by Asahel Curtis.)

Below left: Uprooted tree just after a windstorm in the winter of 1921 on the Olympic Peninsula. The shallow, horizontally spreading root system is typical of forest conifers.

Below: The infrequent windstorms in Puget lowlands endanger life and property. Downed trees on houses in the Lake Sammamish area, 1961.

Winds give us the last examples of the capricious deviations taken by the nearly predictable Puget Sound weather. Seattle has never been known as a windy city, and when the Pacific lows are holding sway over the Sound, winds of any force are almost non-existent. Even when the climate machine shifts gears out over the Pacific or in the northern interior of the continent, changes in wind velocity for us are not usually great. But there are exceptions!

Three windstorms stand out in the annals of natural catastrophes in the Pacific Northwest. In each instance the brunt of the winds was borne by the forests: trees fell like matchsticks in a wind tunnel. Record windstorms are called "blowdowns" in the Northwest, for the great devastation of forests they leave in their wake. The first of these rare windstorms is remembered as "the Great Olympic Blowdown" of January 1921. Though its force was felt in the Sound area, it was the southwestern Washington coast that took the full impact. On the afternoon of January 29, 1921, the typical low pressure barometric readings of an average winter storm began to drop further, just before the lowest reading of 979 millibars (or 28.90 inches) was reached; winds at that time were at 40 miles per hour. But within minutes the velocity increased to 100 mph, peaking a short time later at 113 mph, with gusts up to 150 mph. An eyewitness account was provided by a keen observer, Mr. Perry Hill, in charge of the Weather Station at North Head, at the mouth of the Columbia River near Ilwaco. He and his wife were returning to the weather station when the elements foretold danger. They had the good sense to abandon their car in heavy forest and seek refuge in a clearing. Mr. Hill reported that

> The southeast wind roared through the forest and falling trees crashed to the ground in every direction. A great spruce fell across the roadway within 10 feet of where we stood. Many trees were broken off where their diameter was as much as four feet. Tree tops broke off and sailed through the air, some of the trees fell with a crash, while others toppled over slowly as their roots were torn from the earth. Between 1545 and 1550 [3:45–3:50 PM] the wind shifted to the southwest and the velocity decreased. (Phillips 1962)

Oldtimers remember another severe storm which hit western Washington on October 21, 1934. The death toll in the Northwest from that storm was eighteen, with winds recorded at 70 mph in Seattle and 90 mph in outlying areas.

A later blowdown, christened the Columbus Day "Big Blow," cut a path of devastation across western Oregon and Washington on October 12, 1962. Similar in intensity to the 1921 and 1934 storms, the Columbus Day debacle had a greater impact on human activity, destroying power lines, communications, buildings, and other

built structures, as well as taking a mammoth toll on nearly 10 billion board feet of standing timber. Forty-six people were killed in that storm. The meteorological interpretation of the storm is still a puzzle. It fits neither the character of a typhoon (hurricane) nor of a more common midlatitude cyclone. It is just possible that the Columbus Day storm was the regenerated extratropical tail of Frieda, a tropical storm that had supposedly petered out in the Western Pacific only three days before.

Though the infrequent windstorm may have its epicenter south and west of Puget Sound, much of its might can be felt in the basin itself. Power outages are caused by trees falling across utility lines, massive numbers of conifer branches are whipped off trees, bridges across Lake Washington become awash with windswept waves, and miscellaneous urban flotsam flies through the air. It can be an awesome, and dangerous, spectacle.

Whatever the cause, such cyclonic storms are blessedly infrequent in the Northwest. Their rare occurrence, and the infrequent appearance of other weather eccentricities, should remind us not to rely only on the predictable. Besides its predictability, weather can be fickle, a reminder to humans that they are still subject to uncontrollable forces on the planet.

The rare natural event—an extreme in weather, a devastating geological upheaval, a catastrophic pestilence in a forest—can abruptly change the quality of natural communities or organisms. The so-called "Law of the Mean" is important in accounting for the perpetuation of long-term trends. But the "Law of the Extreme" often marks the end of a trend and initiation of a new one. Fire, vulcanism, cyclonic winds, the advance or retreat of glacial ice, extreme heat, cold, or drought can cause rapid changes in the pattern of life. The history of life in the Puget Sound basin can be interpreted from both the orderly progression of averages or trends and from the near one-of-a-kind events that frequent the corridors of the past.

Ultralocal Weather and Climate

Life is supported within a thin skin of soil, water, and atmosphere— the biospheric surface of planet Earth. Though the quality of the atmosphere is largely determined by global and regional influences, amazingly varied local conditions do exist. For an ant, the weather under a rock can be vastly different from that on the outer surface of that protecting boulder. A seed that becomes lodged on the lee side of a clod of earth is more likely to germinate there than on the drier, more exposed side of the micromountain. And at the human scale, the weather in downtown Seattle can be noticeably different from the weather only a few miles out in suburbia. Variations in topography, at all scales of magnitude, the nature of the surfaces and quality of materials exposed to the atmosphere, as well as the presence, absence, or quality of plant cover, all can produce significant local deviations from the "normal" climate. A whole subdivision of meteorology, aptly named micrometeorology, deals with the measurement and interpretation of climate in small-scale environments, especially at ground level.

We can begin to appreciate local temperature differences in the central Puget Sound area based on a study done by Cliff Mass, an atmospheric scientist at the University of Washington. On a cool November morning in 1987, from 6:00 to 7:30 A.M., Mass and his students took temperature readings all over King County. They recorded appreciable variations within the local region: thus, on November 28, 1987, the high in the early morning was 42 degrees F at Hunts Point, and the low was 25.6 degrees F at Woodinville.

A good place to begin the study of small-scale climates is with the heat budget. The sun's energy is dissipated by reflection and absorption as it passes through layer after layer of the upper and

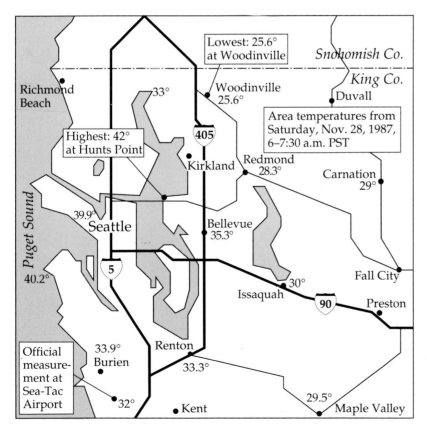

Local variations in temperature for lowland central Puget Sound basin, recorded on November 28, 1987, between 6:00 A.M. and 7:30 A.M. Highest was at Hunts Point on Lake Washington (42°F); lowest was at Woodinville (25.6°F). (Rendering by Robert Hutchins.)

lower atmosphere before it reaches the earth's surface. At the ground, the remaining energy is either reflected or absorbed by the living and nonliving substance of the ground-level environments. If that environment is irregular in form and substance, significant local differences in absorption and reflection of heat will occur. Just think of all the variables in the intricate mosaic of our habitat: land versus water, bare soil versus vegetation cover, density and quality of plant life (open and sparsely spaced versus dense; trees versus shrubs versus grassland, etc.), color of substrate, whether it be natural or man-made (snow, soil, asphalt, cement, painted surfaces, etc.). One can recall the relief upon stepping from a hot parking lot to the adjacent cool park of trees and grass. Each microenvironment has its own heat budget that organisms can sense. By adding the variables of season, time of day, atmospheric moisture, cloud cover, and wind to the factors controlling the heat budget of microenvironments, the array of possible "pinpoint" weathers escalates.

The hilly terrain and the lakes bequeathed to us by the Pleistocene's scouring ice give Puget Sound country the ingredients for distinct microclimates. The irregular topography, with slopes of contrasting exposure and valleys broad or narrow, creates conditions for local air movements. One result is a system of cold air drainages. As each day wanes, cold air, produced at the earth's surface, begins to pour downhill to reach whatever "heat sink" lies at the foot of the terrain. When the heat sink is confined as in a basin, contoured by natural conformations of the land, or by a vegetation barrier, or by an artificial impediment, the cold air is trapped. The garden at the bottom of a cold-air drainage suffers the fullest brunt of nighttime frosts, while neighboring land upslope may go unscathed. Bogs, ponds, and small confined lakes are particularly dependable heat sinks. Minimum temperatures at the edge of a small lake or bog can be eight to ten degrees lower than in the forest border above the body of water.

If lowlying basins are potential "ice boxes," then why is it that temperatures are relatively more mild around the shores of major lakes, Puget Sound, or the ocean itself? The overriding effect of bodies of water is that of the thermostat—keeping temperatures from skittering widely up or down. Gardens along the shores of Puget Sound can safely grow certain plants that would suffer frost damage only short distances from the water. On large bodies of water the thermostat works well; cold air drainage into Puget Sound or Lake Washington is dissipated over the water, not stopped "cold," as in a small basin. The "banana belts" of locally milder climates here and there around the lowland country are linked to these large bodies of water. The successes of Carl English, who grew many relatively tender kinds of trees and shrubs at the U.S.

Army Corps of Engineers' Locks in Seattle, came in no small part from the proximity of the locks to Puget Sound. His good fortune with plants of borderline hardiness has been repeated by many a local gardener lucky enough to live in the right place.

Dirty Air in Puget Sound

Ten A.M., a Tuesday in mid-September, a clear day in Puget land and I should be able to see forever! But no, from my third-story outlook southward over the University of Washington campus, Mount Rainier today is only a dim iceberg veiled by massive haze. Along the skyline, hills and valleys are obscured by a pallid atmospheric smear. And on occasions earlier in the summer, both sun and horizon were separated from vision by a much denser atmospheric load. Air pollution? Yes and no. If by air pollution we mean gaseous and particulate matter given off into the air from hu-

Fishermen on Elliott Bay during a smog alert, December 13, 1985. (Photo by Jimi Lott.)

Above: Open burning at garbage dumps, once common, is now banned in most Puget Sound cities.

Above left: An emission plume from a pulp mill on Commencement Bay, Tacoma.

Below left: Industrial air pollution in Seattle during the early part of this century—before pollution controls were enforced.

man preoccupations with powering a mechanized world, the answer is yes. But there are other sources of haze and smog. The surface of the earth has yielded pollutants to the atmosphere for eons. Volcanic ash, cyclonic winds laden with dust, detritus from weathering processes, and the like, have obscured the sun and beclouded the air over and over again. And living things have made their own dirty air over the ages. The earliest human inhabitants surely witnessed the smokes and hazes from natural fires and from those they may have set intentionally. Wherever there is vegetation there may be a haze of a more subtle origin. Frits Went (1955), noted plant ecologist and physiologist, claims that forests, especially coniferous forests, give off volatile byproducts that react with air and sunlight to produce the characteristic blue haze over vast areas of certain forested landscapes.

The word "pollution" has come to mean many things, mostly unpleasant. The terms thermal pollution, noise pollution, and visual pollution round out the vocabulary for the undesirable byproducts of our twentieth-century societies. In ecological terms, air and water pollution should be interpreted in the context of the normal and efficient recycling of substances that are living or dead and inanimate. Thus, any substance that can be reprocessed by other organisms does not block the system. On the other hand, some pollutants impede a normal reprocessing function. Either the pollutant cannot be recycled by living things or it interferes with—perhaps even poisons—the metabolism of the living system. In this sense, these pollutants are resources out of place.

Some air pollution is a product of the planetary "engine"—smoke, haze, and dust from natural activities ongoing through time immemorial. This fact surely should not put us at ease about the magnitude of dirty air in modern times. The added burden to the air generated by human activity is enormous, and at times and places it is critically dangerous. What are the atmospheric conditions that cause lowlying smogs and other aerial blights? Why are cloudy or rainy days relatively smog-free? Why are some clear days as in winter truly clean and clear, while other cloudless periods are eye-irritating, view-obstructing, and cough-inducing?

The ingredients that will make atmospheric pollution close to the ground are those that produce typical weather at certain seasons, plus some eccentric factors. The sources of pollution are all of the various energy-yielding, combustion-demanding activities set in motion by humans: transportation, commercial and industrial energy consumptions, and the multifarious domestic activities that consume energy. Most energy transformations that humans use are inefficient. The uncombustible portions of the fuel are emitted as smokes or clouds of other tiny particles, or as gasses. Over the

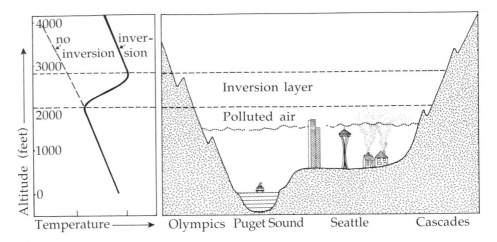

years we have tended to emit these substances into the atmosphere as though it were an infinitely large reservoir. The rationale (and myth) has been that such aerial effluents dilute themselves to harmlessly small amounts, until they become innocuous. We have lately learned to our chagrin and annoyance, and often to our grief, that the dilution dogma seldom works well—if at all. The atmosphere does cleanse itself eventually, but it may require days, months, or even years to rid itself of some pollutants.

Given the human polluter, how does the atmosphere of the Puget Sound basin "package" the pollution in noxious concentrations and turn it back onto the source? The basinlike configuration of the land provides the receptacle for condensing the brew. Infrequent stable atmospheric conditions hold the pall in place; and a lid is placed on the whole mess by temperature inversion.

Look at each of these factors more closely. First, the Puget Sound basin, trending north to south, should act as a funnel for winds coming from the southwest in the winter and from the northwest in the summer. But whenever these winds are insufficient to move the air, it stagnates in the basin. So the combination of a gigantic receptacle for holding stagnant air and a stable atmosphere sets residents up for a spell of bad air, especially if the lid is on. The lid is a creation of a frequent inconsistency in the physics of the atmosphere. Ordinarily, temperature decreases with increase in altitude; air gets progressively cooler the higher it goes. But sometimes this temperature gradient is reversed. Upper warmer air may cap cooler air below. While human activities in cities are adding effluents to the lower layer, the lid of temperature inversion remains in place. This concentrates the smog near the ground, readied now for human consumption. Only when a weather system moves in from the ocean, or wind speeds increase, does the stable air mass with its irritant load disperse.

Temperature inversion in atmosphere puts a "lid" on polluted air. Left: Graph of normal temperature decreasing with altitude (dotted line), and temperature increase (inversion) at c. 2,000 feet altitude (solid line). Right: Cross-section at Seattle of Puget Sound basin during an inversion. (Drawing by Sandra Noel.)

Acid Rain. Dirty air eventually disperses throughout the Puget trough and beyond. But the pollutants do not vanish; they settle out somewhere, on land or at sea. Some of the dispersed pollutants become transformed into acids, as aerosols in the atmosphere. The fallout of "acid rain" onto land and water surfaces can appreciably alter the chemistry—and the life—of soils and bodies of water. Do we have an acid rain problem in Puget country? If we do, it certainly has not reached the crisis stage like that in Europe or eastern North America. There, the evidence is strong that industrially generated air pollution that forms nitric or sulfuric acid is killing forests and the life of lakes.

In the forested lands west of the Cascades, natural acidification is already a way of life, and forest vegetation has adjusted to the relatively high acidity. Furthermore, red alder, a tree that commonly pioneers after logging or fire, causes soils to become yet more acidic, perhaps ten times more acid than from normal rain. Yet lowland conifer forests do replace alder in time. The big question is whether further acidification of soils by human-generated air pollution will adversely affect our forests. The question in the Northwest is being studied, but the answers are not yet fully known. Other aerial pollutants of human origin may turn out to be more critical for forests than acid soils. Ozone and PAN, pollutants from combustions (exhaust from cars, industry, etc.), directly and adversely affect foliage. Ozone concentrations ten times greater than normal have been recorded near Mount Rainier.

"There Is Really No Such Thing As Bad Weather"

Puget country's regional climate nicely illustrates the unbounded nature of any ecosystem. While local ecologies and habitats do have their uniquenesses, their particular attributes are fashioned also from external influences. Climate descends on Puget Sound prevailingly from the southwest out of the Pacific Ocean, but with impressive deviations from the north when frigid Arctic air reaches the basin. Wherever it may come from, weather reaches the basin from beyond—and the ecosystems respond accordingly. Further, our modified Mediterranean-type climate—wet autumns and winters but nearly dry summers—can have major departures from the normal. Extremes of heat and cold, wet or dry, can occur, as can variations caused by local differences in topography. So ecology and climate are intricately interwoven with threads of local to global reach. John Ruskin's words on weather are a comforting end to this chapter: "Sunshine is delicious, rain is refreshing, wind braces up, snow is exhilarating; there is really no such thing as bad weather, only different kinds of good weather."

Land, water, and life interact along the inland sea bordering Bainbridge Island. (Photo by Mary Randlett.)

3 The Inland Sea

"To stand at the edge of the sea, to sense the ebb and flow of the tides, to feel the breath of a mist over a great salt marsh . . . is to have knowledge of things as nearly eternal as any earthly life can be."—Rachel Carson

Remove the islands and smooth out the irregularities of coastline, and Puget Sound now appears as a J-shaped figure with a perimeter of about 200 miles. But a bird's eye view of the real Sound sees its special magic: tortuous, sinuous, indented—adjectives that portray the intricacy of its coastline. Innumerable bays, inlets, promontories, mud flats, and gravelly or sandy beaches form the intricate contours of the shore. Add to the convoluted outline of Puget Sound the myriad islands of all sizes (from the great Whidbey to the smallest bare bird rocks), and the variety and extent of shoreline escalates to a grand total of 2,000 miles (3,220 kilometers). The total surface area of water contained by the Sound comes to 768 square nautical miles; a nautical mile is 6,076 ft.

Up to now I have used the place name "Puget Sound" in almost every context other than its original one: the body of water so named by Captain Vancouver in 1798 for the southern portion of this inland sea. The lowland basin with its mountainous perimeter, its river valleys and deltas, its terrain, and the life that the land supports, all gravitate to the Sound itself. Some call Puget Sound a "miniature ocean," others portray it as one of the largest systems of estuaries in the world, and those with a biological bias describe it as "one of the most productive bodies of water in the world." Indeed, Puget Sound is the most distinctive feature of the landscape in western Washington.

As in other parts of the world, the land at the edge of this inland sea becomes the busiest stage for playing the human drama. All over the world, humans have settled along coasts, greatly modifying their contexts. The shoreline of Puget Sound—and indeed its bottom—still would be boldly revealed as human-altered environments, even if, by magic, the land and water were to be whisked away.

Physical geographers consider Puget Sound to be an estuarine extension of the Strait of Juan de Fuca, defined by a sinuous coastline southward from Admiralty Inlet and Deception Pass to the tide-washed mud flats at Olympia. Since the waters of Puget Sound, including Hood Canal, are continuous with the strait, the setting of boundaries is rather arbitrary; the local phrase, "Puget Sound and adjacent waters," acknowledges the absence of a discontinuity. North Sound, the channels of the San Juan Islands, and the

Puget Sound, showing major hydrographic features and place names. (Map by Nancy Eberle.)

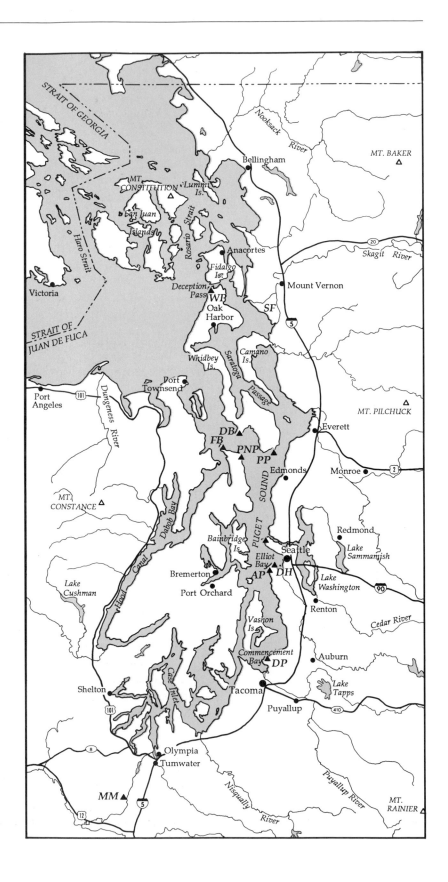

Strait of Juan de Fuca are the "adjacent waters" in a most immediate way. (See Appendix 2 for a discussion of place names.)

What is a sound? An estuary? The definition of "sound" easily fits our image of Puget Sound. The dictionary calls it an "inlet, arm or recessed portion of the sea." But to call Puget Sound an estuary stretches that word's narrow definition as "an arm or inlet of the sea at the lower end of a river"; or in dynamic terms, "an estuary is where the river's currents meet the sea's tide." Since many rivers pour into Puget Sound, it really is more a system of estuaries, not just a single estuary.[1]

Puget Sound is a dynamic body of water in more than one sense. First, there is the unceasing tidal flow of its waters. As a complex estuarine system, Puget Sound is fed by waters from both the land and the sea. Fresh water enters the Sound directly as rain, or from rivers, creeks, trickles, and seeps, and from human discharges via storm drains and treated sewage waters. Fresh water flows into the Sound at an average rate of 140 billion cubic feet a year.

On the saltwater side of the ledger, this dynamic reservoir daily gains and loses water on each tidal cycle from the Strait of Juan de Fuca and the Pacific Ocean. The volume of this so-called tidal prism of water is about 1.27 cubic miles. Visualize a cubical container, somewhat over one mile on each side, filling and draining daily. This awesome amount compares to a total holding capacity of 26.5 cubic nautical miles at mean high water, making Puget Sound one of the world's largest inland seas.

The topographic "vessel" that houses this huge mass of water is a narrow U-shaped submarine trough with numerous lateral canals. Though its average depth at mean low water is 205 feet, there are substantial tracts of deeper water. Each of the four geographically definable basins of the Sound (central Puget Sound basin, Whidbey Basin, South Puget Sound, and Hood Canal) have depths of 600 feet. The deepest hole of all is 930 feet, just off Point Jefferson, only five miles northwest of Seattle. Other deep holes are frequent, especially in the northern sector, where water of 600 to 800 feet is not uncommon. Below the Tacoma Narrows, depths of 300 feet are typical, although a sounding of 546 feet is recorded just off McNeil Island. These extreme depths lead oceanographers to regard Puget Sound as one of the deepest water basins in the conterminous United States.

The waters of Puget Sound lap at many different kinds of shoreline, here sand and water-worn rocks. (Photo by Arthur Grossman.)

1. Puget Sound was designated an "Estuary of National Significance" by the U.S. Environmental Protection Agency in 1988. As with other major estuarine systems (Narragansett Bay, Long Island Sound, and San Francisco Bay), the recognition acknowledges the obvious to those who know and appreciate the uniqueness of Puget Sound. But the recognition does have a tangible element: priority in funding for cleanup and protection of Puget Sound is assured.

The deeper basins of the Sound are partially separated by several submarine dams or ridges, called sills. The Sound is flushed by the action of sea water entering at depth, combined with freshwater supplied by rivers, and then flowing seaward as a dilute surface layer. The three major sills, which restrict the Sound's flushing capacity, are located at strategic positions. One at Admiralty Inlet, the deepest of the sills (218 feet), checks the deeper flow between the Strait of Juan de Fuca and the Sound. The two other major sills are at the entrance to Hood Canal (175 feet at South Point) and at the Tacoma Narrows (145 feet). Other minor sills act as lesser impediments to the turnover of marine and estuarine waters: they are at Blake Island (23 feet), Agate Pass (24 feet), Rich Passage (68 feet), and Hammersley Inlet (11 feet).

How does the submarine topography of the Sound, with its basins and sills, influence the daily and seasonal march of the oceanic tides? And how does this submerged terrain affect the discharge and replacement of resident water with new water? The Sound has for years been a handy laboratory for the oceanographers at the University of Washington, and they now have answers to some of these questions.

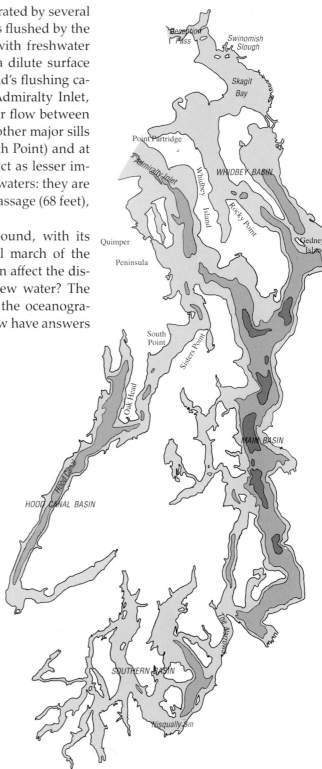

Depth in Meters

0-100
100-200
Over 200

Depth at Sills

Admiralty Inlet 66m
Deception Pass 13m
Swinomish Slough 3m
Gedney Island 97m
The Narrows 44m
Nisqually Sill 31m
South Point 53m
Oak Head 125 m

Variation in depths of Puget Sound at intervals of 100 meters. The deepest places are in the main channel, south from Whidbey Island to below Seattle.

Opposite page: A working model of Puget Sound, showing the southern reaches (Olympia area) at the bottom, and northward to Whidbey Island and Admiralty Inlet at the top of the model. When filled with dyed water and agitated, the model can show tides and currents in action. (Photo by James O. Sneddon.)

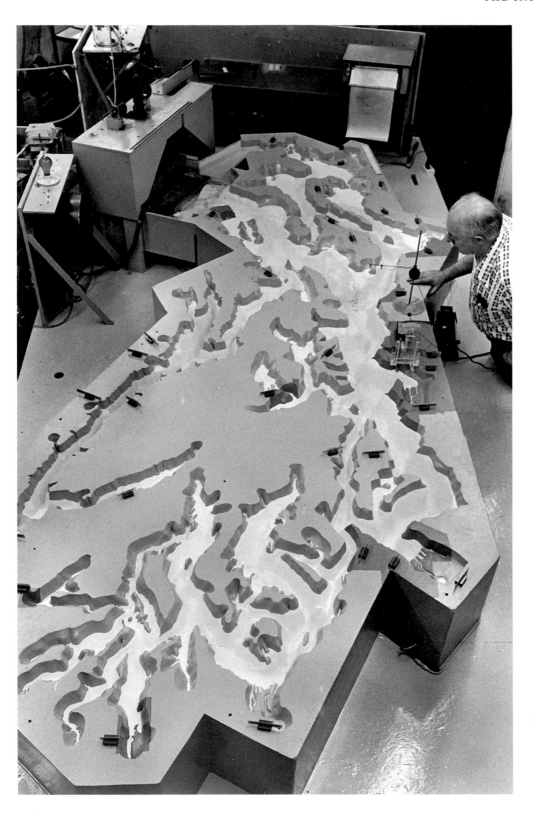

A variety of shoreline types:

Above: Rocky headlands bordering Deception Pass, north end of Whidbey Island. Turbulent flows of tidal water course through the narrow channel into Rosario Strait to the west. (Photo by the author.)

Center top: Low tide exposes rocky (shingle) beach in southern Puget Sound at Tolmie State Park.

Above: Steep eroding bluffs at Cattle Point, southern San Juan Island. Glacial till at top feeds the beach on Haro Strait with sand and cobble.

Left: Undisturbed salt marsh, with salt-tolerant grasses and sedges. (Photo by Mark Sheehan.)

Below left: Mud flats at Discovery Bay, Jefferson County. Salt-tolerant aquatic flowering plants colonizing mud at head of the bay. (Photo by Ron Vanbianchi.)

A seasonal pattern of flow is initiated, far away from the Sound, out in the open Pacific Ocean. In late summer, upwelled dense ocean water flows shoreward at depth into the Strait of Juan de Fuca, to pour over the submarine sills at the entrance of Puget Sound. This dense oceanic water mixes vertically with the less dense surface waters exiting from the Sound at the sills. Tidal flow produces the energy for the mixing. Because of the great inflow of fresh water from the drainage ways on land into the Sound, the volume of near surface water moving seaward over the sills must equal the sum of the influx at depth and the river contribution. The overall result is a net circulation, superimposed on the oscillating flow driven by the tides. On the average, the waters of Puget Sound are effectively replaced twice a year. The major exception, as would be expected, is the deeper water of the lower extremities of that spectacular cul de sac, Hood Canal, and in the deep portions of Dabob Bay, where the replacement time is slowed to about once a year. Given the basin and sill topography of the floor of Puget Sound, it is not surprising to learn that some deeper waters just to the lee of shallow sills are replaced slowly and may become significantly lacking in oxygen as the water ages, a phenomenon of consequence for the type of life that can be supported in such anaerobic habitats.

Above: Sandy beach with forest of conifers and hardwoods down to the water's edge, Tolmie State Park, southern Puget Sound.

Far left: Tilted metamorphic rock makes an impressive coastline in the San Juan Islands. (Photo by Ron Vanbianchi.)

Pollutants discharged from human activities can become an added, and dangerous, burden to the accumulation of natural substances that may pile up here and there in the Sound. While some soluble substances are usually diluted by tidal flushing, particulates bearing toxic materials can settle into the basins bordering the shallower sills. Pollutants in bottom sediments may remain innocuous or become a potent source of toxicity to marine life. The complex interplay between pollutants and marine life in Puget Sound is treated at length in Richard Strickland's *The Fertile Fjord* (see his chapter 7).

Tides and Currents:
The Seaward Ebb and the Landward Flood of Waters

Like the oceans, the waters of Puget Sound are tied to the gravitational pull of the moon and sun. Such celestial influence manifests itself by daily fluctuations in the water level of the Sound. Tidal changes are particularly spectacular here, compared to other localities to the south along the Pacific Coast. Just contrast the daily range in water level (the difference between the highest and lowest tides) for Seattle (11.3 feet), with the same measure for Los Angeles (5.4 feet) and Astoria, Oregon (8.2 feet). As might be expected, there are significant variations in tidal heights even in Puget Sound. At Port Townsend on the northeast tip of the Olympic Peninsula, at the gateway between the Sound and the Strait of Juan de Fuca, the daily tidal range is 8 feet; near Olympia at the "bottom" of the Sound, the range is 15 feet. Life on the shoreline between the tides is at the mercy of severe shifts in environment, from benign and protected conditions while under water at high tide, to demanding exposure during the periods of low tide.

The tidal charts (p. 71) are eloquent testimony to the drastic differences in tidal patterns at different places along the Pacific Coast. Seattle's tidal flux is greater than that of San Francisco but pales in comparison to that of Anchorage, Alaska.

The lunar month with its progression, day by day, of two highs and two lows has a fixed rhythm of its own. But as any fisherman, clam digger, or shorebound naturalist will insist, there is another rhythm of the tides. Its calendar is a whole year, best stated in terms of the four seasons. The annual migration of the earth around the sun produces a change in the lunar monthly pattern. The annual cycle of tidal differences, however, is more subtle than the daily or monthly cycles, as the effect of the sun on the tides is less than that of the moon. One attribute of the annual pattern is the timing of the highs and lows. In winter, for instance, the lowest tides come at ungodly hours for marine biologists and clam diggers—late at night or very early in the morning, but always in the dark! In June the lower low tides are at more accommodating times, between midmorning and midafternoon.

Another seasonal variation is tied to the position of the sun relative to the equator. When the sun is near the equator during March and September, the daily extremes between high and low tides are at a minimum; during June and December, the daily differences between highs and lows are at a maximum.

You can become more familiar with the cyclic changes in the tides by looking at tide tables, in either graphic or tabular form. They are published daily in the newspapers or are in booklet form available at sporting goods stores and boating marinas. With chart or table in hand, observe the tidal changes at some familiar landmark on Puget Sound. (This is an easy pastime in the summer but demanding of fortitude and warm clothing in the winter.) Tidewatchers soon learn that the time of the highs and lows is later by about fifty minutes each day, the lunar day.

Tidal Currents and Wind Waves

The daily rushes of water in and out of all the reaches of the Sound are called tidal currents. Though set in motion by the same forces that activate the tides, the timing and magnitude of the currents are modified by local and regional differences in landforms and meteorological conditions. Variations in topography along the perimeter of the Sound and beneath the water's surface as well as the character of river discharge and weather conditions at any given time greatly modify the celestially controlled tidal currents. Especially variable are the velocities of currents; the greatest rates of flow are in narrow but shallow channels which connect large volumes of water. Thus, the shallow constrictions at Admiralty Inlet, Deception Pass, and the Tacoma Narrows have tidal current velocities of 4.7, 7.2, and 5.1 knots,[2] while in the wider and deeper sectors of the Sound, the velocities are much less.

The direction and speed of winds over the water modify the tidal currents in those areas where tidal currents are slight. Waves generated by winds can either be amplified or reduced by the tidal current. Where the direction of wind waves opposes tidal currents, a steep choppy sea develops, whereas waves traveling in the direction of the current are reduced. Waves on Puget Sound, due to wind, are small compared to those of the open ocean. Oceanic swells have been decreased in their amplitude by the time they reach the entrance to the Sound and are of little consequence. Only

2. One knot equals one nautical mile per hour or 1.15 statute miles per hour.

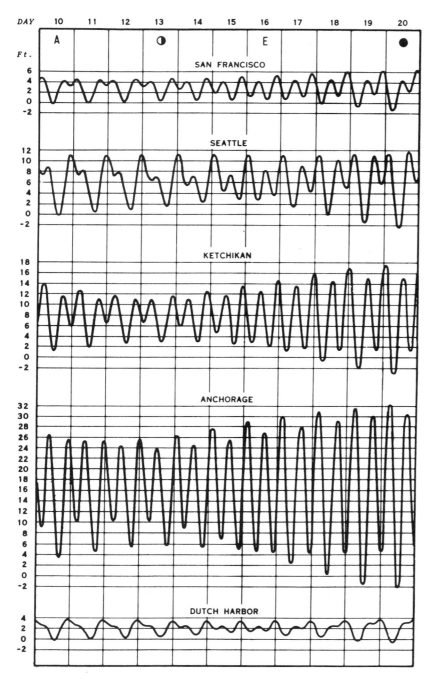

DAY

Lunar data:
A – Moon in apogee
☽ – last quarter
E – Moon on Equator
● – new Moon

Typical tide curves for four Pacific Coast localities over a ten-day period. Tidal amplitudes for Seattle are substantially greater than at San Francisco or Dutch Harbor. Seattle shows tidal inequality well: at certain times the two high waters of a day may differ by more than four feet and the two low waters by more than eight feet. A discussion of tidal curves is on page 69.

to those manning small craft in the Sound or to inhabitants on the shoreline, do the waves created by intermittent wind storms become both a challenge and a danger. During storms, waves four to six feet high can be encountered; the largest waves on record for the Sound were in Dabob Bay (in upper Hood Canal), where they reached a height of eight feet. Waves are limited on the Sound by the fetch, the straight line distance that the wind has to act on the water surface to produce waves.

The Origin of the Submarine Trough System

If Puget Sound were to be drained, one would look into a vast, steep-sided, U-shaped trough. There is little sign from the surrounding topography above the trough to suggest its presence. Though hilly in spots, the above-sea-level land is gentle in slope. How then did the carving of a deep gash down the middle of the Puget basin come about? The answers come from a close reading of the events of the Pleistocene ice ages as they left their mark on the landscape.

During the last maximum glacial activity in Puget Sound, a great tongue of ice completely occupied the space that today is filled with water. The glacier moved into western Washington as a massive outpouring from the continental ice sheet in Canada. Recall from my discussion in chapter 1 that the horizontal spread and the vertical thickness of the Puget Sound lobe of the glacier reached spectacular dimensions. If the ice were at the most 5,000 feet thick as it inched over land above the present sea level, the vertical thickness must have been several hundreds of feet more in the trough of the Sound proper. But was the trough there first, waiting to be occupied by the incoming ice? The answer, elaborated earlier, is no. Rather, the submarine trough was excavated to its current contours and depth by the last (Vashon) glaciation.

The physical features of Puget Sound, as well as the origins of its form are given fuller treatment in two recent Washington Sea Grant publications: R. Burns, *The Shape and Form of Puget Sound* (1985), and J. Downing, *The Coast of Puget Sound: Its Processes and Development* (1983). I deal with the marine biology of Puget Sound in chapters 4, 10 and 11.

Winds and tide acting in concert. On February 2, 1960, a southwesterly gale coincided with an 11.8-foot-high tide at Alki Point, West Seattle. Heavy waves tossed driftwood onto Beach Drive. (Photo by Josef Scaylea.)

Gulls in motion on a Puget Sound beach. The most familiar of shorebirds, it is a common year-round resident and breeding waterfowl. (Photo by Mary Randlett.)

4 Marine Life in Puget Sound

"It is humbling to think that all animals, including human beings, are parasites of the plant world."—Isaac Asimov

Marine biologists are in a special predicament about their domain, the waters of Puget Sound. Whereas the more familiar world of life on land can be sampled directly, marine biologists probe at a distance, with nets, buckets, and dredges, a living world which they perceive only dimly. Our account of Puget Sound marine life, then, must be biased and abbreviated by many deficiencies, all human. Each investigator, casual observer, or research team goes to the Sound to plumb its depths wearing particular blinders. Some biologists are after one kind of organism, others sample only one kind of habitat, and still others are seeking information on the kinds of life important only in human commerce. From that patchwork must come a synthesis, imperfect and incomplete.

Another way of saying this is that there has been no systematic biological survey of the waters of Puget Sound. What has been compiled, though, is so intriguing that we should all share in it. It is the biology of an astoundingly rich and diverse submarine world. Whereas life on land is richest in the tropics, the estuaries and continental shelf of the cool north temperate oceans vie for first place in richness of their marine life.

How is life arrayed in the waters of the Sound? Is it a homogeneous "soup" of algae, tiny floating animals, fish, marine mammals, and birds? Or is it discretely partitioned as semidiscontinuous clusters of organisms attuned to particular habitats? Since life resists cataloguing into discrete categories, it is not surprising that life in Puget Sound is arrayed *both* in continuities and in discontinuities. Some plants and animals are bound to one kind of habitat (a mud flat or a rocky bottom, for instance), while other kinds are found almost everywhere. Exercise with caution, then, the human desire to classify, this time the kinds of habitats.

The physical properties of the basin are far from uniform in any of their dimensions. Superimposed on a sinuous, 2,000-mile-long outline, is the diversity of shoreline. Steep cliffs dominate much of the shore, with only narrow beaches at the toe of the bluffs and headlands. The near vertical rise of cliffs from 50 to 500 feet is made largely of that familiar rubble, the glacial deposits of the ice ages. Only where there are river deltas does the shoreline give way to extensive tidal flats. Narrow beaches come in textures of sand, gravel, or rock, testimonials to the incessant contribution of the bluffs to their replenishment. Mud and fine sand in any extent as a home for beach life are products of rivers like the Skagit, the Stilla-guamish, and the Nisqually.

The tidal wash along the upper shoreline nurtures a rich flora and fauna, though precariously so, because of the daily ebb and flood of protective water. We know most about this intertidal zone of marine life, for we have easy access to it.

Below the influence of the tides is a submarine landscape of great variety: shallow ledges and sills, sloping bottoms, and the deepest troughs of the basin. The habitable bottoms of underwater terrain get their character from processes of onshore geology. Mosaics of sand, clay, and gravel substrates form the predominant settling ground for life, although muds from the dynamic actions of marine waters may thinly coat the coarser materials here and there. The bottom sediments of Puget Sound—the clays, sands, and gravels—come from three sources. First is the erosion of the submarine slopes themselves. The same slopes above water, the nearby bluffs and cliffs, constantly feed coarse and and fine rubble to the water below. But the largest contributors of sediments are the many streams that enter the Sound.

Add to the variety of intertidal and submarine terrain, the pecu-liarities of tidal current and wind/wave action, and hospitable habi-

Above: Giant kelp washed ashore after fall storm. This huge seaweed is an annual plant, living but one year.

Right: Salt marsh, seen here at eye level, is a highly productive tideland ecosystem. This one at the delta of the Nisqually River on southern Puget Sound, accessible to visitors, is managed by the Nisqually National Wildlife Refuge. (Photo by Mary Randlett.)

Left: Tidepool, teeming with marine life, mostly invertebrates and algae; usually in water-worn rock outcrops of the intertidal. (Photo by Robert Tschudy.)

Below: Estuarine habitat where a fresh water stream meets the tidal flux from the inland sea. (Photo by Mary Randlett.)

tats for marine life multiply. Organisms that spend their adult lives as bottom-dwellers form the benthos of the marine environment; benthic plants like kelps and benthic animals like sea anemones are familiar forms of this dimly lit way of life.

Life on submarine terrain is largely a sedentary or sluggish existence, where organisms attach to rock, festoon bottoms, crawl over submarine beaches, or where life perches on other life: plant on plant, animal on plant, and animal on animal. The benthos ranges from the dim world on the bottom of the submarine troughs right up through the intertidal. In the intertidal and splash zones beyond the reach of the tides, marine life commonly sits and waits—the watery world comes to it. Attachment and sedentary ways of making a living take many forms. In the plant world the gamut is from tiny encrusting coatings of algae on rocks, felty patches on sand and mud, and delicate scums, to giant undulating forests of bull kelp and their lesser kin, the sea wracks and other ribbony or feathery seaweeds. And these come in many hues, from bright green to brown to red and even purplish-black.

Benthic animals in their own ways are nearly as diverse as plants in form and size. Though we think of vertebrates of the sea as being freely mobile, some are restricted to shore and to submarine bottoms, and thus are truly benthic. Bottom-inhabiting fish like ling cod, flounder, and petrale sole are rather sedentary. Some

Representative seashore plant and animal life of the coastal intertidal. The diagram shows habitat preferences of marine organisms, and with some exceptions, works for the Puget Sound nearshore zone as well as for the outer coast. (Drawing by Sandra Noel.)

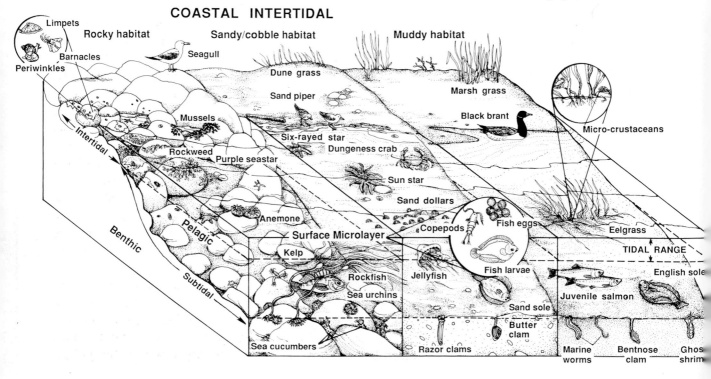

COASTAL INTERTIDAL

Subtidal beds of eelgrass, a marine flowering plant; these productive beds, near Winslow, are home to many marine animals. (Photo by Ron Phillips.)

shore birds seem to stay put in the sense of "attachment" to the intertidal by virtue of their feeding habits. Gulls, sandpipers, phalaropes, and the like, for much of their lives, forage on the intertidal life of the beach, scavenging on its dead remains. It is the animals without backbones, the many kinds of invertebrates, that make the most out of living within and below the tidal flux. The catalogue of invertebrates in Puget Sound easily fills separate books (Kozloff 1983). The different major groups give a glimpse of the variety: sponges; hydroids and sea anemones (sedentary kin of jellyfishes); ribbon worms, round worms, segmented worms; chitons, clams, snails, and limpets; crabs, barnacles, and their other carapaced kin; and finally the spiny-coated relatives, starfish, sea urchins, and sand dollars. In short, nearly every major invertebrate clan has taken up housekeeping in the submarine labyrinth of Puget "canyon-land."

The waters of Puget Sound do more than bathe the sedentary inhabitants of the submerged landscape. Also there, floating and actively swimming, is a plant and animal world free to move around in water. The marine biologist calls this the pelagic zone, the most extensive of the oceanic habitats. For Puget Sound, the pelagic world is never far from shore or bottom. But in the open ocean the very vastness of room for suspended life calls for the distinction between the dwellers of surface layers (in the neritic zone) and the abyssal organisms that know only dimly lit to pitch-dark environments thousands of feet below the neritic layers. Pelagic life in Puget Sound is not markedly different from that of other areas in terms of kinds of organisms present. Indeed, the economy of matter and energy turnovers demands a basic and predictable pattern. The phytoplankton, or floating plants, are microscopic algae that make living substance for themselves and all other life forms from the energy of the sun. They are the food that sets the whole living fabric in motion. Floating vegetation visible to the naked eye is more likely to be some stray kelp or seaweed set loose from its sedentary bottom existence by wind or wave action, a displaced member of the benthos.

The fascinating story of planktonic life in Puget Sound has been told by Richard M. Strickland in *The Fertile Fjord: Plankton in Puget Sound* (1983). The pelagic world of miniature phytoplankton is revealed to us in two ways. We observe it either by the "greening" of the surface waters populated by dense colonies, or blooms, or by painstaking microscopic examination of water samples taken near the surface when the tiny plantlets are not forming blooms. As photosynthetic organisms, phytoplankton should occur only down to depths at the lower levels of light penetration. Whatever the sampling method, the variables in phytoplankton are nearly always the same—great variety in kind and numbers.

Green planktonic life is rich and diverse. Probably no one will ever know just how many kinds exist in the world, they are so small in size and variable as to habitat. Many kinds of green planktonic organisms are known for Puget Sound, and inventorying their diversity is far from done. Experts tell one planker from another by differences in form, color, function, habitat, and so on.

Plankters may occur either as single cells or in simple colonial aggregates of cells. The single-celled types may be shaped like tiny boxes, boats, or balloons; all are invisible to the naked eye. When in cell clusters, the aggregates are usually of a definite and low number: twos, fours, up to a few hundred. These simple colonies may be in filamentous chains, flat plates, or tiny multicellular balls, all of them busy absorbing carbon dioxide and certain dissolved salts from their marine environment and using their photosynthetic machinery for making food with radiant energy from the sun. The food is first used by their tiny selves. But inevitably it will enter the web of pelagic life as food for organisms without the photosynthetic machinery. The assembly line of making fish begins with phytoplankton, or as put by a Chinese philosopher, "Big fish

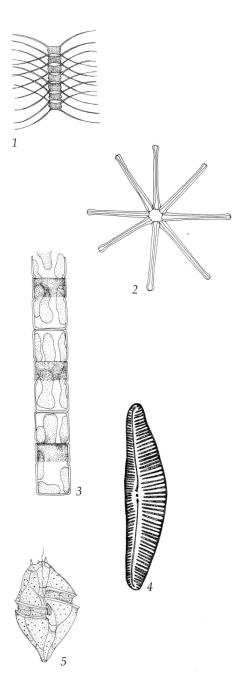

Phytoplankton, the ultimate primary producers in Puget Sound: (1) Chaetoceras, *a diatom; (2) colony of* Asterionella; *(3) chain of* Melosira *cells; (4)* Cymbella, *one of many kinds of diatoms; (5)* Gonyaulax, *dinoflagellate, one of the toxic "red tide" organisms. (Drawings by Sandra Noel.)*

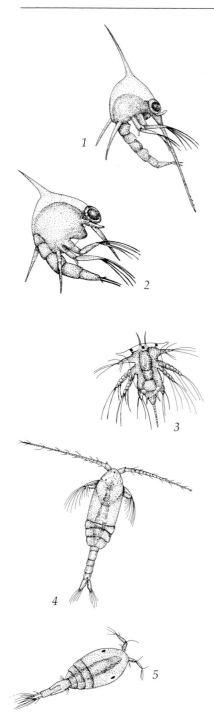

Zooplankton, tiny consumers of phytoplankton. 1-3 are larval stages of crabs and barnacles, while 4 and 5 are tiny adult copepods. (Drawings by Sandra Noel.)

eat little fish, little fish eat bugs, and bugs eat mud." For the marine ecosystem of Puget Sound, read "phytoplankton" for "mud." I suspect that the Chinese sage knew that green mud was alive! Moreover, the "mud" that fuels the aquatic food web embraces more than the floaters. The diatoms and other microorganisms of the bottom (benthos) are copiously eaten, too.

The first harvesters of phytoplankton are their like-sized counterparts without photosynthetic pigments: bacteria, water molds, and zooplankton (animals that float). The bacteria and molds feed mostly on dead organisms; they are the "trashburners" of the sea. Zooplankters are tiny transparent animals, colored green or golden brown only by what they have eaten. They can be single-celled protozoans or multicellular organisms of diverse alliances in the animal kingdom. Of the multicellular types, some may be tiny Crustacea, like miniature shrimp; others may be assigned to animal groups known only by experts in the world of zooplankton. Unlike most phytoplankton, most kinds of zooplankton can move at will with their own means of locomotion, even though this may seem futile when tide currents and wind subvert their efforts. Tiny oars, whiplashes, or flexuous and muscular bodies for swimming give local mobility to such tiny creatures.

Most plant and animal plankton pass their whole lives as floaters; they are eternally pelagic. Yet there are many planktonic organisms that have taken to the buoyant and mobile life as only one brief stage in spinning out a complex cycle of life stages. The sperm, eggs, and larvae of countless invertebrates are pelagic until they grow up into other body forms; or, failing that, they serve as food for other animals or just quietly die and sink into the detritus of the bottom. Life cycles during which spore production alternates with sex cell production are common to a great range of plants, from algae and fungi to flowering plants. Plants and animals of the benthos—kelps, clams, starfish, and their sedentary kin—annually and with great seasonal precision release countless numbers of spores, or sperm and eggs, everywhere in the waters of Puget Sound. A bottle of water from mid-Sound will be a surprising microcosm of microscopic plants and animals—some tiny "adults" whose entire life is pelagic, but others equally minuscule, early stages in a drama of growing up to renew life as bottom or intertidal dwellers.

A Sampling of Undersea Life

We need to flesh out this account of marine life with some examples. My biases lead me to three different portraits of sea life: the kelp beds, the eelgrass meadows, and the fish life of Puget

Sound, each intriguing in its own right. And when examined in detail, each reveals the complexity and diversity of undersea environments and portrays the interconnectedness of things.

Forests in the Sea: Kelp Groves in Puget Sound

Of all the kelps and seaweeds that hug the shorelines of Puget Sound and the open coast, none is more spectacular, evoking mythical sea monsters, than the giant bull kelp, *Nereocystis luetkeana*—*Nereo* (sea nymph) and *cystis* (bladder). (The species name *luetkeana* commemorates the Russian explorer, Count Luetké. An essay on the naming of plants and animals is to be found in Appendix 1.)

Though more common along the outer coast and in the San Juan Islands, bull kelp groves are not infrequent in the waters of Puget Sound. The massive colonies of the plant prefer situations where the sea is in motion. The best beds occupy a zone just below lowest low tide down to a depth of forty to sixty feet (mean low water). The visitor to the beach can get to know this giant marine plant in several ways. The easiest is to encounter the "corpses" of whole plants that litter shorelines after a storm. Stranded on the beach, a typical plant may measure fifteen feet or more, from the anchoring holdfast to the tip of the often tattered blades or fronds. To encoun-

Left: Bulbous float and thick stalk (stipe) of giant kelp, its streamer-like blades missing, detached after a storm. (Photo by Mary Randlett.)

Right: Closeup of kelp blades. (Photo by Victor Scheffer.)

ter bull kelp alive, one must go just beyond the intertidal where exposed parts of the kelp undulate at the surface. From a boat or an overlook on shore, a grove of bull kelp appears as a dense tangle of brownish, streamerlike leaves up to five feet long attached in tufts to a round and hollow, gas-filled float. From the float the plant disappears from sight to descend via a rubbery cord, called the stipe, to its attachment by a tangle of rootlike processes (the holdfast) on a rocky inshore bottom.

Bull kelp plants in Puget Sound can get up to 20 feet long, a prodigious growth for an annual plant of the sea. This same species reaches lengths of 80 feet in the subtidal along the open ocean. One report is of a plant in Alaska waters that attained a length of 270 feet. Note that I said these are lengths attained by an *annual* plant, a species that lives but the span of a year. The kelp's is a way of life similar to giant sunflowers or hybrid corn—but only deceptively so. Events of the annual cycle for bull kelp involve striking changes in the course of a year. Plants like kelp and seaweed are members of a vast clan called the algae. Pond scums, phytoplankton, kelps, seaweeds, and other algae reproduce without flowers or cones, as we shall now see.

In midsummer, when the floating blades or fronds are mature, patches of tissue along the frond stand out as darker and thicker. These patches disintegrate, leaving perforations in the frond. Far from being the results of wear and tear in a demanding environment, the perforations figure in the survival of the species. They are the signs of a stage in a most curious mode of reproduction. Tiny, pigmented swarm cells, capable of swimming by whiplash filaments, are released to the water from the patches of dense tissue; when they are spawned to the open sea, the remaining weakened tissue becomes perforated. Millions of the swarmers are released, but only a small number find a suitable habitat, a rocky bottom of the subtidal.

The swarmers, called zoospores, become transformed into tiny filamentous growths so unlike the bull kelp as to have misled early marine botanists into believing that they had discovered a new algal species. Two kinds of these delicate plantlets result from germinated zoospores; one produces sperm, the other produces eggs. Motile sperm encounter attached eggs, and the life cycle takes another turn. The product of the union of sperm and egg is a tiny plantlet destined to grow rapidly from early spring to summer into a full-grown kelp. Such a roundabout way to produce many kelps from one! But we may read design and strategy into the affair. The tiny swarmers shed from the adult kelp frond spread the species and assure its perpetuity, while the interlude of sex provides the means for hereditary variety so that the species may leave offspring adaptively attuned to different environments. Many other organisms have a similar alternation of sexual with asexual phases in their life histories: ferns, conifers, flowering plants, mushrooms, and most jellyfish. The particular structures in which the alternation is played out may vary. But the common goals of dispersal and genetic variation are achieved.

Intertidal Pastures: The Eelgrass Meadows

If bull kelps thrive in swiftly moving water, another aquatic plant specializes in an equally common but less turbulent habitat. Dense crops of eelgrass, swaying in subtidal waters like wheat rippling in the wind, are at home on muddy bottoms in the lower intertidal and subtidal zones of Puget Sound. One should not read too much into the common name, eelgrass. Known to the botanical world as *Zostera marina,* this saltwater "pasture" plant is only distant kin to the cereal grains, the grasses. But it is a closer relative to grasses than to kelp. In the classification of the plant world, kelps and other seaweeds are members of the loose confederation called algae. Though incredibly varied in body form and mode of reproduction, *no* algae produce flowers or seed. This is just what one would expect if the green way of life began in the sea: plants with primitive modes of propagating themselves persisting as the descendents of ancient marine life. It is unexpected then, to find a plant like eelgrass with flowers and seeds making a success of life in the seas. After all, seed plants evolved on land. Like whales and other marine mammals, eelgrass has taken its heritage of structure and function for terrestrial life and adapted it to life in the sea. In so doing it has become as thoroughly algal in ways other than reproduction as whales have become fishlike. To evolutionary biologists this return of land dwellers to the sea is both predictable and expected. Living things are opportunists. Whenever there exists a way of life as yet unexploited, the chances are that an organism will evolve in structure and function so as to be able to occupy the vacant niche. Very probably, the ancestor of eelgrass was one such opportunist.

Like quack grass on land, eelgrass is gregarious and invasive, spreading by underground stems, or rhizomes. Thin, streamerlike blades, flat and green, grow upward from the rhizomes to festoon the subtidal waters in dense columnar masses. The blades, though delicately thin and narrow, may grow up to six feet long in the lowermost reaches of their subtidal habitat; the blades are progressively shorter in the upper, shallower intertidal areas.

An eelgrass meadow is so dominantly "eelgrass" in composition as to appear having been planted by a single-minded farmer.

Sea wrack (Fucus sp.), a common seaweed of rocky intertidal areas. Also called rockweed or popping wrack, its bladdery tips pop when squeezed. (Photo by Victor Scheffer.)

Monocultures, like fields of corn or wheat, are not common in nature. The price paid for a one-of-a-kind existence is often decimation or extinction by disease or hungry herbivores. This is the costly lesson learned by humans in their practice of agriculture. So how does the natural monoculture of eelgrass survive against catastrophic eradication? Indeed it doesn't in some parts of the world. On the North American side of the Atlantic Ocean, great stretches of eelgrass meadows succumbed to a mysterious "wasting disease" in the 1930s. In one year nearly all the eelgrass beds were destroyed. Populations of all forms of sea life that were dependent on eelgrass were depleted or forced to migrate. Water birds such as the black brant, and other animals, use the plant for food. The thick stands of eelgrass also provide a habitat for many marine organisms.

If monocultures are so susceptible to epidemic onslaughts, why did not West Coast eelgrass pastures succumb? No one knows. The suspected pathogen, a fungus called *Labyrinthula*, is present on Pacific Coast eelgrass. Perhaps, as has been suggested by researchers, the fungus is really a saprophyte, and simply feeds on dead or dying eelgrass tissue. The term monoculture is only superficially valid here. The eelgrass community, actually rich and diverse, may be its own buffer against pathogens. Eelgrass beds only appear to be monocultures. A "pure" stand of eelgrass is more like an untidy weed-infested cornfield, clothed and infiltrated with all manner of smaller plants and animals that may provide the antibiotics needed to keep the eelgrass healthy.

Note the heavy coating of attached algae and tiny invertebrate animals on the eelgrass. (Photo by Ron Phillips.)

Eelgrass has been the specialty of Ronald Phillips at Seattle Pacific University. He has compiled the story of Puget Sound eelgrass in the form of an ecological life history of the plant. Such an account is a detailed biography of an organism: what it is, where it lives, how it makes its living, and its interactions with its environment and other organisms. Phillips (1972) posed the question: How does eelgrass compare with other plants in its capacity to produce living substance from sunlight and inorganic raw materials? Only one other crop, sugar cane, outstrips eelgrass in productivity. Expressed in grams of dry matter produced per square meter of "meadow" per year, the value for Puget Sound eelgrass is 581 grams. Other values for productive agricultural ecosystems do not measure up to eelgrass in Puget Sound. The world averages for wheat, oats, corn, and rice are 344, 359, 411, and 497 grams per meter per year. Looking to natural ecosystems, the values are 446 grams for tall grass prairies in Wyoming and 358 grams for beds of seaweeds in Nova Scotia. Compared to other productive ecosystems, both natural and cultivated, the eelgrass meadow gets high marks as a provider of biomass, both for itself and for all other organisms tied to it in the web of recycling matter.

Eelgrass produces flowers, though not showy ones. All a botanist demands of a flower is that it have one or more stamens that produce pollen and a pistil that accepts the pollen and produces one or more seeds. No decorative petals need be present and eelgrass has none. Sometime in early spring, a special branch emerges near the base of a leaf blade. Within this sheathed and distended segment are alternating rows of pollen-producing and seed-producing flowerlets: the pollen flowers with a single stamen, the seed flowerlets with a single seed-producing portion, the pistil. Drab, yet they fulfill the essential requirements of flowers.

The stamens release thousands of pollen grains to the water. Unlike pollen of land-dwelling flowering plants, the grains, though tiny, are long and filamentous, a most exceptional shape for pollen. Phillips estimates that each pollen chamber contains about 13,500 grains; the waters of an eelgrass meadow should thus be a turbid, cloudy suspension of pollen at the height of reproductive activity. Pollen grains float by chance onto the feathery, pollen-catching tips (stigmas) of the seed-producing flowers. The long grains twine about the stigmas; germination of the pollen and fertilization presumably proceed as in terrestrial flowering plants, though verification is still needed. Pollination (the delivery of pollen to a seed-producing organ) does yield seeds in due course. Each tiny, ripe pistil contains one seed, scarcely as large as a grain of rice. It appears that the seeds are not ejected from the parental home by any complex mechanism. Rather, intact whole plants, as they break

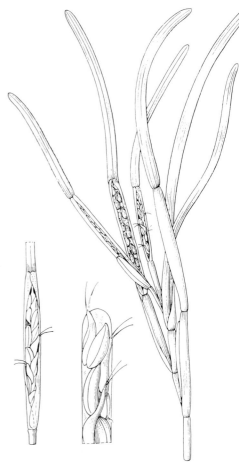

A subtidal flowering plant. A branch of eelgrass with tiny female flowers. Inset shows seed-producing flowerlets and fruit.

away from the home turf, retain their seed-as-offspring, to be released wherever the tattered, detached plant comes to rest. Possibly some seeds are spread by black brant or Canada geese, both voracious feeders on the whole eelgrass plant. Whatever the agents of dispersal, Phillips is sure that the seed-plant mode of reproduction is effective. What better testimonial is there for this successful change of the land-plant way of life to that of the sea, than the spread of eelgrass all along the shores of the Pacific Ocean?

From our vantage point, or that of a Canada goose, eelgrass seems to occur in pure stands. But when viewed up close by shrimp, crab, or microscopic planktonic and benthic organisms, the eelgrass is by no means alone. A wide variety of sea life is harbored in the protective tangle of the eelgrass beds. The plant turns a monotonous stretch of mud and sand into a living landscape where potential microhabitats are vastly multiplied. New places to live are created: the surfaces of leaves, nooks in the crotches of stems, crevices in the flowering stalks and a labyrinth of holes and tiny cracks where the creeping rhizomes enter the mud. And even without settling down on some part of the eelgrass plant itself, swimming and floating life, from plankters to fish, hover and scuttle about in the elfin forest. Herein lies an oft-repeated ecological truth: the presence of plants (or animals) creates homes and ways of life for other animals and plants. In the case of eelgrass meadows in Puget Sound, Phillips found copious growth of diatoms and other algae on the eelgrass blades. This plant-on-plant existence, so widespread in the plant kingdom, on land as well as in the sea, is called epiphytism, and the tenant on the host plant is the epiphyte.

Keeping company with the tiny piggyback algae (the epiphytes) is an array of animals: sea anemones, marine worms, snails, limpets, crabs, and fish. A monoculture it may be to the casual human observer, but for its tenants, the eelgrass pasture is a rich assemblage of many kinds of organisms, living, eating, and dying here.

Given the microtopography of eelgrass plants as housing for other organisms, it is logical that bull kelp beds do much the same. Along the full length of the giant kelp's stipe and blade, there is a felty coating of small plants and animals. James Markham, who catalogued the algal freeloaders of kelp (1969), has reckoned that twenty-three species find homes along the length of the kelp plants. Some species of this epiphytic (plant-on-plant) load may seek a particular level along the host plant for attaining optimal light, but Markham also found that proximity to the bottom is crucial in determining vertical zonation. To determine whether or not a kelp had to be alive to take on the landlordship for other organisms, Markham anchored a sixteen-foot green plastic garden hose on the bottom of a typical kelp bed. Epiphytes took to this surrogate kelp plant in short order and in quantity. Though the lower portion of the artificial kelp was largely devoid of epiphytes, the upper half was readily colonized. Markham concluded that epiphytes care little about the physical or chemical quality of the host; rather, they seek a place to settle down at the same appropriate position above the bottom. The results with the artificial kelp should come as no surprise to the sailor who finds that ropes, pilings, and boat hulls quickly "come alive" when left in sea water for long.

Fishes of Puget Sound

The marine fishes in all their diversity mostly occupy only terminal niches along the intricate chain of the eaters and the eaten, the aquatic food web. Like the many invertebrates in the Sound, fishes have evolved special ways of making a living by exploiting three general trophic (feeding) modes: herbivore, carnivore, and omnivore.

Saltwater fishes vary in size and shape from the large and sleek salmon, trout, and sharks to the little blennies and sculpins of tidepools. Each is closely linked to a specific habit and habitat. Where fish lurk is only a guessing game played by fishermen, but when known can reveal much about fish ecology and life history. Though the kinds of habitats for fishes in Puget Sound are neither as great nor as extreme as in the Pacific Ocean, the range is indeed rich. Close to the Puget Sound shoreline where life is dominated by a daily rhythm of the tides, fish with special attributes occupy tidepools, mudflats, estuaries of freshwater streams, as well as kelp and eelgrass beds. Below the reach of the tides, in the subtidal, fish find two kinds of existence, the pelagic or free-swimming one and the benthic or bottom habitat. The more spectacular and familiar fishes, either avidly sought (or detested) by fishermen, are of the free-roaming type, like salmon, dogfish sharks, ratfish, herring, hake, and some types of rockfish. Mud, sand, or gravel bottoms of Puget Sound provide a special niche for the familiar and often highly palatable bottom fish like the flounder, cod, sole, and most types of rockfish. Just as on land, the inland sea is a multiplicity of habitats, each habitat having its particular breed of exploiter. Fish diversity is no exception. For the different subregions of the Sound, from Olympia out to Port Angeles on the Strait of Juan de Fuca, fish biologists record a total of 211 species of fish. This number includes the rare occurrences of the Bering snailfish, the Pacific angel shark, or the blue lanternfish, as well as such common species as the Pacific cod, coho or silver salmon, and ling cod. But a mere figure of 211 species and the names of a few scarce or common fish say nothing about the variety of fish shapes, or about particular behaviors and habitats.

A sense of the amazing diversity of local fishes can come from a sampling of the suggestive and colorful common names of the fifty-eight families into which they are classified (Table 7). The family level in the classification of organisms groups species that have closely similar attributes. Thus, the family Salmonidae contains all the species of salmon, trout, and their kin (Table 8, pp. 96–97). Often the common names of species within a family are particular variants of the family's common name.

Table 7. Families of Fishes in Puget Sound: Their Colorful Common Names and Latin Equivalents

Sturgeons (Acipenseridae)	Lanternfishes (Myctophidae)
Poachers (Agonidae)	Snipe eels (Nemichthyidae)
Lancetfishes (Alepisauridae)	Brotulas (Ophidiidae)
Thresher sharks (Alopiidae)	Smelts (Osmeridae)
Sand lances (Ammodytidae)	Barracudinas (Paralepidae)
Wolffishes (Anarhichadidae)	Temperate basses (Percichthyidae)
Sablefishes (Anoplopomatidae)	Lampreys (Petromyzontidae)
Ronquils (Bathymasteridae)	Gunnels (Pholidae)
Toadfishes (Batrachoididae)	Righteye flounders (Pleuronectidae)
Lefteye flounders (Bothidae)	Quillfishes (Ptilichthyidae)
Pomfrets (Bramidae)	Skates (Rajidae)
Requiem sharks (Carcharhinidae)	Salmons and trouts (Salmonidae)
Chimaeras (Chimaeridae)	Drums (Sciaenidae)
Herrings (Clupeidae)	Sauries (Scomberesocidae)
Sculpins (Cottidae)	Mackerels and tunas (Scombridae)
Wrymouths (Cryptacanthodidae)	Rockfishes (Scorpaenidae)
Lumpfishes and snailfishes (Cyclopteridae)	Cat sharks (Scyliorhinidae)
Killifishes (Cyprinodontidae)	Graveldivers (Scytalinidae)
Surfperches (Embiotocidae)	Barracudas (Sphyraenidae)
Anchovies (Engraulidae)	Dogfish sharks (Squalidae)
Codfishes (Gadidae)	Angel sharks (Squatinidae)
Sticklebacks (Gasterosteidae)	Pricklebacks (Stichaeidae)
Clingfishes (Gobiesocidae)	Butterfishes (Stromateidae)
Gobies (Gobiidae)	Pipefishes (Syngnathidae)
Greenlings (Hexagrammidae)	Electric rays (Torpedinidae)
Cow sharks (Hexanchidae)	Ribbonfishes (Trachipteridae)
Ragfishes (Icosteidae)	Cutlassfishes (Trichiuridae)
Mackerel sharks (Lamnidae)	Sandfishes (Trichodontidae)
Molas (Molidae)	Eelpouts (Zoarcidae)

An illuminating example is that remarkable group, the lantern fishes, small plankton-feeders with luminescent organs in linear pattern on the body. The three species found in Puget Sound are the blue lanternfish, the northern lampfish, and the California headlightfish (also called theta lanternfish). And then there is the picturesque nomenclature for the many species of sculpins in Puget Sound waters: padded, scalyhead, smoothhead, Puget Sound, bonehead, rosylip, silver-spotted, roughback, sharpnose, calico, mosshead, spinyhead, buffalo, soft, red Irish lord, brown Irish lord, northern, dusky, threadfin, spotfin, longfin, Pacific staghorn, blackfin, great, sailfin, tidepool, saddleback, fluffy, tadpole, slim, darter, grunt, cabezon, manacled, roughspine, and even the ribbed sculpin. No one really knows how all these variant forms of the sculpin way of life sort themselves out in the trophic and habitat scheme of things. The ecological principle of *competitive exclusion* says that two closely related species cannot coexist if they compete for the same resources; one must be eliminated. If the principle works for sculpins, then one species must avoid competition with another by having distinctive food and breeding habits or by occupying a different habitat.

Unlike most terrestrial vertebrates such as the more familiar birds and mammals, the habits and ecological requirements of marine fishes are poorly known or still remain a total mystery. Only the more common commercially harvested or sport fish have been studied sufficiently for us to piece together their ecological life histories and the particular ways they tie into the strands of the aquatic ecosystem. Most study has to be by remote control: dredge or net samplings at various depths, examination of stomach contents, and other indirect probings into this alien world of fish. Fish of shallow waters can reveal more of their habits to skindivers; SCUBA-assisted underwater exploration allows the diver to join the sculpins, rockfish, and perch in their kelp-forested habitats where they can be observed in action.

For a better understanding of the way fish utilize their environments, one may examine the ways different species of fish exist throughout their life-cycle, as well as learn of their habitats, food, reproductive features, and any behavior crucial to their species-specific roles. I have selected one or two fish species from each of the three major habitat types—intertidal, pelagic, and bottom.

The tidepool sculpin or rockpool johnny, *Oligocottus maculosus*, must be familiar to every child and adult who has explored the multicolored and lively tidepools along the Pacific coast. This tiny three-inchling, like its other sculpin kin, has a sharply tapering body, large fins beset with spines, and a large ugly head. More pleasing is its bright coloring (reds, greens, and browns) dis-

Right: A marine dredging party off Friday Harbor, San Juan Island. Buckets of dredged samples on deck for later scrutiny at the University of Washington's Friday Harbor Laboratories. (Photo by Robert Tschudy.)

Below: Fitting device for taking plankton samples in Elliott Bay, Seattle's harbor.

tributed in complex pattern over the body. As is common to the sculpin group of rockfish, this tidepool fish can change color quickly to match its background. Any sign of danger stimulates these little fish into bursts of great speed, darting from one protected spot to another in the tidepool. So common a fish with such distinctive external markings and behavior provokes questions about its life history and habits. What does it eat? Are the spines and coloration for protection against predators? How does it breed? Yet I find next to nothing in the scattered literature on rockfish that pries into the secret life of this little fish. General works on marine life of the Pacific Northwest provide only frustratingly small morsels such as "the coloration is extremely variable, but greenish black tones predominate. Younger specimens are particularly undependable with respect to color, but as a rule they are more sharply marked—especially with white areas—than adults" (Kozloff 1973:136), or "spawning was observed on February 17, 1942, in the English Bay Aquarium. The male clasped the female with one pectoral fin and fertilized the pale greenish blue eggs as they were deposited on a rock" (Clemens and Wilby 1961:301–2). And yet another tidbit, from Ricketts and Calvin, "It is a small fish with a sharply tapering body, a large ugly head, and large pectoral fins. It is red-brown and prettily marked" (1968:163).

Another sculpin fares much better in the literature on fish of the intertidal and adjacent subtidal. The marbled sculpin, or cabezon (*Scorpaenichthys marmoratus*), has been taken at nearly all the sampling stations around Puget Sound (DeLacy et al. 1972:282–83). It may be even more abundant than its smaller cottid relative, the tidepool sculpin. But unlike the majority of sculpins that rarely exceed eight inches in length, the cabezon is a giant among sculpins, reaching two and a half feet in length and weighing up to twenty or twenty-five pounds. Eminently edible, though its flesh is slightly bluish, it is much esteemed by shoreline and dockside fishermen. In the National Geographic Society's *The Book of Fishes*, the cabezon

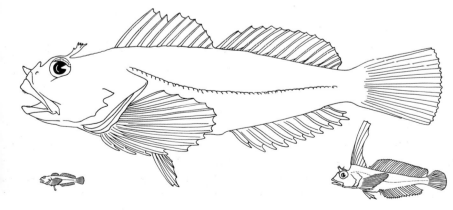

Three sculpins of the Family Cottidae, showing the range of size and ornamentation of this diverse fish clan: the big cabezon (Scorpaenichthys marmoratus) *at top, the tiny tidepool johnnie* (Oligocottus maculatus) *at left, and the elegant sailfin sculpin* (Nautichthys oculofasciatus) *at right. (Drawing by Michael Emerson.)*

gets deserved attention. I quote from the chapter, "Treasures of the Pacific," written by Leonard P. Schultz, ichthyologist of the U.S. National Museum:

> [The cabezon's] color is highly variable, usually mottled with rich dark brown or reddish brown, and greenish above, lighter below. It is often variously spotted with reddish or creamy yellow. Fish living in the kelp and fucus beds are usually predominately brownish, while those inhabiting green algae or eelgrass are mostly greenish. In fact, the marble sculpin (or cabezon) imitates the colors of objects in its immediate surrounds so well as to be difficult to see except in motion.
>
> The skin, without scales, has a wrinkled appearance. The head is large with numerous spiny projections, as in most other marine sculpins. The mouth, too, is large, with sharp teeth, enabling feeding on anything available, such as small fish, [other] sculpins, crabs, and shrimps. Above the eyes and on the snout are large featherlike flaps of skin, or tentacles.
>
> The marbled sculpin in the Puget Sound region has been found to spawn during the spring, usually March and April or later. It deposits its eggs, poisonous if eaten, on the tops of large rocks or old pilings extending from six inches to a foot or two above the beach. The eggs, small, variable in color, but usually yellowish to wine red or purplish, adhere to one another compactly.
>
> At low tide a single exposed rock or pile may display several distinct batches of eggs, each batch varying in color and in a different stage of development. Eggs laid a week or more are in an advanced state, and if placed in a jar of sea water, after exposure to sunshine, they will hatch immediately like popping corn. The larvae, pale greenish and nearly transparent, swim about actively in the jar. If not too crowded and if kept cool they will live for several days. Along the beach in the vicinity of the piling, older larvae have been taken in plankton nets. (1939:241)

The starry flounder (*Platichthys stellatus*) is a familiar representative of a remarkable adaptation to the bottom habitat. Along with sand dabs, halibut, sole, and other bottom-feeding flounders, the starry flounder's adult body is warped into a flattened shape, most unlike the streamlined submarine-shape of the typical pelagic fish. How the typical fish body is compressed, yet still retains both eyes on top of the now flattened surface is a miracle of adaptive geometry, spun out over evolutionary time. The young of flatfish have the normal, upright, symmetrical body with eyes on each side of the head. "Very soon a metamorphosis takes place, during which one eye migrates to the opposite side of the head, so that eventually both eyes are on the upper or darker-colored side. The fish then settle to the bottom and swim horizontally" (Clemens and Wilby 1961:203–4).

*Starry flounder (*Platichthys stellatus*) a common flatfish of mud or sandy bottoms in Puget Sound. The asymmetrical body with eyes and skin pattern on the right (upright) side are telltale features. (Drawing by Michael Emerson.)*

The starry flounder is one of the most common right-eyed flounders in Puget Sound.[1] It lives on sandy bottoms usually at shallow depths. In False Bay, San Juan Islands, Schultz (1939) found starry flounders abundant in the shallow water at low tide, partly buried in the sand. He had "no difficulty in capturing enough for a big dinner by the simple expedient of slipping up and stepping on them." The fish gets its name from the star-shaped pattern of rough scales on the upper, eyed, side of the animal; added distinguishing marks are the several black bars on the fins. Like so many of the flattened bottom fish, the starry flounder is excellent eating; it is filleted and usually sold along with other bottom fish as sole.

The flounder way of life is a sluggish one in which food-getting and concealment to avoid larger predatory fish consume most of the daily adult life. Flounder diet is a smorgasbord of crabs, shrimps, worms, clams, and small molluscs. Small fish like the black-bellied eelpout (*Lycodopsis pacifica*) also are common items of food.

A clue to the bottom-feeding habit is finding nipped-off clam necks in the flounder's stomach. The necks (actually the water siphons) of the clams are "browsed" when protruding just above the sandy surface of the bottom. In Puget Sound, the starry flounder spawns in the early months of its third year of life; the eggs and larvae are pelagic, floating freely in the currents of the sea. It has been observed that the young often enter freshwater streams for some distances but achieve adulthood back in salt water. Like the intertidal sculpins, the flounder/sand dab way of life has been abundantly exploited. Fifteen distinct species take up the flattened shape with rotated eyeballs, adapting to shallow or deep bottoms of Puget Sound.

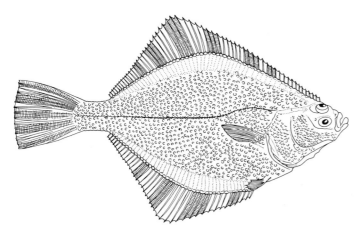

1. Most local flounders have both eyes on the right side, though three species are left-eyed. The starry flounder, however, may have both types of eye position throughout its range and in about 50-50 proportions.

Members of the salmon clan (trout, steelhead, char, and salmon) figure conspicuously in the ecology of Puget Sound and its fresh-water tributaries. No other aquatic resource has so educated the public to the ecological significance of water quality, proper management of drainages, and shoreline as has the favorite sport and commercial fishes of the Family Salmonidae. We need to gain a good understanding of life histories, environmental requirements, and other critical attributes of these highly prized fish if we are to exercise our citizens' prerogatives of *quis custodiet ipsos custodes* ("who will watch the watchers?") with intelligence.

The salmonids form a small natural grouping of fishes, including Atlantic salmon, trouts, chars, and five Pacific salmons. Puget Sound waters are the home or transient way-station of the coastal cutthroat trout (*Salmo clarkii*), the rainbow trout and steelhead (both forms of one species, *Salmo gairdneri*), the dolly varden (*Salvelinus malma*), and all five Pacific salmon species (the pink salmon, *Oncorhynchus gorbuscha*; the coho or silver salmon, *Oncorhynchus kisutch*; the chinook or king salmon, *Oncorhynchus tshawytscha*; the chum or dog salmon, *Oncorhynchus keta*; and the sockeye salmon, *Oncorhynchus nerka*).[2] Of course, the chinook and coho, more familiarly known as the king and silver salmons, are the prime objects of sport and commercial fishing in our waters.

All members of the salmonid group (salmon, char, and trout) are to varying degrees migratory (see Table 8). The most spectacular migrations are the underwater voyages of adult salmon, cutthroat and steelhead, between fresh and salt water in the three-to-five-year reproductive cycle of these species. The coho or silver salmon exemplifies the general pattern. Adult fish, mostly three-year-olds, begin their spawning route from the Sound or from the open ocean into lowland streams in late summer through late autumn. Once having reached suitable stream habitats, usually smaller tributaries with gravelly riffles, the fish pair in a simple courtship followed by synchronous release of eggs and milt (sperm). The eggs and sperm must fuse within a minute; in one and a half minutes, released sperm are dead, and eggs at the end of four minutes become impervious to sperm. The female continues to agitate the gravelly nest so that the fertilized eggs become buried under two or three inches of sand and gravel. Silt or mud from a stream laden with erosional runoff is fatal to the tiny embryonic life. While the finer particulates would choke off oxygen, coarse sand and gravel permit life-giving gas exchange.

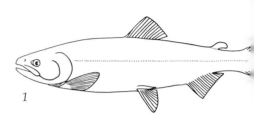

1

Fish of the salmon and trout family (Salmonidae) found in Puget Sound and adjacent marine waters, drawn to scale to permit comparisons: (1) sockeye salmon (Oncorhynchus nerka, also red salmon); (2) chum or dog salmon (O. keta); (3) coho salmon, male spawning; (4) pink or humpy salmon (O. gorbuscha); (5) steelhead (or rainbow trout) (Salmo gairdneri); (6) chinook or king salmon (O. tshawytscha); (7) coho or silver salmon (O. kisutch). (Drawings by Michael Emerson.)

2. The Latin names of salmon species almost defy pronunciation. The first or genus name (*Oncorhynchus*) means "hook nose" (a feature of mature males), whereas the various species names are Russian, Indian, or Kamchatkan in origin.

Finished with spawning, the adult fish die. Once they entered fresh water on their way to the spawning grounds, the adults had stopped eating. Their upstream movements required great exertion in overcoming rapids, falls, fish ladders, and other challenges to the instinctive upward urge. Exhausted and often battered, most adults seem truly unable to survive beyond the final exertion of spawning. Yet some fish finish spawning without any visible signs of physical deterioration. Healthy looking fish have been kept alive in aquaria for some time after spawning. But they too will soon die. Death of a spawned-out fish is a mystery to the fish biologist seeking a functional explanation. Perhaps the "will to live" some day might be expressible in scientific terms, but for now we must be

Table 8. Fish of the Salmon Family (Salmonidae) in the Puget Sound Basin

Names and Habitats	Distinguishing Body Features	Migratory Behavior	Spawning/Hatching	Other Features
1. Steelhead, *Salmo gairdneri* Southern Calif. to Gulf of Alaska	Absence of red dash on underjaw; no teeth at base of tongue; short head; compressed body; 3 ft. 9 in., up to 36 lbs.	Anadromous* (repeated) 3rd–5th year of life; enters fresh water anytime of year.	Winter–spring; late spring young 1–2 yrs in fresh water.	May travel far in open ocean; at sea eat squid, crustaceans, and fishlike herring, etc.
a. Rainbow trout, *Salmo gairdneri* (syn: Kamloops trout)	Purplish colored band along each side of body; otherwise like steelhead, but smaller.	Non-migratory, fresh-water.	May–June in streams; hatching in inlet streams of lakes.	Feed on insects, insect larvae when small; on leeches, large insects, molluscs, and fish (kokanee) when large.
2. Brown trout, *Salmo trutta* (syn: Lochlevn trout) Introd: Calif. to Vancouver Isl.	Black spots below lateral line, each with halos of pink or red; no red dash below lower jaw.	Weakly anadromous.	Nov.–Dec. in small streams; fry emerge in spring.	Introduced species, not common; food similar to cutthroat trout.
3. Coastal cutthroat trout, *Salmo clarkii* (Syn: sea trout, small specimens in sea water) No. Calif. to S.E. Alaska	Teeth on back of tongue; bright red gash below lower jaw (="cutthroat"); long head, rounded body; 2 1/2 ft., up to 17 lbs.)	Anadromous; seaward young remain in estuaries to feed on salmon fry.	Feb.–May; young remain in fresh water for indefinite periods.	Voracious fish-eaters when large, taking kokanee, sticklebacks, and salmonid fry; some populations never leave fresh water.
4. Dolly Varden, *Salvelinus malma* No. Calif. to Bering Sea	Pale yellow spots on back, and red to orange spots on sides; length to 3 ft. and up to 30 lbs.	Both sea-run and non-migratory; uncommon in Puget Sound; though abundant in Alaska.	Spawning migrations in fall; sea-run in spring.	Named for calico-gowned Dickens character; destructive of salmon eggs and fry.
5. Brook trout, *Salvelinus fontinalis* (syn: speckled char) Introd: No. Calif. to S.E. Alaska	Red spots on side of body; dark olive-green markings on back and dorsal fin; up to 2 ft. 10 in. long, and up to 9–12 lbs.	Anadromous on Atlantic coast; introduced here, may be anadromous.	Spawning in autumn months; fry emerge in spring.	Larger fish feed on other fish.
6. Pink salmon, *Oncorhyncus gorbuscha* (syn: humpback-males, at time of spawning) Range: No. Calif. to Bering Sea (*onco* = hooked; *rhyncus* = snout)	Spawning males with compressed body and prominent hump behind head; small scales and oval black blotches on tail fin; length to 2 1/2 ft., 3–5 lbs. but up to 10 lbs.	Anadromous; spawning runs staggered, odd- and even-yeared; usually in lower tidal reaches of streams.	Late Sept.–early Nov.; late Feb., going to sea soon after hatching.	Hooked snout of spawning males; "gorbuscha" = "humpback" in Russian

Table 8. (*continued*)

Names and Habitats	Distinguishing Body Features	Migratory Behavior	Spawning/Hatching	Other Features
7. Coho salmon, *Oncorhyncus kisutch* (syn: jack salmon, 2nd year males; blueback, early 3rd year fish; silver salmon in U.S. No. Calif. to Bering Sea	Black spotting confined to back and upper lobe of tail fin; pale flesh along base of teeth in lower jaw. Length to little over 3 ft.; ave. 6–12 lbs., but up to 31 lbs.	Anadromous at short distance from sea or to upper tributaries of larger streams; mostly stay one year in streams.	Nov.–Dec.; fry appear in April.	Feed on herring, sandlance, and other small fish at sea. Gamiest of all sport-fished salmon, though do not usually take lure in fresh water.
8. Chinook salmon, *Oncorhyncus tshawytscha* (syn: jacks, 2–3 year males; gulse, immature of both sexes; tyee salmon, spring salmon in B.C. waters; king or quinnat salmon in U.S. waters) So. Calif. to Bering Sea	Black spotting on back and on upper and lower lobes of tail fin; black pigment along base of teeth in lower jaw. Length to 4 ft., 10 in., and 10–50 lbs. at maturity (126 lbs. possible)	Anadromous; two runs: April–June and Aug.–Nov.	Spawn larger streams well upriver in Oct.–Nov.; hatch winter or spring. Young may go to sea directly or stay in fresh water up to 15 months.	"Tshawytscha" = local name in Kamchatka. Mature in 3–7 years; food as with coho. A favorite sport fish at sea.
9. Chum salmon, *Oncorhyncus keta* (syn: dog salmon) No. Calif. to Bering Sea	Absence of large black spots on body and tail fin; tips of all but dorsal fins tinged black; dusky streaks or bars across sides in mature fish in fresh water. Length to 3 ft. 4 inches; ave. 8–18 lbs but up to 33 lbs.	Anadromous; migrates not far from salt water; young go to sea immediately.	Latest of fall spawners.	"Keta" is Russian for salmon. Does not take lure or bait; commercially caught by purse-seining. Called "dog" salmon because of large teeth of breeding males or since formerly used as dog food.
10. Sockeye Salmon, *Oncorhyncus nerka* (syn: kokanee, kickaninny, red salmon, little red fish, silver trout, blueback salmon; "jack" sockeye are 3rd year males) So. Oregon to Bering Sea	Absence of black spots and presence of large number of long, slender gill rakers. Length to 2 ft. 9 in.; 5–7 lbs., but up to 15 1/2 lbs.	Anadromous; adults seek lake-fed streams after spending 3–4 years at sea.	Summer–early autumn; spring hatching, young enter lakes to stay 1–3 years.	"Kokanee" = land-locked sockeye. Feed on plankton when young; crustaceans when at sea. Highly prized as canning fish; not a sport fish.

Note: Anadromous refers to migrating up rivers from the sea for the purpose of spawning.

content with the vague idea of a salmon's fulfillment of its destiny: reproduction and death. Unlike the Pacific salmon, the Atlantic salmon, as well as the Northwest's native cutthroat and steelhead, may live after spawning and return to the sea; some may return to fresh water, to spawn a second or third time.

Hatchlings emerge after about two months of development in the sand of an upstream riffle. The tiny fish, with yolk sac still attached, begin feeding. In some species, fingerlings, up to four inches long, remain a year or two in the natal stream, feeding on aquatic insects and worms. They are then ready for the trip to salt water. Their migration traces in reverse the route of their parents. Once in salt water, each fish is caught up in its own programmed migratory destiny. Coho (silver) and chinook (king) salmon may leave the Sound and head north to the west coast of Vancouver Island and the coastal waters of British Columbia. A lesser number venture as far south as Grays Harbor in southwestern Washington. While at sea young coho and chinook grow robust on a rich fare of herring, sand lance, and other small fishes, as well as a variety of crustaceans (shrimp and their kin) and squid. After three or four years of free-roaming life, the adult fish enact a final chapter of their inherited and encoded script, using particular clues from their surroundings for guidance. As mature fish, they are now ready to return to their freshwater birthplace. At this time, coho and chinook salmon differ in size. Adult coho (or silver salmon) average three feet in length and 6 to 12 pounds, though 31-pounders have been caught. Chinook, the king of Pacific salmon in size, reach up to four feet, ten inches long and usually weigh 10 to 50 pounds; 126-pounders have been reported.

Coho, and to a lesser extent chinook of Puget Sound waters, differ in migratory behavior from fish of the same species from other areas. Sizeable numbers remain in the Sound, never migrating to the open sea. These fish grow more slowly and achieve smaller size at maturity; they are the prime inducement for spring and summer sport fishing in the Sound. Later, the autumnal "madness" that grips the salmon sport fisher is brought on by the predictable inbound migrants from the open sea, the larger "hooknosed" silvers.

The salmon caught by an eager fisherman could well have been interrupted in one of the longest migratory patterns of any of the marine fishes. Most late summer fish entering the Sound from the open ocean have completed one or more great circuits of the eastern North Pacific, heading north from Vancouver Island up the Alaskan coast and out and down the great Gulf of Alaska arc. By the time a fish like the chinook or coho has entered the stream of its birth to spawn, it may have traveled as many as 10,000 miles. Such

A salmon's mighty leap in search of an upstream spawning site, after leaving Puget Sound. (Photo by Josef Scaylea.)

an amazing feat of oceanic navigation might make a fisherman reluctant to interrupt this remarkable voyage with hook and line. It is too bad the fish are not palatable to humans *after* spawning.

The "how" of salmon migration has received considerably more attention than the "why." Data recovered from tagged or fin-clipped fish (technically called "mark-release-recapture" data) have provided fairly reliable clues to the paths of migration. For the pink salmon of southeastern Alaska and British Columbia, the oceanic migration pattern is most accurately known.

*Migration—and reproduction of
new salmonid life—is over for this
spawned-out humpback salmon. (Photo
by Mary Randlett.)*

While at sea, it is clear that the salmon do not aimlessly wander
in search of food, biding their time until full-grown. On the contrary, migration studies by United States, Canadian, Japanese, and
Russian fisheries biologists clearly demonstrate oriented movement. Celestial navigation, sun orientation, and sonar (sound
echolocation of submarine topography) have all been proposed
(and shot down) as explanations. A recent, as yet untested, hypothesis for a guidance mechanism is an electrical one. Lynwood
Smith and his colleagues at the University of Washington School of
Fisheries believe that the fish "navigate [by] electrical voltages generated by the ocean currents as they pass through the earth's mag-
netic field. The electrical voltages are only about 0.5 microvolts per
centimeter (0.0000005 volts), but the voltages are always oriented
crosswise to the direction of the water movement. Thus, any fish
capable of detecting the voltages could follow the ocean current
anywhere" (1967). According to this hypothesis:

There are two characteristics of salmon behavior which the electrical
hypothesis explains very nicely. One is that salmon swim downstream in the ocean currents most of the time. Since the ocean cur-

rents in the North Pacific form large spirals, a salmon following one will return to the coastline somewhere near where it departed. We also know from tagging experiments conducted by fisheries scientists in western United States and Canada that ocean migrations of salmon form large circles which resemble the pattern of the ocean currents. The other [characteristic] is that salmon swim downstream actively rather than drift with the current. Thus these migration routes are sought actively and deliberately, and not just random wandering or drifting. . . .

[Even so] salmon sometimes migrate in straight lines without regard to the direction of the ocean currents. Such behavior is not readily explained by the hypothesis, but no other hypothesis explains it any better.

This intriguing hypothesis, even if tested and found acceptable, only explains the guidance of oceanic migrations. When the fish is within 100 yards of its birthplace, another guidance mechanism must come into play, one that appears to be connected with the sense of smell. Perhaps some distinctive odor from the old spawning-hatching area spreads all the way down to the estuarine beginnings of the upward route. Such an idea is appealing, but apparently is not the case. Aubrey Gorbman, also at the University of Washington, has evidence to indicate that the returning salmon "home in" on a whole series of olfactory cues all along the route of their return in fresh water. Remembering that in science one answer provokes a series of new questions, one wonders how these electrical and olfactory cues operate in the fishes' guidance system. We will have to wait on answers to this tantalizing line of questioning; there are simply no sure answers as yet. It is now assumed, however, that the process is wholly inherited, not learned, as the salmon moves from one segment of the stream to the next, "reading" its underwater directions.

The migration of salmon is fraught with peril. Predation, disease, and injury take their toll of initial downstream migrants. Beginning with an arbitrary 1,000 fingerlings, only 100 get back to the estuary after the swim downstream and the long tour of the oceanic currents. The loss is further aggravated as the fish go upstream. Only 10 to 15 of the original 1,000 get back up to spawn, but nearly all (90 percent) of that hardy band of survivors will have returned to within 100 yards of their original gravel bar or riffle birthplace. This low return for an initial high egg investment is not unlike the vital statistics for many other pelagic animals with external fertilization and no maternal care. The low return for salmon is both a product of their own natural life cycle and, of course, the efficient fishery in the estuarine and coastal waters.

Why migrate at all? The lake or stream where they were born surely seems a safe place to live out a life. There is even more reason to stay in fresh water given the demanding bodily changes imposed on the downstream migrants preparing for a wholly new life in salt water. Despite this logic, Dr. Smith believes that the success of these anadromous fish is fostered by a long residence in the sea, where there is abundant and nutritious life for growth. Moreover, since it is more economical from a metabolic standpoint to keep on the move than to stay put, the fish continue to move into new sources of food.

An intriguing sidelight to the migratory activity of salmon concerns the behavior of the fingerlings in fresh water. Until they are ready to migrate, they swim against the current, close to their birthplace, out of the faster water. But when the urge to migrate downstream overwhelms them, the young fish begin swimming full tilt downstream in the fastest water at the center of the stream. They can reach salt water in only a few days when thrust by their natures to face the next phase of their existence.

Habitat Changes

The late nineteenth and twentieth centuries have been turbulent times for our native biota on land and in the water. Violent fluctuations in population numbers of many species have followed in the wake of people's intentional and accidental changes to habitats. Some species have gained in numbers, others decreased, and still others are now extinct. Introductions of alien plants and animals also have had their impact on the native flora and fauna. Fish populations too have suffered from disturbance of habitats. For the salmonid fishes, destruction of spawning grounds, pollution of streams, modifications of waterways by dams, streambank and bottom changes, all have seriously reduced the populations of some salmonid species, especially in streams where the free-flowing waters have been interrupted by dams. On the Columbia River all salmon production has been eliminated above Grand Coulee Dam, and its barrier is too high for the operation of fish ladders. The additional dams downstream, either now built or planned along the Columbia and its major tributaries like the Snake, the Yakima, and the Wenatchee, could have a disastrous effect on the continued vitality of the salmon fishery in this great river system. In an experimental release of fingerlings some years ago, the U.S. Fish and Wildlife Service found that a 15 percent mortality occurred in downstream migrants at Bonneville Dam. This loss might be assumed to occur at any other dam encountered by the fingerlings. If so, the effect of additional dams could be devastating to the valuable fish resource.

On the credit side of the human-and-fish ledger, are the farflung programs of fisheries rehabilitation in Washington State, with the

Salmon, the "unlimited" resource of the late 19th century, now must be husbanded with great care and foresight.

A Puget Sound catch of salmon around the turn of the century.

Stocking the Cedar River near Seattle with fingerling trout. This method, used for decades, is still effective today.

cooperative efforts of the state Department of Fisheries, federal agencies, and the fisheries research activities at the University of Washington. The coordinated efforts to bring the salmon supply back up from its all-time low in the 1930s is based on four essential requirements for a successful fishery: (1) a proper proportion of returning mature fish must be allowed to spawn upstream (adequate escapement); (2) the spawning grounds must provide the appropriate conditions of cold, clear fresh water with *gravel* beds; (3) the waters, both salt and fresh, must be free of significant pollution; and (4) these waters must contain sufficient food. Adequate escapement is achieved by regulation of fish harvesting and restrictions of time and place imposed on both commercial and sports fishermen. Time of year, numbers caught, and types of fishing gear used are all restrictions familiar to those who fish for fun or profit. Estuary and stream protection as well as rehabilitation are continuing efforts to assure the perpetuation of suitable spawning grounds. Periodic attempts to weaken the State Shoreline Management Act are symptoms of the political pressures in conflict with concerns for stringent protection of fish habitat.

The system of hatcheries in the state is one way to compensate for loss of spawning habitat. After eggs of captured mature fish are fertilized at the hatchery, the young are reared in hatchery ponds until the appropriate time for their release for the downstream migration. Hatchery production of fingerlings still does not supplant the need to maintain high quality natural habitat. Efforts of the fish biologists must be accompanied by the actions of an enlightened public: private industry, agriculture, forestry, as well as individual citizens. Many Puget Sound streams can be saved for the critical stages in fish production as well as for aesthetic and valid environmental reasons if sound ecological practices are adopted. From time to time, the public has been offered proposals for managing major rivers like the Skagit and the Nisqually to preserve and enhance what is left of their free-flowing, natural character. The response has been about evenly divided between those who are concerned with the environment and the productivity of the rivers' fisheries, and those who have other interests at stake. Only through some consensus on preservation can the integrity and interconnectedness of things in ecological context be preserved or restored.

The introduction of alien animals to any new habitat can have far-reaching consequences. If it succeeds (that is, if the species reproduces and increases in abundance), the niche these alien animals come to occupy either may have been unoccupied by an indigenous species or the newcomers' niche may overlap and thus be competitive with that of one or more native species. Plant and animal introductions in other parts of the world have upset ecological equilibria, locally or on a regional scale. Witness the rabbits on San Juan Island or the scrap fish species (carp and other spiny-rayed types) in some of our freshwater lakes.

Alien fish in saltwater Puget Sound, unlike those in lakes, have not made a serious impact on native species and in fact have added interest to sport fishing in certain instances. The occasional striped bass taken in Puget Sound is undoubtedly from small outlier populations, as the center of the striped bass fishery is in the San Francisco Bay area. "Stripers" were introduced from eastern waters to the Sacramento River drainage in the late nineteenth century.

The American shad, planted in the Columbia River in the 1880s, is a herringlike fish not uncommon in Puget Sound. Attempts to introduce alien salmonids in the Pacific Northwest have met with mixed results. The Atlantic salmon, planted in British Columbia waters, has not succeeded. The brown trout (*Salmo trutta*) is rather widespread in British Columbia, but it was not found in 1972 Puget Sound samplings. The successes in most fish introduction programs are with the native species, that is, the reintroduction of species previously eliminated. The program of steelhead reintroductions is a spectacular case in point. Release of hatchery fish has greatly increased the numbers of this highly favored sports fish.

Puget Sound with its many bays, estuaries, and inlets affords a rich array of habitats to put sound fish ecology to still another test. Aquaculture, or fish farming, is being tried in pilot studies at several locations about the Sound. In addition to the intensive culture of seaweeds and shellfish, the growing of edible fish is being tried in "rearing pens" at several places in the Sound. In such confined underwater "farms," supply of food to the fish, controlled rearing conditions, and harvest can be managed to provide a profitable yield.

Two cautionary thoughts on fish-farming must be voiced. First, some kinds of intensive aquaculture, especially of fish, may pollute waters locally. Fish food for farmed fish, waste products from the fish, etc., can be a noticeable and harmful side effect of the enterprise. Then, artificial manipulation of populations may come with a genetic liability. Natural populations that once entered the many streams bordering the Sound were a rich sampling of the hereditary variability within each salmonid species. Managed populations, however, represent only a fraction of that variability. Hence, like so many land-based crops, fish cropping also becomes an agribusiness with a monoculture hazard. The reduction in genetic variation can only impair the long-run ability of fish populations to cope adaptively with disease and other environmental challenges.

Marine Birds of Puget Sound

Seaweeds, crabs, limpets, and other sedentary intertidal life are all closely pinned down to the shoreline habitat and its tidal wash. In contrast, marine birds are attached to Puget Sound shorelines by a looser tether. They can leave the coastline at will, and often can be sighted well away from coasts. But they are inevitably drawn back to shore habitats by their evolved needs for the food, shelter, or nesting sites that the shoreline provides.

Marine birds are a special avian breed. They eat, reproduce, and find shelter in and around salt water. The spectacular successes at being any kind of a shorebird dramatize evolutionary histories that fostered adaptations galore to seaside living. Coping with shoreline and marine habitats means acquiring special structural, functional, and behavioral "fixes" for getting and processing food, avoiding predators, and finding places to breed. And marine birds do it all in a variety of ways.

Birds that specialize in marine ways of life can be found in several different shoreline and saltwater habitats. Rocky shoreline is the least frequent habitat type. Outcrops of lavas and basalt do occur, mostly on the northwestern part of the Sound. On rocky coasts the bird-watcher may encounter oystercatchers, turnstones, tattlers, and sandpipers, all deftly picking out a living with their stout, pointed bills. In intertidal and tidal shallows below rocky beaches, the vegetarian brant and harlequin ducks may be seen.

Sand, pebble, and cobble are the most common ingredients of shorelines along the Sound. Gritty textures of sand and loose rock accommodate marine birds in variety that feed on the rich invertebrate and algal fare. Look for killdeer, pigeon guillemots, kingfishers, and the ubiquitous gulls ransacking sand and cobble beaches for food.

Black oystercatchers at shoreline.
(Drawing by Tony Angell.)

The richest marine bird habitats—mud flats and salt marshes—are also the most vulnerable to human disturbance. Much of this ecologically highly productive habitat is now gone—filled in, dredged, or otherwise obliterated. Already lost are the once rich estuarine "nurseries" at the mouths of the Duwamish and Snohomish rivers. Yet some are left on Puget Sound. The best displays of mudflat and saltmarsh habitats are in the deltas of major rivers like the Skagit and Nooksack to the north, and the Nisqually to the south. The birdwatcher will be overwhelmed by the variety of bird life in these estuarine habitats. The amount of plant biomass these environments produce for ultimate bird consumption is awesome, more than the nearby lowland forest. Besides serving as refueling stops for major bird migrations, the vegetation and dependent invertebrate life of the flats and marshes can also support a resident bird diversity, as well as host those that breed locally and then move on.

The great variety of bird life found in estuarine flats, marshes, and other marine wetlands consists of both marine-oriented species and freshwater birds, collectively called waterfowl—not an unexpected mixture, since the estuary is where salt water mingles with fresh. This nutrient-rich habitat supports brant, snow geese, and whistling swans at the intertidal shoreline, while such shorebirds as dunlin, sandpipers, and plovers in countless numbers extract a rich living here in fall and winter.

A more elusive marine habitat is open water. Yet any boater or ferry passenger can witness birds on open stretches of our inland sea. Birds that fly over or land in open water include gulls, terns, cormorants, scoters, grebes, and loons, most common in the fall.

Guidebooks to marine birds and waterfowl are a natural outcome of this distinctive type of bird life. *Marine Birds and Mammals of Puget Sound*, by Tony Angell and Kenneth Balcomb, for example, is

Belted kingfishers. (Drawing by Libby Mills.)

Pigeon guillemots. (Drawing by Libby Mills.)

Above left: The western grebe is a common winter resident throughout Puget Sound. Major gatherings of this bird are in waters from Bellingham and Samish bays to the eastern San Juan Islands. (Photo by Mary Randlett.)

Above right: Sandpipers feeding on tidelands. (Photo by Mary Randlett.)

Left: "GBH" to birdwatchers, the great blue heron is a familiar year-round resident in salt- and freshwater localities and, as here, in the brackish water of an estuary. (Photo by Mary Randlett.)

Right: American avocet. (Drawing by Libby Mills.)

a fine volume in the Washington Sea Grant Series, "Puget Sound Books." The very readable and informative text is matched by Angell's peerless drawings of the birds and mammals.

Marine birds beautifully illustrate the diverse ways a group of organisms can optimally utilize a set of habitats. This highly specialized segment of bird life offers a particularly clear ecological lesson. Specialized structure and function inevitably accompany partitioning of the natural economy; take, for example, the variety of bill sizes and shapes. Some are highly specialized, like the snow goose's beak for extracting eelgrass or bullrush shoots or like the long sturdy beak of the oystercatcher which pries loose limpets from rocky shores. Other marine birds have evolved a generalist's syndrome of structure and function. Gulls and eagles, for instance, can take a wide range of living and dead organic matter from the shoreline. The switch from predator to scavenger is easy for these generalists among marine birds.

Matching habitat and its resources with evolved structure and function of marine birds can become vividly rewarding by a little homework. The first step of the lesson is to make comparisons of contrasting marine bird types with the aid of a field guide. The descriptions of bird activities are the raw materials for the "take-home" lesson. Try these pairs of comparisons to get an initial sense of sharp contrasts in adaptive modes: cormorants versus oystercatchers, turnstones versus guillemots, eagles versus gulls, and grebes versus harlequin ducks. Test your knowledge in the field by bird-watching along Puget Sound shorelines. Be assured of at least two rewards: first, a deeper appreciation of the multiplicity of Darwinian "fixes" for exploiting habitats, and, second, an awareness that the "fixes" are not absolute. The ingenuity of birds can add an element of unpredictability to their behaviors.

Top: Waterfowl (gulls and snow geese) periodically leave Puget Sound shorelines to forage in lowland fields of the Skagit Valley. (Photo by Mary Randlett.)

Right: A mixed flock of trumpeter and tundra swans; both are common winter migrants on Puget Sound and in fresh water habitats, here in the Skagit River delta; they feed in both estuarine and freshwater habitats as well as in farmers' fields in the northern Puget basin.

Marine Mammals of Puget Sound

Two major groups of marine mammals are represented in Puget Sound: Order Carnivora (Suborder Pinnipedia), seals and sea lions; and Order Cetacea, whales and porpoises. All their members are repatriates to the sea. They are warm-blooded, air-breathing, milk-giving animals whose ancestors deserted the land millions of years before Puget Sound was formed.

The dramatic shift by a terrestrial vertebrate to a sea-going life was achieved by evolutionary adaptation in small increments, spanning millions of years. So thorough was the conversion of a land-based life to marine existence that cetaceans (whales, porpoises, and dolphins) are helpless now on land. Such features as the persisting mammalian reproduction (young developing in the mother and nourished from the secretion of milk) and the breathing of air are reminders of their great evolutionary journey back to the sea—as mammals. The seals and their kin (pinnipeds) are more closely allied to other carnivores like dogs, cats, bears, and other terrestrial predatory mammals than they are to whales. The fossil

Killer whale (Orcinus orca) in a spectacular over-water, whole-body display. Orca pods (herds or schools) are frequent in inland waters from Puget Sound north into mainland British Columbia and Vancouver Island coastal waters.

Right: Victor B. Sheffer, eminent naturalist and conservationist, on the shore of Puget Sound.

record supports this view in that the cetaceans and the carnivores were evolving along separate paths, long before the pinnipeds separated from their carnivore relatives.

Whales and other cetaceans are uncommon today in the busy waters of Puget Sound; one cannot predict when and where they will appear. Six or seven species have been recorded there. Three species of baleen or "whalebone" cetaceans (Suborder Mysticeti) are known from the Sound: little piked whale or minke whale (*Balaenoptera acutorostrata*), the only baleen whale apt to be seen in this location; humpback whale (*Megaptera novaeangliae*), with a few recorded sightings within the past century; finback whale or fin whale (*Balaenoptera physalus*), because an adult was trapped in a log boom at Shelton in 1930 (before it escaped, visitors actually walked on its back). Each year a small number of gray whales (*Eschrichtius robustus*) venture into Puget Sound, some to as far south as Tacoma and Shelton. The gray and other great whales may be expected rarely to blunder into the Sound, since the open ocean is their home.

Of the toothed cetaceans (Suborder Odontoceti), the following have been seen (Scheffer and Slipp 1948; Scheffer 1975): killer whale (*Orcinus orca*), often called "blackfish" (perhaps 300 individuals enter the Sound in a year); false killer whale (*Pseudorca crassidens*) (an individual was shot at Olympia in 1937); harbor porpoise (*Phocoena phocoena*), fairly common until the 1950s, now perhaps gone from the Sound. Before commercial fish traps were banned from the Sound, harbor porpoises were occasionally trapped along with the fish they were chasing.

The killer whale has evoked the greatest interest of all the local cetaceans. They are common, spectacular, capable of generating controversy over their behavior, and, above all, a magnificent example of adaptation to the ocean-going, predatory way of life. Victor Scheffer, marine mammalogist and writer-naturalist, gives a fine, detailed account of the killer whale. I quote from his article, "The Killer Whale" (Pacific Search Leaflet 1967):

> The killer whale cruises in all months of the year through waters of the Northwest. It ranges, in fact, through all seas of the world, to the very limits of polar fast ice. No one knows its numbers, though for the State of Washington several hundred would probably be a closer guess than several thousand.
>
> In the North Pacific Ocean the male attains a known length of 27.2 feet and an estimated weight of 9 tons, the female, a known length of 22.9 feet and a known weight of 7.9 tons. (Lengths up to 31 feet for males and 27 for females have been reported by Japanese whalemen.) The newborn calf is about eight feet long and weighs an estimated 1,000 pounds. The large triangular dorsal fin of the male attains a height of 5.6 feet, that of the female about three feet.

The color pattern of the adult is striking black and white with some gray. The white areas on the adult are yellowish or light yellowish-brown on the newborn. All-white individuals (albinos) have often been seen around Vancouver Island.

The killer whale is highly social, habitually traveling in packs of two to 40 individuals. "Family togetherness" is a way of life. Females and young are said to stay slightly apart from the bachelors and bulls. Locally, the social instinct of the killer whale has been exploited for the purpose of capture by firing a 16-inch harpoon into the back of the largest male, presumably the group leader or "pod bull." A brightly-colored float trailing from the harpoon allows the hunter to follow the group for days or weeks.

Is the killer whale a peril to man? Roger Caras, in his 1964 book *Dangerous to Man,* says that "there has not been one single authenticated attack."

The name "killer" originated, of course, from the whale's habit of taking warm-blooded prey. His enthusiasm for the job of satisfying his appetite comes from a survival instinct similar to that of a hungry wolf in a herd of sheep; it is often mistaken for a so-called joy of killing. The killer is the largest and swiftest of the marine mammals that eat warm-blooded prey. Its top speed is about 30 landmiles per hour. J. H. Prescott saw a male killer leap clear of the water holding an adult sea lion crosswise in his jaws. The teeth are stout, deeply rooted and conical, numbering about 46 to 50 in the adult. Evidently they take quite a beating, for in old whales they are often worn to the gum-line, or even to a depth where the pulp cavity is exposed and infection sets in.

The main food items, fishes and squids, are not the ones which fill our literature with accounts of "savage" attacks upon sea birds, seals, sea otters, porpoises, and whales. Killer whales undoubtedly attack their marine associates very efficiently. The evidence comes from stomach examinations, from eye-witness stories, and from observations of the parallel scars, spaced like killer whale teeth, on the backs of seals and whales. The bloodiest stories tend to be untrue or distorted.

Though the killer whale has great recreational appeal, it has no commercial value in the United States. In Asian waters it is hunted for its fine, clear oil, its fresh meat for human food, and its scrap meat for fertilizer and fish bait.

Is the chasing of killer whales in our local waters legal? Ethical? Humane? Since 1965, six whales have admittedly been killed by Seattle showmen; many others have been quietly killed or mortally wounded by harpoons, drug-syringes, and nets. All were legally destroyed. No laws of any kind protect the smaller cetaceans of North America. Should individuals have the right to harass and maim wild animals which belong to all residents of the Pacific Northwest? The highly integrated social behavior and intelligence of this mammal will allow him to learn through experience, sensitized by the bloodshed of his fellows, to avoid areas of known danger. Must we all lose the thrill of seeing these magnificent beasts free, unalarmed and approachable because individuals seek profit or fame?

Of the Puget Sound pinnipeds, only the harbor seal (*Phoca vitulina*) is common. In 1978 there were as many as 7,000 seals in all marine waters of Washington, most of them living in Grays Harbor and Willapa Bay. The Puget Sound population has been estimated at 2,600 (Angell and Balcomb 1982). Their numbers were steadily reduced by hunters and by loss of habitat up to the enactment of the federal Marine Mammal Protection Act of 1972. Harbor seals reach a length of five feet and an extreme weight of 300 pounds. They propel themselves with their hind flippers and run a smooth, silent path through the water. They often sink below the surface so as to swim better at high speeds. They are usually most visible when they haul out on a reef, sand bar, or beach. Their diet is exclusively fish and shellfish, though salmon are not taken in nearly the quantity assumed by fishermen. In turn, the harbor seal is also prey. Its most effective predator is the killer whale; a seal so threatened will haul out or seek shelter in shallow water.

While other kinds of seals may make an occasional appearance in Puget Sound, the harbor seal is not only the common Puget Sound resident but is the only seal to breed in these waters. The pupping season spans late summer, from mid-August to mid-September. Usually a single pup is born, following a gestation period of nine months. Pupping areas are often the more secluded sand bars and reefs in the Sound as well as the haul-out areas in estuarine sections of tributary streams to Puget Sound.

The northern (or Steller's) sea lion (*Eumetopias jubatus*), the northern fur seal (*Callorhinus ursinus*), and the elephant seal (*Mirounga angustirostris*) are occasionally sighted or have been collected in Puget Sound. None is at all common.

Although sea otters (Order Carnivora, Suborder Fissipedia; *Enhydra lutris*) lived in Washington waters before the last individual was killed by hunters about 1910, they did not, for unknown reasons, enter Puget Sound. Even now, after reintroduction on the outer coast, they have not appeared in our inland waters. Their skeletal remains have not appeared in Indian middens in the enclosed waters of the state. Sightings of "sea otters" in Puget Sound are actually cases of mistaken identity. Their look-alikes, river otters, do cavort on Puget Sound shorelines, even taking up residence in man-built structures near the water.

Tony Angell's captivating scene of a curious harbor seal in a kelp bed. These fish-eating mammals, though supposed to compete severely with human fishermen for salmon and other edible fish, mainly dine on those fish not sought for by, or even palatable to, humans.

The forest floor under old-growth western hemlock and Douglas fir often displays a wealth of shrubs, sword ferns, and other herbs.

5 Life on Land

Lowland Forests

Modern inhabitants have so thoroughly changed the landscapes bounding Puget Sound that the present scene bears little resemblance to the unbelievable grandeur of pre-European times. The Spanish explorers at Nootka Sound, and Captain Cook on the outer coast, followed by Captain Vancouver, intrepid eighteenth-century circumnavigator of Puget Sound, encountered on our shores an evergreen forest of majestic and awesome dimensions. Only the beach or the deck of a ship was a sanctuary of open space in those early times. Even the coastal Indians stayed mainly near the water's edge and traveled rivers when they had reason to penetrate the great timbered maze inland.

Yet this immense evergreen landscape was but a few moments old in geologic time. The forest reinvaded barren land in early postglacial times, beginning less than 13,000 years ago, and it is now already diminishing in quantity and virgin quality since our brief 150-year tenancy of the land. Before primeval lowland coniferous forest becomes only memory, it should claim our attention, both sentimentally and biologically. Familiarity with forests can nurture respect and promote the patience and understanding necessary to ensure the forests' preservation and restoration—here and there around Puget Sound.

Lowland Coniferous Forest: The Dominant Life Form

All ecological questions about terrestrial life around Puget Sound can be reduced to a deceptively simple one: What is the structure and function of any land-bound ecosystem? A full understanding of the words "structure" and "function" would suffice to explain how a living landscape of several thousand square miles works. Ecologically speaking, structure means organization of many parts at different levels of size and complexity: from individual plants and animals upward through populations and communities of organisms, to the largest aggregate, the living fabric on land. What about function? Though it may be redundant to say that function is how structured things work, it is ecologically meaningful to say that a forest functions by the interactive workings of its many parts—trees, flowering shrubs and herbs, animals in variety from bugs to bears, and those levelers of all living matter, the microbial and fungal "trashburners." And all that interwoven life is supported and powered by solar energy and terrestrial matter—light, atmosphere, soil, and water.

Structure and function are inseparable components of all biological systems. The way living things are put together from molecule and cell to whole beings determines the ways they work. And to come full circle, all the many activities required to sustain life demand particular structures. Saying that structure begets function and function begets structure is intentional and profoundly meaningful in the search for an understanding of life.

Is all the life on land within the Puget Sound basin a single ecosystem? Or is it a web of interconnected, yet separable ecosystems? The reader may shrug this off as a question for philosophers or hairsplitters. But the question does illuminate a vexing problem: can any part of the living environment be distinct and independent of any other neighboring segment? In practical terms, any local segment of the whole environment seems to stand apart, as does a sphagnum bog ecosystem, a Douglas fir ecosystem, or a subalpine meadow ecosystem. Each has unique attributes—particular plants, the producers; characteristic animals, the consumers; and microbes, the decomposers—all set in motion by the matter and energy of that particular habitat's allotment of earth, air, water, and light. But here is the dilemma: a bog grades into the adjacent Douglas fir forest, and a Douglas fir forest blends upward into a Pacific silver fir forest. The living landscape is a continuum, separable into subordinate and partially distinct groupings more for ease of comprehension than from natural causes. (See page x.)

Looking at Puget Sound life on land as either one ecosystem or many has merit: one big ecosystem, and even that an arbitrary one when the ocean and the crest of the Cascades are the breachable boundaries; or, if many, then a series of not-so-discrete ecosystems each with some unique feature or set of attributes. This indecision reminds us that an ecosystem is an abstraction for dealing with the openendedness and interconnectedness of living things and their life-support contacts with the physical universe.

A good place to start is with any sample of relatively undisturbed terrestrial plant life near sea level. In earlier times, such a sample would have been forest, dominated by coniferous evergreen trees. Alas! hardly anywhere along the shores of Puget Sound can we expect to find samples of old-growth forest not modified by humans. We will have to be content with samples in some stage of regeneration.

The forest often meets the inland sea in Puget country, stunningly so in the San Juan Islands; here a forested promontory on Cypress Island looks down on Rosario Strait. (Photo by the author.)

Just as life in the waters is powered by the sun and the green plant, so it is on land. To dissect out the elements of structure and function in a forest, one must do the obvious: look at the trees and associated vegetation. Animals and microbes must wait their turn, as they do at nature's table, for food and shelter that forest plants provide. Human observers—botanists, foresters, or curious naturalists—look at groupings of plants in two ways. The first is taxonomic: what species of plants and other organisms are present in a representative sample of the forest? The simplest inventory gives the kinds of organisms present; the published result is a local flora. Such a species listing for plants, however, disregards critical quantitative attributes like frequency, abundance, dominance, and other estimates of the degree of importance that one species may have relative to another. The checklist, combined with statistics on the relative abundance and the frequency of occurrence of each plant species, gives an accurate, though static, view of community composition. This is called the *floristic* approach to ecosystem description.

Another way of analyzing a living landscape is less preoccupied with an inventory of kinds of organisms present. Rather, it portrays the form, pattern, and biomass (quantity of living matter produced) of the plant community in both qualitative and quantitative terms. This is called the *vegetation analysis* approach. Here the observer may record species, but will emphasize life form (trees, shrubs, herbaceous plants) and determine vertical stratification from the emergent canopy of tree tops down to the moss layer on the forest floor. Often the ecologist renders the analysis in diagrams of forest profiles. Contrasts between vegetation analysis (form and function of the green landscape) and floristics (inventories of what grows on a piece of land) are portrayed in the diagram on page 121. Having no preference for either method, I will use both floristic and vegetational portraits for an interpretation of this evergreen land.

The kinds of organisms (species) present in a living landscape give it unique character. But just what is a species? Biologists tend to avoid closely defining species in an abstract sense, since the attributes of a species vary from one kind of organism to another. Yet there are some general qualities of a species that we should keep in mind. As a collective view of a particular kind of organism, a species usually consists of many individuals, even uncountable millions, with like features of structure and function. Local samples of species are populations of individuals that bear close identity to each other and that are distinguished from other but similar kinds. Thus, the two-needled shore (or lodgepole) pine and the five-needled western white pine (both species of the genus *Pinus*) may coexist in the same forests. Yet all individuals of each retain their unique species-specific trademarks. The key to such internal integrity is heredity; individuals of a species interbreed with each other but rarely do so with other but similar "kinds." (See Appendix 1 for an account of the naming of organisms.)

Major Terrestrial Communities of Plants and Animals

The geography of life on land is often fitted into a scheme of lifezones. When zones are used to delimit what appear to be discrete groups of organisms, it is well to retain an image of the intricate overlap in nature of individual species as well as groups or communities of species. Only rarely does one species have limits of tolerance to environmental conditions that neatly coincide with those of other species in the community. Rather, most species have tolerance ranges that only partially overlap. Consider, for instance, two evergreen dominants of Northwest forests, Sitka spruce and Douglas fir. Along the coast and in low inland valleys, the two coexist. But Douglas fir far outstrips Sitka spruce in its tolerances for different environmental conditions, and thus the fir commonly occurs well beyond the distributional limits of Sitka spruce. Since a plant community is composed of several species with *partially* overlapping tolerance ranges, discontinuities of communities and zones are partial and their leading edges are blurred.

Below left: Range of Tolerance (survivability) of a hypothetical plant species to varying environmental conditions. Survivorship decreases as species encounters unfavorable environmental conditions. (Rendering by Robert Hutchins.)

Below: Survivorship curves for Sitka spruce and Douglas fir. The two can occur in the same forest only where their tolerance ranges overlap. This overlap can occur even though the tolerance range of Sitka spruce for temperature and rainfall are much narrower than those of Douglas fir. (Rendering by Robert Hutchins.)

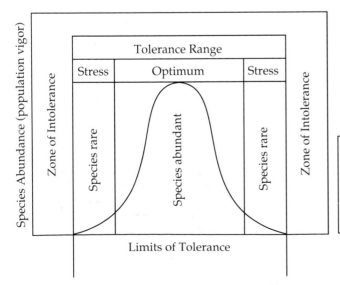

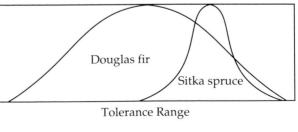

Species:
Shore pine
Douglas fir
Madrone
Grand fir
Salal
Moss and
    licorice fern
Fawn lily
Chocolate lily
Camas
Lommolommol
Lichen
Wild onion

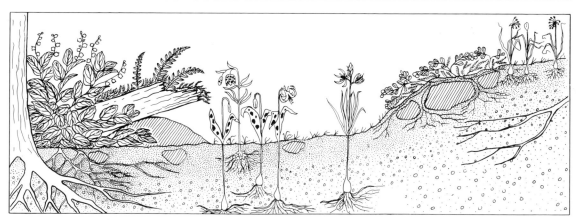

Identical forests of trees and plants in the understory can be analyzed either as vegetation types without regard to kinds (species) of organisms, or can be identified species by species.
A. Vegetation along a topographic gradient. An open Douglas fir forest near Deception Pass.
B. A "slice" of A with vegetation shown as the tree canopy, the shrub and sapling understory, and the herb (ground) layer.

C. Floristic diversity emphasized in a "slice" of B: from left to right: tree, Arbutus menziesii (madrone); shrubs, Gaultheria shallon (salal) and Vaccinium sp. (huckleberry); herbs, Polypodium glycyrhiza (licorice fern) on log, Erythronium oreganum (fawn lily), Fritillaria lanceolata (checker lily), Camassia esculenta (camas), Polytrichum commune (pigeonwheat moss), and (far right) Allium cernuum (nodding onion). (Drawing by Linda Wilkinson.)

With due regard for the world as it really is, the ecologist yields to the practical need for ascribing "zones" to our region's plant and animal life. At least in this way an overview of major vegetation patterns can be had. Two major schemes of zonation have been used for the Northwest, both based on the response of vegetation to change in climate with increasing elevation. Coincidence of climate and elevation with particular kinds of plants produces clusters of species often dominated by one or a few coniferous evergreens. These clusters, highlighted by their dominant trees, constitute the zone. Table 9 compares the two leading systems of zonation. To many, the Merriam life-zone scheme is most familiar. It has been taught to students since the turn of the century. Learning the catechism of "Humid Transition," "Canadian," "Hudsonian," and "Arctic-Alpine" reveals very little about the qualities of each zone; after all, the names were coined to be applicable to contour lines of life in many different areas of North America. Each Merriam life-zone, delimited as a span of altitude on mountains of middle temperate latitudes, was thought to be comparable to the continent-spanning bands of life at high altitudes; hence, the names Canadian, Hudsonian, and Arctic. In fact, a presumed "law" of distribution states that an increase of 300 feet in elevation is approximately equivalent to one degree (70 miles) of latitude, or 500 feet per 100 miles of distance poleward. This would mean that a vegetation-viewing trip in Mount Rainier National Park from Longmire at 2,761 feet to Paradise at 5,557 feet would be comparable to a jaunt of approximately 560 miles to the north. Or, in Merriam's life-zone terms, one would pass from the Canadian Zone to the Hudsonian Zone, with its attendant shifts in latitude, plant life, and climate as though one were to travel from Montreal to Fort George on Hudson's Bay. But does life really behave that way? The elevation-and-latitude correlation is only a crude approximation; yet, vegetation at high elevations at 55 degrees north latitude does resemble that of habitats at lower elevations in more northerly latitudes.

A simpler scheme of zones, using dominant tree species, has been adopted by forest ecologists of the Pacific Northwest (Franklin and Dyrness 1973). Of the several vegetation zones recognized for the entire Pacific Northwest, only three occur in the Puget Sound basin: (1) the Western Hemlock (*Tsuga heterophylla*) Zone, which ranges from sea level to lower montane slopes of the basin; (2) the Pacific Silver Fir (*Abies amabilis*) Zone in the midmontane altitudinal belt; and (3) the Mountain Hemlock (*Tsuga mertensiana*) Zone at upper forested levels. Possibly a fourth zone should be included, the Timberline-to-Alpine Zone, since the region does have a high treeless rim where countless drainage systems get their start.

Zones of vegetation in the Puget Sound basin. The lowland forest zone (Western hemlock-Western red cedar) is the most widespread, while the alpine zone, above timberline, is confined to only the highest (mostly volcanic) peaks.

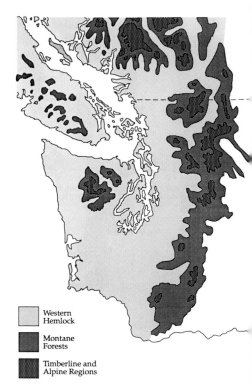

☐ Western Hemlock

■ Montane Forests

■ Timberline and Alpine Regions

A scheme that includes only three or four zones of necessity overlooks marked variations in plant and animal life within a given zone. For example, Douglas fir (*Pseudotsuga menziesii*) often dominates in most of the present lowland forests that would nevertheless be included within the Western Hemlock Zone. There is no inconsistency here to the plant ecologist: a vegetation zone is more than a belt of similar plant life bounded by elevation and associated climate. "Zone," and the adjective "zonal," in the jargon of the ecologist, means a belt of *climatic climax vegetation*, where the dominant species reproduce to maintain a steady state (i.e., climax), generation after generation. In the lowland forest, western hem-

Table 9. Comparison of Two Schemes of Vegetation Zones, Western Washington to Cascade Crest

Elevation	Vegetation Zones (Franklin and Dyrness 1973)	Merriam's Life Zones (Jones 1936)	Dominant Woody Vegetation
	Alpine	Arctic-Alpine	Treeless; perennial herbs and low shrubs
6000 ft.	Upper (Parkland) subzone		Alaska cedar, mountain hemlock, subalpine fir, whitebark pine
	Tsuga mertensiana (mountain hemlock)	Hudsonian	Mountain hemlock, Alaska cedar, Pacific silver fir
5000 ft.	Lower (forested) subzone		
4000 ft.	*Abies amabilis* (Pacific silver fir)	Canadian	Pacific silver fir, western hemlock, western red cedar
3000 ft.			
2000 ft.	*Tsuga heterophylla* (western hemlock)	Humid Transition	Western hemlock-western red cedar climax Douglas fir subclimax
1000 ft.			
Sea level	*Picea sitchensis* (Sitka spruce)		Sitka spruce, western hemlock, western red cedar, Douglas fir

lock is the dominant climatic climax species. It is compatible with regional climate to such an extent that it replaces itself in the forest, crop after crop. Though other tree species like Douglas fir or red alder (*Alnus rubra*) may be more common in any particular forest stand, western hemlock eventually tends to replace a Douglas fir stand. In such situations the Douglas fir is said to be a seral or successional species, self-reproducing with vigor during early and middle periods of colonization of bare land, but eventually to be succeeded and displaced by the climatic climax dominant, western hemlock.

An additional proviso is needed, though, to fully characterize a zonal vegetation. Only on deep loamy soils of good drainage and in places where the terrain is undulating (neither too steep nor too flat) will the zonal or modal association with its dominant tree species occur.

An early attempt to capture the grandeur of forested landscapes in the coastal Northwest. This 1789 view of a Northwest coastline has a tropical look to it, hardly representing the distinctive coastal evergreen conifer forest.

The Western Hemlock Zone

The most spectacular coniferous forests in the world are still found within the zone potentially dominated by western hemlock (*Tsuga heterophylla*). In Puget country, it was the Western Hemlock Zone that formed the sky-reaching wall of evergreens bordering aboriginal people's shoreline existence. And it was western hemlock country that overawed the early European explorers and settlers to our land. The immensity of the lowland forested expanses was almost too great a challenge for the brush and pen of these early visitors to Puget Sound. The artists and writers of the time attempted to record a primeval scene unparalleled in their previous experience, as witnessed by their ornate and often fanciful portrayals.

Prose that strived to capture the virgin quality and hugeness of the forest seems paltry when compared to the real scene. One such attempt at describing the nearly indescribable comes from the journal of Archibald Menzies, surgeon and naturalist to Captain Vancouver (Menzies 1923). On June 6, 1792, while stationed on board H.M.S. *Discovery*, which was anchored in upper Puget Sound, he writes:

> We cannot quit Admiralty Inlet without observing that its beautiful Canals & wandering navigable branches traverse through a low flat Country . . . thus diffusing utility and ornament to a rich Country by affording a commodious and ready communication through every part of it, to the termination of the most distant branches. . . . The general appearance of the Country from this station was as follows. To the South West of us a high ridge of Mountains ran from the outer point of de Fuca's entrance in a South East direction,—gradually increasing in height to form the rugged elevated peaks of Mount Olympus. . . . To the South East of us down Admiralty Inlet was seen through a beautiful avenue formed by the Banks of the Inlet, Mount Rainier . . . which did not diminish but rather apparently augmented its great elevation & huge bulky appearance; from it a complete ridge of Mountains with rugged & picked [sic] summits covered here and there with patches of Snow and forming a solid & impassable barrier on the East Side of New Georgia, running in a due North direction to join Mount Baker. . . .
>
> Between us & the above Ridge & to the Southward of us between the two Mountains already mentioned a fine level Country intervened chiefly covard [sic] with pine forests abounding here and there with clear spots of considerable extent & intersected with the various winding branches of Admiralty Inlet. . . . These clear spots or lawns are clothed with a rich carpet of Verdure & adorned with clumps of Trees & a surrounding verge of scattered Pines which with their advantageous situation on the Banks of these inland Arms of the Sea give them a beauty of prospect equal to the most admired Parks in England.
>
> A traveller wandering over these unfrequented Plains is regaled with a salubrious & vivifying air impregnated with the balsamic fragrance of the surrounding Pinery, while his mind is eagerly occupied every moment on new objects & his senses rivetted on the enchanting variety of the surrounding scenery where the softer beauties of Landscape are harmoniously blended in majestic grandeur with the wild & romantic to form an interesting & picturesque prospect on every side. (Menzies 1923:47)

The inquiring mind craves further understanding that comes from facts and figures. The plant ecologist sees the Western Hemlock Zone as a mosaic of species bound together by history and coinciding tolerance ranges. The ecologist recognizes that past events can determine which species might stock any particular piece of the globe. In the Pacific Northwest, the glacial activity of the Pleistocene and those glacial after-effects of the post-Pleistocene created a raw seed bed for the species that hung on near the southern edge of the continental ice sheet. Presumably all the species present in the contemporary vegetation (save introductions by humans from other continents) were recruited from the plant communities that hovered close to the ice. Forests of western hemlock were in existence during the last Ice Age, surviving on coastal terrain beyond the frigid tension zone bordering the ice.

The overriding determinant of western hemlock's ability to colonize the land in countless numbers is climate, both regional climate and suitable microclimates created by topography. The western hemlock way of life is benign. It is a forest type that thrives in a mild, moist (maritime) climate. Average monthly temperatures range from 38°F in January to 66°F in July; precipitation comes mostly as rain distributed fairly equally throughout the year, but with the greatest amounts between October and April. Western hemlock country gets an average annual rainfall of thirty-two inches (in Bellingham) increasing to fifty-two inches in Olympia. These and other critical climatic data for the Western Hemlock Zone are given in Tables 10, 11, and 12.

A particularly crucial statistic is the amount of solar radiation available to vegetation for photosynthesis. For 229 days of an average year, the central Puget Sound area is cloudy—not just partly cloudy, but completely overcast. Should not this be a deterrent to optimal growth of forest species, not only for dominant trees but for the shaded understory associates—herbs, shrubs, and the ground layer of mosses and lichens? Bright sunshine and thriving cornfields surely go together, but what about hemlock forests? Plant physiologists have learned that the lowland forest species of the hemlock belt photosynthesize best under light conditions below those of a bright midday in summer. The light that gets through the cloud cover is more than ample to power the "solar batteries" in cells of hemlock needles and sword fern fronds. Perhaps it should not be surprising that the forest vegetation does best in just that particular climate which can be depended upon year after year and century after century. An evolutionary bargain was struck eons ago between plant and environment to yield a successful, adaptive compromise.

Recall that the phrase "Western Hemlock Zone" stands for an

Table 10. Climatic Data from Typical

Station	Elevation (feet)
Monroe	120
Seattle City	14
Seattle-Tacoma Airport	386
Snoqualmie Falls	440
Bremerton	162
Shelton	22
Longmire	2762
Tacoma	127
Aberdeen	365

Note: Data from Phillips 1965, 1968

Stations within the Western Hemlock Zone

Temperature (°F)					Precipitation (inches)		
Average annual	Average January	Average January Minimum	Average July	Average July Maximum	Average annual	June through August	Average annual snowfall
51.2	38.0	31.9	64.1	75.8	46.76	4.91	10.1
53.2	41.2	36.8	65.6	75.1	34.10	2.78	8.6
51.1	38.3	33.0	64.9	75.6	38.94	3.34	14.4
50.1	37.7	31.5	63.0	77.1	60.30	5.93	16.9
51.0	39.4	33.8	64.2	75.8	38.66	2.61	7.9
51.1	38.4	31.7	64.3	77.6	64.29	3.59	8.3
45.1	30.3	24.3	61.2	74.9	82.43	6.73	177.7
52.1	39.9	34.8	64.4	74.1	37.06	3.04	12.1
50.3	39.7	—	60.1	—	84.54	6.00	—

Table 11. Cloud Cover at Seattle-Tacoma Airport (daily averages)

	Percent Frequency of Cloud Cover		
	0–3 (scant)	4–7 (moderate)	8–10 (heavy)
January	12	7	81
April	25	14	61
July	49	11	40
October	23	12	65

Note: Data from Phillips 1968.

Table 12. Percentage of Annual Precipitation by Months

	Seattle	Aberdeen
January	15.2	14.8
February	11.4	11.7
March	9.7	11.1
April	5.7	6.9
May	4.6	4.1
June	4.1	3.0
July	1.8	1.8
August	2.1	1.9
September	4.8	4.5
October	9.6	10.7
November	14.6	12.8
December	15.8	16.9
	100.	100.

Note: Data from Church and Fritschen 1968.

abstract concept as well as a particular belt of vegetation dominated at some stage in forest regeneration and in optimal situations by western hemlock. Only under ideal conditions of moisture, drainage, and topography is the lowland country forested with self-sustaining western hemlock as the prime species. In fact, the forest ecologist sees at least three major forest types within the Western Hemlock Zone. These three forest associations are named by their

Far left: Old-growth Douglas fir with abundant younger western hemlock.

Above: A Darius Kinsey photo from the early 1920s records a maturing forest of western hemlock.

dominant tree and shrub (or herb) components as follows: Western Hemlock/Sword Fern, Western Hemlock/Cascade Oregon Grape, and Douglas Fir/Salal. Other ecologists would add to this list still more plant communities, depending on their methods of describing vegetation types. A close look at some of these forest communities is in order, for residents of Puget Sound country are in daily contact with the variant themes of western hemlock communities—or their latter-day remnants.

The Western Hemlock/Sword Fern community and the Western Hemlock/Cascade Oregon Grape community are the two groupings where hemlock dominates in the forest. In such a forest, hemlocks of gigantic size will grow in open spacings of 50 to 100 stems per acre. Mature trees can reach an average diameter at shoulder height of 3 to 4 feet, and tower 175 to 225 feet into the air. Hem-

Above right: Western red cedar can be a local dominant in western hemlock forests, as here in the Snoqualmie-Mount Baker National Forest.

locks are compatible with other forest conifers. Western red cedar is by far the most common tree associate in the wetter hemlock sites. Though not as tall, the cedars may outstrip hemlock in diameter due to their massively buttressed and tapered lower trunks. Occasional individuals of Douglas fir and western yew join western hemlock in typical forest communities.

Old-Growth Forest

Mention "old-growth forest" in mixed company of conservationists and foresters and you are enmeshed in a red-hot controversy. "Decadent" or "over-mature" forests, "spotted owls," "ancient" trees, or "a race of giants" are just some of the buzzwords that can set off a lively debate. After years of emotional exchange on the pros and cons of preserving old-growth stands, without much substance to back up claims from either side, the issue is now supported by several major research studies. Two Forest Service documents summarize the attributes of old growth: "Ecological Characteristics of Old Growth Douglas-Fir Forests" (Franklin et al. 1981) and "The Seen and Unseen World of the Fallen Tree" (Maser and Trappe 1984). An eloquent version of these research reports can be found in the March 1986 issue of *Audubon Magazine* ("The Decadent Forest" by Kelly and Braasch), and the book, *Fragile Majesty*, by Keith Ervin (1989).

Lowland conifer forests begin to take on the attributes of old growth at from 175 to 250 years. Old growth is in its prime at 350 to 750 years. A perceptive naturalist senses the unique qualities of old growth, in contrast to young forest stands. Trees in old growth vary markedly in size, from seedlings, saplings, and young trees (age 50 to 100 years) to huge specimens with massive trunks free of lower branches. Spacing of old trees is greater than in the dense, even-aged stands of the young forest. Though amply shaded, the forest floor develops a substantial understory of tree seedlings, shrubs, and herbs that thrive on filtered sunlight. Young forests may be so dense as to prevent the development of appreciable understory. Logs and canopy branch debris liberally litter the forest floor. Standing dead trees and decapitated snags in all stages of decomposition are conspicuously intermixed with the living trees of the forest.

Despite the evident and singular quality of old growth, scarcely any of its dominant plant species are either exclusively or dominantly confined to the old-growth forest. Major tree species, as well as most of the understory plants, can be found at nearly every stage in the growing, maturing forest. It is the particular way they manifest themselves—by size and luxuriance of the dominants, as well as by the diversity of the understory—that achieves the unique old-growth look.

If any ecological grouping of plants is optimally developed in old-growth forests, it has to be those curious non-green flowering members of the orchid and heather families. Displays of the pure-white phantom orchid, the Indian pipe, and the ghostlike, spectacular candy-stick and pine-drop are best seen on the organic forest floor of old-growth stands. These amazing flowering plants that appear to "live on death," are discussed further on pages 180–85.

Vertebrate animals (especially birds and mammals) can be the most telling characteristic indicators of old growth. Seven bird species find optimal forage and nest sites in old-growth habitats; they are the goshawk, northern spotted owl, Vaux's swift, pileated

woodpecker, Hammond's flycatcher, pine grosbeak, and Townsend's warbler.

Six different mammals live in the forest canopy, staying largely arboreal. The northern flying squirrel and the red tree vole are the best-known acrobats of this lofty way of life. Three mammals (a vole, a mole, and the marten) are ground-dwelling in old growth.

The northern spotted owl heads the list of those animals most closely dependent on old growth. Spotted owls have selected—or, in Darwinian terms, have been selected for—a highly specialized nesting site. They prefer the cavities created in old living trees with broken and hollow tops. Clearly this is a habitat found predominantly in old-growth stands. Hence, as old growth disappears in lowland Puget country, so will the spotted owl. It is now only rarely sighted (or merely heard calling?). Put another way, it is very likely that the major support for preservation of old growth will come from the urgency to preserve the habitat of the spotted owl and other vertebrates closely tied to old-growth forests.

The old-growth forest eloquently dramatizes the ecological adage: "Everything is connected to everything else." The trees, the subordinate plant life of the understory, the animals, and all the rest of the seen and unseen organisms of the forest ecosystem, create a grand symbiosis—a self-perpetuating, mutually advantageous system of life. Moreover, the living, the dying, and the dead all coexist; life and death are inseparable and indeed interdependent. Vast amounts of plant and animal biomass, as soon as life ceases, enter the recycling circuitry. The "trashburners" of the forest floor (fungi, bacteria, and invertebrate animals) process the remains for use in the rebirth of new generations of forest life. But more than reprocessing biomass, the intertwined life and death—the living forest with the dead logs, stumps, and other forest litter—perform additional life-support functions. Decaying logs act as sponges to retain water through the summer's drought. And the ever-present downed timber creates microcosms of local habitats, sheltering plant and animal life that could not survive on hot, dry mineral soil once the forest is gone. The prodigious decay also becomes a hospitable root-run for new plant life, from tree seedlings on nurselogs to shrubs and herbs of the understory and forest floor. Where the logs and fallen limbs fall in the path of streams, they act as

Death begets life in conifer forests.
The natural recycling of dead biomass
includes the turnover of everything
from needles and pollen cones to huge
fallen trees. (Photo by Mary Randlett.)

natural check-dams to runoff and foster their own aquatic recycling "industry."

Besides recycling existing nutrient elements, the forest can extract new nutrition from the atmosphere. The canopies of old-growth trees are festooned with lichens. These living attachments (epiphytes), with their dual alga-fungus plant bodies, can convert atmospheric nitrogen into a form usable by plants, if the algal member of the team is a blue-green alga. Canopy epiphytes, like ferns, mosses, and algae, also "comb out" moisture and particulate matter from the air, a gain in nutrition and water that adds to Nature's economy.

When old growth is described as decadent or overmature, the intent is clear. The trees must be harvested before they become

Tree trunks and limbs often carry a luxuriant load of epiphytes, mostly mosses and licorice fern. (Photo by Bob and Ira Spring.)

An early method for felling old-growth Douglas fir: "axe men on spring-boards" notched into a huge Douglas fir.

useless or even detrimental to the forest (or to the forester). In ecological terms, overmature stands are assumed to be on a one-way trip to oblivion. In this view, the forest, like Shakespeare's Seven Ages of Man, has a beginning and an end. *If this were true,* then old-growth forests would be transient actors in a drama of eventual, inevitable change. But if we view the symphony of life-with-death in the old growth as a system in perpetual motion, then old growth should be looked upon as having gained the limitless plateau of maturity, set for eternal existence. Barring fire and other capricious calamity, the mature forest has no life span. When it attains the status of what we have called old growth, the forest then has gained the versatility and ecological flexibility to reproduce itself in perpetuity. As long as the regional climate persists, so will the mature forest persist. Aged or ageless, that is the question. The current studies of mature forest stands seem to come down on the side of ageless.

Old-growth stands of colossal western hemlocks, western red cedars, and Douglas firs with their rich understory vegetation can still be found occasionally at lower elevations in the Puget basin. None are at sea level and thus do not give the spectator the shoreward view of stately forest seen by early explorers. Most contemporary stands are in the hinterland of the basin, at around 1,000 feet elevation, often miles from Puget Sound. Because of their elevation and distance from the Sound, such old-growth stands intergrade in species composition with the next higher, the Pacific Silver Fir (*Abies amabilis*) Zone (for a detailed account of this zone, see chapter 8).

But nowadays, seekers of the pristine lowland forest type cannot be choosers. Rather, they rejoice in the good fortune of its token preservation in scattered localities in western Washington. Most of the 800,000 acres of old-growth forest are in public ownership. Listed here are some of the most outstanding samples of this grand forest type.

Mt. Rainier National Park: (1) Ipsut Creek and the lower Carbon River drainage; (2) between the park entrance and Longmire on the road to Paradise; (3) Lower Stevens Canyon road between Ohanapecosh and the Trail of the Patriarchs. The trail ends only about a mile from the highway at a magnificent grove of mammoth western red cedar, western hemlock, and Douglas fir.

Olympic National Park: (4) the lower Dosewallips River, just inside the park; (5) the Staircase area, Skokomish River. Just beyond Puget Sound proper are the fine old-growth stands on the north side of the park: (6) the lower Elwha River valley, west of Port Angeles; (7) Heart of the Hills campground area, on the road to Hurricane Ridge. From here, the world-famous temperate rain forests of the west side are within easy striking distance from Puget Sound.

Mt. Baker National Forest—Snoqualmie: (8) Boulder River trail, above Boulder Falls, twelve miles west of Darrington; (9) Lake Twenty-Two Trail, south fork Stillaguamish River; (10) North Fork Nooksack River,[1] Highway 542, ten miles east of Glacier; (11) Asahel Curtis Nature Trail, Highway I-90, about three miles west of Snoqualmie Pass.

State Land: (12) Federation Forest State Park, fifteen miles southeast of Enumclaw, on State Highway 410; (13) Lewis and Clark State Park, twelve miles south of Chehalis; (14) Rockport State Park, Skagit River valley.

---

1. Numbers 9 and 10 are Research Natural Areas with no public access except along the highway or established trail. Research Natural Areas, mostly federal and state, preserve for scientific and educational purposes, representative samples of major vegetation types in the United States (Franklin et al. 1972; Dyrness et al. 1975).

It is still possible to witness old-growth forest in Puget lowlands. A superb example is the Federation Forest on Highway 410 about 15 miles east of Enumclaw. (Photo by Ruth and Louis Kirk.)

County/City Land: (15) "Pioneer" forest in Schmitz Park, West Seattle.

To visit old-growth forests in Puget Sound country, consult also *Visitors' Guide to Ancient Forests of Western Washington,* by the Dittmar family.

An Example of Community Types in the Western Hemlock Zone

Before characterizing the several variant western hemlock communities, ecological theory and practice must be comprehended. "Community" and "association" are words inevitably encountered in the literature of plant ecology. They represent a human urge to distill some discrete order out of the endless variety in green landscapes. Any sample of vegetation exhibits variety—few to many kinds of plants. Only rarely does one encounter a pure stand, a monoculture of just one species. This is especially true for old-growth stands within the Western Hemlock Zone. Living with the dominant conifer are other less frequent cone-bearing evergreens, as well as species from all other realms of the plant kingdom. Any sample of vegetation is a grouping (association) of different species. The aggregations of species, each as a large or small population, constitute the community. Harder to define, of course, is the nature of the forces that bind or bring together diverse species into one community. Chance, past events, and similar tolerances for environmental conditions can superficially account for the cohabitation of western hemlock with other species unrelated by heredity.

The western hemlock/sword fern association is recognized by the dominating presence of the sword fern (*Polystichum munitum*), forming dense patches of lush three-to-five-feet-high evergreen plumes on the forest floor. When the trees are gone (logged or burned) the sword fern may persist (though stunted) to tell of a prime habitat for growing hemlock and cedar.

Other species are common cohabitants with western hemlock and sword fern. Douglas fir is not uncommon even on the more moist sites optimal for western hemlock; in fact, some of the largest trees in such a forest may be Douglas fir. Western red cedar may be so common as to share dominant status with western hemlock in the forest canopy. Sword fern shares the understory shrub layer of the forest with three common woody species: red huckleberry (*Vaccinium parvifolium*), Cascade Oregon grape (*Berberis nervosa*), and trailing blackberry (*Rubus ursinus*). Less frequent on these flat, moist, but well-drained sites will be isolated specimens of vine maple (*Acer circinatum*). And at ground level, besides seedlings of all of the above, another distinctive assemblage appears—a cover-

Table 13. Common Names of the Most Common Plants
of the Western Hemlock Zone

Trees	Shrubs	Herbs
Western hemlock	Scouler's willow	Sword fern
Western red cedar	Vine maple	Deer fern
Douglas fir	Salal	Evergreen violet
Red alder	Red huckleberry	Foam flower
Bigleaf maple	Cascade Oregon	Twin flower
Black cottonwood	grape	Western trillium
Madrone	Devil's club	False lily-of-the-valley
		Wild ginger

Note: Tables 14, 15, and 16 provide fuller lists of plants in the three strata: tree, shrub, and herb.

ing of perennial herbs, mosses, and lichens. As can be seen in Table 13, the number of species sharing the western hemlock habitat is substantial. That so much plant variety can coexist in a patch of forest bears witness to the fine adjustments each species has made in exacting from the habitat its share of resources—light, moisture, and soil minerals.

Portraits of Lowland Trees

"Except during the nine months before he draws his first breath, no man manages his affairs as well as a tree does."—George Bernard Shaw

The codominant conifers of the western hemlock/sword fern association merit closer inspection.[2] Whole-tree impressions of hemlock, cedar, and Douglas fir, along with some of their ecological attributes, will assist in their recognition. (See Table 14.)

WESTERN HEMLOCK (*Tsuga heterophylla*). Old specimens of western hemlock have massive, straight trunks, free of limbs from ground upward to 75 feet or so. The first branches, though out of reach, have a graceful droop to their tips. This pendulous profile repeats itself all the way to the top of the tree. The most characteristic feature of western hemlock, when viewed from a distance, is the pendant terminal growing tip or leader. Pendant terminal leaders are not easily seen from the ground in a forest of old-growth giants. But look around at eye level. The drooping leader is easy to

2. Books that deal with the Sound region's plant life abound. For trees, the classic manual *Forest Trees of the Pacific Slope* by Sudworth (1908) and the more modern *Northwest Trees* by Arno and Hammerly (1977) should be consulted.

Table 14. Trees of the Western Hemlock Zone

Species	Abundance	Size (height/diam. in feet)	Habitat
Evergreen			
Western hemlock (*Tsuga heterophylla*)	****	150/3	Flats and slopes
Western red cedar (*Thuja plicata*)	****	150/3	Moist flats and lower slopes
Douglas fir (*Pseudotsuga menziesii*)	****	200/6-8	Flats, slopes, ridges
Western white pine (*Pinus monticola*)	***	125/3	Flats, slopes on sandy soils
Shore pine (*Pinus contorta*)	**	30/1	Swamps, prairies and coastal; islands
Yellow pine (*Pinus ponderosa*)	*	150/3	Gravelly prairies at Ft. Lewis
Grand fir (*Abies grandis*)	**	125/3	Flats and headlands near Sound
Sitka spruce (*Picea sitchensis*)	**	150/3	Moist bottoms
Juniper (*Juniperus scopulorum*)	**	30/2	Dry slopes and headlands San Juan Islands
Western yew (*Taxus brevifolia*)	**	30/1-3	Moist flats and slopes
Madrone (*Arbutus menziesii*)	****	30-80/1-3	Drier slopes and headlands
Golden chinquapin (*Chrysolepis chrysophylla*)	*	50/1	Dry forests, west side Hood Canal
Deciduous (Hardwoods)			
Bigleaf maple (*Acer macrophyllum*)	****	100/4	Bottoms and slopes
Red alder (*Alnus rubra*)	****	60/2	Flats, slopes, near water
Black cottonwood (*Populus trichocarpa*)	***	100/4	Valley bottoms
Western flowering dogwood (*Cornus nuttallii*)	***	50/1.5	Flats, slopes with Douglas fir
Scouler's willow (*Salix scouleriana*)	****	50/1	Openings in forest
Birch (*Betula papyrifera*)	**	50/1	Flats from Marysville north
Rocky Mt. maple (*Acer glabrum*)	**	40/1	Forested slopes
Quaking aspen (*Populus tremuloides*)	**	30/1	Usually wet areas
Bitter cherry (*Prunus emarginata*)	***	40/1	Openings in forest
Garry oak (*Quercus garryana*)	***	40/1	Gravelly prairies and parkland
Ash (*Fraxinus latifolia*)	**	50/2	Low-lying wet areas bordering rivers
Wild crabapple (*Pyrus fusca*)	**	30/0.5	Wet brushy thickets
Hawthorn (*Crataegus douglasii*)	**	30/0.5	Wet brushy thickets
Pacific willow (*Salix lasiandra*)	**	50/1	Low-lying wet areas
Cascara (*Rhamnus purshiana*)	***	40/0.5	Second-growth and forest openings
Vine maple (*Acer circinatum*)	****	40/1	Tree-like in openings
European mountain ash (*Sorbus aucuparia*)	**	40/1	Suburban woods (an escape)

Note: **** common, *** frequent, ** infrequent, * rare.

Western hemlock branch with maturing seed cones.

spot at the tips of sapling hemlocks. Young trees in the stand reveal other identifying characters. Any fresh branch is clothed with symmetrical flat arrays of smallish, closely set needles, dark green above and nearly white beneath. Hemlock's small needles are irregular in length, varying from one-half to three-fourths of an inch, which gives a ragged look to the edge of the flat frond of needles. Young trees are precocious cone producers and old giants leave a litter of their spent fecundity on the forest floor. For such a huge tree, the cones of hemlock seem absurdly small, not more than three-fourths to an inch long. They are made of thin papery scales, overlapping one another, tightly so before opening and spreading apart when the tiny one-eighth-inch-long seeds are shed.

Another whole-tree characteristic that is the hallmark of western hemlock is its choice of starting place. Dead trunks, preferably of

Western hemlock with its telltale pendulous branches and drooping leader. (Drawings by Ramona Hammerly.)

Douglas fir, when brought to earth, are prime horizontal "nurseries" for western hemlock seedlings. This nurse-log phenomenon persists for many years. While the hundreds of seedlings on a single downed log continue to grow, the nurse-log melts further into the ground. What was once a dense crop of seedlings is now reduced to a few saplings with their roots fully penetrating the decayed nurse-log to the soil. For a time a young hemlock seems to be straddling a fallen giant; then at a later stage all that one sees of the nurse-log is a faint mound at the base of the maturing hemlock. All stages of this reprocessing of old conifers to make new ones are to be seen in most older stands of hemlock. The alluvial benches just above any of the river drainages into Puget Sound—like the Skagit, the two forks of the Stillaguamish, the Snoqualmie, and the Nisqually—are prime areas to look for western hemlock bountifully replacing itself in this remarkable manner.

Western hemlock best exemplifies the "nurse log" effect; one of the many seedlings of hemlock can persist on a downed log to reach the soil. Here an old hemlock still shows its attachment to the nurse log. (Photo by Bob and Ira Spring.)

Up to thirty years ago, old-age hemlock was abundant. Turn-of-the-century loggers had their eyes only on prime timber, Douglas fir and cedar; hemlock was shunned as a useless, "weed" tree. Hemlock does make good lumber; yet, prejudices are hard to shake off. Only in the 1930s did western hemlock come into its own, then to serve the expanding paper-pulp industry with its most needed raw material, alkali-resistant alpha-cellulose that is the essential molecular ingredient of the long, stringy, yet strong fiber cells of its wood. In 1953, Donald Culross Peattie reasoned that western hemlock seemed an inexhaustible resource for the foreseeable future. As a crop to be "farmed" and wisely husbanded on a thirty to sixty-year rotation, this kind of inexhaustibility is probably true. But mature stands that were once everywhere around lowland Puget Sound are fast disappearing. Only in the sanctuary of national parks, natural area preserves, or in as yet unlogged old-growth forests will patriarchal stands be found by naturalists in the 1990s. By their disappearance, a quality of primeval nature will have gone from Puget Sound, never to return.

WESTERN RED CEDAR (*Thuja plicata*). The several Indian tribes around Puget Sound found western red cedar or canoe cedar of immense value in their daily lives. The native cedar was so plentiful in the wetter sites of lowland Puget Sound that it could be harvested at will, a seemingly unending gift of Nature. Its tough stringy bark was harvested in long strips, then either shredded for padding or woven, plaited, or sewn to make clothing. The wood was worked into timbers and planks for the imposing longhouse and the more modest special-occasion shelters.

Cedar is the wood of the famed Northwest Indian canoe. From cedar came the outfitting of this seaworthy vessel in sails, ropes, and bails. House posts, carved from cedar, adorned dwellings and served ceremonial and functional needs similar to the totem poles of the coastal Indians north of Puget Sound. Hilary Stewart's lavish book, *Cedar* (1984), provides an exhaustive list of items made from cedar. Her account bears witness both to the versatility of the tree and to the ingenuity of the Indian craftspeople. The earlier classic work on native plants by Erna Gunther, *Ethnobotany of Western Washington* (1945; reprinted in 1973), also highlights the value of cedar to North Coast Indian cultures. Gunther's book was compiled at a time when Indian elders were alive to tell of their ancestors' ways of life.

Western red cedar is the easiest conifer of the lowland forests to identify. No other evergreen around the shores of Puget Sound has minute flattish scales instead of needles for leaves. Examine closely even the smallest branchlet of cedar to see a mosaic of tiny green, wedge-shaped "tiles," each pointed at the tip. The paired leaves (each not more than a sixteenth of an inch wide and long) are dovetailed like symmetrical shingles in opposed ranks to clothe the smallest twig completely. The sweet smell of crushed cedar foliage is another unmistakable recognition signal to sniffers of herbage.

On all but young saplings, cedar branches take on a characteristic look. Each lower branch is bent into an S-shaped curve that is an unmistakable mark of this cedar. Starting from the trunk, the limbs sweep upward, then curve gently down, and finally curve up again at the tip, a shape to remind one of the draftsman's French curve or of a Dutchman's pipe.

Cedar vies with western hemlock in its capacity for prodigal seed output. The small brownish cones, borne in dense clusters on branches from any part of the tree, turn upward on the branch as they mature. Each half-inch long conelet consists of four pairs of elongate scales, scooped out like tiny rowboats; each scale of the longer middle pair bears two small seeds, winged for aerial dispersal. But the seed of this species is not as efficiently airborne as western hemlock's. Released from 150 feet in the air, cedar seeds travel only up to 400 feet from the source. Under only slightly different conditions, hemlock seeds have been known to move more than three times that far. The rare cyclonic storms such as the devastating Columbus Day blow of 1962, however, can carry seed much greater distances.

Even more than western hemlock, western red cedar is a tree of damp to wet woods. Sudworth, in his 1908 botanical classic, *Forest Trees of the Pacific Slope,* writes: "[Western red cedar is] confined to regions of abundant precipitation and humidity, chiefly to wet or moist flats, beaches, gentle slopes, river bottoms, in and about swamps and wet springy places, and in cool moist gulches and ravines. [The trees are] of gigantic size on deep, rich, moist bottoms in the vicinity of the coast." You can almost wring water out of that description!

Moisture and shade afford the most favorable conditions for germination and establishment of seedlings. Tiny cedars, looking like little ferns, are as much at home on nurse-logs as are crops of juvenile western hemlock. Prolific seed output and high germinability on decaying wood, coupled with preferences for moist habitats, closely link both species to the same ecological conditions. The two share a high tolerance for shade in infancy and early youth. This shade tolerance may account for much of both species' success in perpetuating their kind.

DOUGLAS FIR (*Pseudotsuga menziesii*). Ecological theory predicts that, given enough time—decades to centuries—a community of species that can perpetuate itself will reach a dynamic steady state,

Below: Old-growth Western red cedar (Thuja plicata) is massive in form, especially at its base with the flared, buttressed lower trunk. The fibrous bark is a distinctive feature. Specimens like this can be seen just south of Eatonville along the University of Washington's Pack Forest nature trail. (Photo by Bob and Ira Spring.)

Right: Western red cedar frequently grows in wet sites in lowland Puget country, often next to standing water. (Photo by Jerry Franklin.)

the climax condition. For moist sites on flat to gently sloping to-pography, hemlock and cedar should become supreme. Yet, not all lowland areas have a hemlock-cedar suitability. Past geological events have given the land great diversity of slope, exposure, drainage, and soil quality. Drier habitats on west- and south-facing slopes cannot support hemlock and cedar. In their place, Douglas fir is nearly always found. The combination of Douglas fir and salal (*Gaultheria shallon*) is the most characteristic plant association on Puget Sound headlands, bluffs, steep and summer-dry slopes, and similar habitats of limited available moisture. In pristine or rela-tively undisturbed conditions, this association is impressive: large, evenly spaced Douglas firs tower over a nearly impenetrable shrub layer of evergreen salal.

In Puget Sound country Douglas fir is seen most frequently in association with vegetation of drier sites. Yet its broad tolerance for moisture—from optimal to stressfully reduced—as well as its com-patibility with other forest dominants, assure its presence in al-most every habitat except the wettest or driest. Douglas fir is com-mon even in hemlock-cedar forests. Most ecologists believe that when found with hemlock or cedar, it has persisted from a time

Below: Succession, exemplified here in a sequence of lowland forest stands, is the replacement of one vegetation type (and its species) by another over time. Succession gives way to climax vegetation when a plant community reaches a steady state (replacing itself by itself). (Diagram by Linda Wilkinson.)

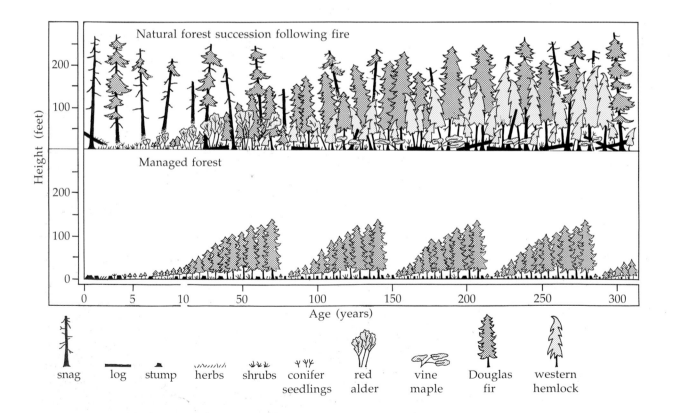

when the community was in some earlier stage of development. Douglas fir can become established in almost any but the most extreme habitats (moist or dry) since it competes well with other juvenile stages of tree species. Douglas fir is moderately intolerant of shade and can readily colonize open habitats. Only when it begins to furnish shade for seedlings of other species, does the struggle for dominance begin. On wetter sites, hemlock and cedar then become established in the shade of Douglas fir, eventually to oust their benefactor. This slow-moving drama of replacement is nearly universal in occurrence and is referred to by ecologists as succession. Plant species that coexist in a community for only a brief span of vegetational time are caught up in the drama of succession. Douglas fir clearly is a successional species in habitats where hemlock or cedar will eventually become the self-perpetuating dominants. And dominance here has special meaning. Though Douglas fir may appear to be the prime forest component throughout most of the successional time span, it eventually fails to reproduce itself since its seedlings cannot tolerate deep shade.

So versatile a tree as Douglas fir is not ousted everywhere by potential climax species. In fact, Douglas fir is its own climax species

Douglas fir (Pseudotsuga menziesii) is the common coniferous evergreen of Puget Sound country, dominant in old-growth, second-growth, and "tree farm" stands as well as the tree of urban and suburban landscapes.

Above: Old-growth Douglas fir stand with lower trunks free of side branches. (Photo by Bob and Ira Spring.)

Right: Old-growth Douglas fir, with young western hemlock. In time the hemlock may replace the fir. (Photo by Bob and Ira Spring.)

on drier habitats where its seedlings thrive in a sunny glade opened by a chance fallen monarch of its own species. The Douglas fir-salal association can in this way be its own self-perpetuating alliance, just as can the wetter forest of hemlock and cedar.

So much of the quality of life—human life and the lives of many other terrestrial organisms—is bound up with Douglas fir in the Pacific Northwest that a thorough acquaintance with the tree is called for. First, take its name. Pinning down a secure botanical name for this ever-present tree has been a particularly vexing adventure. At once a conifer and yet unique in numerous of its attributes, the question in the eighteenth century of how to link Douglas fir with any of the existing botanical groupings provoked indecision. It was first placed in the genus *Pinus*, which around 1800 was a catchall for most cone-bearing trees, besides serving as a generic haven for those trees still recognized as pines. Yet members of *Pinus* in the modern sense all have their needles clustered in bundles of constant number; this would exclude Douglas fir. So, dissatisfied with including it in the genus *Pinus*, botanists tried other solutions. It could more handily be absorbed in either *Abies* (true firs) or *Tsuga* (hemlocks); indeed, both solutions were tried in the nineteenth century. Then, in recognition of the singular features of cone and foliage, French horticulturist Elie Abel Carrière in 1867 proposed the generic name of *Pseudotsuga*. Here Douglas fir now resides, along with four other species.

Left: Black bear in a Douglas fir.

Center: A second-growth stand of Douglas fir, with some cedar, near Tumwater. (Photo by the author.)

Right: A managed "forest" of Douglas fir—a Christmas tree farm—on Kitsap Peninsula west of Seattle. The tall single tree was left as a seed source. (Photo by the author.)

The search for a stable species name for Douglas fir became almost as tortuous as was finding a generic name. It takes a clever botanical lawyer to trace the intricate history to the present full (binomial) name for our kind of *Pseudotsuga*. It was only in 1950 that the decision to settle on *Pseudotsuga menziesii* was made. Now, if the tree in question had been an insignficant member of the flora, the change would have been accepted without objection. But a tree whose role in human endeavor is so central could not suffer a name change without hue and cry. Foresters, horticulturists, and even botanists were not prepared to see the old familiar name of *Pseudotsuga taxifolia* give way to the new one. Appeals to the botanical rulemakers were made; but, in accepting the rule of honoring prior published names, *Pseudotsuga menziesii* had to take precedence, once it came to light. By now, the new name has become firmly established and is easily used by all who need the Latin names of plants. But should some botanical sleuth find a published name in even the most obscure source that antedates the present specific name, *menziesii*, then the confrontation between stability of names and priority of names would surface again. Appendix 1 is devoted to the lore of the naming of organisms—plants, animals, and microbes.

Pseudotsuga means, literally, "false-hemlock." It was applied by Carrière to denote conifers that had hemlock-like features, yet possessed distinctive features of their own. Five particular variations on the *Pseudotsuga* theme are known, two in North America and three in Asia. Of the five, Douglas fir is by far the most successful species, both in sheer numbers of its kind and in its great geographic range in western North America.

For the Douglas fir, *menziesii* commemorates Archibald Menzies of Aberfeldy, Scotland, the first European to collect specimens. Menzies served as surgeon-naturalist with the Vancouver Expedition in Puget Sound in 1792. Though we acknowledge Menzies' right to being the namesake for the Northwest species of *Pseudotsuga*, we may wonder why the tree has never commonly been called the "Menzies fir" rather than Douglas fir, which has been its name for many years.

Douglas fir, as *the* common name, has nearly the same sterling integrity as does *Pseudotsuga menziesii*. David Douglas gave more of his life to discovering the botanical riches of the virgin Northwest than did any other early plant explorer and collector. Even before disembarking at the mouth of the Columbia River in 1825, he recognized a tree which "may prove to be *P. taxifolia*" (he refers here to *Pinus taxifolia*, the name given Menzies' collection of Douglas fir). Soon after Douglas had recognized, collected, and sent to England specimens and seeds of this much-named "fir-spruce-hemlock-pine," his collection was given the name *Abies douglasii*. As this botanical name and others, like *Pinus douglasii* and *Pseudotsuga douglasii*, began to appear in botanical literature, the common name, Douglas fir, slipped into common usage. At least five other common names exist: Douglas spruce, yellow spruce, red spruce, Oregon pine, red fir, and Douglastree. Oregon pine is frequently used as the name for the lumber processed from the tree. Donald Culross Peattie, in writing of western trees (1953), likes "Douglastree" best because "it leans on no analogies [to other conifers] and still does honor to that noble pioneer among explorer-botanists of the Northwest, David Douglas." Despite such logic, I predict that Douglas fir will be *the* name of preference for years to come.

Beyond the name is the daily encounter with the tree. In parks, arboreta, open spaces, gardens, and vacant lots in Puget Sound suburbia, nearly anywhere outside a fir-built dwelling, Douglas fir is there. Its needles, branches, and cones—the organic rain from a winter's blow—appear on the doorstep, lawn, and gutter. The pliant, yet tough cone of Douglas fir assures easy recognition. It is two to four inches long, roughly egg-shaped, and consists of fifteen to thirty papery scales arranged in a symmetrical spiral around the hidden axis. Each larger scale bears two winged seeds next to the basal attachment. When mature and dry the cone scales are well separated at their tips so that the seeds may easily escape. Each cone scale has along its lower surface a telltale tonguelike projec-

The hallmark of Douglas fir is its distinctive cone with the trident (three-pronged bracts) extending beyond the seed-bearing scales.

tion from the base of the scale to well beyond the free tip of each seed-bearing scale. This so-called bract of the cone-scale is forked like a broadly three-pronged pitchfork, or devil's trident. Children fancy the notion that the bracts are the tails of mice scampering back into the cone.

Besides the distinctive cones, there are other features that mark Douglas fir. Its buds are elongate and pointed, like tiny cigars with dark brown papery wrappings. Except on the upper branches, the needles are mostly 3/4 to 1½ inches long, radiating outward from the twig rather than lying in one plane.

Distinctive features of older Douglas firs include countless small leafy twigs hanging as long slender pendants from large horizontal limbs, and deeply furrowed bark, which may be eight to ten inches thick. Outer bark is dark reddish-brown to black; inner bark—often exposed along the deep fissures—is a mottled buff color. By association and experience, even a blindfolded woodsman should be able to smell and feel his way to a successful identification of Douglas fir. However, in an even-aged, second-growth forest, the bark of younger trees is still smooth, like young hemlock, grand fir, or Sitka spruce. Only when the telltale trident-armed cones are present is identity assured. So, with whatever help is at hand (picture book, mental image, intuition, or skilled teacher) stroll into any evergreen landscape nearby and become acquainted with this tree. You will be meeting one of nature's more glamorous and thoroughly successful productions.

OTHER TREE SPECIES. Up to this point I have characterized lowland western Washington vegetation by its major plant associations and the dominant cone-bearing species in each. Hemlock, cedar, and Douglas fir make an easy-to-learn trio. Yet if these were the only tree species in Puget Sound country, the arboreal landscapes would be rather monotonous. Several other tree species occur in and around the urban setting, some frequent, others rare. There are at least eight additional evergreens. Seven are cone-bearing species: Sitka spruce, grand fir, Rocky Mountain juniper, western yew,[3] western white pine, ponderosa pine, and lodgepole pine. Only one of the eight is a flowering evergreen, the remarkable madrone.

There are several species of deciduous hardwood trees that decorate Northwest forests at each season of the year, some breathtakingly so in the fall. The list of deciduous hardwoods includes bigleaf maple, red alder, flowering dogwood, paper birch, bitter cherry, willow, cottonwood, ash, and (when arborescent) vine maple. It is

3. Yew has its seed in a fleshy red berry (an aril), the juniper in a gray berry; both have their pollen in cones.

tempting to do a thumbnail sketch of each, but as other writers have done well by them (see, for example, Arno and Hammerly 1977, Brockman 1979, Peattie 1953, or Sudworth 1908), I will single out only a few favorites. Table 14 has capsule summaries of each tree species.

The keen observer is sure to encounter "islands" of Puget Sound forest in which the dominant tree is a five-needle pine, western white pine (*Pinus monticola*). Its recognition is easy even from a distance. The white pine silhouette is one of exceptional symmetry: slender horizontal branches reaching out from the trunk in evenly spaced whorls, three to five branches at each node or stem joint, leaving clear, vertical gaps (the internodes) on the trunk between nodes. Another silhouette feature is the pendant cones suspended like sausages from the tips of the upper branches. Up close, the identity of western white pine is even easier: no other pine in lowland western Washington has five needles to the cluster; also, the long (5 to 8, or even up to 15, inches long), slightly bent, and cigar-shaped cone is a key feature. In the Seattle area, a good place to see western white pine in abundance is just north of the city limits, between Northeast 175th Street and the county line, and bounded east to west by 15th Avenue Northeast and Aurora Avenue North. Possibly unusual soil conditions here are propitious for the establishment of western white pine, where it grows often with western hemlock. Western white pine seems to outgrow the other common conifers in exceptionally well-drained sandy soils.

The only member of the true firs (genus *Abies*) that thrives in the lowland forest is grand fir (*Abies grandis*). My most memorable encounter with this stately tree was at sea level, near Foulweather Bluff on Kitsap Peninsula. Near The Nature Conservancy's Rawson Preserve there are some beautiful old specimens of grand fir, interspersed with Douglas fir and hemlock. The huge trunks here have aged enough to display the grayish-brown furrowed bark, not unlike that of Douglas fir.

Young and old, specimens of grand fir are the quintessence of symmetry. Horizontal to gently arching branches project from the trunk in regular intervals and in whorls of five to eight at each node, though much more densely so than with western white pine. The ultimate branchlets are clothed with glossy dark green needles that project stiffly from the twig, like teeth of a double-edged comb. The undersurface of the leaves is conspicuously white, from the persistent waxy bloom that coats the rows of minute air pores, or stomata. Older twigs that have lost some of their leaves gain a recognition feature consistent in all species of *Abies:* the detached needle leaves a circular depressed scar on the twig, giving the leafless section of branch a smooth appearance, in contrast to the

Grand fir (Abies grandis) is a familiar though infrequent evergreen of exquisite symmetry, often growing just back of Puget Sound shorelines. (Photo by the author.)

Western white pine (Pinus monticola), with five needles per cluster, frequents both sides of Puget Sound. (Drawings by Ramona Hammerly.)

rough surface of branchlets of Douglas fir, hemlock, or spruce. A hunt for a cone of grand fir on the ground will be in vain. All true firs develop sizeable cones, erect on the uppermost branches; but inevitably the cones fall apart at maturity to shed seeds and cone scales. Only if a squirrel has been at work in the tree's crown to drop fresh immature cones to the ground, will the passerby get a glimpse of the usually inaccessible cones of grand fir. In the Puget Sound area, grand fir is only an infrequent companion of the more common conifers, especially on the deeper, moister soils. A most likely habitat for this tree is just back of the headlands and shoreline bordering the Sound. East of the Cascades where it grows at somewhat higher elevations, grand fir is more common and may be found in nearly pure stands.

Hardwood trees must have been uncommon around Puget Sound in prehistoric times. Vast, unbroken stretches of coniferous evergreens dominated the landscape. Yet maple, alder, and cottonwood were here then, for they were collected by Menzies and Douglas. To understand the primeval role of hardwoods, it is necessary to seek out the few remnants of undisturbed lowland forest, especially in Mount Rainier and Olympic national parks. Bigleaf maple (*Acer macrophyllum*), red alder (*Alnus rubra*), and black cottonwood (*Populus trichocarpa*) are largely restricted to floodplains and borders of streams. They succeed by being specialists when under the domination of virgin, climax forests of conifers. But let fire or the axe eliminate the conifer canopy and one or more of these three hardwoods will make an impermanent but bold stand in the successional struggle. Red alder is the most adept at colonizing bare mineral soil after fire, clearcut logging, or flood.

Within the first hundred years of Western tenancy of the lowlands, red alder has moved out of its riverine habitat to become the ever-present early colonist on nearly every deforested area in the region. As second or third generation coniferous forests are once again harvested, there will be a ready seed source of alder nearby to lay claim to the denuded land. By the first snowfall a newly created bare site will be seeded; one can find alder seed on fresh snow. By late summer of the next year, alder seedlings as thick as grass will be knee-high, holding the soil tenaciously against further erosion. One pound of alder seed contains 660,000 potential new plants, each capable of aerial dissemination; no wonder that almost any patch of bare ground will green up with alder come spring.

Not only prolific in seed output, alder is precocious. In ten years' time, a young tree will produce pendant tassels of pollen flowers and the robin's egg-sized oval seed "cones." Alder's pioneering tendencies serve well those coniferous species that may come later

*Red alder (*Alnus rubra*) occurs everywhere in Puget country, along streams, on logged-over land, and in suburbia. Pure stands ("monocultures") of alder are typically associated with wetlands or during early succession following fire. (Photo by Mary Randlett.)*

Right: Up close, red alder is unmistakable with its large toothed leaves and woody seed "cones." (Drawing by Ramona Hammerly.)

*Old big-leaf maple trees (*Acer macrophyllum*), once confined to streamside and other wet habitats, are now everywhere in Puget country. Their massive, squat lower trunks usually branch skyward into several erect trunks, reaching 75 to 100 feet above ground. Right: A medium-sized big-leaf maple at the edge of a meadow, Nisqually river delta. (Photo by Mary Randlett.)*

in the march of succession. Besides the rain of its deciduous leaves to add a rich compost to the soil, the roots of alder have acquired the legume's trick. Just like alfalfa and clover, alder can turn atmospheric nitrogen into a form of nitrogen that can enter the tissues of plants and thus become a part of the ecosystem's supply of protein-making nitrogen. Alder roots develop a knot of twisted and coiled rootlets as a result of a benign infection. In contrast to the bacterial guest in the nodules of clover and other legumes, the infectious agent is a mold-like actinomycete (*Frankia alnii*). It makes its home in the tissues of alder's nodulated roots, where it takes nitrogen out of the air to make it usable to the tree. In return, the alder roots furnish other nutrients to the nodule-forming microorganism.

The wet west side of the Cascades fosters abundant growth of plants-on-plants (epiphytism). Here mosses and ferns festoon a big leaf maple.

Bigleaf maple (*Acer macrophyllum*) has much of the same pioneering capability as red alder. Though confined to wetter slopes and flats as an infrequently encountered species of climax communities, this robust maple responds to disturbance with alder-like aggressiveness. But unlike alder, it rarely pioneers in pure stands. Of the three species of maple in western Washington, *Acer macrophyllum* carries off first prize for statistics. Both in height and in basal diameter, older specimens are massive; two to three or even up to five feet in diameter gives imposing bulk to the short sturdy trunks of this maple. Usually not more than ten feet from the ground, the squat trunks branch and the huge primary limbs soar forty to fifty feet upward; the whole aspect of bigleaf maple is an upswept look, striking in winter. The leaves, often up to a foot in width and shaped like some giant's hand, give shade in summer and then go out in a blaze of yellow glory in the fall.

Bigleaf maple plays host to a variety of epiphytes, especially mosses, lichens and ferns. Although spectacularly seen on maples of the wet west-side valleys of the Olympic Peninsula, the epiphyte load can be substantial on maples in Puget country. The masses of epiphytes on the trunk and upper branches now are known to be more than casual ornaments. Bigleaf maple actually sends out aerial roots into these pads of greenery and thereby aids the nutrition of the host tree. This discovery was no mean feat for Nalini Nadkarni, a forestry student at the University of Washington. She spent many hours high in the canopy of the trees to learn this secret.

Bigleaf maple packs its future generations in big, winged seeds, arrayed in stiff pendant clusters. A large tree will produce millions of seeds dependably year after year. The short-lived maple seed germinates quickly and copiously after helicoptering to earth. The prodigal number of tiny seedlings in spring on a lawn, parkway strip, or in the open forest makes for later intense competition for light and other resources.

The other two maples in our lowlands merit mention. Nearly as ubiquitous as bigleaf maple is vine maple (*Acer circinatum*). Rarely does this species take on the stature of a tree. In mature forests, it spreads outward in an intricate tangle of branches; in this vinelike shrub form, it stays within fifteen feet of the ground. In open habitats vine maple is a dense upright shrub or small tree from ten to twenty feet in height. The seven-lobed leaves, though much smaller than those of the bigleaf maple, make up in crimson fall beauty for their lesser size. The third maple is much less often encountered in the central Puget Sound area, but is not uncommon in the more northern part of the basin, especially on the San Juan Islands. Douglas maple (*Acer glabrum douglasii*) is thought to be a coastal variety of the shrubby Rocky Mountain maple of the eastern Cascades and beyond. It often appears with vine maple as a shrubby look-alike, but has distinctive, three- to five-lobed and toothed leaves. Douglas maples on favored north slopes in Whatcom, Skagit, and San Juan counties can approach the size of middle-aged bigleaf maples.

Puget Sound residents easily learn of the presence of black cottonwood (*Populus trichocarpa*) in their surroundings, even before seeing the tree. In early summer, the air in the vicinity of the native cottonwood comes alive with tiny cottony tufts. In each silky parachute is embedded an even more minuscule seed. Airborne cottonwood seed land everywhere, sprouting in gutters and cornices of buildings as well as on any moist mineral soil. I regularly find cot-

*Black cottonwood (*Populus trichocarpa*), a miracle of prodigious growth, occupies alluvial flats and wet places in the lowlands and also persists in farmland and urban areas. This grove shelters barns at the Nisqually National Wildlife Refuge. (Photo by Mary Randlett.)*

Right: A branch of cottonwood foliage with its triangular (deltoid) leaves. (Photo by Mary Randlett.)

tonwood seedlings coming up in greenhouse pots, the soil of which had been sterilized before planting; the seed drifted down through the greenhouse ventilators. Such a tiny seed has a grand paternity and potential. Germlings grow vigorously in moist soil to become 7-foot saplings in a year and 45-foot trees in seven years. Our black cottonwood is the largest of the poplar clan in all of North America. Mature trees, upwards of two hundred years old, will range from 80 to 125 feet high and have massive trunks, 3 to 4 feet in diameter. Peattie (1953) says that in the early days of the Northwest, old patriarchs got to 200 feet high and 7 to 8 feet through. High fecundity and seed viability, coupled with remarkably rapid growth, make this tree a real success story for moist, valley-bottom soils.

The shiny, almost leathery leaves of black cottonwood are large and distinctive in shape. The broadly rounded base tapers to a tip, giving the leaf a triangular or deltoid outline; the edge of the leaf is finely saw-toothed. On young saplings the leaves may be six inches broad and eight to ten inches long; on older established trees these exuberant dimensions are diminished to two to four inches in width and six inches in length. The sticky, long-pointed leaf buds give off a distinct fragrance in the spring. This is such a hallmark that species of *Populus* are as well known as balsams or balsam poplars as they are as cottonwoods. The word "cotton" does have a place in the tree's life history. The mature seed capsules, clustered in pendant tassels, open in mid-June to release the season's progeny, cottony clouds of tufted seeds. It is this gossamer down, keeping the fragile seed aloft, that led to the name cottonwood.

It just may come to pass that the fuel in your gas tank will eventually come from black cottonwood. The phenomenal growth rate of young cottonwood trees is currently being exploited as a managed renewable resource. Black cottonwood has become the prima donna of forest trees for a number of reasons. Its rapid juvenile growth, its ease of vegetative propagation (cloning), its quick re-sprouting after harvesting, and the valuable chemical properties of its total biomass (wood, bark, leaves, etc.) have led to the formation of a cooperative research group of forest geneticists, biochemists, and botanists. Their research is aimed at understanding cottonwood biology and using that knowledge to improve upon yield and quality of this native poplar's biomass. The means to this end is "biotechnology," the use of modern techniques of genetic engineering to effect a rapid improvement in the inherited qualities of cottonwood and to devise means of rapid clonal propagation and harvest of desired strains. Improved cottonwood, when grown commercially, can deliver more than biomass for conversion to alcohol for the gas tank. Fiber for paper, textiles, etc., as well as many chemical byproducts, are the expected returns for converting this native hardwood to short-term rotational forestry. As forest biotechnology grows in know-how and accomplishments with black cottonwood, other forest species, conifers and hardwoods, will be tested for their potential in rapid biomass production.

An ally of cottonwood is the quaking aspen (*Populus tremuloides*), which can occasionally be seen in lowland Puget Sound country. The leaves tremble and quiver just like the aspen that grows in such spectacular stands east of the Cascades. The flattened leaf stalk (petiole) responds to the minutest breath of air. Aside from the distinctive quivering of the leaves, the aspen is easy to tell from the black cottonwood by its smooth gray-green bark and the smaller and more broadly triangular leaves. One can expect to find small groves of aspen along water courses and in semipermanent wet places here and there throughout the gravelly outwash prairies east of Olympia.

The madrone (*Arbutus menziesii*) is in a class by itself, apart from the distinction of being the region's only common broad-leafed evergreen tree. Foliage, bark, flower, and fruit of madrone consummate one of Nature's most ornamental works of art. The large leathery leaves, glossy green in hue, clothe the tips of the smooth twigs and branches. The orange to pea-green twigs merge with other larger branches and main trunk where the inner bark is polished to a bold reddish brown sheen as the outer bark continues to

*The Pacific madrone (*Arbutus menziesii*) thrives in urban and untamed drier sites, usually well-drained and exposed. Above: The distinctive smooth and flaky bark of madrone. (Photo by Frank Brockman.)*

peel away. In late spring this striking green on orangey-red image becomes the backdrop for thousands of candelabras of white flowers. Each flower in the many-flowered clusters is an exquisitely fashioned pearly goblet, narrow at mouth and flaring toward the base—a perfect miniature of a brandy snifter. By late summer the distinctive pea-sized fruits have matured into bright orange, warty spheres, reminiscent of small strawberries.

Occurring as pure stands in small groves, or more often as individual trees intermixed with Douglas fir, the madrone is to be found time and again around the Sound where well-drained soils and west-facing exposures afford a dryish habitat. Nowhere else in its extended range from Southern California to British Columbia does madrone become such an integral part of urban landscapes as it does in Puget Sound. All stages of its singular beauty are displayed throughout the year in garden, park, and open space: from the bold leafy seedlings to the patriarchal specimens of massive trunk and irregularly branched open crowns. Particularly fine specimens can be seen at Lincoln Park in West Seattle, on Magnolia bluff in full exposure to the Sound, and at Point Defiance Park in

A dramatic vista framed by madrones looking west from Seattle across the Sound to the Olympic Mountains. (Photo by Josef Scaylea.)

Madrone's floral kinship to garden favorites in the heather family, like manzanita or strawberry bush is revealed in this portrait. (Drawing by Ramona Hammerly.)

Tacoma. Pure stands of madrone occupy a whole west-facing hill-side in the Innis Arden residential area at the north edge of Seattle and rocky promontories along the Chuckanut Drive south of Bellingham. Many fine older madrones are suffering a devastating, wasting disease. Some trees are killed and others are severely damaged by the pathogen. Yet healthy saplings do appear to be replacing the infected trees.

Green Companions in the Understory

All but the most dense stands of forest support shrubs and herbs on the forest floor. So dense can be a young stand of fir or hemlock that very little light penetrates the upper canopy. This absence of undergrowth is called the "green shade effect." As second-growth forests mature, natural thinning of the stand occurs. Eliminated are "suppressed" trees, those whose upper leafy branches never could penetrate to sunlight through the overtopping canopy of adjacent dominant trees. By middle age and maturity, the remaining trees are farther apart, with considerable open ground between tree trunks. Light can then penetrate to the forest floor, even though its intensity is substantially reduced and it is only intermittently available.

The rich mosaic of shrubs, herbs, and ground-hugging mosses beneath the forest canopy stretches endlessly through an old-growth forest, giving visual delight and variety as the eye wanders

*A host of evergreen and deciduous shrubs, tolerant of low light, can carpet the forest floor. The evergreen salal (*Gaultheria shallon*) often forms impenetrable thickets waist high and taller. Though common and thus taken for granted, it is an elegant evergreen in leaf, flower, and fruit. (Photo by the author.)*

downward from leafy ceiling above to the mossy carpet underfoot. Ecologists see structure in a vertical section of forest. In simplest form, the strata are three or four in number: trees, shrubs, herbs, and the moss-lichen layer. (See Table 15.)

The shrub layer in the lowland forest. In the deep shade of undisturbed mature forest only four or five shrub species are commonly found. They are salal (*Gaultheria shallon*), Cascade Oregon grape (*Berberis nervosa*), red huckleberry (*Vaccinium parvifolium*), and Scouler's willow (*Salix scouleriana*). The two evergreens, salal and Oregon grape, were favored in the diet of Northwest Coast Indians. Salal berries were washed and pressed into loaves that might weigh as much as ten to fifteen pounds. Just before being eaten, the dried and pressed berries were soaked, then dipped in seal oil. Though European palates might balk at such a mixture, this food was nutritious and highly prized by Indians. Salal leaves were brewed or chewed for their medicinal properties; dried leaves also were mixed with those of kinnikinnick (the trailing manzanita) as smoking tobacco. Cascade Oregon grape was used as a food and

Table 15. Shrubs of the Western Hemlock Zone

Species	Occur-rence	Abun-dance	Habitat
Evergreen			
Evergreen huckleberry (*Vaccinium ovatum*)	W	****	In forests of all age-classes, Kitsap and Olympic peninsulas
Salal (*Gaultheria shallon*)	W	****	In forests of all age-classes
Oregon grape (*Berberis aquifolium*)	L	**	Openings and gravelly prairies
Cascade Oregon grape (*Berberis nervosa*)	W	****	Dense shade of woods
Oregon box (*Pachystima myrsinites*)	L	**	Coastal bluffs, wooded slopes
Rhododendron (*Rhododendron macrophyllum*)	L	***	Kitsap and Olympic peninsulas in forest
Labrador Tea (*Ledum groenlandicum*)	W	**	In most bogs
Bog laurel (*Kalmia polifolia*)	W	**	In most bogs
Gorse (*Ulex europeus*)†	L	***	Gregarious where escaped
Mt. balm (*Ceanothus velutinus*)	L	**	Dryish openings; Kitsap and Olympic peninsulas
Manzanita (*Arctostaphylos columbiana*)	L	**	Dry areas, Kitsap and Olympic peninsulas
Kinnikinnik (*Arctostaphylos uva-ursi*)	W	***	Dry flats and slopes; openings and woods
Hybrid manzanita (*Arctostaphylos x media*)	L	**	Disturbed woods and Christmas-tree farms, Kitsap Peninsula
Twinflower (*Linnaea borealis*)	W	****	In deep woods
English Holly (*Ilex aquifolium*)†	L	**	Suburban woods (an escape)
Deciduous			
Scouler's willow (*Salix scouleriana*)	W	****	Forests and openings
Hazelnut (*Corylus cornuta*)	W	***	Forests and openings
Sacaline (*Polygonum sachalinense*)†	L	**	Disturbed sites; weedy
White virgin's bower (*Clematis ligusticifolia*)	L	**	Disturbed sites; vine
Mock orange (*Philadelphus lewisii*)	W	**	Open woods, dryish sites
Whipplea (*Whipplea modesta*)	L	**	Woods; Hood Canal area
Redflowering currant (*Ribes sanguineum*)	W	***	Open woods and clearings
Stinking currant (*Ribes bracteosum*)	W	**	Near water in forests
Prickly currant (*Ribes lacustre*)	W	**	Near water in forests
Hardhack, spiraea (*Spiraea douglasii*)	W	***	Bogs and swamps
White spiraea (*Spiraea betulifolia*)	L	**	Clearings and rocky openings in forest
Ninebark (*Physocarpus capitatus*)	L	**	Damp openings and woods
Ocean-spray (*Holodiscus discolor*)	W	***	Drier open woods
Rose (*Rosa gymnocarpa, R. nutkana*)	W	****	Forests and openings

Table 15. (*continued*)

Species	Occurrence	Abundance	Habitat
Salmonberry (*Rubus spectabilis*)	W	****	Damp openings and woods
Thimbleberry (*Rubus parviflorus*)	W	****	Forests and openings
Dewberry (*Rubus ursinus*)	W	****	Forest floor and groundcover in clearings
Himalayan blackberry (*Rubus procerus*)†	W	***	High bramble thickets in disturbed sites (escape)
Indian plum (*Oemleria cerasiformis* = *Osmaronia cerasiformis*)	W	***	Open moist forests
Mountain Ash (*Sorbus aucuparia*)†	L	**	Escape from cultivation, in 2nd growth forest
Serviceberry (*Amelanchier alnifolia*)	W	***	Open woods and clearings
Scot's broom (*Cytisus scoparius*)†	W	***	Cleared areas, abandoned fields, etc.
Bush lupine (*Lupinus arboreus*)†	L	***	Sand and gravel bars, headlands, dunes above Sound
Tree tea (*Ceanothus sanguineus*)	W	**	Open woods
Poisonoak (*Rhus diversiloba*)	W	**	Clearings and open slopes near water, southern Puget Sound
Vine maple (*Acer circinatum*)	W	****	Forests, openings
Rocky Mt. maple (*Acer glabrum*)	W	**	Forested slopes, North Cascades and San Juan Islands
Buffalo berry (*Shepherdia canadensis*)	L	***	Dry rocky woods and headlands, San Juan Islands
Prickly-pear cactus (*Opuntia fragilis*)	L	*	Dry open headlands, San Juan Islands and Sequim area
Devil's club (*Oplopanax horridum*)	W	***	Wet woods
Creek dogwood (*Cornus stolonifera*)	W	***	Along streams and lake borders
Fool's huckleberry (*Menziesia ferruginea*)	W	**	Forest understory
Blueberry (*Vaccinium alaskense*)	W	***	Forests, damper sites
Red huckleberry (*Vaccinium parvifolium*)	W	****	Forests
Wild cranberry (*Vaccinium oxycoccus*)	L	***	Sphagnum bogs
Blue elderberry (*Sambucus cerulea*)	L	**	Gravelly prairies and other dryish sites
Red elderberry (*Sambucus racemosa*)	W	***	Forests
Squashberry (*Viburnum edule*)	L	**	Damp places in woods
Oregon viburnum (*Viburnum ellipticum*)	L	**	Damp places in woods
Snowberry (*Symphoricarpus albus*)	W	***	Dryish open forests and clearings
Honeysuckle (*Lonicera ciliosa*)	W	**	Dryish open forests
Twinberry (*Lonicera involucrata*)	W	**	Wet places

Note: W = widespread, L = local; **** common, *** frequent, ** infrequent, * rare, † introduced.

The low-growing evergreen, Berberis nervosa *(Cascade Oregon grape), thrives in the filtered sunlight of old growth. It often cohabits with sword fern. (Photo by W. Marten.)*

dye plant. Indians ate the ripe berries fresh; in recent times, following the fashion of the white man, the berries were made into jam. The roots of Oregon grape yielded a yellow dye used in basket-making.

It has been the custom of pioneering whites to disdain the common native plants of the new and alien surroundings, tending rather to replace the natives with plants from the place of origin. Salal, Oregon grape, and other natives were eradicated as fast as forest was transformed into homestead and settlement. The superior ornamental quality of the native shrubs was recognized first by wealthy English patrons of early plant collectors. Long before our own twentieth-century gardens began to use salal and Oregon grape as choice ornamentals for the woodland garden, the European gardener was skillfully cultivating them. The most ludicrous example has to be that exquisite harbinger of Puget Sound springtime, the red-flowering currant (*Ribes sanguineum*). Long after it had become a favorite in European gardens, it was "introduced" from England to the Pacific Northwest as a choice garden shrub.

One other shrub of the shaded woods merits special mention. The red huckleberry (*Vaccinium parvifolium*) specializes in growing

The native rhododendron (Rhododendron macrophyllum) is best seen on the west side of Puget Sound, Kitsap Peninsula, and Olympic Peninsula along Hood Canal. It favors the understory of Douglas fir and western hemlock. (Photo by Asahel Curtis.)

on logs or on the top of stumps. Birds and their fondness for the tasty red fruits account for seeding the huckleberry on these perched habitats. There is scarcely a stump in our forests that does not have growing from it one or more kinds of plant spread by birds. Red huckleberry with its small oval leaves, twiggy angular stems, and red berries is an easily recognized member of the natural stump garden.

Where forest has yet to reappear after logging or the trees are less dense, as in a more exposed habitat, the shrub layer may be enriched with still other species. To be sure, the environmental tolerance of salal is broad enough to encompass almost any forest habitat, from damp shady places to the rigors of dry sunny openings. Yet, other shrubs besides salal can be expected in a variety of lowland habitats. The most common are ocean-spray (*Holodiscus discolor*), red-flowering currant (*Ribes sanguineum*), mock orange (*Philadelphus lewisii*), serviceberry (*Amelanchier florida*), Oregon box (*Pachistima myrsinites*), salmonberry (*Rubus spectabilis*), thimbleberry (*Rubus parviflorus*), bittercherry (*Prunus emarginata*—it may even become a large tree), Indian plum (*Osmaronia cerasiformis*), snowberry (*Symphoricarpos albus*), hazelnut (*Corylus cornuta*), and wild rose (*Rosa* spp.)—quite a respectable list of shrubs for a region that is usually thought of as a land of coniferous forests. The fabric of the whole forest ecosystem has many threads, and the mosaic of the shrub layer is by no means insignificant. Beyond its contribution to ecosystem stability, it brings pleasure to the human eye, providing variety within the expanse of forest. And the shrub layer affords a treasure of garden plants for the tamed urban landscape. My book, *Gardening With Native Plants of the Pacific Northwest* (1982), describes the uses of many of the native plants of our region.

The herb layer in the lowland forest. The forest floor beneath a mature stand of trees and shrubs can support a moderately rich assemblage of shade-loving herbs, ferns, mosses, and lichens. From the more extensive list in Table 16 there are certain outstanding examples (see pages 190–93).

One of the most typical inhabitants of the deep forest is the sword fern (*Polystichum munitum*). Clumps of this beautiful evergreen fern, two to even five feet high, may dominate the landscape of a forested bottomland, terrace, or lower slope. So closely associated is this fern with the most productive of forest habitats that the forester may use robust, abundant stands of it as an "indicator" plant to predict a high potential yield of a tree crop.

Sword fern was used as food, household material, and medicine by Indians. The rhizome (underground stem) was peeled and baked. The Quileutes of the outer coast found baked fern and salmon eggs a tasty combination. The long featherlike fronds or leaves were used in cooking (to line the fire pit, and to lie under food on drying racks) and as a mattress material. They were even used in play: "Children of the [coastal] Klallam and Makah tribes play an endurance game, seeing who can pull off the largest number of fern leaves [most likely the leaflets or pinnae], saying 'pila' with each one, in a single breath" (Gunther 1973). I hesitate to mention this anecdote, lest it suggest to children a game of defronding this most excellent fern.

Europeans found a different and more highly exploitative use for sword fern that continues to flourish today. Around the Sound, the evergreen fronds are harvested in great quantity as florist greens. As an ornament in a shady garden, it is unsurpassed. Yet rarely is sword fern intentionally introduced into the garden; rather, it is

Salmonberry (Rubus spectabilis) (Drawing by Libby Mills)

Left: Vanilla leaf (Achlys triphylla) can form large colonies over the forest floor, spreading widely by underground stems (rhizomes). (Photo by Bob and Ira Spring.)

Below: Herbaceous natives of the forest floor are truly epitomized by the dwarf dogwood (Cornus canadensis), yet indeed it is a relative of the shrub and tree dogwoods. Its fall display of showy red berries gives it another common name, bunchberry. (Photo by Bob and Ira Spring.)

Left: Formidable, yet lovely, devil's club (Oplopanax horridum) selects wetter sites in the lowland to mid-montane understory, often forming large, uncrossable colonies. (Photo by Bob and Ira Spring.)

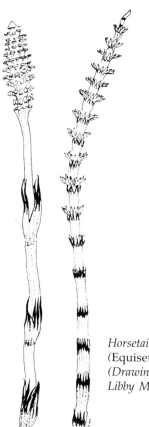

Horsetail (Equisetum sp.) (Drawing by Libby Mills)

Woodland ferns and their allies are often conspicuous plants in the forest understory; evergreen and deciduous ferns often coexist with club-mosses and horsetails.

Right: Sword fern (Polystichum munitum) in spring, its new fronds unfurling. (Photo by Bob and Ira Spring.)

Left: Deer fern (Blechnum spicant) is another common woodland evergreen fern, easily recognized by its thin fertile (spore-bearing) leaves (fronds) and the leafier vegetative fronds. (Photo by Mary Randlett.)

Below: Giant horse-tail (Equisetum telmateia), though an unwanted intruder in gardens, is at home in the wetter areas of forest openings. It is distant kin to true ferns. (Photo by Mary Randlett.)

either a holdover from the once natural forest or an arrival as a volunteer sporeling. Fern spores are common in the pollen and spore "rain" that reaches the soil each season. Development of the spore into a tiny sexual plant is precarious business, yet some of the sporelings succeed, giving rise to a good crop of young spore-bearing sword ferns.

Many herbaceous flowering plants grow on the forest floor. One, the wild ginger (*Asarum caudatum*), surely looks as though it were an escapee from the tropics. Though a ground-hugging species, it has big (four to six inches) heart-shaped, aromatic leaves and the most curious flowers. The latter, often hidden under the big leaves, are large thimbles with three long tails projecting from the rim of the floral cup. The reddish-brown fringed flowers may be pollinated by fungus gnats that ordinarily are addicted to decaying fungi. Despite the curious flowers and their possible role in cross-pollination, wild ginger more often indulges in self-pollination. Such a letdown is not uncommon for plants with showy flowers!

How animals have accommodated to plants and vice versa is now known as coevolutionary biology. Wild ginger and its most voracious predator, the slug, provide a neat case of such biological interaction. Both the native tan slug and the introduced dark brown slug eat the leaves of species of wild ginger. The marbled-leaf ginger of southwestern Oregon is much more palatable to slugs than the western Washington species. That difference in slug dietary preference was enough to start Rex Cates on a long-term study of the slug-ginger system (1975). Cates discovered that our native ginger, *Asarum caudatum*, has two distinct races, one more palatable than the other. Both forms coexist in the lowland forests, but the palatable one occurs in wetter sites often disturbed by spring runoff, grows faster, and flowers earlier than the unpalatable form. Cates concluded that both forms of wild ginger in Puget Sound forests are "trying" to outdo the predatory slug: the palatable one does so by growing fast and flowering earlier, while the unpalatable form relies on its anti-slug chemistry to keep ahead in the herb-herbivore race.

It is now believed that many such plant-to-animal interactions have evolved and continue to evolve, each member of the coevolving pair buying survival time from generation to generation. The next time you see insects chewing or sucking away on plants, think of the probable compromise that predator and prey may have struck to coexist. By the way, the tropical look of ginger has foundation in fact. Nearly all of the more than four hundred species in the family (*Aristolochiaceae*) of wild gingers and Dutchman's pipes are tropical, where they are well known for their bizarre flowers elegantly contrived for pollination by flies and beetles.

Wild ginger (Asarum caudatum) *has a tropical look about it (and is kin to a tropical family), yet it is at home in wetter forest habitats in lowland Puget country. (Photo by Bob and Ira Spring.)*

Another herb inhabitant of the lowland forest ecosystem in damp habitats also comes from a long line of tropical relatives. Skunk cabbage (*Lysichitum americanum*) somehow looks out of place in a temperate conifer forest; the huge, platter-shaped leaves and the massive yellow "flower" would seem more at home in a lush tropical vegetation. Skunk cabbage is one of the few temperate members of a predominantly tropical clan, the aroid (Araceae) family. The indoor gardener will be familiar with some of these imports from the tropics: anthuriums, caladiums, and philodendrons. The massive yellow "bloom" of skunk cabbage is not a flower. Each emergent yellow flag of early spring is part of an aggregate unit, an inflorescence or flower cluster. The yellow cloak, called the spathe, encloses a club-shaped stalk, the spadix. The latter structure is studded with small greenish-yellow florets, each yielding pollen and capable of ripening into a berrylike, inedible fruit.

The spathe-spadix "syndrome" is a design of great variety throughout the tropical members of the aroid family. The remarkable aroid contrivance of the hooded flower cluster (spathe and spadix) has been shown to be Darwinian in function; that is, adaptive for mutual benefit of plant and animal. Many species of aroids are visited by insects which become trapped in the lower funnel-shaped portion of the spathe, lured by the fetid odors emitted by the aroid inflorescence. Once within the floral trap, beetles or flies pollinate the flowers of the spadix as they seek escape. In some aroids, the odors, propagated by high temperatures in the spadix at the height of flowering, are accompanied by other floral contrivances to keep the insects entrapped for a time. The net result—pollination—is the climax to a complex interplay between insect and plant.

Could our temperate aroid, the common skunk cabbage, have a similar pollination syndrome? Until 1986, there were only hints and rumors suggesting that little staphylinid beetles were the pollinators. Now we know that rove beetles (of the staphylinid group) closely track the floral biology of *Lysichitum* (Pellmyr and Patt 1986). The beetles are lured to the inflorescence by fragrance and color. They then utilize the spathe-spadix structures as a mating site and for food. During their stay in the spathe, the rove beetles are presumed to bring about pollination.

Skunk cabbage is a food for some wildlife, mostly bear, deer, and elk (and banana slugs, too). Northwest coastal Indians incorporated skunk cabbage into their daily lives, occasionally as food, but more often in household tasks. Rhizome, leaf-stalks, and "flower," all were eaten by some Indian groups. The item was usually well cooked for a sound precautionary reason: aroids commonly are toxic, yet are used around the world in the human diet. Our own

Swamp lantern, or skunk cabbage (Lysichitum americanum*), lights up swampy ground in the spring with its soft yellow "blooms." (See text for the real flower story.) (Photo by Bob and Ira Spring.)*

skunk cabbage is probably no exception in possessing a toxic principle. The chemical, calcium oxalate, is crystallized into long needles, often barbed; the needles may occur in packets in special cells. The net effect is acute anguish when a fresh sample of aroid tissue is eaten. The mouth becomes aflame with an irritation that no antidote can alleviate, since the pain is due to the injection of bundles of these tiny needles into the lining of the mouth. Because of this highly irritating state of the fresh tissue, aboriginal peoples all over the world boil, often repeatedly, their choice of food aroid. Northwest Indians performed precautionary cooking of skunk cabbage. In this way the tiny needles (raphides) of crystalline calcium oxalate are removed. One wonders why the toxic property of skunk cabbage does not bother the animals that browse on it. Somehow animals can detoxify plants known to be poisonous to humans.

Besides their occasional use as food, the big leaves of skunk cabbage were employed as wrappings or underlinings in the Indian kitchen ("Indian waxpaper," fide N. Turner). Many different medicinal properties were ascribed to skunk cabbage: an infusion for internal disorders, a poultice for skin afflictions, an abortifacient, and an aid to childbirth. Though the latter two uses may appear antagonistic, both may take advantage of some muscle-stimulating effect of the plant.

So striking a plant is skunk cabbage, from its bright yellow emergence in the spring to the green luxuriance of summer and early fall, that it is not surprising that the plant plays a role in Indian legend. Erna Gunther's account of one such myth from Chinook-speaking Indians of the lower Columbia River is worth quoting in its entirety:

> In ancient days [so say the Kathlamet Indians] there was no salmon. The Indians had nothing to eat save roots and leaves. Principal among these was skunk cabbage. Finally the spring salmon came for the first time. As they passed up the river a person stood upon the shore and shouted: "Here come our relative[s] who[se] bodies are full of eggs. If it had not been for me all the people would have starved."
> "Who speaks to us?" asked the salmon.
> "Your uncle, skunk cabbage," was the reply.
> Then the salmon went ashore to see him, and as a reward for having fed the people he was given an elk-skin blanket and a war club, and was set in the rich, soft soil near the river. There he stands to this day wrapped in the elk-skin [the yellow spathe] and holding aloft his war club [the spadix]. (1973:23)

Such an inappropriate name, skunk cabbage, for this elegant herb! It is only faintly skunk-like (mephitic) in odor, and is not a member of the cabbage family. Two other common names, yet to supplant the current unsavory epithet, merit adoption: swamp king or swamp lantern.

One by one, wet meadows, pastures, and swampy places around Puget Sound give way to asphalt and concrete. Skunk cabbage may never be wholly exterminated but will become rare enough to be legendary in the annals of the white man's tenancy of the land. Would that every community around Puget Sound had the foresight to preserve a sample of these rich damp habitats, so much the home of skunk cabbage and other moisture-loving things.

The forest floor is a stage for yet another silent drama of plant and animal. Two of our most spectacular spring beauties, bleeding heart (*Dicentra formosa*) and western trillium or wake-robin (*Trillium ovatum*), use the boundless energies of ants to expand the ranges of their populations. Seeds of these two plants possess fleshy outgrowths on the surface which are nutritious tidbits for the ant colony. Ants gather the seeds, pack them off to their nests, and devour the food body (the elaiosome) on the seed surface, leaving the seed intact, ready to germinate well away from the parent plant. The lovely pink flowers of *Dicentra* are borne aloft in *pendant* clusters over fernlike leaves. As the seed capsule matures, the pendant position persists. Then, when the capsule releases its shiny black seed, the seeds fall directly to the ground. Rolf Berg, who studied the ant-seed syndrome in many different plants (1969), devised a simple experiment to test the potential of the surface food-bodies attached to certain seeds in attracting ants. He placed seeds of various species, some with food appendages and others devoid of them, in likely ant-collecting sites. He then observed the rate of removal of the contrasting kinds of seeds. *Trillium* and *Dicentra* seeds were selectively and avidly sought by ants while the seeds of other species were ignored.

Trillium's venture into the ant-seed dispersal enterprise is remarkably similar to that in *Dicentra*, an unrelated species. Our lovely woodland trillium, a relative of lilies and grasses, draws ants into its way of life long after the captivating show of early spring bloom. Each flowering stalk comes from an underground stem; usually the flowering axis bears only one three-part, large white flower (often fading to pink or even red) perched just above three broad and horizontally radiating leaves. When the fruit begins to ripen after flowering, its short stalk bends to one side and the drying, expanding fruit begins to split open. Seeds then fall to the ground, often in viscous clusters. Less frequently, the entire unopened capsular fruit falls to the ground where it then opens. By either method, *Trillium* seeds, once on the ground, attract ants which seek the lustrous oil-rich cap of tissue on one end of the seed. Berg performed dispersal experiments with *Trillium* seed. He

Trillium (T. ovatum) *is one of the earliest spring flowers on the forest floor, often in bloom just after snows are gone. (Photo by Josef Scaylea.)*

found that ants eagerly sought them, rapidly examined the fleshy appendage of the seed, carted off the seed, and were followed soon after by other ants returning to take the rest of the seeds to the nest. Using ten seeds each of *Trillium*, wild ginger (*Asarum caudatum*), and hedge-nettle (*Stachys ajugoides*), barely twelve minutes elapsed before all seeds but the hedge-nettle were taken. As might be expected, wild ginger seeds also have a nutritional attraction for ants, while no such specialization exists for *Stachys*. Haste is essential for ants to use the fleshy appendage of *Trillium* seeds, because it dries up quickly and ceases to be attractive.

Natural history of such intriguing phenomena as the ant-seed interactions has only barely begun in western North America. The probability of turning up other cases of mutual exploitation is high, given the diversity and common coexistence of many kinds of plants and animals in our region. Anyone with the faculties of patience and cautious observation and the power of reasoning can begin to add to the now rather barren pages of natural history for this Northwest corner of the world.

Mosses of the lowland forest. In most places in the hemlock, cedar, and fir forests of lowland Puget Sound, the forest floor is a green carpet where mosses form the predominant turf. Remove the moss layer and much bare soil and humus would be exposed. The humid lowland forest zone provides just the right environment—subdued light, moderate temperatures, and adequate moisture—for the nurture of a moss-and-lichen layer, the lowermost stratum of the multilayered forest. The life-zone at sea level is the richest in mosses. Of the eighty different species for the lowland habitats, forty-five are forest inhabitants.

Two common growth forms are exhibited by mosses in our area. Many species have an erect habit, with the long-stalked spore capsule borne above a tiny erect leafy shoot. Usually the individuals of this growth form (called acrocarpous) occur in such dense and tufted clusters as to form the "pile" of a mossy rug. The other life form consists of plants with many-branched horizontal stems that form a diminutive, fernlike frond. These pleurocarpous mosses bear their tiny spore cases on laterally placed stalks. Both growth forms coexist in Northwest woods. Thus the filmy acrocarpous (erect) species, *Leucolepis menziesii,* will occur side by side with our most exquisite pleurocarpous (spreading) plant, *Hylocomium splendens.* So temperate and accommodating is the lowland forest environment that the mosses are exuberantly successful on nearly every possible substrate, though with a strong species-by-species selectivity.

Forest species of mosses select three different kinds of substrates: living trees, rotten logs and stumps, and soil. For the most part these habitat preferences are closely adhered to. A tree-inhabiting species will not turn up on other substrates. It is the tree-inhabiting species of mosses and lichens that join with ferns and club mosses to produce the rain-forest effect: festoons of epiphytic greenery draped on trunks and limbs of forest trees, usually hardwoods like bigleaf maple. The rain-forest phenomenon is not restricted to the misty, rainy west side of the Olympic Peninsula. Some of the more moist river valleys draining into Puget Sound, like the lower Stillaguamish and Skagit rivers, put on a good rain-forest show, too. Lest one is tempted to think of mossy coniferous forests as tropical paradises, it should be remembered that the phrase "rain forest" was borrowed from its original context from the tropics. Only by faint resemblance to the epiphytic (plant-on-plant) luxuriance of the lowland wet tropics do our temperate wet forests qualify as rain forests; the best compromise is to think of them as *temperate* rain forests.

Fern moss (Hylocomium splendens) *can form extensive, mossy carpets on the forest floor. (Photo by Ruth and Louis Kirk.)*

Lichens in the lowland forest. Favorable temperatures, optimal moisture, and subdued light, which bring forth an exuberance of mosses on the forest floor and lower tree trunks, encourage another group of plants—the lichens. The brown, gray, green, and even black tones of these dual algal-fungal organisms add visual diversity to the forest habitat. A lichen is an intricately woven synthesis of green or blue-green alga and colorless fungus. The two components are so marvelously fused that they develop one unique lichen body in unison. Such is the wonder of the organic world: the whole is greater in complexity than the sum of its parts. What is accomplished by such an intricate mix of alga and fungus in one plant body? The algal component, usually a filamentous or single-celled species, makes organic nutrients photosynthetically, as well as other metabolic essentials. The fungal component provides the webbing and structure to hold its nutritional partner in place in a protective and form-making coating of fungal tissue. Since the fungal partner provides the attachment to the substrate (rock, soil, or woody plant) and provides the greater proportion of lichen tissue, uptake and storage of water and minerals may be the prime role of the fungus.

Though infinite in variety, the form of lichens can be sorted into three broad categories: crustose, fruticose, and foliose. In crustose forms the lichen plant body tenaciously clings to the substrate, usually bark or rock; crustose lichens resemble flakes of paint or bits of plastic adhering to a surface. Alder bark is transformed in color and design by several crustose lichen species. The fruticose type of lichen is an erect, often branched form, most frequently in dense aggregates; they appear as tiny ghostlike trees or shrublets on soil and rotting logs. Foliose lichens, those fringed, scalloped, or tattered sheets of plasticlike substance, are nature's expression of crochet, needlepoint, and origami. They festoon the forest and decorate the forest floor in endless color, form, and texture. Trunks and branches of both conifer and hardwood bark can be coated with foliose lichens, from the big, flabby, buff-colored lobarias to the spaghetti tufts of the grey and black parmelias. The foliose habit is the predominant lichen form of the forest.

To be so ubiquitous, the lichen's powers of reproduction are prodigious. In theory, spores from the fungal component, generated by a complex sexual fusion, must find both a suitable microenvironment for germination *and* the germling must come into contact with the proper algal partner (or symbiont) in order to regenerate the adult lichen. This chancy way to assure propagation of one's own kind is doubtless rare; other more sure-fire means of reproduction have evolved. The two most common methods of propagation, both asexual, are by simple fragmentation and by soredia.

Lichens, intimately interwoven living fabrics of algae and fungi, thrive on soil, rock, dead woody substrates, or on live plant hosts. Above: Foliose lichen festooning a conifer branch. (Photo by Mary Randlett.) Below: A dense carpet of foliose lichens, mixed with mosses on a forest floor. (Photo by Bob and Ira Spring.)

Dried lichens easily fracture into flecks and pieces of the composite algal-fungal tissue that are carried by gusts of wind far and wide. The ultimate in survivorship is the soredium (pl., soredia); each soredium is a microscopic speck composed of one algal cell enmeshed in the yarn of fungal filaments. Nearly all lichens produce soredia in pustular masses here and there on the plant body. Like spores and pollen, soredia form a significant component of the airborne fallout of the atmosphere. But of this living dust in the air, surely the soredia have the greatest prospects for success. On landing in a suitable habitat, the tiny packet of alga-plus-fungus can become a new plant, uncomplicated by sexual reproduction.

The role of lichens in the economy of the forest biome is difficult to estimate. The algal-fungal partners constitute a special kind of primary producer and thus convert atmospheric carbon dioxide, water, and light energy to organic carbon, the energy-rich base of all ecosystems. Yet in comparison to other producers in the forest, the lichen contribution is small. Moreover, the recycling of lichen-captured matter and energy is slow. A few animals, like elk, eat lichens in our region, but the bulk of lichen bodies simply decompose, to release their matter and energy. Even the classic role of lichens as the initial colonizers and preparers of bare ground or newly exposed rock surfaces has little application to succession—the sequence of plant species replacement—in the forest community. Forest succession in the area, usually initiated by logging, fire, or other human-induced disturbance, most often bypasses the moss-lichen stage. Instead, seed plants, usually weedy ones, are early colonizers. Yet it would be wrong to dismiss lichens as having no significant roles in forest ecosystems. Some foliose lichens are now known to convert atmospheric nitrogen to a form usable by plants. That large flabby lichen inhabiting crowns of trees, *Lobaria oregana* (lung wort), makes three to seven pounds per acre of usable nitrogen per year in an old-growth forest.

Lichens can serve as detectors of the health of an urban ecosystem. Like canaries that are used by miners to test for poisonous gases underground, lichens are biological indicators of urban atmospheric pollution. The strong correlation between the presence and abundance of lichens and the proximity and intensity of atmospheric pollutants is well known. In a high pollution zone, lichens that would grow on rock, soil, or vegetation simply are not present. As one moves out from the high pollution concentrations, lichens increase in abundance and variety. Seattle's pattern of lichen abundances is no exception. David Johnson (1979) found that lichens increase northeastward away from the pollution centers of the industrialized lower Duwamish River delta and downtown Seattle.

Mushroom hunters expect the greatest productivity from the rich organic layer of the forest floor. The variety of fleshy fungi on standing forest biomass and on the ground is staggering: Many more species of fungi live in forests than do all other kinds of plants. Right: Fly amanita (Amanita muscaria), poisonous. (Photo by Victor Scheffer.)

Shaggy mane (Coprinus comatus). (Photo by Catherine Ardray.)

Far right: Gem-studded puffball (Lycoperdon perlatum). (Photo by Catherine Ardray.)

Fungi and the lowland forest ecosystem. Each fall in Puget Sound country, a special breed of nature watchers turns out in force to stalk some of the forest's most elegant productions—mushrooms and their allies. After the first fall rains, the rich organic debris and humus of forest floor comes alive with a great variety of the fleshy fungi: chanterelles, boletes, inky caps, bracket fungi, amanitas, and many others. Until the fall "explosion" of mushrooms, the nearly continuous network of *underground* fungal plant substance goes unnoticed, yet is ever present, feeding on the remains of the forest, the organic litter of seed plants and ferns. What appears in fall are the fleshy tips of this vast fungal "iceberg," the many and varied kinds of spore-producing fruiting bodies that have emerged from the underground meshwork of fungous growth.

For the seeker of mushrooms and their kin, there are but two kinds, those that are edible and those that are not; in the "are not" category are both poisonous ones and others with no claim to palatability. But to the botanist who specializes in fungi—called a mycologist—there is a much more complex catalogue of fungal diversity. The mycologist recognizes two major groups of fleshy fungi: the club fungi (Basidiomycetes) and the cup fungi (Ascomycetes). The Basidiomycetes group embraces the mushrooms, toadstools, bracket fungi, pore fungi, puffballs, and numberless other variations on the feature common to the group—the club-shaped, microscopic basidium, each of which bears four spores. For sheer quantity and variety the "basidios" take first prize among the fungi in the region's lowland forests; yet no one has a final count on how many kinds may occur. Though mycologists at the University of Washington, under the leadership of Daniel E. Stuntz and Joseph Ammirati, have been busy over the years compiling the catalogue of this diversity, each generation of students discovers still more species. To account for Basidiomycetes in all their shapes, sizes, and colors, the conservative rough estimate of 3,000 species in the Northwest must suffice.

Yellow chanterelle (Cantharellus cibarius). *(Photo by Catherine Ardray.)*

Essentially all species are wholly or partially saprophytic; that is, they live on dead organic matter. The incessant rain of plant material onto the forest floor—leaves, cones, limbs, and whole trees—becomes the nutritive basis for fungal life. In the unceasing recycling of matter and energy in forest ecosystems, the fungi play a key role. In the terrestrial portions of Puget Sound, the fungi are prime decomposer organisms, restoring to the system the nutrients bound into the bodies of primary producers (green plants) and consumers (animals). Without them, the system would grind to a halt, clogged with unconsumed organic and inorganic foodstuffs—in a word, polluted. One ecologist has said that pollution is merely deflected production; by that definition, when fungi and other decomposing "trashburners" are not around, production is deflected and pileups of unrecycled matter occur.

Besides playing a dominant role in melting down dead organic matter, fungi act out a more subtle role in the economy of the forest. Many Basidiomycetes serve as intermediaries between soil and the roots of tree species, acting as a kind of auxiliary root system. The subterranean portions of such fungi as the boletes (pore fungi) are tufts (the aggregate mycelia) of filamentous strands (hyphae) that can make intimate connection with the roots of trees and other green seed plant species. What is accomplished by this symbiotic arrangement? At the very least, the fungus acts as the converter and pipeline to the host green plant for inorganic mineral nutrients; in return the roots of the host plant provide organic carbon and growth-promoting hormones to the fungus. So intricate is the intimate growth of fungus and root that distinctive root-to-fungus

The red-belted polypore (Fomitopsis pinicola) *is a common shelf or bracket fungus on trees. (Photo by Mary Randlett.)*

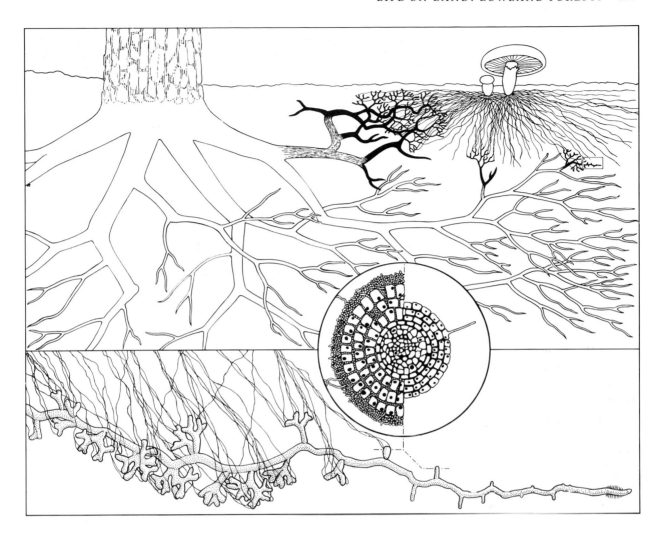

The intricate and hidden world of mycorrhizae where fungi and trees are linked. Below ground the tree roots and fungal tissue (hyphae) make connection. The circular inset is a cross-section of a tree root with its "coating" of fungal tissue. At bottom, a conifer root with (left) and without (right) mycorrhizal branch roots. (Drawing by Michael Emerson.)

formations occur, called mycorrhizae. Most green plants of the forest are thought to develop mycorrhizal associations; at least it is known that the dominant tree species like fir, spruce, hemlock, etc., develop this partnership. The mutualism of the fungus-root complex enhances the growth of both parties.

Other major groups of fungi may yield plant bodies (sporocarps) large enough to catch the eye of the human observer. Among the Ascomycetes (the cup or sac fungi) there are the colorful tiny saucers of the cup fungi, as well as the morels and their allies. Another and most startling group of forest-inhabiting fungi includes the small and delicate slime molds. They reveal their distinctive character in two stages. Initially, the slime mold appears to be just that, a thin, viscous dab of protoplasm that oozes in amoeboid fashion over decaying vegetable matter, engulfing solid bits of food en route. Then the most marvelous transformation takes place: the naked protoplasmic "scum" takes on highly distinctive form and color to become the spore-producing phase. The tiny spore cases, not much longer than a head of a pin, cluster on decaying wood to form bright flecks of color (yellow, orange, red, brown, and black) on logs and twigs of the forest floor. Like most other fungi, the slime molds and the sac fungi have joined forces with the bacteria to process the ceaseless accumulation of plant and animal debris. All these trashburners collectively decompose tons of natural litter each year, returning locked-in substances to further use in the ecosystem.

Other living trashburners. Though the larger fleshy fungi epitomize the decomposer's function in the ecosystem, much biodegradation is accomplished by other organisms. Perhaps the bulk of the natural composting process—turning forest litter into soil—is done by microorganisms. In the world of microbes where plant and animal form and function become blurred, the diversity and numbers of tiny organisms are beyond reckoning. Any sample of the soil mantle covering the rocky substrates of Puget country would disclose a multitude of protozoa, filamentous fungi, bacteria, algae (both blue-greens and greens), all detectable only with the microscope and by special culturing techniques. Tiny invertebrate animals add further variety to the living soil; they, too, are part of the recycling function. Nearly invisible arthropods (insects, terrestrial crustaceans, spiders, and mites) and worms (both the familiar and visible earthworms and the ever-present but invisible nematode worms) inch their way through the soil, turning organic matter into reusable matter and energy for the soil segment of the ecosystem. The microscopic world of the soil is an ecosystem in itself, and, as with any segment of the living environment, soil is interconnected with other elements of the larger ecosystem. Soil has its own microclimate and physical surroundings of forest. Soil ecosystem processes display the dynamic aspects of ecosystems in general: producers (algae), consumers (protozoa and invertebrate animals), and decomposers (bacteria and fungi) are distributed throughout the soil mantle in intricate food webs, carrying out the vital reclamations of substance. See Appendix 5.

Flowering plants as consumers, not producers. One remarkable group of consumers in the forest soil ecosystem is an assemblage of flowering plants bound together by their unique nutritional character. Though members of quite unrelated plant families—orchid, snapdragon, and heather families—these atypical nonphotosynthetic flowering plants either function as parasites on host green plants, or behave much like mycorrhizal mushrooms, living off dead organic matter and host plants. The parasitic flowering plants are limited in number and are not in the mainstream of the recycling function. Two parasitic kinds in the family Orobanchaceae, the ground cones (*Boschniakia*) and species of the broomrapes or cancer-roots (*Orobanche*), occur sporadically around Puget Sound. They can be expected in dryish open habitats, especially in clearings within the forest or on exposed brushy to grassy sites. Ground cone is a parasite on the roots of salal and possibly other members of the heather family (Ericaceae). It has been noted as fairly common on the Kitsap Peninsula. This peculiar plant looks like a reddish brown or yellowish pine cone perched upright and slightly embedded in the soil. What might be taken for the scales of a pine cone are the brownish two-lipped flowers tightly clustered around the conelike axis. Devoid of functional leaves, the above-ground structure consists merely of scales and flowers. Each ground cone plant produces a prodigious quantity of seeds; a single plant of *Boschniakia* may produce more than a third of a million seeds. Upon germination, the rootless seedling forms a tuberlike growth around the root of a host plant. The tuber, with attachments to the host root, enlarges indefinitely, sometimes attaining a diameter of several inches.

The broomrapes, smaller in all respects than the ground cones, send up from the connection to the host plant, a single flower stalk not over three to four inches high. Each stalk bears a few flowers or only a single showy tubular flower, two-lipped and either yellow or purple. Unlike the long-lived perennial ground cone, the broomrapes appear to be annual plants, completing their germination, parasitizing of a host, and flowering in one season. The broomrapes parasitize a wide variety of green plants, most commonly members of the sunflower (Compositae), stonecrop (Crassulaceae), and saxifrage (Saxifragaceae) families. Broomrapes are frequently encountered in dry, exposed habitats, especially on the headlands and islands in and around Puget Sound, and they are frequent in the San Juan Islands.

Still another flowering parasite should be mentioned, though it is only rarely found in the undisturbed forest ecosystem. A tangle of yellowish-green threads enmeshed on some hapless shrub or herbaceous plant is sure to be a species of dodder (*Cuscuta*, in the morning glory family, Convolvulaceae). Also called "love tangle" or "coral vine," the dodders can be expected to appear on a variety of vegetation in open dryish habitats from the gravelly outwash prairies around Tacoma and Olympia to the rain-shadow prairies near Sequim and onto the San Juan Islands. Dodders, though kin to morning glories and bindweeds, bear no easy resemblance to their green relatives. They are indeed marvelously contrived for a parasitic existence, living on a variety of seed plants. The most likely place to see dodders is in salt marshes of western Washington. Here a widespread species of dodder (*Cuscuta salina*) uses a salt marsh plant, the fleshy-jointed pickleweed (*Salicornia*), as its host. Soon after germination, the dodder seedling, growing upward in a spiral fashion, encounters a host plant. After initial infection, the stringy, leafless threadlike stems repeatedly infect the host as they grow, eventually enveloping it in a loose tangle of yellowish-green filaments. When full grown and on a fairly large host species, the total length of the branches from a single dodder plant can equal a half-mile.

Among examples of plants growing on other plants, there is the case of the dwarf mistletoes that grow on various cone-bearing trees. Akin to the large, showy mistletoes of oaks and of Christmas-time decor, the dwarf mistletoes are much reduced in size over their more southerly kin. In the Puget Sound region they are all parasitic on conifers. Expect to find the small clusters of mosslike greenish outgrowths on the leafy branches of western white pine or lodgepole pine. Dwarf mistletoes can severely impair the growth of conifer hosts, as they kill, probably by starvation, the host branch outward from the point of infection. The most eye-catching manifestation of this parasitism is frequently encountered on the east slopes of the Cascades, where the dryish coniferous forests consist largely of Douglas fir, yellow pine, and lodgepole pine. Heavy infestation of one species of dwarf mistletoe (*Arceuthobium douglasii*) causes the formation of dense and often grotesque branchlets anywhere on the host. These so-called "witches brooms" are infected branches of Douglas fir from which the tiny parasite frequently emerges as a slender shoot no longer than a fir needle. Actually the major growth of the parasite is within the tissue of the fir. The course of the parasitism leads inevitably to the death of the host tree. First the "witches brooms" appear on any of the side branches of the tree, then the top of the tree dies (the "spike-top" of the logger), foreshadowing the death of the whole tree. Unlike the larger leafy mistletoes whose sticky seeds are spread by birds, the seeds of dwarf mistletoes are violently self-propelled. Their explosive discharge may take them distances of up to twenty or thirty feet. The seeds are fully prepared with a sticky coating to stay put at the end of their ballistic path.

Since the tiny leafless stems of dwarf mistletoes are green, one wonders if mistletoes are really parasites in the fullest and most dependent sense. In fact, they do possess chloroplasts, the intracellular dynamos of the photosynthetic process. But despite this potential capacity for autotrophy (self-feeding), there is little doubt that their greater dependence for nutrition is on their hosts; they can draw nutrients from the host tree year-round. Their existence

Non-green flowering plants are scattered through the lowland forest floor habitat. They seem to mimic fungi in their dependence on decaying plant material for food. But their lives are a bit more complicated. (See text, pages 183–85). The most widespread and diverse of them are members of the Heath and the Orchid family.

Right top: Calypso bulbosa. *(Photo by Bob and Ira Spring.)*

Right bottom: Coralroot orchid (Corallorhiza *sp.). (Photo by Ruth and Louis Kirk.)*

is assured, for even if the host is killed, the sure-fire method of explosive seed dissemination perpetuates the parasite.

Beyond parasitism, what other ingenious nutritional tricks might have been evolved out of the basic format of a flowering, seed-producing plant? A natural evolutionary shift would be for a flowering plant to simulate fungi and bacteria by feeding on dead organic matter and still retain the essences of their flowering plant heritage. Such nutritional specialization was for years thought to have occurred in certain orchids (Orchidaceae) and wintergreens in the heather family. These non-photosynthetic flowering plants were commonly called saprophytic angiosperms, freely translated to mean flowering plants that derive sustenance from dead organic matter. That notion has now given way to a new interpretation. More about that in a moment.

All such flowering plants lacking chlorophyll are small herbaceous species of the humus-rich forest floor. Some are truly spectacular in form and color. While green terrestrial orchids carry on photosynthesis, two kinds of terrestrial orchids of our lowland forests have lost their photosynthetic independence. The coral-root orchids (species of *Corallorhiza*) often grace an otherwise barren forest floor with a delicate touch of color. Single stems or a cluster of as many as a dozen slender stalks up to two feet high appear in spring; these fleshy leafless wands of pale purple to pink bear rows of small pink and purple striped orchid flowers along their tips. It is the knotted, short, rootlike processes that suggest the common name, coral-root orchid. The other non-green orchid is elusive, but what a sight when found! The phantom orchid (*Eburophyton austiniae*) is completely colorless, as white as a ghost. It is taller than the coral-root and has larger, showier flowers. To encounter one in the woods is to see a pale but exquisite ghost of some more brightly colored green-leaved orchid.

Non-green members of the Ericaceae (Heather or Wintergreen) family are so diverse in size, shape, and color as to defy a single description. Their quaint common names hardly reveal any thematic character: candystick or sugarstick (*Allotropa*), Indian pipe (*Monotropa*), pinefoot (*Pityopus*), pine sap (*Pleuricospora*), pine drops (*Pterospora*), and leafless wintergreen (*Pyrola aphylla*)—all names that bear witness to their curious shapes and habits. Their white, flesh-colored, or red-striped stalks that emerge from the forest floor hardly reveal their heather affinities. It is the fleshy urn-shaped flowers that show kinship to the Ericaceae family. Like the non-green orchids, these leafless ericads pop through the forest duff in the most unexpected places. And it is only by accident that the wandering naturalist encounters one of these elusive forest dwellers.

Left: Pine drops (Pterospora andromedea). (Photo by Bob and Ira Spring.)

Far left, top: Phantom orchid (Eburophyton austiniae). (Photo by Victor Scheffer.)

Far left, bottom: Indian pipe (Monotropa uniflora). (Photo by Asahel Curtis.)

To call all these bizarre non-green plants "saprophytes" is to beg the true definition of the term. Strictly speaking, the saprophytic plant should gain its nutrition directly from dead organic matter; this is the true mark of vegetable scavengers like fungi and bacteria. In the case of colorless or non-green flowering plants that are not parasites, fungi themselves may act as intermediaries in relaying food substances from an organic source (decaying vegetation) to the orchid or ericad. Recall the mutualism performed by mycorrhizae, those intimate unions of fungus filaments with tree roots. It is suspected (and now known in the case of *Monotropa,* the Indian pipe) that mycorrhizal associations—fungi linked either between dead organic matter and the non-green flowering plant or between green plant and colorless flowering plant—provide the lifeline for these curious inhabitants of the forest floor. Such a bizarre nutritional arrangement was sure to call forth a special term: *achlorophyllous mycotrophic angiosperms,* which translates, "flowering plants without chlorophyll that utilize fungi in their nutrition."

Fire in the Puget Lowland

Fire has interrupted the placid continuity of lowland forests for eons. Old-growth western hemlock–Douglas fir stands under natural conditions—no suppression of fire—can have a life expectancy of from 500 to 750 years. But this is not to imply that there is a regular, recurrent fire cycle of that time span for old growth. Unlike yellow pine forests east of the Cascades, with frequent and predictable fires, west side forests burn infrequently and without any discernible periodicity. But when fires of natural causes do occur, under conditions of high fuel buildup and late summer drought conditions, severe crown or surface fires can kill entire stands of old growth. All components of the ecosystem are affected: canopy trees and understory killed, animals either driven out of the fire zone or killed; in short, all life in the forest can be terminated following a severe fire.

Yet life does return to a fire-killed forest. Around 200 years after a major fire, a new edition of the same ecosystem approaches maturity, taking on the attributes of the old-growth stand it has succeeded. Though fire is an abrupt termination of life, the replacement of old growth by yet more old growth is the hallmark of succession: pioneer vegetation replaced by mature forest, over and over again. This assured replacement, whether rapid following fire or windstorm, or slow as single old trees fall to make room for new ones, is fueled by natural recycling. In the case of tree death by fire or other causes, that death begets life (Franklin et al. 1988).

Twenty years after the trees of a forest stand have been killed by

fire, a juvenile forest will have begun using the nutrient capital from old snags now mostly down on the forest floor; the charred remains of the old forest are continuously decomposed by microbial "trashburners." At this twenty-year stage, trees are saplings newly born from seed "raining" in from nearby unburned stands, or from the seed in the crowns of burned trees. The young western hemlock, western red cedar, and Douglas fir at this stage are heavily browsed by animals, but eventually escape herbivores to become the "framework" for the maturing forest. Early stages in this replacement process are marked by a rich herb cover on the forest floor, mostly pioneer plants; its biomass as herbage, fruits, or seeds attracts birds and game in variety (Agee 1981).

In time, the twenty-year-old sapling stage is transformed into an even-aged stand of young trees, often so densely stocked that light penetration is drastically reduced at ground level. Walk into almost any dense thirty- to fifty-year-old stand and witness this abrupt

Fire has always been a natural part of Pacific Northwest forest ecology, mostly caused by lightning during the late summer drought period. But human-started fires have also taken their toll of forest stands. These two forest fires were in lowland mixed conifer stands, one southwest of Mount Rainier, the other on the Olympic Peninsula.

dimming of light, the so-called "green-shade effect." The forest with closed canopy is nearly devoid of ground-level vegetation.

This densely packed, even-aged forest is only a transient stage. The once-closed canopy begins to open up as less successful trees (suppressed trees) die, eventually putting their substance back into the nutrient bank. By age 200 to 250, an old-growth form to the forest emerges. Widely spaced boles of living trees overtop a multi-layered understory of shrubs, tree seedlings, or saplings and herbs. The "death-into-life" cycle is enhanced by rotting snags and other biodegradable returns to the soil. The remaining live trees increase their girth and continue shoot and lateral branch growth. Trees of this maturing epoch can live on to 500 or more years in the absence of wind or fire.

Fire is not a simple variable in the matrix of forest influences. Given the variety of habitat types in Puget Sound country, the occurrence and intensity of fire will depend on local rainfall patterns,

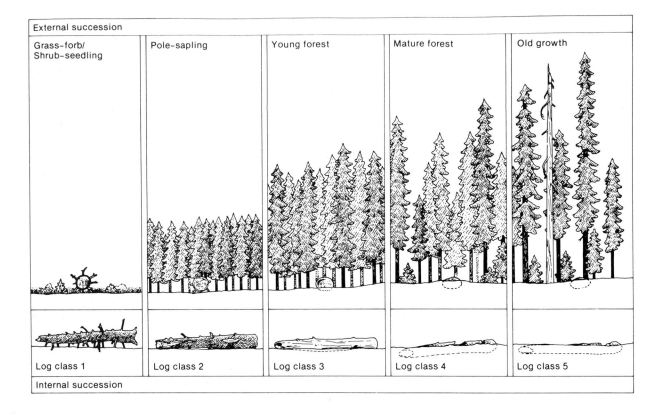

fuel buildup, and qualities of the habitat (open and exposed versus closed and protected); events of forest disease and pest infestations add yet another variable. Like other strands of the ecosystem network, fire is connected to everything else.

One variable in the effects of fire is the differing susceptibility of tree species to injury or death by fire. There is reasonable agreement among forest ecologists that Douglas fir is the species most resistant to fire. Least resistant is Sitka spruce, with western red cedar and western hemlock in between. Can it be that conifers cope with fire by evolving "defenses" against it? Is there a fire-adapted species? While it is reasonable to expect that evolution may have fine-tuned the trait of fire resistance, it is hard to prove.

Fire by natural causes surely has been a "constant" (or persistent variable) in the history of the region's vegetation. Lightning is the most common cause of forest fire, especially when coupled with drought conditions of late summer and a generous buildup of fuel, alive and dead. Fires caused by humans came late to the Pacific Northwest. How soon after aboriginal people arrived in the New World could the first forest fire have started? While hard to pin down, we can be sure that in Indian cultures fire was used to burn

Decaying log biomass becomes living forest tree biomass in this diagram of forest succession and log decay.

vegetation. All over the west, the evidence is compelling that Indians and fire went together. Deliberate use of fire to burn vegetation in Puget lowland was probably restricted to grasslands, including our own Puget Sound "prairies." Indians set fire to the prairies to drive game and to perpetuate the open grasslands for the harvest of camas and other bulbs. In so doing, adjacent forest could have been ignited too. It is not so clear that coastal Indians caused fires in old-growth hemlock-cedar-Douglas fir forests. Fire was used to girdle cedar trees and to hollow out cedar logs for canoes. But this confined use of fire probably did not lead to setting whole forests afire. Unfortunately, fire-scarred bark on old-growth trees does not tell us if the fire was natural or man-induced.

With the coming of Europeans, the frequency and magnitude of forest fires increased, up to a point in time. Prior to deliberate fire protection, begun in the early 1900s, fires associated with all kinds of human (mostly non-Indian) activity often raged out of control. Some major fires devastated thousands of acres, turning midday to darkness in lowland Puget Sound. The nearest thing in western Washington to the great Tillamook burn in northwestern Oregon (1933), was the more than 200,000-acre Yacolt burn of 1902. And in the Puget Sound basin proper, many major fires, like the Big Beaver (Skagit River area) fire of 1926, and the Deming fire (1960s), have consumed whole forested regions, despite deliberate fire protection.

All timbered lands in the Puget basin are now "managed." Besides national parks where forests are managed as wilderness, public and private forest lands are either into first or second generation growth after logging or fire. Fire now becomes both a tool and a hazard in these more intensively managed lands. The burning of logging debris—slash burning—is the most common and rudimentary use of fire. Controlled burning in young to maturing forest stands could be used here on the wet side of the mountains. Its intent would be to improve the forest tree crop by eliminating "unwanted" competing vegetation, downed thinned trees, etc. Those of us brought up in the Smokey Bear epoch will shudder at first in witnessing intentional use of fire in forests. And even more we may question deliberate withholding of fire control in nearby national parks. Fire in our west-side forests is a given; how it is to be used or controlled in a deliberate way is yet to be determined.

Table 16. Some Herbaceous Plants in the Western Hemlock Zone

	Abundance	Habitat
Tall: over 3 feet		
Sword fern (*Polystichum munitum*)	****	Moist forests
Lady fern (*Athyrium felix-femina*)	****	Swamps, streams in forest
Bracken fern (*Pteridium aquilinum*)	****	Dry forests, clearings
Goat's beard (*Aruncus sylvester*)	***	Moist places in forest
Fireweed (*Epilobium angustifolium*)	****	Dry woods, clearings
Cow parsnip (*Heracleum lanatum*)	***	Moist woods, openings
Hedge-nettle (*Stachys cooleyi*)	**	Moist woods, openings
Tiger lily (*Lilium columbianum*)	**	Openings in forest
Bull thistle (*Cirsium vulgare*)†	***	Disturbed sites
Canada thistle (*Cirsium arvense*)†	***	Bad weed in disturbed sites
Nettle (*Urtica dioica*)	***	Damp woods, openings, disturbed sites
Tansy ragwort (*Senecio jacobea*)†	***	Bad weed in disturbed sites
Tansy (*Tanacetum vulgare*)†	***	Bad weed in disturbed sites
False hellebore (*Veratrum spp.*)	**	Local on deep, damp soils; meadow and forest border
Teasel (*Dipsacus fullonium*)†	**	Disturbed sites, pastures
Foxglove (*Digitalis purpurea*)†	***	Edge of woods along roadsides and in clearings
Mullein (*Verbascum thapsus*)†	**	Roadside weed
Toadflax (*Linaria dalmatica*)†	**	Roadside weed, mostly on gravelly prairies
Wormwood (*Artemisia spp.*)†	***	Roadside weed
Orchard grass (*Dactylis glomerata*)†	****	Weed and pasture grass
Tall meadow oatgrass (*Arrhenatherum elatius*)†	***	Weed and pasture grass
Rye grass (*Elymus glaucus*)	***	Open woods, clearings
Beachgrass (*Ammophila arenaria*)	***	Sand dunes
Cattail (*Typha latifolia*)	***	Bordering swamps and standing water
Sweet clover (*Melilotus alba*)†	**	Roadside weed

Note: **** common, *** frequent, ** infrequent, * rare;
† = introduced weed.

Table 16. (*continued*) 191

	Abundance	Habitat
Medium: 1 to 3 feet		
Colt's foot (*Petasites frigida*)	***	Moist to dry openings in woods and roadsides
False Solomon's seal (*Smilacina racemosa*)	**	Open forests
Twisted stalk (*Streptopus amplexifolius*)	***	Shade of dense forest
Trailblazer (*Adenocaulon bicolor*)	***	Openings in forest
Yarrow (*Achillea millefolium*)	***	Prairies, clearings, disturbed sites
Pearly everlasting (*Anaphalis margaritacea*)	****	Openings in woods, clearings
Bleeding heart (*Dicentra formosa*)	***	Deep forests
Sweet cicely (*Osmorhiza nuda*)	***	Dryish forests
Oxeye daisy (*Chrysanthemum leucanthemum*)†	****	Roadsides, pastures, etc.
Large-leaved avens (*Geum macrophyllum*)	***	Forests and clearings, usually disturbed
Hawkweed (*Hieracium albiflorum*)	**	Forests and clearings, usually disturbed
Checker lily (*Fritillaria lanceolata*)	**	Prairies, openings
Balsamroot (*Balsamorhiza deltoidea*)	**	Prairies, dry meadows
Camas (*Camassia quamash*)	***	Wet places in prairies, meadows
Swamp lantern, or skunk cabbage (*Lysichitum americanum*)	***	Bogs, swamps, springy places
Goldenrod (*Solidago spp.*)	***	Roadsides, meadows
Lupin (*Lupinus rivularis*)	**	Roadsides, prairies
Resinweed (*Grindelia integrifolia*)	***	Coastal bluffs
Youth-on-age (*Tolmiea menziesii*)	***	Deep woods
Fringe-cup (*Tellima grandiflora*)	***	Deep to open woods
Alum-root (*Heuchera micrantha*)	***	Clearings, rocky places
Horsetail (*Equisetum telmateia*)	****	Wet disturbed sites
Deer fern (*Blechnum spicant*)	***	Deep woods
Rein-orchid (*Habenaria dilatata*)	**	Wet places in forest openings
Velvetgrass (*Holcus lanatus*)†	***	Roadside and pasture weed
Brome grass (*Bromus carinatus*)	***	Roadside and pasture grass
Nodding trisetum (*Trisetum cernuum*)	**	Woodland grass
Blue grass (*Poa pratensis*)†	***	Introd. pasture grass
Sedge (*Carex spp.*)	***	Grasslike, with triangular stems; usually in wet open sites

Table 16. (*continued*)

	Abundance	Habitat
Low: less than 1 foot		
False lily-of-the-valley (*Maianthemum dilatatum*)	***	Often gregarious in deep woods
Western trillium (*Trillium ovatum*)	***	Deep to open forests
Vanilla leaf (*Achlys triphylla*)	***	Deep forests
Bunchberry, dwarf dogwood (*Cornus canadensis*)	***	Deep forests
Bead lily (*Clintonia uniflora*)	***	Deep forests
Rattlesnake plantain (*Goodyera oblongifolia*)	**	Deep to open forests
Star-flowered false Solomon's seal (*Smilacina stellata*)	**	Forests, wet clearings
Willow-herb (*Epilobium paniculatum*)	***	Weed of 2nd growth forests
Star flower (*Trientalis latifolia*)	***	Open to deep forests
Bedstraw (*Galium triflorum*)	**	Open to deep forests
Coralroot orchid (*Corallorhiza maculata*)	**	In dense shade of forest
Foam flower (*Tiarella trifoliata*)	****	In deep to open woods
Strawberry (*Fragaria vesca*)	***	Clearings, meadows, open forest
Evergreen violet (*Viola sempervirens*)	***	Deep forest
Stream violet (*V. glabella*)	***	Wet forests
Twin flower (*Linnaea borealis*)	****	Damp woods
Sidebells pyrola (*Pyrola secunda*)	***	Moist to dry forests
Pink pyrola (*P. asarifolia*)	**	Moist forest
Stonecrop (*Sedum spathulifolium*)	***	Rock outcrops often near coast
Fawn lily (*Erythronium oreganum*)	**	Open woods, clearings
Shooting star (*Dodecatheon hendersonii*)	**	Spring-wet places in prairies
Harebell (*Campanula rotundifolia*)	**	Gravelly prairies

Note: **** common, *** frequent, ** infrequent, * rare; † = introduced weed.

Table 16. (*continued*) 193

	Abundance	Habitat
Inside-out flower (*Vancouveria hexandra*)	**	Open woods and road-sides from Tacoma south
Self-heal (*Prunella vulgaris*)	****	Weed of damp shady places
Calypso (*Calypso bulbosa*)	**	Sporadic in deep woods
Oak fern (*Gymnocarpium dryopteris*)	***	Gregarious in deep woods
Licorice fern (*Polypodium glycyrhiza*)	***	Usually on bark of bigleaf maple
Wild ginger (*Asarum caudatum*)	***	Moist woods
Sheep sorrel (*Rumex acetosella*)†	****	Weed of waste places
Groundsel (*Senecio vulgaris*)†	**	Weed of waste places
Bitter cress (*Cardamine oligosperma*)	***	Weed of dryish openings
Buttercup (*Ranunculus repens*)†	***	Weed of wet places
Wood sorrel (*Oxalis oregana*)	***	Deep woods
Indian paintbrush (*Castilleja miniata*)	**	Local, in openings, prairies, rocky places
Plantain (*Plantago lanceolata*)†	****	Weed of waste places
Cat's ear (*Hypochaeris radicata*)†	****	Weed of fields, prairies, waste places
Dandelion (*Taraxacum officinale*)†	****	Weed of disturbed sites
Miner's lettuce (*Montia sibirica*)	***	Wet woods, clearings
Sea-rocket (*Cakile edentula*)	**	Dunes along coast
June grass (*Poa annua*)†	****	Lawns, pastures, waste places

Cougar (Felis concolor) roams from the lowlands to the subalpine (as seen here), with foraging territories of many square miles.

6 Animal Life in the Lowlands

"A mouse is miracle enough to stagger sextillions of infidels."—Walt Whitman

The Lowland Forest ecosystem, from its primeval state to the present, has been dominated by plant life. In a parochial way, I suppose botanists should delight in the importance assumed by the plant life they name, study, and file away. It is true that, unlike on a coral reef or the Serengeti grassland plains of Africa, animals are inconspicuous in the living landscape of Puget Sound country. (Of course, this observation does not apply to humans, who in the twentieth century have populated much of the lowland landscape.) But zoologists would reject any dearth-of-animals assertion. Even though animal life in Puget country may not be conspicuous, animals *are* there, in variety.

The ecological view is to look at the whole ecosystem fabric as a unity, rather than simply as catalogues of plants and animals. A plant-biased reading of the natural landscape is indeed one-sided. Animals help shape regional ecosystems; they do make their mark on their surroundings. They eat, move, mate, and sleep their way through the green world, leaving the vegetation altered in ever so many ways: clipped, chewed, packed, bent, uprooted, molded into shapes for nests, digested, and cast upon the land again. It is hard to imagine what a hemlock-cedar forest would look like were there no animals in it. No ecologist has ever built an animal-proof exclosure around an entire forest, and if that were possible, the barrier would have its own altering effects on the vegetation.

Another way to grasp the profound interdependence of plant and animal takes us back to the beginning of "biotime" on the earth. Biologists are now in a position to make cautious guesses about the sequence of events leading from a geochemical planet to one stocked with life. The earliest unicellular life was heterotrophic. Simple life fed upon molecules of organic substances created spontaneously and stored in the ancient oceans. According to a prevalent theory, as this rich oceanic "soup" became depleted, some of the simple heterotrophs (other-feeders) evolved the steps to independence from this limited organic resource.

The ultimate step was the development of full-scale machinery for carrying on photosynthesis. Thus, the plant, at first a simple unicell with photosynthetic capabilities (autotrophic), was a latecomer in the long trial period for the coming of life on the planet. If

195

this notion is true, then a further idea demands attention: plants must have served as food for animals from the very start of their two divergent nutritional modes of life. If it cannot be decided whether primordial life were plant or animal, then surely it can be labeled in functional terms as *heterotroph* or *autotroph*. Animal-plant interdependence is not only close, it has undergone eons of reinforcement.

Links in the Forest Food Chain

The recognition of the interdependence of plants and animals leads us to the nutritional dynamics of the system. If an aphorism for the aquatic world is "big bugs eat little bugs, and bugs eat mud," then the adage for land dwellers is "one hill, one tiger." For tiger, substitute cougar, and the poetic, Oriental view of nutritional interdependence is cast in a Northwest setting. Solar energy, transformed into the substance of green plants, is passed along from organism to organism within the ecosystem. Animals seize bites of the organic energy-in-matter around them in a great variety of ways. In fact, much animal diversity can be equated with diversity of modes of making a living. The broad categories of this diversity are three: herbivores, carnivores, and omnivores—eaters of plants, animals, or both. The first animal link in the food chain beyond plants is herbivory, a specialty of insects galore, birds of many feathers, and a spectrum of fur-bearing animals. Some of these plant eaters have a specialist's palate and others assume the role of a generalist with wide-ranging appetite.

Herbivory has its peril. Inevitably, poised along the food chain is the carnivore, to take its tithe of herbivore flesh for the sake of survival. Plant-eating mouse, butterfly, bird, or deer falls prey to a meat eater and the passage of energy-in-matter proceeds along the food chain. The omnivore simply makes a more efficient harvest—a smorgasbord—of the available plant and animal prey.

A detailed account of the animals of Puget country is beyond the scope of this book and would be a rather unrevealing list of "who's who" in the lowland forest. More rewarding will be a close look at certain key animals in the ecosystem as they figure in food chains and food webs. For identifying a particular animal in lowland habitats, you should consult the various guidebooks on animals of Puget country, listed in the "For Further Reading" section of the bibliography.

Analyzing the lowland forest as an ecosystem where the matter and energy of living things are transformed appeals to all who view nature as a unitary whole. It should be simple to connect one organism with another in order to represent the total food web of a

The "actors" in a foodweb for a lowland forest ecosystem: primary producers (trees, shrubs, and herbs), animal consumers (carnivores: bear and owl; herbivores: deer, squirrel, birds, banana slug, and hemlock looper in inset), and decomposers (fungi on stump and log). (Drawing by Phyllis Woolwine.)

hemlock-cedar forest by listing all the organisms found in the system and then drawing in connecting lines to show the passage of food along the system. For various reasons, however, a complete and accurate food web cannot be made. First, a complex tangle of lines and loops would develop. Foods at any trophic level do not move in simple, straight paths. Take the biomass of a conifer: Douglas fir needles pass into the food web in many directions. They are eaten by a variety of herbivorous animals (insects and mammals); then a lesser but diverse array of carnivores and omnivores consume the flesh of those eaters of Douglas fir needles. Finally, the waste matter from both herbivores and carnivores becomes the life-giving substance for decomposers like fungi and bacteria, or detritus-feeders like protozoans and small invertebrates. Yet another circuit can develop, revealing the flexibility of the system. The Douglas fir needles may bypass the herbivore-carnivore sequence to be turned directly into elemental matter by insect detritus-feeders and by decomposers. And if this sequence of trophic events—a small strand in the total forest ecosystem's food web—shows considerable indeterminacy, much greater is the unpredictability of sequences in the sum total of all such food chains or webs. (See Table 17.)

Furthermore, ecologists are ignorant of specific steps in many trophic pathways. As might be expected, the Douglas fir-herbivore link has been well studied because of the economic importance of the fir, but other pathways involving noneconomic plants and their consumers are largely unknown. What food webs are traceable from such sources as salal, ocean-spray, rattlesnake plantain, skunk cabbage, and all the rest of the common or rare plants that are not utilized, and therefore rarely studied, by western man?

There is no need to be intimidated by either complexity or the state of ecological ignorance. The armchair ecologist can create simulations of food webs, modifying them as information becomes available. The idea of a dynamic network of feeding levels *does* form a central thrust of contemporary ecology. Our task is to take the generalized model—producer → consumer → decomposer—and adapt it to a particular local ecosystem and at any level of complexity we choose. The fitting of the general model to some specific "subroutines" has already been attempted for sectors of the Puget Sound ecosystem, and by a most exceptional scientific effort.

Teams of scientists in the Pacific Northwest joined together during the 1970s in the International Biological Program (IBP) to seek fuller understanding of the region's coniferous forest ecosystem. In the larger perspective of the worldwide IBP effort, the Coniferous Forest Biome Project was one of five projects tackling the complex analysis of major ecosystems in North America. Other biomes under similar long-term, team study were grassland, deciduous forest, tundra, and desert. As the objectives of the Coniferous Forest Biome Program exemplify those of other biome or ecosystem programs, the local team's goals illustrate the total ecosystem analysis planned by IBP. I quote from their preamble:

> We seek a basic understanding of coniferous forest ecosystems . . . in order to develop new theoretical approaches and to recognize and define ecological limitations on management and opportunities for increasing production of fiber, food, water, and wildlife. The overall strategy includes identification of the major components and processes, both physical and organic, and definition of how they are interrelated.

Table 17. Generalized Food Web for Lowland Forest

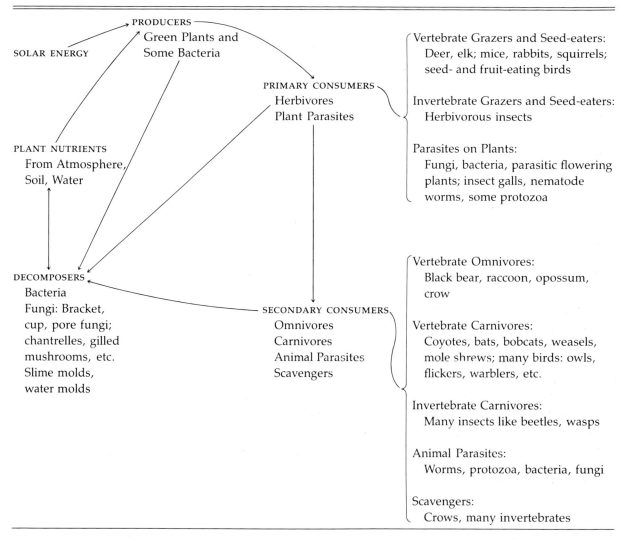

Starting with this broad thematic statement, the Biome team began gathering and analyzing data, and published the final report of its ten-year study (Edmonds 1982). To get at the interplay between animal, plant, and physical environments, the Biome program concentrated on three objectives: the creation of an ecosystem model, the identification of the interdependent subsystems of that overall model, and investigations of particular processes and phenomena at the plant-animal interface.

How the Coniferous Biome scientists have looked at our regional ecosystems can first be visualized in the abstract. The series of charts presented here should be viewed as a sequence of nested

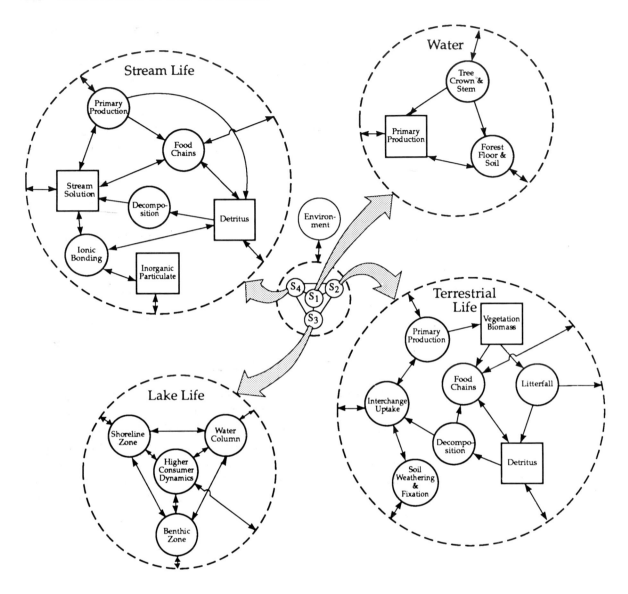

compartments, proceeding from the most general overview to the interactive subunits of the whole system.

Within the total environment of the Coniferous Forest Biome, the IBP team defined four major subsystems: life in streams and lakes ("stream life" and "lake life" subsystems), the soil-soil, soil-water, water-forest tree interface (the water, or "hydrologic" subsystem), and the plant-animal-microbe interactions of the terrestrial phases of the ecosystem ("terrestrial life" subsystem). In the mind's eye it is possible to enter this multidimensional maze at any point, at once to be caught up in the many strands of the environmental web. We will focus on only one subsystem, the terrestrial

Lowland forest ecosystems modeled as a series of interconnected, "nested" living and nonliving components: S_1, water; S_2, terrestrial life; S_3, lake life; and S_4, stream life. Animals are represented either as consumers or in food chains.

life, and then zero in on the third-order subsystem, food chains (see chart, opposite).

The IBP Coniferous Biome ecologists divided the food chains into two subsets, each with herbivores and carnivores. The *grazing food chain* consists of animals consuming the living products of vegetation and their predators. The eaters and the eaten are the familiar forest foragers like deer, elk, bear, cougar, birds (both herbivorous and carnivorous), as well as the less noticeable herbivorous and carnivorous animals without backbones—insects, slugs, earthworms, and others. The other subsystem consists of *detritus feeders:* their food is the bits and pieces of dead organic matter from the continuous rain of litter onto the forest floor, plus the partially decomposed forest humus and waste products of other animals. The detritus feeders share the organic feast with the fungal and bacterial decomposers in turning the dead and decaying biomass into the substance of their own bodies and in liberating substance for the never-ending process of renewal.

It should be possible to go a few steps further than the IBP fourth-level subsystems of grazing and detritus food chains. The animals that make up these two subsystems in a lowland forest food web could form an impressive catalogue. Even such a listing, though it would add familiar names to the generalized diagram of grazers and detritus feeders, would not allow us to put together a simplified food chain. What is needed now are particular organisms that can be linked by their trophic requirements. We now examine certain food chains, each involving a different organism. A caution, though: any specific, simplified food chain is an abstraction, lifted out of the environmental fabric where the interconnected strands exceed our capacity to portray them.

Large Mammal Consumers of the Forest's Productivity

The most conspicuous forest consumers are deer and elk. These browsing animals make a noticeable impact on the lowland vegetation by nibbling many kinds of plants. Two species of deer have been prevalent in the Puget Sound area. The black-tailed deer, a lowland, west-side cousin of the mule deer of eastern Washington, is now the most common. The other species, the Columbian white-tailed deer, in earlier times was common in the open prairie country from the Cowlitz River south to the Willamette Valley of Oregon; it is now restricted to the low, marshy islands and flood plains along the lower Columbia River.

Nearly any kind of plant of the forest understory can be part of the deer's diet. Where the forest inhibits the growth of grass and other meadow plants, the black-tailed deer browses on huckleberry, salal, dogwood, mountain ash, vine maple, hazelnut, and almost any other shrub or herb. In clearings within the forest, herbs such as grasses, sedges, hedge-nettle, skunk cabbage, and fireweed are favorites. But all this is fair-weather feeding. What keeps the black-tailed deer alive in the harsher seasons of plant decay and dormancy? One compensation for not hibernating is the built-in urge to migrate, especially so for mule deer on the east side. Deer may move from high-elevation browse areas in summer down to the lowland vegetation in late fall. Even with snow on the ground, the high bushy understory is exposed; also snow and wind bring down leafy branches of cedar, hemlock, red alder, and other arboreal fodder. The fall and spring crops of fungi are consumed, as are the mosses and lichens that festoon trees. Plant protein, carbohydrate, and fats thus are copiously turned into the flesh and sinew of deer all year around.

The numbers of deer have fluctuated markedly since the entry of Europeans into Puget Sound country. The early explorers and settlers told of abundant deer in the early 1800s and yet almost in the same breath bemoaned the lack of this succulent game animal in early times. Lewis and Clark arrived at the mouth of the Columbia River on November 14, 1805, in nearly starved circumstances. They had experienced great difficulty finding game west of the Rockies and not until the second of December did they kill their first elk. To keep forty men alive that winter, they consumed approximately 150 elk and 20 deer. And when game moved out of the lowlands in early spring, the expedition decided to return east rather than face possible starvation. Later on in the early years of the nineteenth century, when Fort Vancouver became the headquarters for the Hudson's Bay Company, deer populations continued to fluctuate. David Douglas, Scottish botanical explorer of the 1830s, found a disturbing change in the animal life around the fort during the period between his first visit in 1825 and his final contact with the fort in 1832. A recent biographer (Morwood 1973) states:

Deer, mostly Columbian black-tailed deer (Odocoilus hemionus *subsp.* columbianus), *are common in forests, brushy areas, and clearings in Puget Sound. (Photo by Bob and Ira Spring.)*

> Though he had been absent for only two years [1829–30, back in England], Douglas found that civilization had encroached with giant strides upon the fort. Many of the great Douglas firs had been cut to feed the new saw mills, while others had been simply felled and burned to clear the land for agriculture. More than two hundred acres were under cultivation, providing stands of wheat, corn, and vegetables and a famous apple orchard. . . .
>
> Douglas found the changed landscape depressing and complained of "too much civilization." The deer which once picturesquely dotted the meadows around the fort were gone, *hunted to extermination* [my italics] in order to protect the crops. Even Indians were rarely to be seen plying the river or trooping into the fort to trade foreign trinkets.

Reduction in numbers of game should have boded ill for their survival in later times. A worsening of the plight of deer was to be expected as white settlers encroached on the land, logging, burning, and clearing, eventually replacing a wilderness landscape with roads, cities, towns, and factories. No doubt the numbers of deer declined still further. Recall the fate of the Columbian white-tailed deer, now in a protected status as small populations along the lower Columbia. But for the black-tailed deer, human pressure has had just the opposite effect. Wildlife zoologist Helmut Buechner (1953), in reviewing the nature of biotic changes in our state through recorded time, says that "since the early 1940's the state has had more deer than at any other time in its history, the winter population fluctuating around approximately 320,000[1] deer (mule and black-tailed deer) which will yield about 65,000 of either sex and any age annually for an indefinite period."

The causes of this population rebound are consequences of other human actions. First, the major predators of deer—wolves, cou-

Explorers like David Douglas observed that in the early nineteenth century game had become scarce around settlements. Here, at Fort Vancouver, the clearing of forest for lumber, buildings, and livestock, plus hunting pressure, probably caused the reduction in numbers of game animals.

1. The estimated population of deer statewide for 1983 was 434,310, up substantially from Buechner's figure for 1953. Numbers of black-tailed deer for the Puget region came to 97,450 in 1983.

gar, and lynx—have been greatly reduced in numbers. Second, conservation has been insured by limiting times for and types of hunting. But the most profound reason for the restoration of high population numbers has been the fate of the forests. Great tracts of lowland country deforested by logging, fire, or both, have become ideal feeding grounds for deer. In addition to finding an increase of suitable browse, like huckleberry and vine maple, Arthur Einarsen, longtime game biologist in the Pacific Northwest, found *quality of browse* in the open areas to be substantially more nutritive. When he compared the chemical and nutritive content of plants grown in the shade with that of plants grown in the open, the differences were remarkable. The protein content of shade-grown vegetation was much lower than that for plants grown in clearings.

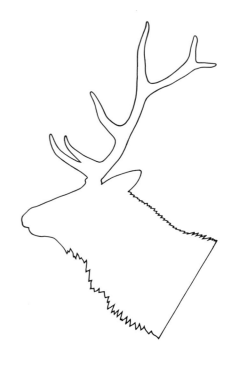

Though the mule deer migrates fifty miles or more from summer to winter range, the west-side black-tailed deer spends most of its life in the area in which it was born. Neither black-tailed nor mule deer form herds, though two to four may band together. When foraging is severely impaired in the winter, they may assemble in the best (or last remaining) foraging areas. The black-tailed deer breed in November and December; females may then be herded in harems to mate. A young doe will give birth to a single fawn (after some two hundred days of gestation). An older doe will often produce twins, though three or four fawns from one doe may occasionally occur. Does may mate precociously at seven months, but more commonly are not mated until the second year. The fawn at birth weighs a little over six pounds (2.7 kg), is protectively spotted, camouflaged from predators, and is able to walk. Intermittently during the day, the doe leaves her young in dense underbrush where the fawn rests quietly and unobserved. The mother comes back to nurse her fawn about every four hours. Fawns can begin nibbling on vegetation when only a few days old, but are dependent on the mother for milk for at least six weeks. After weaning, the young females may tag along after their mothers for a year or more; the males usually leave during the first year. Black-tailed deer have a life span of about ten years in the wild, though in captivity, twenty-year-old individuals have been recorded.

What is the fate of deer biomass in the endless cycle of matter and energy? Natural predators can hardly account for much predation of black-tailed deer in modern times. Lynx and wolves are nonexistent now, and the cougar is a rare predator. Humans have assumed the role of dominant "predator." Intentional predation, called hunting for big game, takes the major number of deer. The estimated population of black-tailed deer in 1967 was 225,000, of which 32,000 were killed by hunters.

But what happens to that large reserve of nearly 190,000 animals

Fawn in a camouflaged setting. (Photo by Bob and Ira Spring.)

Sketches for recognizing the three large herbivores in Puget country: elk (left), Columbian black-tailed deer (middle), and Columbian white-tailed deer (rare and local, right). (Silhouettes by Michael Emerson.)

that escape gunshot predation? Between birth and natural death, a span of about ten years, the deer are subject to a variety of mishaps. No one has ever estimated the number killed by cars. Death may come by starvation during especially severe winters or by other stressful circumstances (overpopulation, short supply of browse, etc.). West-side deer were decimated during the winter of 1968–69, yet the Washington State Department of Game reported that the mild winter of the next year brought on good crops of fawns, to restore the populations. An exceptional consequence of the severe 1968–69 winter is recounted by Earl Larrison (1970) for eastern Washington. A massive campaign to feed hungry deer caused them to congregate in farmyards and along highways. As a consequence, automobiles and domestic dogs killed many of the deer banded together for the charitable feeding. More deer were killed than starved that winter, at least in six eastern Washington counties. This well-meant charity with its sad aftermath epitomizes the ecological epigram: "We can never merely do one thing."

The passage of deer substance into the human social system (as meat, trophies, kills by dogs and vehicles, etc.) is not the end of the story. Only the fraction of those deer eaten by humans becomes human protoplasm; the balance is dissipated by decomposers. Just as flesh and blood goes to ashes and dust, so goes the forest's productivity of forage into deer, ultimately entering the soil-air environment of the forest ecosystem.

Besides the black-tailed deer, the other large herbivore in western Washington is the elk. A magnificent animal to behold, the Canadian elk or wapiti might be confused with a large specimen of black-tailed deer. But unlike the deer, the elk has a conspicuous dark brown mane on the neck, and antlers with lateral points coming from a main beam or axis (like the white-tailed deer); even the largest black-tailed deer would not match the elk in size. A mature elk may weigh up to a thousand pounds. Elk in the Puget lowlands are not nearly as common as deer.[2] They occur in a few scattered herds: north of Seattle on the Nooksack River; along the drainages of the Green and White rivers in King and Pierce counties; and south to the Columbia River. The major elk populations west of the Cascades are on the Olympic Peninsula, mainly on the west side of the Olympic Mountains. Zoologists recognize the Olympic Peninsula form as subspecies *roosevelti* of the Canadian elk (*Cervus canadensis*). From its native habitat, the brown Olympic or Roosevelt elk has been transplanted to most of the present west-side localities and elsewhere in the West.

2. 1983 population estimate for elk in the Puget Sound region was 4,480, and 56,535 statewide.

*Roosevelt elk (*Cervus elaphus *subsp.* rooseveltii) *in forest clearing.*

Elk, like deer, thrive on the rich shrub browse that grows back on logged-over or burned forest land. It is the elk herds on the west side of the Olympic Peninsula that best exemplify the effect of browsing animals on stature, configuration, and species composition of vegetation. The low-lying river valleys in Olympic rain-forest country would become impervious thickets of understory brush if it were not for the prodigious herbivory of Olympic elk. The trimmed park-like vistas underneath the conifer canopy along the Queets, Hoh, and other west-flowing rivers are testimony to the magnitude of elk and other animal predation on green plants. Wildlife managers have demonstrated the landscape impact of browsing game on vegetation with the device of game exclosures. Game-proof fences are erected around a plot of land, and the contrast between browsed land outside the exclosure and the dense understory of herbage within the exclosure is dramatic. Results from two exclosure studies, one on the Cedar River watershed just east of Seattle and the other on the Olympic Peninsula (Quinault River), though in quite different areas and forest types revealed similar conse-

Elk exclosure on Olympic Peninsula. Dense vegetation within exclosure and heavily browsed area outside.

quences. Shrub vegetation decreased while grass and grasslike plants increased outside the exclosure where big game could browse. But inside the fenced exclosure, shrub vegetation increased and grasses diminished. Apparently vegetation that grows at ground level is favored under the impact of the animals. The number of conifers per unit area was found to increase outside the exclosure, probably due to the more open landscapes created by animal activity. Consumption of herbage and trampling of vegetation are the major causes of change in vegetation wrought by big game animals.

The most omnivorous of our large game animals is the black bear. Familiar in national parks and zoos, comical to observe, yet dangerously unpredictable, the black bear's reputation is enriched by fact, fable, and festival. Every summer the little town of McCleary, west of Olympia, stages a Bear Festival which includes the consumption of "bearburgers" and bear stew by tourists and locals. And in years past, the festival tolerated a collateral event, the picketing of the festival by a few "SOB"s (intrepid and determined members of

"Save Our Bears"). The principal sacrificial actor in this peculiar folk drama is the black bear (*Ursus americanus*), who pays with its life for having been caught up in a conflict between economic needs and a disturbed forest ecosystem.

The area around McCleary has been intensively logged over the years and is now managed for the sustained yield of uniform, even-aged timber. This new ecological strategy has affected the feeding behavior of bears and also has helped sustain their population. In earlier times, food in old-growth forests was either sparse or highly varied. In the 1980s, the dense even-aged forests often exclude the berry-yielding undergrowth so important in the diet of black bears. As versatile omnivores, the bears (or at least some individuals) have shifted their feeding to the very species that humans harvest: forest trees. Black bear damage to Douglas fir, in particular, is said to be extensive in many western Washington areas. Chris Maser describes this new animal-tree-human syndrome, with some unexpected conclusions. "Black bear damage to young Douglas fir forests has been extensive enough in some areas to cause concern for the timber crop. On the other hand, thousands of acres of such forests harbor populations of black bear and sustain no damage. It seems apparent, therefore, that factors other than the mere presence of the bear are involved" (1967:34).

What is the nature and extent of bear damage to trees, and what are those "other" factors? Bears inflict the most damage to young trees, in the fifteen- to forty-five-year age classes. A bear that has learned to select the sweetish, soft, and pulpy tissue just under the bark will eat away on any part of the young tree trunk, from the butt up to heights of forty to fifty feet. The damage done high in the tree often is a complete girdling of the young trunk and is thus more severe than the slashing of bark at the base of the tree. Both claws and incisor teeth are used to get at the sapwood. But what induces bears to extend their already wide-ranging diet to conifer sapwood, and especially Douglas fir? Maser feels that only certain individual bears get the knack of feeding on fir sapwood. And they are led to the habit by those practices of second-growth tree farming expected to yield the best or quickest timber. When a dense stand of fir saplings is thinned early ("precommercial thinning"), the leafy limbs beneath the crown of each tree may persist well down on the tree trunk. These trees are easily climbed by those bears that have found Douglas fir a palatable food source. However, in dense, unthinned second-growth stands, bear damage is much less; lower branches have been self-pruned and the trees cannot be easily climbed. It would seem that in an open stand, bears can climb the more limby trees with ease to reach the tastier sapwood of the upper crown. A moral—or at least a piece of a con-

Severe black bear damage to Douglas fir on a forest research plot, Lewis County. (Photo by Michael Wooton). A new strategy to divert bears from eating Douglas fir is to feed the bears a tasty substitute for bark. Pet food laced with pinene (an aromatic conifer extract) seems to work, and is now being tested on tree farms in western Washington.

*Black bear (*Ursus americanus*).*

servation ethic—seems to emerge from the "bear eats fir" story. Rather than convert bear to stew or "bearburger" for the McCleary festival, timber managers might institute the practice of removing lower limbs of trees that remain after precommercial thinning. In this way, we can have bears and timber too (though the price of two-by-fours may have to reflect the cost of the delimbing).

The next link in the passage of matter and energy along the forest food chain is the carnivorous consumer. Each carnivore is uniquely designed to utilize the flesh that was plant. Carnivores range in size and kinship from large mammals like the cougar, fox, coyote, and bobcat, to tiny invertebrates like the bug, beetle, and spider. And in between are predatory birds, small carnivorous mammals, reptiles, and amphibia. My abbreviated bestiary of Puget Sound country should include an account of at least one carnivorous mammal. I choose the cougar (puma, or mountain lion, *Felis concolor*) to be symbolic of the flesh eaters, not only because of its sheer magnificence of form and function, but because of its great ecological lesson. Almost no other predatory mammal in western North America has been so maligned in word and abused in deed as the cougar. The flesh sought by the cougar is a nutritional and ecological necessity, imposed by the drama of evolution acted out over stretches of geological time. The interactions between the hunter and the hunted are endlessly complex, affording the biologist a clear example of an interdependent coevolutionary system. In the case of the cougar, its prey has evolved patterns of defense in response to the adaptive skills of the catlike hunter. Such challenge and response on the part of prey and predator achieves a kind of shifting balance: neither too many prey, nor an overabundance of predators. Thus it is with the cougar and its prey. Although the cougar may be forced to take a variety of smaller mammals, deer are the prime targets of the cat's prowess at stalking and taking food on the hoof. A single cougar probably takes no more than seventeen deer a year. Given this level of predation, it is evident that our expanding deer population is not in much danger from over-exploitation by cougars. Using game census data for the entire state (in 1985, about 528,000 deer and 1,500 cougar), I estimate 23,500 deer as potential prey for Washington's cougar population. Besides indicating a supply and demand with a comfortable margin of safety, this ratio of deer to cougar tells a more fundamental story. Whether the measure be energy, biomass, or numbers, there is always a marked decrease in absolute numbers of predators as contrasted with their prey. This applies to all levels in the food web: plant to herbivore, herbivore to carnivore, and, indeed, from one carnivore to another. See page 225 for food pyramid diagrams.

The contest between cougar and deer, as told by Victor Cahalane in his *Mammals of North America* (1961:264), is one of wiliness in both potential victim and its stalker. The watchfulness and escape behavior in the deer are a near match for the hunting prowess of the cougar; indeed, the cougar fails to catch its prey at least two out of every three tries. After the surprise of attack is gone the cougar makes only a fitful attempt to chase its quarry, so fleet is the deer.

In 1968 game biologists estimated that there were about four to five hundred cougar roaming their miles-wide territories throughout the wilder areas of the state. The most recent census (1985) is up to fifteen hundred animals, based on county-by-county "harvest" figures. The discrepancy between five hundred and fifteen hundred is probably more a product of better information than real increase in population numbers. Estimates are hard to come by for the number in western Washington, where there may be as many as five hundred individuals, with most of these on the Olympic Peninsula.

The intervention of humans in the balance between prey and predator in the Olympics led to unexpected consequences. In 1904 a bounty was placed on cougar. Then in 1906, a ten-year ban on the killing of elk was initiated. These measures were taken to restore the apparently dwindling numbers of Olympic elk. In 1909 additional protection was afforded the elk by establishing the Mount Olympus National Monument (a forerunner of the present Olympic National Park). By 1915, signs of elk overpopulation and food shortage became evident. The strained links in the food chain were rattled loudly enough for game biologists to take another look at the management of elk in the Olympics. In 1961 bounty payments on cougar were halted, and in 1966 this native predator was classed as a game animal.[3] With these partial measures the cougar was afforded a modicum of protection. If it can avoid the dogs and guns of hunters as well as elude other human influences on its natural habits, the cougar may survive. The Washington State Department of Wildlife figures do allow us to infer that an increase in numbers of cougar is occurring, beginning from about 1965 to the present. This elegant animal, so superbly shaped and powered for its natural predatory function, should continue to be a working partner in perpetuating the natural economy of the forest ecosystems.

It is tempting to read simple cause-and-effect into the coincidence between the decrease of cougars by bounty hunters and the trend to overpopulation of the elk. The classic case of the Kaibab

3. During the many years of cougar bounty the annual "harvest" (a euphemism for kill) ranged from 40 to 250; the peak years were in the mid-1940s. At present, about 200 cougar a year are killed by hunters, a harvest closely scrutinized by the Department of Wildlife.

deer in northern Arizona, when carefully reinvestigated, shows the fallacy of a simple explanation. The prevailing dogma has been that populations of mule deer living on the Kaibab Plateau along the North Rim of the Grand Canyon were regulated at an optimal number by their natural predators, mainly cougar and coyotes. Then humans intervened to protect the deer by eliminating the predators. The result was an epidemic outbreak of deer that oversaturated their environment, with 60 percent of the mushrooming number of deer dead from starvation and disease in the severe winters of 1925 and 1926. The intended lesson from this presumed conflict between human intervention and natural balance struck between prey and predator was simple. Serious and often disastrous consequences will result from interference with the harmonious equilibrium of an ecosystem.

But those who used this example and then drew a conventional conclusion had not checked the original data or reviewed all the circumstances attending the buildup and crash of the deer populations. A second look was taken by Graeme Caughley (1970). He began with the undeniable fact that deer populations did increase and then suffered a dramatic decline following overgrazing of the habitat. But the estimates of population sizes at that time ranged from 30,000 to 100,000, not very reliable data to begin with. Moreover, although Caughley recognized that predator extermination was current at the time of the deer increase, cattle and sheep were also removed from the Kaibab area. The removal of domesticated browsers and grazers could have reduced the herbivore pressure on the vegetation, thus providing deer with greater food supply. Caughley concluded that "data on the Kaibab deer herd . . . are unreliable and inconsistent, and the factors that may have resulted in an upsurge of deer are hopelessly confounded" (1970:56).

The Kaibab deer story emphasizes the need for caution in drawing conclusions from ecological coincidences. In the case of the elk overpopulation and cougar bounty hunters on the Olympic Peninsula, it would be oversimplifying to say that decrease in cougar numbers caused increases in the elk population. Fire, logging, differences in weather from year to year, changes in land use and management, all may have contributed to the overbrowsed conditions and consequent elk starvation in the second decade of this century.

What behavioral traits does the cougar have that secure for it some hope of survival in the chancey game of life? The animal is largely a nocturnal hunter, neatly timing its food-getting activities with the active hours for deer, its major prey. The home ranges of the cougar lie in the wild, remote parts of Washington State. Within wilderness, the cougar stakes out an immense territory for hunting, roaming areas as large as fifty square miles. Only during mating periods is the solitude of the lone animal broken. The mating ritual lasts a scant two weeks. After the union is consummated, mates behave with hostility toward each other. The average litter will have up to three kittens. After initial and intensive maternal care, the kittens can handle food from fresh kills brought in by the mother, and by two months or so the lively youngsters go out hunting with their mother. The mother-offspring tie may last up to two years, while the young cats learn all they can about cougar ways of survival. This is a good beginning for a life of up to a dozen or more years.

The cougar has been branded a killer of humans and domestic animals. However, the typical animal shuns people and therefore is usually remote from cattle and sheep. Some livestock, though, are killed by cougars, and there are a few authenticated stories of cougars killing people. Most of the latter incidents involved older animals, which were incapable of killing wild game, or else a cougar carrying the rabies virus (probably acquired from dogs). Cougar experts have also attributed some attacks on humans to mistaken identity: a man wearing a fur jacket is taken for a prey animal. Humans rarely encounter cougars in the wild—an encounter is brief, with both parties going in opposite directions! No doubt some animals learn to prey on livestock; open-range cattle, sheep, and even horses have been known to succumb to those occasional "killer" animals that have acquired a taste for easy flesh.

Cougar (Felis concolor)

As to the cougar's presumed exorbitant inroads on deer populations, we have already put that exaggeration in proper perspective. And to the fact that the deer versus cougar balances are nicely struck, we can add that no more than 50 percent of the adult cougar's diet is venison; the balance is taken from the flesh of small animals like skunks, dogs, and porcupines. There is increasing recognition on the part of game biologists and others that cougars should be permitted a continuing place in the ecological firmament. New and more enlightened laws of protection should aid the animal's survival. The long-range threat to cougar existence is the year-by-year disruption of more and more of its habitat. Everywhere throughout its vast range—from the Strait of Magellan to Canada—areas of desert, forest, scrub, and jungle are succumbing to axe and bulldozer, and cougar habitat is forever lost.

Small Herbivorous Mammals: Squirrels, Mountain Beaver, Mice, and Other Rodent Kin

No other group of vertebrate mammals better deserves the herbivore label than does the great group of rodents. What they may lack in size and elegance, rodents make up for in sheer numbers and effective ways of making "flesh from grass." Myriad kinds of rodents find sustenance in the vegetation of nearly every land mass on our planet, and yet all are equipped with the same basic implements for feeding. Four incisor teeth (two upper and two lower) make gnawing on or chiseling away at bark, roots, succulent stems, leaves, and seed a ceaseless and efficient business. The roster of rodents in the lowlands of the Pacific Northwest is impressive even when expressed only in the variety of rodent ways of doing business. Chipmunks, squirrels, mice, rats, beaver, voles, moles, and gophers are familiar names that tell the patterns of "making out" in a vegetarian's world.

The quantity of rodent biomass that scurries, burrows, jumps, and even glides through the forest biome must be impressive. No census exists of the total populations of all kinds of Puget Sound rodents, but it is safe to guess that their total biomass would exceed the total for the bigger, more spectacular herbivores like deer and elk. I have chosen three very different rodent species to illustrate the central position of the rodent clan in the forest food web.

The mountain beaver, *Aplodontia rufa*, is a true prototype rodent. The ancestry of this shy creature goes back to the beginning of the Tertiary, at a time when the land was subtropical and the dog-sized ancestor of the modern horse had begun to make its way up the evolutionary tree. A vegetarian with unspecialized structure and behavior can be counted on to be successful, and *Aplodontia* is no

Mountain beaver or sewellel (Aplodontia rufa), a most primitive rodent, is restricted to humid parts of western North America from coastal California to southern British Columbia. And it harbors the largest flea in the insect kingdom! (Photo by Michael Wooton.)

exception. About the size of a cottontail rabbit, this fur-bearer gnaws its way through the greenery that so commonly blankets the ground in logged-over and other scrub lands in Puget country. The brushy slopes and damp alder bottoms abound with their burrows, pitfalls for anyone who stumbles through the underbrush jungle. Their tunnels are not especially engineered for the harvest of roots. Rather, the mountain beaver relishes only succulent stems and leaves above ground. Probably the tunnels are simply the safest way for the little beast to traverse dangerous terrain where predators are poised. The mountain beaver emerges from its burrow at will to sample all manner of vegetation. Sometimes the burrows are close enough to water that they become underground water mains. Yet apparently the animals are not evicted by their self-made subterranean canals. Though the animal may fell a small tree in the manner of a true beaver, it prefers bracken shoots, salal, alder, and other kinds of brush plants. Apart from the occasional tree-felling, there is no good reason to call *Aplodontia* the mountain beaver, since it is scarcely beaverlike in size, habit, or body form, and is less often in the mountains than in the lowlands. In fact, the catalogue of common names for *Aplodontia* is a list of misnomers. Sewellel, mountain boomer, chehalis, whistler—none of these reflects the nature of the animal. As suburbia encroaches on secondgrowth forest and abandoned farmland, the mountain beaver and humans cross paths of incompatibility. A vegetable garden or a

Douglas fir sapling responds with multiple shoots after being cut near ground level by a mountain beaver. (Photo by Michael Wooton.)

Deer mouse (Peromyscus maniculatus). (Drawing by Linda Wilkinson.)

back yard of shrubs and annual plants may border on a brushy woodlot home of *Aplodontia*. Many gardeners have fed mountain beavers their hard-won vegetables or ornamental plants. It is to be hoped, though, that this direct descendent of Mesozoic rodents will not be exterminated.[4]

The word "mouse" most likely evokes images of furry kitchen scavengers, or of cabins and campsites in the woods plundered of accessible food (with little "calling cards" left as recycled tokens of the visit), or a host of other comic or unsavory impressions. Yet our most common native mouse, the deer (or white-footed) mouse, *Peromyscus maniculatus,* hardly deserves the stigma of human disgust, for it is fastidious in its personal grooming, is harmless, and may even make a tractable pet. From central Alaska to Mexico City and nearly all lowland habitats from the Atlantic to the Pacific define the almost continuous and vast range of this species. Though there are fifty-five species of *Peromyscus* in the world, none is so widespread, common, and environmentally versatile as *P. maniculatus*. This species is recognized by its large membranous ears and unusually long tail. Though superficially like the house mouse (*Mus musculus*), that bold urban pest imported from Europe, the deer mouse is shy, clean, and downright engaging in its habits. Mostly nocturnal, deer mice are often met scurrying across trails on the forest floor late at night. Not infrequently they enter cabins and other human habitations in search of food. In such close quarters their shrill buzzing and rapid thumping with the feet raise a noise that outshadows their size and presence. As with most rodents, deer mice eat small seeds of almost any kind of plant. Though

4. A curious footnote to the mountain beaver story: this singular relic of the Tertiary sports a record-breaking parasite. The world's largest flea (*Hystrichopsylla schefferi*), 6–8 mm. long, lives exclusively on *Aplodontia*. Its species name commemorates the father of Puget Sound naturalist Victor Scheffer; Theo Scheffer, a fine naturalist in his own right, did the definitive study on the mountain beaver in the 1920s (T. Scheffer 1929).

Deer mice in typical poses in an opening in the woods. (Drawing by Linda Wilkinson.)

largely herbivorous, they do feed on adult and larval insects, and even are known to eat their own kind and to scavenge the carcasses of larger vertebrates. Only one species of mouse native to Washington is largely carnivorous: the grasshopper mouse lives on insects and spiders, though it may include the deer mouse occasionally in its diet.

More than any other North American mammal, the white-footed deer mouse has commanded the attention of biologists studying the dynamics of evolution. Darwinian change results from the processes of mutation and recombination of hereditary elements (genes), followed by the retention or rejection of those genes by the selective action of the environment. The accumulated minute changes in heredity are then fashioned into detectable, adaptive modes of life. All these aspects of change operate at the level of populations, well within the bounds of what the naturalist may define as a species. Since a wide-ranging species like *Peromyscus maniculatus* occurs in many different environments, the particular local agents of natural selection will yield different adaptive modes—populations uniquely fitted to local or regional habitat conditions. Over sixty variants or geographic races have been designated for this single successful species, one large, presumably interfertile community of individuals that share in a common reservoir of genes.

The small (microevolutionary) events that initiate a distinctive geographic or ecological race can be any unique and discontinuous factors of environment: climate, soil or vegetation differences, or nature of the predator pressure on populations of the deer mouse.

The classic studies of deer mice by Sumner (1932) and Dice (1940) revealed both gradual and abrupt separation into races in response to equally gradual or abrupt environmental conditions. Painstaking observation and experiment have confirmed the hypothesis that these racial differences are evolutionary responses in the Darwinian mode: the preservation of favored heritable variants by natural selection. The deer mouse not only holds an influential position in the economy of the region's habitats, but it has also made a contribution toward testing evolutionary theory.

Tree Squirrels: Arboreal Herbivores in the Lowland Ecosystem

More noticeable a group of rodents than mice are the tree squirrels of lowland forests. There are both native and introduced tree squirrels in western Washington. One of the introduced tree squirrels is more than familiar to urbanites. The eastern gray squirrel (*Sciurus caroliniensis hypophaeus*) is a pest in gardens and parks, though it does give us easy contact with a clan of tree squirrels (the North American genus *Sciurus*) that is ordinarily shy of city and suburban life. But the price paid for the aesthetics of squirrels in town is more than enough for some gardeners. Planted seed, buds of all kinds of plants, roots, bulbs, and tubers of ornamentals are all on the gray squirrel's menu. Earl Larrison defends their presence: "This was a commendable introduction, as the Western Gray Squirrel, native to certain areas of the state, seems not to care for urban life. The eastern squirrel, therefore, affords countless thousands of persons the opportunity to see at least one species of the tree squirrel genus, *Sciurus*, North America's largest and finest group of squirrels" (1970:71). But I hear contrary testimonials from those who see gardens and parks looted by these bushy-tailed marauders. As is true of so many introduced plants and animals, the eastern gray squirrel finds a wholly unoccupied niche to which it easily acclimates; so, pest or prize, it is probably here to stay.

Of the two native squirrels, by far the most common in the area is the chickaree or Douglas squirrel (*Tamiasciurus douglasii*). Its less common counterpart is the western gray squirrel (*Sciurus griseus griseus*). The two species illustrate a neat partitioning of the available environment in terms of food and habitat. The western gray squirrel occupies a niche that closely conforms to the distributional range of the Garry oak (*Quercus garryana*). In fact, this squirrel comes only as far north as the northern limit of the continuous distribution of the oak, the gravelly prairies just south of Tacoma. It does not occur in the discontinuous patches of oak to the north. Why this is true is one of those perennial mysteries of plant and animal distribution. Acorns and pine seeds are the choicest of

The raccoon is a common smallish carnivore of the lowlands. It is seen in rural to highly urban habitats and is well-known for its catholic tastes in food, captured or scavenged.

foods for this squirrel, but a variety of other plant foods round out its diet. Theo Scheffer, Northwest naturalist, pointed out years ago that the western gray squirrel may contribute to the molding of the natural landscape by its particular predations (1952). It avidly seeks the tender cambial layer within the bark of Douglas fir and yellow pine. By girdling saplings, the gray squirrel thus inadvertently helps keep conifers from encroaching on the oak prairies of Pierce and Thurston counties.

The chickaree or Douglas squirrel is truly at home in the coniferous forests of Puget Sound. Where the gray squirrel is a success in the oak prairie habitat, the Douglas squirrel thrives on reproductive output of cone-bearing trees. In fact, the whole pattern of survival for the gray squirrel would lead to its downfall in dense coniferous forests. Its habit of caching food items one at a time and its lesser agility make the gray squirrel ready prey to martens and other coniferous forest predators. The gray squirrel just cannot make it in Douglas squirrel country, though there are records of its trying.

The noisy scolding of the little brown Douglas squirrel is a familiar sound in the woods, especially away from urban disturbance. Douglas squirrels are smaller than other tree squirrels and are distinguished by their dusky olive back and orangish-yellow underparts. From midsummer to fall, their chattering call and busy harvest activity enlivens the forest scene. The results of their summer harvest are the large caches of cones in stumps, under logs, or even in slow-moving streams. During winter they have an easy trip from the nest (often an abandoned woodpecker's hole in a tree) down through a tunnel in the snow to the centralized cache. If the gray squirrel's habitat is snowbound, on the other hand, it must search under snow for the single food items it cached in the soil, thus exposing itself to predation. In a nutshell, a niche is a set of survival strategies optimally fashioned for one kind of organism; just one part of that strategy cannot be exploited by another, though similar, species with any hope of long-term success.

Accounts of the natural history of most small mammals of this region are the meager sums of random observations made by different naturalists over the years. Most records are barely more than the identification and classification of kinds of animals with some scant additional notes on their habits and habitats. But for the Douglas squirrel, we have a goldmine of recent information on behavior, life history, and food preferences, in the thorough studies of Chris Smith. Smith's "Interspecific Competition in the Genus of Tree Squirrels, *Tamiasciurus*" (1965) states a problem fundamental in ecology: How do two closely related species that may live in the same area partition the life-sustaining resources of their shared

The Douglas squirrel, or chickaree (Tamiasciurus douglasii), *is a prodigious consumer of cones, here eating a Douglas fir cone. (Drawing by Linda Wilkinson.)*

habitat? The red squirrel (*Tamiasciurus hudsonicus*) and the Douglas squirrel (*T. douglasii*) can coexist in certain areas of the Pacific Northwest, though mostly to the north and northeast of the Puget Sound area. In order to answer the question he raises, Smith needed to know how each species utilized the resources of its environment when not overlapping in the geography of their distributions.

Tree squirrels, like most mammals, have developed a particular communal behavior as an adaptive response to the challenges of survival. The social organization in Douglas squirrel populations emphasizes a specific pattern of territoriality and a breeding behavior that constitutes a finely tuned adjustment to their coniferous forest habitat. Each individual squirrel, male or female, stakes out a defensible territory of from about one-half to three acres in extent.

Territories are actively defended by the chasing of intruders and/or by intimidation with territorial and aggressive calls. The territorial call is also used to advertise ownership when there is no immediate threat. The boundary of a territory can often be plotted accurately to within ten feet by marking the spot from which the owner gives its territorial calls. The ownership of the major cone-bearing trees near a boundary appears to be understood by both the owner and its neighbor. (Smith 1965:15)

The resource defended within a territory by a single Douglas squirrel is the seed cones of Douglas fir (or other conifer), which can be stored over winter. In fact the importance of correlating the seed cone resource with territory is borne out by exceptional occurrences of the breakdown of the usual territorial defenses. On numerous occasions, Smith found pairs of Douglas squirrels foraging in the same tree, but their appetites were being satisfied not by seed cones, but by pollen cones, a food resource that cannot be stored.

Territorial defense is achieved by both aggressive actions and by distinctive calls. The territorial call is one of five distinct sound patterns in the vocal repertoire of the squirrel. It serves both to advertise ownership of the territory and to warn other squirrels seeking to contest ownership of the territory. The other distinctive vocalizations perform other functions of social behavior, such as protection against predators (the alarm call), warning other squirrels of the aggressive intent of the caller (the aggressive calls, both loud and soft), and the appeasing call used during breeding periods by males approaching a female.

Since individuals, male or female, aggressively defend their own territorial resources, such behavior, if rigorously followed, would deny the species the opportunity for perpetuation. Territoriality must break down temporarily to allow for breeding, and it does so in a characteristic manner. A female in heat allows males to approach her within her territory. Though several males will gather for the occasion, one male succeeds as her mate by warding off other males. This breakdown of territoriality, then, coincides with the period of heat in the female, lasting only for a few days.

The forest habitat is a precarious world for squirrels. They are continually confronted with the dangers of predation, as well as challenged by territorial aggression, competition for mates, and a finite and varying supply of food. Food-getting consumes most of the time and energy in a squirrel's daily routine. To determine how food consumption balances with time and energy spent in food-getting by the busy squirrel, Chris Smith examined in great detail the food resource (energy-rich cones, fleshy fungi, etc.) and the feeding activities of the squirrel. Douglas fir cones are a rich source of squirrel energy. Other cones, such as lodgepole pine and ponderosa pine, are harder to utilize, a point worthy of closer scrutiny a bit later. Size of a stable territory conforms to an area of forest that would supply 0.7 to 2.9 times the annual energy needs for the occupant of that territory. Thus territorial size is likely to be adjusted to the amount of available food; this can be a highly variable value. In a poor cone year, territory size should increase. In years of cone

Douglas squirrel. (Drawing by Libby Mills.)

crop failure the territory owners may even emigrate to other areas. Moreover, the age, density, and type of the forest stand will influence size of territory.

These dynamic interactions between herbivore and plant food resource are surely the products of some parallel evolutionary changes in both the eater and the eaten. Smith conjectures that the conifer food resource may have evolved "strategies" to reduce the loss of cones through predation by squirrels. One strategy would be to have unpredictable cone crops (some good and some bad years) built into the genetic program of Douglas fir. Another likely "antiherbivore strategy," he suggests, involves various impediments to cone harvesting and seed extraction evolved by the conifer species so as to force the squirrels into spending untenable amounts of time and energy in food extraction. The cones of lodgepole pine and ponderosa pine have prickles, tough and protective cone tissue around the seeds, and are placed at difficult-to-chew positions on the twig. But antiherbivore strategies are likely to be matched with adaptive changes in the herbivores, too, so that the coevolutionary "race" seems not to have a winner.

The interconnectedness of things—living and inanimate—is beautifully revealed in the story of the northern flying squirrel (*Glaucomys sabrinus*) and its environment. Hardly a flier, the flying squirrel is largely arboreal (and nocturnal) and can glide from branch to branch in old-growth forests. Its primary foods are in the trees (foliose lichens in winter) and on or in the ground in summer and fall (underground fungi akin to truffles). We have already alluded to the conifer-fungus connection: the mycorrhizal link between trees and mushrooms. This is a system of mutual aid in which tree roots and fungi, intimately interwoven, nourish and water each other. But who spreads around the fungal spores to ensure new mycorrhizal linkages? Flying squirrels, of course, along with other herbivores. This story is fully told in Chris Maser's provocative book, *The Redesigned Forest* (1988).

Sluggish Herbivores

To say that slugs are not everybody's favorite animals is something of an understatement. Downright disgusting to most humans, slugs are not even avidly sought after by predators—birds, frogs, and snakes. Yet their very unpalatability is part of their success story. Slugs, like their close kin the snails and many of their marine relatives (whelks, limpets, clams, and oysters), have secured for themselves sure and unique niches over most of the world.

Not only are slugs efficient herbivores in their native haunts, those species transplanted to new habitats often successfully establish themselves—weeds, in a word! Our own urban landscape is infested with at least three common species of slugs, all introduced from Europe. The most ubiquitous of these introductions, *Arion ater* (the large black slug of gardens) is probably the one memorialized in Theodore Roethke's poem:

> When I slip, just lightly, in the dark,
> I know it isn't a wet leaf,
> But you, loose toe from the old life,
> The cold slime come into being,
> A fat, five-inch appendage
> Creeping slowly over the wet grass,
> Eating the heart out of my garden.
> From *Words For the Wind*

Our one conspicuous native slug catches the eye as it inches along over the green forest floor. It is the banana slug, *Ariolimax columbianus*, busy from spring to fall, taking its tithe of the green luxuriance of forests. I shall come back to that tan "loose toe from the old life" in a moment, to fit it into our view of the forest ecosystem. But first a closer look at the general biology of those marvelously contrived compost-makers is in order.

Three cornerstones of slug success are its mucus or slime production, its efficient food-getting mechanism, and its high reproductive potential. The protective mucus that covers the body and leaves a silvery trail is made in the bloodstream and is forced out of the circulatory system under pressure. Mucus prevents dehydration and serves as a lubricant when the slug is on the move, intensively so when courtship and mating are under way.

Slugs are outfitted with efficient devices for locating, "chewing," and digesting their vegetarian diet. As they glide over leafy ter-

The native banana slug (Ariolimax columbianus) *is a voracious herbivore, rasping its way through mostly native vegetation. Unlike the introduced slugs that abound in Puget country (e.g.,* Arion ater), *the banana slug is rarely found in gardens. (Photo by D. Herren.)*

ritory, they are able to distinguish edible from distasteful plants. What gardener has not despaired of trying to maintain some choice plant against the selective feeding of the choosy slug! The sensuously probing tentacles serve triple duty in feeding, smelling, and "seeing" slug habitat. Probably the sense of smell is the most acute, so that a slug can bypass plants with noxious chemicals to concentrate on safer food.

Common to most gastropod molluscs (slugs and snails) is the rasping tonguelike organ, the radula. Armed with thousands of tiny burs or "teeth," the renewable radula scrapes plant food into tiny digestible bits. Herbivory is then consummated by an efficient digestive system. And so again is played out the form and function theme: efficient implements to utilize a food resource, even if it means that the plant victims may be in someone's garden.

After feeding and growing all summer long, slugs mate. Wreathed in their mucus halo, two adult slugs attend to procreation in a most economical way. Both mates have male and female sex organs. Such hermaphroditism is frequent among mollusks, although reciprocal cross-fertilization rather than self-fertilization is the object. Sperm are exchanged during the slimy embrace, followed by internal fertilization and the eventual hatching of eggs already beginning development. A single slug can lay more than one thousand eggs in the fall, finding safe caches for them in the soil, under rocks, in rotting wood, or in vegetation. The embryonic progeny overwinter in a tough gelatinous or even calcareous shell of the egg until the warm days of spring. Thus, a season of successful grazing and growing is followed by a gilt-edged reproductive insurance for the future. For species of slugs that are "annuals," continuity demands the success of the egg-laying venture.

Our native banana slug seldom invades the urban garden. It eats a variety of forest plants, as well as mushrooms, fallen fruits, animal matter, and dung. Anyone who hikes the woodland trails has seen this five-inch long greenish-yellow "banana" fingering its way over the mossy forest floor.[5] Like their introduced relatives that have taken so well to urban garden greenery, the native *Ariolimax columbianus* has its food likes and dislikes. What they do find palatable, slugs eat voraciously; they recycle 11 percent of the forest biomass annually. Interactions between herbaceous "prey"—the plants—and the predator—the native slug—have been the object of intensive study by University of Washington biologists. The fascinating coevolutionary story featuring slugs and wild ginger was told in chapter 5.

A pair of native banana slugs exchanging sex cells (and genes). (Photo by Victor Scheffer.)

---

5. Another color phase with purplish spots is not infrequent.

Insects and the Forest Ecosystem

Nineteen seventy-three was a big year for outbreaks of tussock moths in Washington forests. Thousands of acres suffered severe tree loss through epidemic outbreaks of this little moth, which in the caterpillar stage feeds voraciously on Douglas fir needles. Other years, the chief insect pest of the forest may be the hemlock looper, the spruce budworm, or some other herbivore that attacks conifers. The many different kinds of insects that make their living off the biomass of the forest fill whole textbooks and keep forest entomologists busy year after year.

The economic impact of insect damage to forests can be staggeringly great, so it is important to understand the ecology of forest insects. Moreover, their role in the ecosystem dynamics of the forest has a fascination all its own. As the plant species native to our forest have evolved over geologic time, so have the countless kinds of insects, each adapting to some niche within the web of forest life. Herbivorous insects may be generalists, taking sustenance from a wide variety of plant hosts; others have taken the evolutionary pathway of narrow specialization by pinning their survival to close reliance on only one or a few host plant species. The pyramid of biomass—plants underpinning herbivores and herbivores feeding carnivores—is clearly illustrated by the pattern of insect life in the forest. Herbivorous insects, mainly either defoliators or eaters of bark, wood, or cones, form a massive tier of consumers astride the still more massive base of the pyramid—the primary producers, plants. The herbivorous insect tier of the biomass pyramid sustains a much lesser biomass of predacious insects, specialists in carnivory or parasitism on the flesh of herbivores. Insect-eating birds also must be figured into this carnivore tip of the pyramid (more about them later). Some carnivorous beetles and parasitic wasps that prey upon insect herbivores can serve as biological control agents of insect pests. But when the numbers of herbivores reach epidemic proportions, such biological control may be ineffectual.

Insects exploit the primary productivity of the forest in many different ways. For insects and other small animals, an individual tree of Douglas fir or western hemlock is a honeycomb of places to live (microhabitats) and ways to make a living (niches). Roots, trunk, branches, foliage, cones, all provide a coarse-grained partitioning of the living topography of the tree and thereby generate habitat diversity. These parts of the tree are further subdivided into places to live, eat, develop, and die, such as upper, middle, and lower levels of the main stem: crown, bole, and buttress; or branches and twigs; or outer and inner bark; or wood; or external as well as internal tissues of leaves (young and old); or cone scales versus young

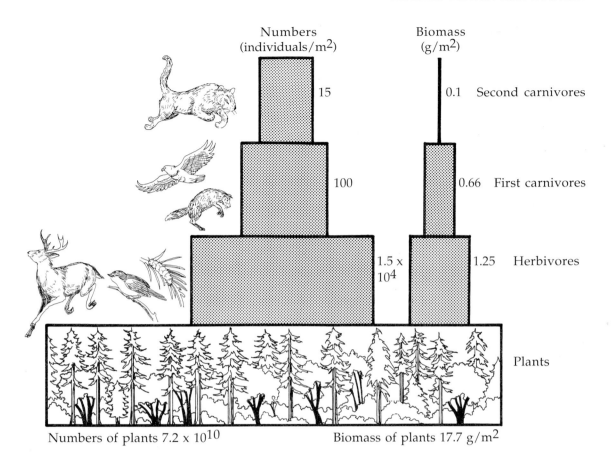

Numbers
(individuals/m^2)

Biomass
(g/m^2)

15 — 0.1 — Second carnivores

100 — 0.66 — First carnivores

1.5 x 10^4 — 1.25 — Herbivores

Plants

Numbers of plants 7.2 x 10^{10} Biomass of plants 17.7 g/m^2

Food pyramids dramatize the loss of matter and energy as plants (primary producers) are consumed by herbivores and they in turn are eaten by carnivores. One kind of food pyramid (center) portrays the diminishing numbers of organisms feeding on the living "tier" beneath them; the other (right) shows the relative volume of living substance (biomass) consumed. Both kinds of pyramids depend on the primary producer base—the lowland forest. (Drawing by Sandra Noel.)

or mature seeds; and so on. Thereby the topography and feeding resources of the host tree are further subdivided, providing a fine-grained environment for insects. Even the continuous rain of arboreal detritus (dead leaves, branches, bark, fallen cones, etc.) extends the niche opportunities to other insects, detritus feeders, adaptively distinct from those occupying the live tree.

To say that moths are the major defoliators of forest trees is subtly misleading. More precisely, moth species in the Order Lepidoptera (Class Insecta) go through a complex life history in which the larval stage, the caterpillar, is the voracious herbivore. The adult moth may not eat at all, or may find its nutrition harmlessly in floral nectar. The Douglas fir tussock moth (*Hemerocampa pseudotsugata*) is a prime example of defoliation-by-caterpillar. In the late summer, adult moths fulfill their only destiny: reproduction. Eggs are laid by the sedentary wingless female on top of the cocoon from which she has emerged. The egg masses are covered by a frothy white substance that the female mixes with hair from her abdomen. These conspicuous egg masses attached to empty cocoons are found on all parts of the tree and adjacent shrubs. The small hairy

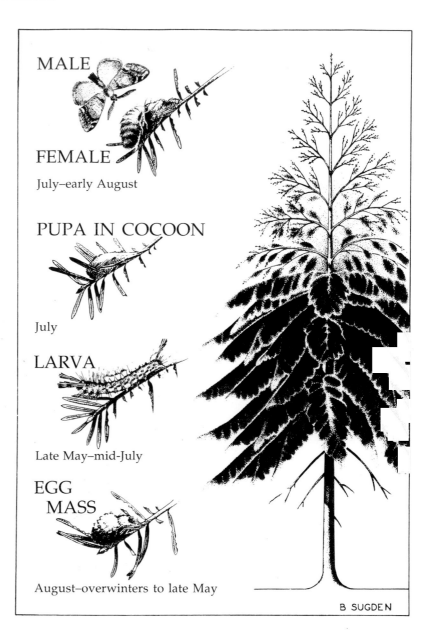

MALE

FEMALE

July–early August

PUPA IN COCOON

July

LARVA

Late May–mid-July

EGG
MASS

August–overwinters to late May

B SUGDEN

Life cycle of Douglas fir tussock moth,
a major defoliator of a variety of conifers.

caterpillars emerge from the eggs in late spring to feed and grow. The caterpillars first attack emerging new foliage by girdling the base of the expanding leaf buds. The small growing larvae can easily be spread by gravity and wind to other parts of the tree where feeding is resumed. Tussock moth caterpillars on the move create a remarkable pattern in the forest. They swing into new sites on long silken threads that form a meshwork of webbing in the forest.

At maturity, the caterpillars are conspicuous and colorful. Forest entomologist F. P. Keen writes:

> When full grown they are from 3/4 to 1 inch long, with gray or light-brown bodies and black shiny heads. Two long brushes, or pencils, of black hairs fully 1/4 inch long, suggest horns, directly behind the head, and a similar but longer tuft is at the posterior of the body. On the upper side of the first four and on the last abdominal segments are dense, light-brown, or cream-colored tufts of hairs about 1/16th inch long, and numerous red spots. Along the sides of the body are somewhat broken, narrow, orange stripes, while the lower side of the body is nearly naked, with the prolegs only sparsely covered with hairs. (1952:92)

At times of epidemic outbreaks, the huge numbers of caterpillars do an enormous amount of damage to Douglas fir stands. As defoliation begins from the top of the tree downward, a heavy infestation is seen by the airborne observer as a scorched-brown swath through the forest. And on the ground, one forester tells me that a massive outbreak is actually audible: the sound of caterpillars eating in unison!

Another defoliator, the hemlock looper, provides an instructive set of contrasts with the tussock moth. Though the preferred host of the hemlock looper is western hemlock, in epidemic outbreaks foliage of all vegetation may be eaten. Eggs on the bark, branches, and twigs hatch in spring to produce 1/4-inch long larvae that climb into leafy branchlets high in the tree. By midsummer, the larvae are 1-1/2 inches long and take a larger toll of hemlock foliage. At this stage the looper lives up to its name as a greenish-brown, diamond-marked "inch worm" that propels itself along a twig by a looping "gait."

Like the tussock moth, larvae of the hemlock looper can lower themselves into new feeding territory by means of silken webs. An epidemic outbreak may turn the forest beneath the canopy and ground vegetation into one massive cobweb. After pupating in the late summer—an event of startling transformation from caterpillar into moth—the adult hemlock looper moths emerge from pupa cases, unprotected by a cocoon. Both sexes are capable of flight; they mate, lay eggs, and do nothing more. As eggs, the new generation is poised for next season's herbivory. Keen describes the look of a forest when adult looper populations have reached explosive proportions: "During an epidemic [the moths] are so abundant as to give the impression of a snowstorm in the woods; creeks, springs, and rivers are covered with the dead bodies, and tree trunks are plastered with them until heavy rains wash them into the ground or carry them away" (Keen 1952:99).

Keen tells of a similar insect mass "fallout" in Colorado:

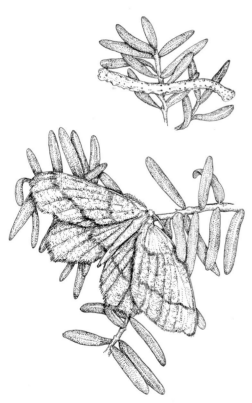

Larva (caterpillar) and adult of the western hemlock looper. The larvae feed on a variety of conifers, especially devastating to western hemlock. (Rendering by Sandra Noel.)

During the flight period of 1949, the air was so full of [Engelmann spruce] beetles that the ones that happened to fall into a small lake in the infested area and washed ashore (although only a minor fraction of the total flight) were so numerous as to form a drift of dead beetles a foot deep, 6 feet wide, and 2 miles long. Those flying southeast over 18 miles of open country settled on a plateau of previously uninfested forest and killed 400,000 trees in one mass attack.

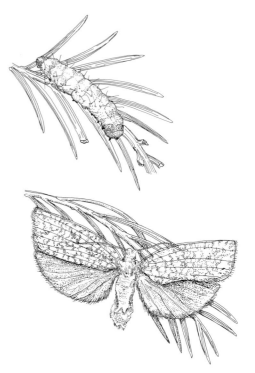

In the mid-1970s, spruce budworm (*Choristoneura fumiferana*) epidemics ran a close second to those of the tussock moth in devastating Washington forests. Driving over almost any of the highway passes east of the Cascade crest, travelers saw miles of brown forest. Although pines were spared, vast acreages of Douglas fir, all of the true fir species (except noble fir), larch, and Engelmann spruce were badly defoliated by the spruce budworm. Spruce budworm is the caterpillar stage of a small moth, grayish with brown markings. The moths emerge from pupal cases in the summer and soon lay eggs on conifer foliage. In about ten days the young caterpillars emerge, only to envelop themselves in a hibernating shroud until the next spring. Then the real damage begins: the caterpillars begin feeding on the tender young needles just starting growth. The loss of trees of all age classes can be tremendous. For those only damaged by the budworm predation, growth and yield will be severely curtailed. Also many weakened trees become part of the total mortality in later years as they are most subject to other types of infestation. Spruce budworm had not gone on a rampage in the Puget Sound basin during that outbreak.

An entirely different niche is exploited by bark beetles and their kin. Many different species of Coleoptera (beetles with tough outer wings) live in the nutritive inner bark of all our species of conifers. Their larvae or grubs thrive on the tender and rich substance of food-conducting and growth tissues (phloem and cambium) just outside the sapwood of trees. Though outward symptoms of infection show only a general debility of crown and canopy foliage, the best evidence of their activity is a symmetrical network of galleries and tunnels engraved within the inner bark and adjacent sapwood. The labyrinth of tunnels and galleries are the works of both adults and larvae. Male and female adult beetles bore their way into the inner bark, depositing boring dust and excrement behind them; egg galleries are then excavated. Larvae hatched from eggs are veritable pulp makers—pale legless creatures, all head and chewing apparatus. They begin their own system of galleries as they consume bark and grow to pupal stage. The miracle of metamorphosis now turns a wormlike grub into a shiny black beetle. Adult beetles soon emerge to attack new host trees, to exploit other parts of the same tree, or to drop to the ground where they over-

Spruce budworm (left, top), the larval stage of the adult budworm moth (left, center), is a voracious feeder on buds and foliage of mostly spruce, true firs, and Douglas fir. (Rendering by Sandra Noel.)

Galleries on the surface of sapwood formed by bark beetles. (Photo by Bob and Ira Spring.)

winter. And thus begins another round of infection, with the added prospect of more progeny.

Inner bark must be a secure microhabitat to support so many insect species. Every species of conifer and hardwood has the potential of having several species of bark-eating predators, not just one. And the tree biomass devoured is gargantuan. The annual loss of timber in all the western states to bark beetles is estimated at 2.8 billion board feet. Healthy trees under normal, nonepidemic conditions can resist beetle infection. Apparently the flow of pitch in the inner bark of vigorous trees repels the adult beetle invader. Dead or dying trees, weakened by defoliating insects, fire, blowdowns, or adverse climatic effects, are easy prey to beetle infestations.

The cyclical or even capricious fluctuations in numbers of forest insects are classic problems for biologists who study the dynamics of populations. The population ecologist uses the census data of the forest entomologist as a basis for constructing mathematical models of rise and fall of insect populations. All known physical variables of environment (light, temperature, moisture) as well as biological variables can be evaluated simultaneously with population numbers to project a given state of the population. Usually such predictive models are tested with the aid of computers; in fact, the exercise of forecasting population potentials—outbreak or just steady state—is called computer simulation. What has been done for forest insects can now be fruitfully applied to other types of populations on a global scale. The technique lends itself to forecasting the consequences of manipulating physical and biotic resources in ecosystems dominated by humans. Some day political decisions and drastic socioeconomic changes in human ecosystems will proceed from this kind of systems forecasting.

Knowing the quality of the vegetation and its physical setting is critical for predicting the dynamics of insect populations. The kinds of plant species present (trees, shrubs, and subordinate plant life) and their relative abundances determine the presence and abundance of herbivores. The more diverse in composition is the forest, the more varied the insect fauna, both carnivorous and herbivorous species and their vertebrate predators, especially birds. A forest with only a single dominant tree species and scant variety in the understory flora is more likely to be the scene of an epidemic outbreak than a species-rich ecosystem where population numbers of one species may be regulated by competition with another. The vitality of the forest plant community also may affect the way an insect population grows. That older forests are more susceptible to insect attack than younger stands is a myth that seems to die hard. Vigor of the forest, rather than age per se, is probably the key determinant of susceptibility. Disturbance, natural or anthropogenic, of the forest tree community can accelerate insect predation on the weakened trees. Fire-damaged or wind-thrown trees as well as logged forests are often the sites of epidemic outbreaks. In the physical environment, climate is overriding in its capacity to effect rates of increase in insect populations. Variations in temperature, moisture, and drought serve to promote or inhibit population trends.

Most insect populations are maintained at nonepidemic levels in the forest due to the interaction of any or all of the influences just discussed. Yet all organisms are inherently bent on acting out the compound interest law of increasing their numbers exponentially. This evolved reproductive stratagem is called the *intrinsic rate of natural increase,* or the *biotic potential.* Though it may differ in degree for different species—birds with three to five eggs per female per season versus the hemlock looper with one hundred eggs—the reproductive potential, if realized, could exhaust the species' environmental resources. Unlimited exponential increase is never realized, since the food resource *carrying capacity* is eliminated first. Other checks on population increase (collectively called *environmental resistance*) serve to dampen or wholly check the intrinsic rate of natural increase. For herbivorous insects, these environmental checks are usually climate, parasites, predators, and disease. Hypothetical growth curves can illustrate alternative outcomes that depend on these several variant factors:

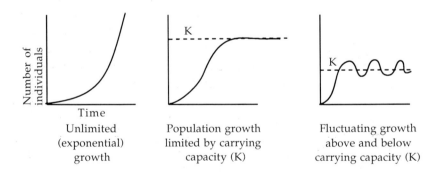

Unlimited (exponential) growth	Population growth limited by carrying capacity (K)	Fluctuating growth above and below carrying capacity (K)

Ecologists may still argue over details of such population trends. They will differ on whether the significant environmental resistance is a function of density in numbers of the population (crowding, stress, predation, parasites, etc.) or is imposed independent of density in population numbers and thus is under external controls of climate and other physical causes. In an ecologist's terms, density-dependent or density-independent controls may be difficult to distinguish. But the big truth is there for all to see. The growth potential of populations puts pressure on the environmental resistance, and vice versa. When environmental resistance is weakened, the growth curve will rise until another level of resistance is met. Remove a predator, weaken the resistance of the host tree, or have an unseasonably mild regime of climate and the population explodes. The question facing forest managers then becomes: Can we afford to delay remedial action (use of control measures such as pesticides, etc.) until some other environmental resistance heads off the outburst of population growth by the forest insect? Considerable damage to a forest may occur before self-arrest sets in.

The same dilemma confronts us now on a global scale. The human potential for increase has taken an alarming course. Shall we wait for environmental resistance in the form of famine, disease, and other more psychosocial disruptions to drastically cut off our own biotic potential? Or shall we seize the chance that is not available to other animals, to control our own population numbers before the apocalyptic controls by natural causes take over? It may seem a far cry from hemlock loopers to humans, but both share in the same fates that are innate in the biological urge to multiply. The human species cannot afford to forget the lessons that can be read from outbreaks of forest insect pests.

Not all insects conflict with man. Many lead innocuous, yet fascinating lives (see the stories about "ant plants" in chapter 5). Ants of the forest floor have adapted their food habits to seeds of certain plants, and in turn the seeds have evolved responses to ant behavior. Seeds of forest-floor plants like the bleeding heart (*Dicentra formosa*), inside-out flower (*Vancouveria hexandra*), and trillium (*Trillium ovatum*) produce an outgrowth (the elaiosome) on the surface of the seed that sends ants into a frenzy of activity. The nutritious and ornamental elaiosome is eaten by ants but only after the seeds are taken home to the ant nest. In this way seeds are dispersed away from the parent plant so as to provide a greater chance of germination and establishment of the progeny, away from competition with the parent plant. This remarkable device for assuring wide dispersal for seeds by ants is widespread in the plant world and is called *myrmechory* (ant dispersal).

Insects can be the "weeds" of the animal kingdom; they have accompanied settlers in all their ventures into the New World. Nearly all the introductions have been unintentional. Insect eggs or larvae have accompanied the shipments of grains and other foods, ornamental plants, ballast of ships, and other articles of transoceanic commerce. The list of introduced insects continues to grow as commerce and travel intensify. Of the hundreds of non-native insect species now in Washington State, there are 168 alien beetle species alone. Ordinarily the introduced species are most closely associated with urban life or with agriculture. But some introductions may move out into the wilds to compete with native insects or to find an unoccupied niche; once established they may affect the well-being of lowland forest ecosystems. A fairly recent introduction, the European pine shoot moth, has given foresters, nursery owners, and home gardeners a scare. The larvae of the moth bore into the new buds of ornamental pines (Scotch and mugho pines, in particular) to destroy completely the developing leaves. The caterpillar may then extend its destructive burrowing by eating its way as much as six inches down into the shoot tips. The net effect in the tree is to arrest shoot growth and cause deformities of the tip. The pest probably came west in infected nursery stock. At the moment it is widespread throughout western Washington but largely restricted to ornamental plantings of introduced pines. However, the threat of outbreaks into native pine stands is a real one, especially as control by pesticides under forest conditions is not practical.

Forest entomologists are not waiting until the pine shoot moth gets out of hand. A new approach in insect control is being tried on this potentially serious pest. The technique utilizes the potent capacity of female moths to lure males. The lure is a chemical one, produced by the female; all such substances are called pheromones (lit., carry + hormone) by the behavioral biologist. The biochemist can extract the native hormone from female moths, determine its chemical structure and synthesize it in the laboratory. This has been done for the sex attractant pheromone of the pine shoot moth. The synthetic pheromone can be used to locate new infestations and to aid eradication. Since the pheromone, placed in moth traps, attracts males, the captive moths can be sterilized and released to mate without issue; or they can be infected with a disease, or killed outright at the trap. The use of synthetic pheromones in insect control is just coming into its own. It may seem a cruel hoax to play sex tricks, but the need for control may override any humanitarian thought about sex life in moths. Moreover, this type of biological control of a pest has far less impact on the rest of the forest ecosystem than would a chemical pesticide.

Since most of the insects introduced have been species that compete with humans for plants of economic value, their control—if not eradication—is of prime importance. Chemical controls, though widely used, often have side effects that harm nontarget organisms. Biological controls, both intentionally applied and natural ones, are ideally the least ecologically disturbing. In addition to the novel use of pheromones described above, natural or introduced predators and parasites of particular insect pests may control pest numbers without any adverse effects on other organisms in the environment. The caterpillar of the cinnabar moth illustrates

The papery nests of hornets and yellowjackets are often seen in brushy areas; the encounter with the occupants may occur first and with sudden pain. (Photo by Josef Scaylea.)

the method of biological control, both its strengths and weaknesses. In this instance, the target pest is the undesirable plant, tansy ragwort (*Senecio jacobaea*). The moth caterpillars may seem to be effectively checking the spread of the weed around Puget Sound. But, again, "We can never merely do one thing." It now turns out that the insect feeds on native senecios, none of which are noxious weeds.

Bald eagle and its nest atop a snag. This elegant raptor is occasionally seen near shorelines of Puget Sound and major rivers. (Photo by Josef Scaylea.)

Birds in the Lowland Forest Ecosystem

The observer of wild nature can feel true solitude in the lowland forest. When far enough away from human activity there can be times when only the sound of vegetation breaks absolute silence— the gentle rustle of foliage in the wind or, if the imagination tempts, the sound of plants ever growing. Yet the animal world is there, eating, reproducing, and trying to avoid being eaten. Only the occasional petulant scolding of the Douglas squirrel or the sound of some bird breaks the silence. Though intermittent and momentary in revealing themselves, birds are there in good numbers. Nearly two hundred species are common residents or migrants in the Puget Sound basin. This figure includes birds of a variety of habitats: from the built environments of cities and towns, to coastlines, meadows, cutover brushlands, and old-growth forests. About forty different bird species have been recorded for forested land at low elevations; this estimate is based on censuses of birds observed in the brush and young trees of cutover land, partially logged fir-hemlock forest, and old-growth stands (see Table 18).

To see birds in the forest takes patience, keen hearing, and good field glasses. Only then does the forest take on a subtle animation: birds quietly going about their business of feeding, defending territories, mating, or avoiding predators. Some are hopping and flitting in short spurts as they forage in the underbrush, others are creeping up and down tree trunks seeking insect larvae of all kinds, and still others are feeding throughout the leafy canopy of the trees in prescribed patterns. Closer observation could disclose that foraging of birds in nearly every stratum or layer of the forest "architecture" is not random or accidental. Different species of birds tend to zero in on a particular sector of the structural pattern of the forest. The word "niche" is here most apt for the unique behavioral and life-support activity of a particular species of bird. It is this niche aspect of Puget Sound bird life that I want to pursue further.

Amateur bird-watchers have provided valuable data to professional biologists who study the relationships of birds to their habitat and niche. Annual bird census statistics often form the critical raw data for more intensive research programs. Lone amateurs, Audubon chapters, and other outdoor groups turn their many hours of bird-watching into valuable statistical summaries. In fact much of our present understanding of how birds parcel out resources and territory—their niche—is based on observations recorded by amateur naturalists.

How are the distinct survival requirements of different bird species in a forest satisfied? There are two approaches to how many bird niches there are in the forest. The most direct approach to bird ecology is to look for the available kinds of food and resources used for reproduction and for protection against predators. Another approach is more speculative and indirect, drawing upon the ideas of Darwinian evolution to explain how different adaptations to features of the habitat could have evolved. Though both approaches are needed to understand niche specialization and habitat preference, the first approach—examining the variety of available niches—will sharpen our view of why birds do what they do in such specific ways.

The most likely resources for forest-dwelling birds are seeds and insects. Now if all birds were able to eat all types of seeds or insects, then a given sample of forest might support only two kinds of birds, just seed and insect "generalists." The generalist behavior is not what we commonly find in nature, however; the forest supports more than two species. Food items come in different sizes and shapes and are found in distinctively different microhabitats within the forest. Even more diversification of food resources is available, since the same kind of seed or insect may occur in more than one kind of microenvironment. Thus, a species of bark beetle may live on newly fallen logs, on the lower trunks of standing trees, in the bark of upper limbs, and even in the bark of different tree species. The possibility of increasing the variety of places to find food is great, given the architectural richness of a forest stand. It is no surprise then to find that different species of birds share the food resources of the forest by foraging in largely nonoverlapping sectors of the forest structure.

A now-classic study by Robert MacArthur (1958) of five species of warblers that coexist in New England pioneered this idea of coexistence by habitat preference. The different warblers behave as though they have partitioned the food resources of a tree into zones: one species frequenting the lower branches and trunk, another the middle stem and branches, another foraging in the upper and outer foliage of the canopy. Though there is some overlap of warblers foraging within these zones, the coexistence of different warblers in the same forest seems to depend on preference of each warbler for a particular sector of a tree's geometry. Since MacArthur's analysis, similar studies of resource partitioning have been reported not only for other forest bird communities but for other kinds of animals as well. The same phenomenon should occur in lowland forests around Puget Sound. For coniferous forests there the model would have to be expanded to include more than

Table 18. Characteristic Birds of Lowland Forest Habitats

Deciduous Woods	*Coniferous Forest*
Sharp-shinned hawk	Harlequin duck (rivers)
Cooper's hawk	Red-breasted merganser (rivers)
Ruffed grouse	Cooper's hawk
Screech owl	Blue grouse
Great horned owl	Ruffed grouse
Long-eared owl	Spotted sandpiper (streams)
Rufous hummingbird	Band-tailed pigeon
Yellow-bellied sapsucker	Screech owl
Downy woodpecker	Great horned owl
Traill's flycatcher	Pygmy owl
Western flycatcher	Spotted owl
Black-capped chickadee	Saw-whet owl
Bewick's wren	Vaux's swift
Robin	Pileated woodpecker
Swainson's thrush	Hairy woodpecker
Ruby-crowned kinglet	Hammond's flycatcher
all Vireos	Western wood pewee
Yellow warbler	Olive-sided flycatcher
Orange-crowned warbler	Steller's jay
MacGillivray's warbler	Gray jay
Bullock's oriole	Common raven
Western tanager	Chestnut-backed chickadee
Black-headed grosbeak	Red-breasted nuthatch
Purple finch	Brown creeper
House finch	Dipper (streams)
Rufous-sided towhee	Winter wren
Pine siskin	Robin
Chipping sparrow	Varied thrush
White-crowned sparrow	Swainson's thrush
Fox sparrow	Golden-crowned kinglet
Song sparrow	Audubon's warbler
	Wilson's warbler
	Western tanager
	Purple finch
	Pine siskin
	Red crossbill
	Slate-sided junco

Note: From Larrison and Sonnenberg, *Washington Birds: Their Location and Identification* (Seattle Audubon Society, 1968).

*The spotted owl (*Strix occidentalis*) is an uncommon predator of flying squirrels and voles in old-growth forests. (Drawing by Linda Wilkinson.)*

Red-tailed hawks
Swifts
Swallows
Fly catchers

Overstory canopy

Pileated woodpeckers
Sapsuckers
Pygmy owls

Understory canopy

Brown creepers
Nuthatches

Shrub layer

Thrushes
Towhees
Winter wrens

Ground vegetation

different species of the same kind of bird. Unlike the New England forests, Northwest forests do not support large "species flocks" like those of the five warbler species. In the Northwest, coexistence through distinct preferences in feeding mostly involves different, often unrelated species of birds. But the ecological idea is there to be tested nonetheless: habitat diversity can promote species diversity, to provide rich exploitation of our forests by birds.

How do birds cope with the different habitat types that have come into being in recent times? Change in forest composition now goes on in lowland Puget Sound at an intensity and magnitude never before witnessed by the forest-dwelling fauna. The patchwork of successional vegetation types—from clearcuts and brush fields to older but even-aged maturing stands—was not even paralleled by the border zone of forest and glacial outwash plains of the early post-Pleistocene.

A study of how birds fare in the mosaic of habitat variety that once was continuous forest was carried out by John Bowles of the University of Washington (1963). Bowles chose three contrasting habitats in a lowland forest setting to see how bird species distribute themselves within and between the distinct set of niches found in the three sites. Plot A was a wind-damaged forest that had been completely logged to salvage the blow-down timber; it had regenerated only to brush species and a few young conifers. Plot B had been selectively logged to remove old Douglas fir, but still retained a relatively closed forest canopy; brush species, however, had moved into the more open forest floor. Plot C was in a

Four layers of a mature forest, from upper canopy to ground vegetation, with the birds that typically inhabit each.

mature Douglas fir forest which had little undergrowth. The size of the plots within each of these forest stand types was small enough (3–5 acres) to allow a complete tally of all birds seen or heard at a given period of observation. Bowles made thirty-four visits to the three plots over a period of eighteen months.

Bowles summarized his observations into a useful overview of how birds utilized the three different habitats (Table 19 and p. 241). More birds, both in absolute number and in species, found food and shelter in the logged-over, brush-covered Plot A than in the other two less disturbed sites. A total of 841 individual birds in 36 species were observed in Plot A (logged, brushy), 555 individuals and 31 species in plot B (disturbed forest), and 640 individuals and 29 species in the mature forest stand of Plot C. Now if the niche idea for birds is largely a matter of specific feeding habits, then Bowles' census figures, plus his observations on where the birds were most often seen, could tell us how insect- and seed-eating birds utilize each of the three different habitats. In the logged habitat, the birds chiefly utilized the foliage-searching niche (foliage insects as food) or the ground-seed niche. In the undisturbed forest of Plot C, most of the species of birds were those that can effectively use the timber-searching niche (birds seeking bark beetles, etc.). Foliage-seeking species were also present. In the open disturbed forest stand the niche preferences were found to be somewhere in between the first two plots. The Bowles study, then, permits the conclusion that the structural quality of the vegetation does make a difference in the way birds utilize the habitat: logged habitats that have recovered to the brush-field stage may provide niches not available in the mature forest, and vice versa.

Bowles' study on habitat preferences embraced all the birds in a patch of forest. In contrast, William Sturman (1968) examined the habitat choices of two closely related chickadees. The black-capped chickadee and the chestnut-backed chickadee commonly occur as permanent residents in lowland western Washington. During their breeding season they show strong habitat preferences. The black-capped chickadee forages mainly in hardwood trees while the chestnut-backed prefer conifer stands. Even when each may utilize the same tree species, the foraging behavior differs. The chestnut-backed chickadee forages higher in the trees and nearer the ends of branches than does the black-capped. Sturman's field studies neatly support the notion that related species have evolved ways to partition the resources of the habitat.

Our intuition is to favor the notion that the variety of birds increases as the kinds of trees in the forest increase. Tree diversity begets bird diversity, is the conventional wisdom. Hence pure stands of alder should support only a few species of birds. But Ed

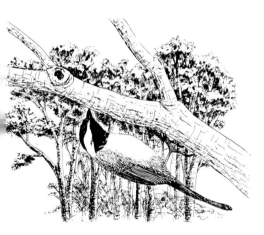

Foraging behavior in two chickadee species. The black-capped chickadee (top) prefers hardwoods, while the chestnut-backed chickadee more often forages in conifers and near the ends of branches. (Drawings by Pamela Harlow.)

Table 19. Most Common Birds of the Three Habitat Types Studied by Bowles (1963)

Plot A (Brush following logging)

1 Swainson's thrush	9 Hairy woodpecker
2 Varied thrush	10 Black-headed grosbeak
3 Western tanager	11 Rufous-sided towhee
4 MacGillivray's warbler	12 Olive-sided flycatcher
5 Robin	13 Wilson's warbler
6 Song Sparrow	14 Orange-crowned warbler
7 Junco	15 (Pine siskin)
8 Rufous hummingbird	16 (Band-tailed pigeon)
	17 (Evening grosbeak)

Plot B (Forest opened by disturbance)

		Key to plants, Plots A-C
18 Brown creeper	24 MacGillivray's warbler	A = alder
7 Junco	25 Red-breasted nuthatch	B = blackberry
19 Golden-crowned kinglet	26 Chestnut-backed chickadee	C = cottonwood
20 Varied thrush	9 Hairy woodpecker	CE = cedar (or western red cedar
21 Pileated woodpecker	3 Western tanager	
22 Audubon's warbler	17 (Evening grosbeak)	CF = coltsfoot
5 Robin	15 (Pine siskin)	D = Douglas fir
23 Winter wren	16 (Band-tailed pigeon)	DF = deer fern
		E = elderberry

Plot C (Mature, undisturbed forest, little understory)

27 Pygmy owl	26 Chestnut-backed chickadee	F = fireweed
19 Golden-crowned kinglet	2 Varied thrush	H = huckleberry
9 Hairy woodpecker	15 (Pine siskin)	HM = western hemlock
25 Red-breasted nuthatch	17 (Evening grosbeak)	S = salal
18 Brown creeper	16 (Band-tailed pigeon)	V = vine maple
		W = willow

Note: Birds in parentheses were seen overhead, but only rarely landed in the plot. Numbers match those in the figure on page 241.

Stiles (1973) was able to demonstrate that mature alder stands were well stocked with kinds of birds; diversity of bird species increased with the maturation (successional stages) of the alder. Apparently older alder stands have greater architectural diversity (more vertical layers of foliage) than do younger ones. Put another way, there are more niches for different kinds of birds in older alder stands. Diversity of forest structure, even within a mature alder "monoculture," is arrayed vertically from forest floor to upper canopy.

The coming of Europeans to the Pacific Northwest in the eighteenth and nineteenth centuries has had its effect on the bird life,

Opposite page: Differences in bird diversity in three contrasting forest settings. Plot A: Brush vegetation after logging. Plot B: Forest opened by disturbance. Plot C: Mature, undisturbed forest with little understory. Numbers refer to bird species listed in Table 19. (Rendering by Pamela Harlow.)

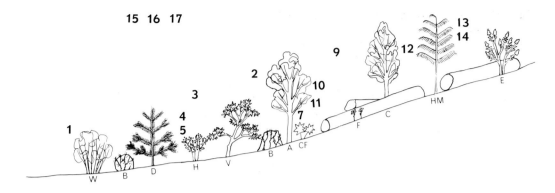

Plot A

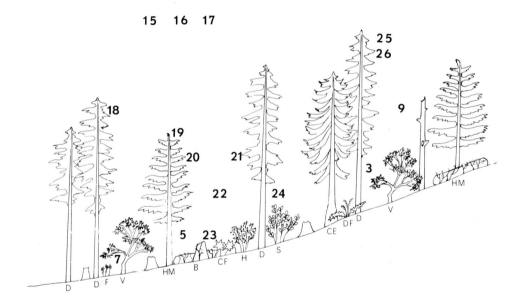

Plot B

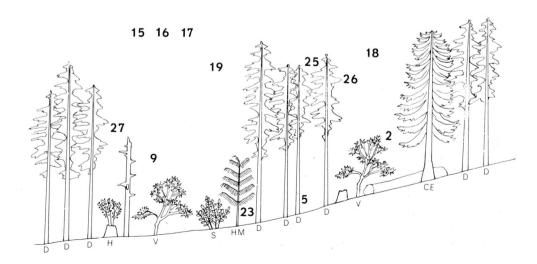

Plot C

as with all other biota. Helmut Buechner lists seven types of alterations in the avifauna of the state, some of which apply to the Puget Sound region:

> 1) The complete extirpation of three large, magnificent species . . .
> the California condor, trumpeter swan [now returning to northern
> Puget lowland, Skagit County], and the whooping crane; 2) the elimi
> nation of the white pelican . . . as a breeding bird; 3) the naturaliza
> tion of one Asiatic game bird, the chukar partridge . . . and two Euro
> pean species . . . the ringneck pheasant . . . and the Hungarian
> partridge . . . ; 4) the addition of substantial populations of two other
> European birds . . . the English sparrow . . . and the rock dove . . . ;
> 5) the recent spread of the starling . . . , which took 60 years to cross
> the continent; 6) the greater abundance of some native species . . . ;
> and 7) the marked reduction of other native species, some reach
> ing such a low level that extirpation appears almost imminent.
> (1953:172–73)

Buechner highlights these changes for Washington State in a useful summary (Table 20). Published in 1953, his study is probably a "period piece" now, since birds less abundant then are mostly rarer today and some birds such as the starling, then in an upsurge of abundance, still continue to increase. A 1990 version of the Buechner bird list (Table 20a), prepared by Dennis Paulson, appears on page 245; it is just for the Puget Sound region. Appendix 4 lists birds (and other vertebrates) of Washington that are of special concern: either uncommon or rare, or else so little known as to be considered in an undetermined status.

It is not surprising that massive changes in vegetation should affect the composition of bird fauna. The losses (or gains) in numbers of bird species and in size of population of a given species are routinely recorded in the bird censuses taken over the years. But there is a more subtle consequence of changes in avifauna brought about by changes in vegetation. The existing vegetation itself can be affected. Consider the nature of birds as niche specialists. Some thrive as seed eaters, others seek foliage insects, and still others live on bark insects. Change the relative density and proportions of any of this fauna and the plant community will be altered. For instance, change in numbers of seed-eating birds could alter the quality and quantity of seed dispersal and establishment. Although birds may destroy some seed by eating them, they more than compensate by assuring the dispersal of many kinds of plants. For another example, recall that insectivorous birds, foraging on foliage or bark of trees, aid in reducing the density of insects that feed on plants. A decline in the numbers and kinds of insect-eating birds reduces control on insect herbivores, which attack trees and other plant growth.

The web of life is a *food web* whose strands radiate and interconnect in many and subtle ways: plants as primary producers and birds that directly or indirectly consume that productivity can generate a web of unexpected complexity and fragility.

Some of the largest birds in Puget Sound are at home over water and on land. Left: Two bald eagles on alder snags, near Manchester State Park on Kitsap Peninsula. (Photo by Larry Staagall.)

Above: Glaucous-winged gulls leave marine habitats frequently to forage inland (especially in garbage dumps and other waste places). (Photo by Bob and Ira Spring.)

Table 20. Some Changes in the Bird Fauna of Washington, to 1953

Alien Birds Now Naturalized

Chuckar partridge
Rock dove (pigeon)
English sparrow
Hungarian partridge
Ringneck pheasant
Starling

American Birds Now Naturalized

Scaled quail
Bobwhite quail
Valley quail
Mountain quail

Native Birds Now More Abundant and/or More Widespread

Mallard
Ruffed grouse
Canada grouse
House finch
Brewer blackbird
Bullock oriole
Song sparrow
Killdeer
Bank swallow
Western meadowlark
Eastern kingbird
Western kingbird
Western mourning dove

Native Birds Threatened with Extinction

Sage grouse
Trumpeter swan
Sandhill crane
Belted kingfisher
Sharptail grouse
White pelican

Native Birds Now Completely Extirpated

Whooping crane
California condor

Alien Birds Unsuccessfully Introduced

Bamboo partridge
Golden pheasant
Chinese quail
Swinhoe pheasant
Silver pheasant
Reves pheasant
Sand grouse
Tragopan pheasant

American Birds Unsuccessfully Introduced

Gambel quail
Mearns quail
Wild turkey

Native Birds Now Less Abundant

Great blue heron
Long-eared owl
Spotted owl
Lewis woodpecker
Franklin grouse
Turkey vulture
Whistling swan
Hermit warbler
Bald eagle
Red-breasted sapsucker
Brewer sparrow

Note: From H. Buechner, "Some Biotic Changes in the State of Washington," in *Washington Territorial Centennial Number,* Research Studies of the State College of Washington, 1953.

Canada geese are now permanent residents in Puget Sound, congregating on lake shorelines, in local parks, and on lawns. (Photo by Bob and Ira Spring.)

Table 20a. Some Changes in the Bird Fauna of Puget Sound, to 1990

Alien Birds Now Naturalized

Gray partridge
Ring-necked pheasant
Rock dove
Eurasian Skylark
European Starling
House sparrow

American Birds Now Naturalized

Canada goose (Puget Sound
   breeding populations)
American black duck
Wild turkey
Northern bobwhite
California quail

*Alien Birds Unsuccessfully
Introduced*

Chilean tinamou
Bamboo partridge
Golden pheasant
Chinese quail
Swinhoe's Pheasant
Reeves' pheasant
Tragopan
Sand grouse

*Native Birds Essentially
Extirpated from the Region*

(No evidence that either California condor or whooping
   crane ever occurred in the Puget
   Sound area)

Yellow-billed cuckoo

*Native Birds Now More Abundant
and/or Widespread Than They
Were 100 Years Ago*

Mallard
Gadwall
American coot
Killdeer
Glaucous-winged gull
Caspian tern
Mourning dove
Barred owl
Anna's hummingbird
Cliff swallow
Barn swallow
American crow
American robin
White-crowned sparrow
Red-winged blackbird
Brewer's blackbird
Brown-headed cowbird
House finch

*Native Birds Now Less Abundant
and/or Less Widespread Than
They Were 100 Years Ago*

Northern goshawk
Peregrine falcon
Mountain quail
Marbled murrelet
Spotted owl
Common nighthawk
Lewis' woodpecker
Olive-sided flycatcher
Horned lark
Purple martin
House wren
Western bluebird
Hermit warbler
Lazuli bunting
Vesper sparrow

Note: From Dennis R. Paulson, Museum of Natural History, University of Puget Sound, Tacoma, WA, 1990.

7 Lakes, "Prairies," and Other Nonforested Lowland Habitats

"If one way be better than another, that you may be sure is Nature's way."
—*Aristotle*

Though forests surely dominated the lowland scene, life-nourishing habitats on land, other than forest, could be found in the Puget basin long before the coming of western settlers. If eighteenth-century aerial photographs of the region were to exist, they would show gaps in the mantle of primeval forest. These "islands" of nonforested land occur within each of the prevalent forested landforms: valleys, terraces, slopes, and upland flats. The late Pleistocene, followed by its postglacial scourings of the land, left indelible imprints, the boldest of which account for the absence of forest where forest should be. Some stretches of land without forest would have been the drainage ways and sinks on the southern fringe of the Vashon lobe of the continental ice sheet, where glacial ice and meltwater pockmarked and scoured the surface of the land. Well after the retreat of the ice, the most common manifestations of postglacial engineering were the depressions in the land that eventually filled with water. These nonforested and often water-filled landforms have persisted since before recorded human history as thousands of gullies, sinks, lakes, ponds, and streams. What grows in the fresh water of these postglacial depressed landforms is of considerable interest and significance to humans, the dominant users of the landscape.

Lakes and Ponds

Nearly all lakes in the Puget Sound basin, from sea level to timberline, are the products of glacial processes. At low elevations the last continental ice sheet gouged depressions out of bedrock or preexisting alluvial deposits to form the basins that would fill with water as the ice melted or receded. Many lakes of the south Puget area near the terminus of the great Vashon ice sheet were formed by detached blocks of glacial ice, mixed with sand and gravel, which became stranded and upon melting formed the depressions called "kettles." In other places, postglacial landslides and damming of valleys with glacial detritus created natural dams that filled

Mima mounds, southwest of Olympia. Late afternoon aerial view. (Photo by Bob and Ira Spring.)

247

with surface runoff to become still another version of a lake born of glacial action.

Montane lakes, though above the direct influence of the continental glacier, owe their existence to depressions rasped out of bedrock by montane glaciers that receded during the presence of continental ice. During the late Pleistocene, montane glaciation covered vast areas of the Cascades and Olympic ranges, much surpassing their more modest expression in the present "interglacial." As a result, nearly every lake from the crest of the Cascades down along the lower reaches of the western slope owes its existence to the local glaciers that originated on the high slopes, grew, and scoured out pockets in their paths.

Glaciation formed montane lakes in diverse ways. The most spectacular lake form of glacial origin is the cirque lake that so plentifully occurs at the headwalls and high sources of montane valleys in the Cascades. A cirque is an amphitheater-like depression that was excavated out of high-country rock by scouring, 'plucking' of rock from walls, and loosening of rock through freeze-and-thaw cycles. Rock material embedded in the glacial ice of the youthful basin rasped the depression still deeper. Most cirque lakes (like Gem Lake near Snoqualmie Pass) have a bedrock bottom, though glacial rubble may form a dam at the outlet.

Further down the montane valley, another glacial process can form valley lakes; Lake Dorothy in the Alpine Lakes Wilderness is a good example. Erosional activity of the glacier in the floor of the valley may cause the valley bottom to overdeepen. The depression thus formed becomes a lake as the ice retreats. Valley lakes, often in stepwise sequence, are not uncommon at middle altitudes in the Cascades; they are usually larger than the jewel-like higher cirque lakes at the heads of valleys. A variant of the valley lake is one formed by damming with glacial drift or by glacier-caused landslide (Pete Lake). Here the lake-forming processes simply dammed an existing mountain stream. Examples of each of those lake types are plentiful in the Alpine Lakes country of the Cascades, a stunning landscape extending from Snoqualmie Pass north to Stevens Pass.

Altogether, montane and continental glacial action have given western Washington more than 3,000 lakes; and this number includes only those over one acre in surface area. Of these, 1,567 lakes are above 2,500 feet and are classed as "high lakes." Yet much of this glacier-made scenery has an impermanence born of the continuous workings of glacial and biologic processes. Everywhere in the Puget Sound basin, stages in the inevitable erasure of lakes can be detected. Mass wasting or the plucking of rock from the walls and steep shorelines of high lakes as well as sedimentation from upland erosion start the filling-in process, just as soon as the lake basin

Types of montane lakes in relation to topography, position, and nature of structural materials (bedrock, glacial drift, or avalanche debris). Cirque lakes (top) are usually just below alpine ridges; the other three lake types form farther down in valleys. (Rendering by Linda Wilkinson.)

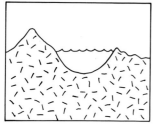

Cirque lake

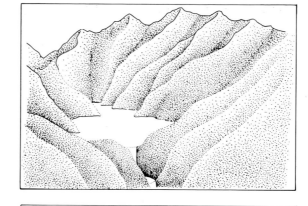

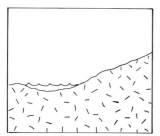

Overdeepened valley lake

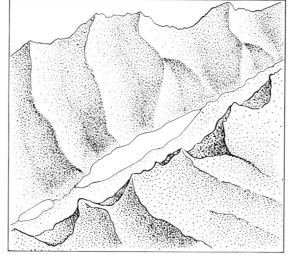

*Overdeepened valley lake
with drift dam*

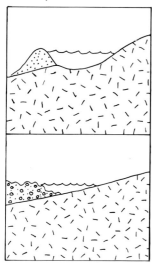

Landslide-dammed lake

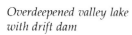 *Bedrock*   *Glacial
drift*   *Avalanche
debris*

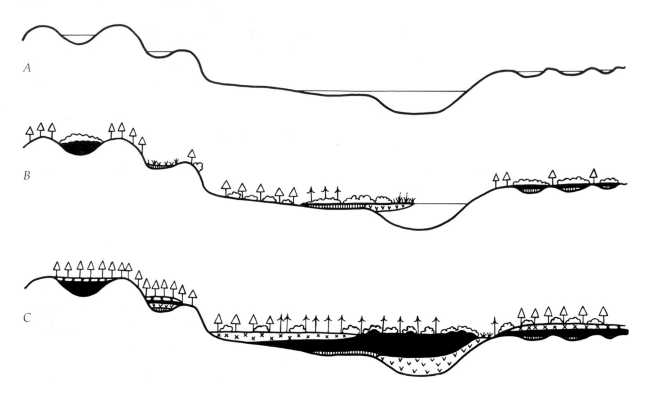

becomes free of glacial ice. Add to geological processes of basin filling by sedimentation, the biogenic processes of organic sedimentation and encroachment by land vegetation along the shore, and the life history of a lake, from its beginning to its final disappearance, can be retraced—a portion of its course detectable in a human lifetime.

Lake succession in several ponds and one lake: A, before becoming vegetated; B, partial filling in by vegetation; C, late stage with lake and bog replaced by forest. (Rendering by Michael Emerson.)

The Physical Environment for Life in Lakes

The quality of life in lakes is dependent on three critical attributes ever present in the physical environment: light, temperature, and nutrients, with their fluctuations extended over time and in aquatic space. Sunlight penetrates the full depth of a shallow lake, but only to a fraction of the total depth of a deep lake. Yet, it is in that upper sunlit stratum of water that the vital photosynthetic activities of the floating algae (the phytoplankton) and rooted aquatic plants occur. The depth to which light may penetrate varies as a result of light quality itself and as an effect of dissolved materials and particles in water. When the sun is directly overhead at midday in the summer, light penetrates deeper than at other times of the day. Turbidity of biological origin may be due to the shadowing effect of a rich population of living organisms, or may be due to the concentration of organic remains of life activities. Finely suspended sediments from upland erosion also reduce the clarity of the water column. Students of lake biology (limnologists) use a simple device to estimate the transparency of the water column. A white plate about ten inches in diameter is lowered on a metered line until it disappears from sight. Visibility of this Secchi disc, so named to commemorate an early Italian limnologist, may vary from less than five feet up to fifty feet and more; the clearer the water the greater the depth of visibility. The simple Secchi disc has been a critical tool in detecting changes in water clarity due to pollution.

For any but the most shallow of ponds, the temperatures of the lake water varies with depth, often abruptly so. In midsummer the layering of waters at different temperatures is particularly striking. The first few feet may vary but little from a relatively warm 20°C (68°F) followed by a sequence of lower temperatures over the next several feet downward. In the deeper lakes, the lowest and deepest stratum may show no change; its lowest temperature reaches to the bottom of the lake. So universal and predictable is this thermal stratification that it has evoked its own set of names identifying the layers and the associated phenomena. The accompanying standard graph of lake temperature stratification specifies the three lake strata.

This steep gradient of summer water temperatures serves to stratify life in deeper lakes and to compartmentalize processes at each distinct level. Cool fall air temperatures, coupled with winds, destabilize the thermal gradient of summer until the entire water column becomes the same low temperature. This so-called "fall overturn" achieves uniform temperature throughout the depth gradient. "Overturn," a common term in lake biology, is a bit misleading. There is no actual rotation of the layers of water. Rather, in autumn, the top layer of water, the epilimnion, gradually becomes thicker (extends deeper) and gets cooler until it finally encompasses the entire water column and the lake then is uniform in temperature from top to bottom. Wind and gravity thus produce the fall overturn, which becomes stabilized as a uniformly low temperature throughout the winter. In those lakes that freeze, the top will be at 0° Celsius (32°F) and frozen, but the rest of the water column stays at or near 40°C (39.2°F), following the fall overturn. The sun's warmth in spring begins to heat the water column to start the thermal gradient on its summerward progression. The spring overturn thus restores the thermal stratification of summer, just as the fall overturn was its undoing.

In addition to light and temperature, nutrient quality of the lake water is a further determiner of the biological poverty or richness of a lake. Lake nutrients, both organic and inorganic, come either

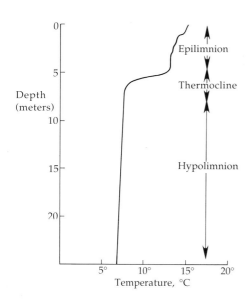

Temperature of lakes changes with depth. The temperature gradient is for the period of summer "thermal stratification."

from runoff from the adjacent drainage basin or from the recycled elements in the lake itself. The level of nutrients is the crucial attribute for the productivity of a lake. Nutrient level is not a simple matter of input-output, however; it is dependent on a great many other factors, especially light, temperature, geology of the nearby drainage basin, regional climate, the surrounding upland terrestrial vegetation, and ongoing biological activity of the lake itself. In fact the nutrient status of lakes is the basis for a biological classification of lakes. Lakes are either nutrient-poor (oligotrophic, little nourished) or nutrient-rich (eutrophic, well nourished), but with the inevitable reservation that there are gradations between these extremes, and often some lakes go from oligotrophic to eutrophic conditions, or even the reverse.

The nutrient or trophic basis for cataloguing and analyzing lakes draws upon all operational factors, biologic as well as physical, to characterize the particular qualities of a lake. Thus, the typical oligotrophic lake which is low in food resources—both organisms and dissolved nutrients—will have considerable transparency. Shallow or deep, an oligotrophic lake has its greatest volume of water as the lowermost (uniformly colder) layer, the hypolimnion. Moreover, the numbers of planktonic organisms will be low in the oligotrophic lake, so that productivity is low. With little planktonic fallout to the lower depths there is no great depletion of oxygen in the deeper reaches of the lake. Such conditions can foster thriving populations of cold-water bottom fish like trout. Oligotrophic lakes, though typical of the upper montane habitats in western Washington, may well have existed in the early stages of lake succession at lower elevations, shortly after deglaciation. An oligotrophic lake in the lowland forest habitat may change its nutrient character. Eutrophication (increase in the nutrient supply) of an oligotrophic lake is a probable fate of low elevation lakes, if not through the natural causes of fertilization from runoff and mineral recycling on land, then surely in the wake of human activity—the inevitable source of nutrient enrichment for lowlying lakes in the Puget Sound basin.

Looking east to Lake Washington, just beyond Seattle skyline, and the Cascade Range; Puget Sound's Elliott Bay and West Seattle (Duwamish Head and Alki Point) in foreground. Aerial taken on August 7, 1990.

In the late 1950s, sights all too familiar to Seattle residents were signs posted at many places around the shore of Lake Washington: "Warning, Polluted Water! Unsafe For Bathing." Water quality, in what once had been a lake of near pristine and clear water, had so deteriorated that it was in danger of becoming unusable for recreation. The alarmist's view of the eutrophication of Lake Washington is to see the lake as dying, with death certain unless the trend is reversed. Limnologist W. T. Edmondson, a longtime student of the lake's biology, is worth quoting (pers. comm.) on this misconception: "I am particularly sensitive to the "dead lake" myth. A heavily enriched lake is no more dead than a big, thriving city with a large cemetery is dead. A lake eutrophied with secondary effluent, as was Lake Washington, has a higher rate of photosynthetic production and supports a larger population of many kinds of organisms than before (so it is livelier). Eutrophication is reversible, death is not."

Lake Washington, before the dramatic improvement in its water quality, was off limits to bathers, young and old.

The most obvious sign of change in the lake was evident to even the most casual observer: a dramatically rapid loss of clarity of the water. No longer could a swimmer or fisherman see the lake bottom along the shallower depths near shore, nor could the limnologist get visibility readings from the Secchi disc at depths recorded in years past. Dr. Edmondson and his associates were quick to fix the blame for the new and distressing color on a common water plant of other nutrient-rich lakes. The culprit was *Oscillatoria rubescens*, a member of the primitive blue-green algae, so called because of the color of some members of the group. The tiny filaments of *Oscillatoria* actually appear brownish-purple when they grow in massive populations called "blooms."

The unpleasant sight and attendant foul smell of waters in Lake Washington were recognized as early symptoms of a familiar series of events, well documented by lake biologists in Europe. A number of Swiss lakes had taken the same turn for the worse that Lake Washington was now experiencing; in such lakes as Zurichsee and Lake Constance the process had gone much further.[1] The enriched European lakes were the key to understanding the complex of biological and physical changes that could send a lake along a course to stagnation. Eutrophication is the now familiar term for what was happening. The word entered the local political arena in the 1960s when farsighted citizens teamed up with the limnologists to spearhead an area-wide campaign of support for a program to arrest and turn back the eutrophic trend in the lake. The implementation of

1. Though only coincidental with the eutrophic lakes of Switzerland, it seems prophetic in hindsight that in 1850, Lake Washington was called Lake Geneva (presumably after its great European counterpart).

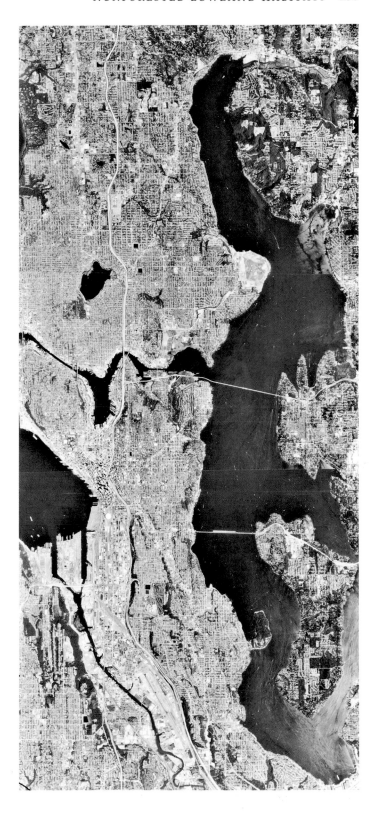

Aerial view of Lake Washington, July 14, 1984: lower (southern) portion of the photograph shows Renton and Mercer Island; center shows Bellevue on right, and Ship Canal, Seattle, and Elliott Bay waterfront on left; and top (northern) portion shows Kenmore-Kirkland area. Little natural vegetation surrounding the lake was left by 1984.

that program and its quick success in the late 1960s and early 1970s is now part of the Puget Sound region's record of active concern for preserving environmental quality.

Eutrophication in Lake Washington. In the late 1940s, Lake Washington was chosen as an object for scientific study by Professor W. T. Edmondson, newly arrived at the University of Washington. Lake Washington appealed to his scientific curiosity in a most particular way. Here was a great body of fresh water in the heart of a growing metropolis into which inadvertent "chemists"—people in the lake's drainage basin—were dumping chemicals in such quantities that they were sure to produce detectable change. In short, the chemical modifications to the lake provided Edmondson with a massive experiment, one that he could never bring off on his own and yet an experiment that he could monitor in its early stages. It was first necessary to inventory the current status of chemical, physical, and biological processes ongoing in the lake. Data from these baseline studies in the early 1950s could then be matched against changes in those same properties and processes that were sure to come as the lake was "fed" by its innocent custodians on shore. It might be said that 1950 was too late to begin monitoring the grand experiment of eutrophication, for undoubtedly eutrophic transformation of the lake's biology had already had a good half-century head start. But some kinds of ecological research cannot depend on a pristine environment for a baseline. Moreover, an earlier study of the lake in 1939 by Victor Scheffer, a student of that noted aquatic biologist Trevor Kincaid, could provide some crucial reference points.

Lake Washington is one of the major bodies of fresh water in North America and is second only to Lake Chelan in size for the state of Washington. It is 22 miles long, from the shoreline at Renton to the water's edge at Kenmore; and its width ranges from one to four miles. The lake surface covers an area of 50 square miles (32,000 acres) and has a shoreline perimeter of 58 miles, excluding the 13.5 miles added by Mercer Island. Lake Washington is 214 feet deep just off Madison Park, the deepest part of its basinlike contours. The present shoreline is recent in origin. In 1916, the lake level was lowered ten feet in making the Ship Canal link between the Sound through Lake Union to Lake Washington. Yet, even with this recent alteration of shoreline, there is variety along the present perimeter—sandy beach, marsh, pebble and gravel shingle, and even rock wall. This assures diversity of habitat for the aquatic life of the lake margin.

Like all other deep fresh-water lakes of temperate regions, Lake Washington develops a pronounced thermal gradient in the vertical water column during the summer. The maximum temperature

W. T. Edmondson poses by Lake Washington, the object of his scientific research for nearly forty years. Edmondson and colleagues can be credited with the crucial studies that led to reversing the lake's eutrophication trend. (Photo by Benjamin Benschneider.)

Below: Lake Washington can be turbulent, here with heavy waves during gale-force winds, November 1981. (Photo by Peter Liddell.)

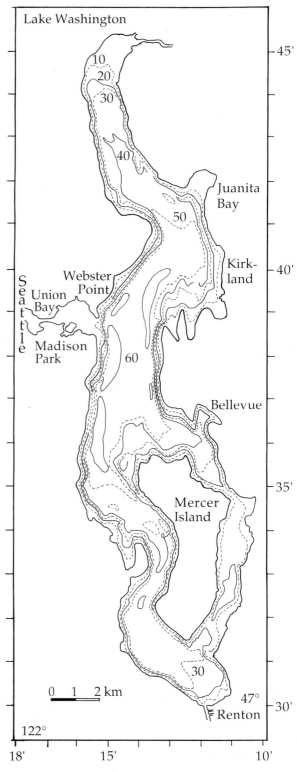

Right: Variations in depth of Lake Washington. Depth contour lines are in meters. (Rendering by Sandra Noel.)

Two Seattle area lakes and their once-wooded shorelines, around the turn of the century. Above: Lake Washington; left: Lake Union.

at the surface of the upper stratum has been recorded at 22°C (71.6°F) in August. During the period of high surface-water temperatures of summer, the thermocline varies with depth as follows: 0–10 meters, 21.2°C; 10–20 meters, 12.1°C; 20–30 meters, 8.7°C; 30–40 meters, 7.6°C; 40–50 meters, 7.0°C; and 50–60 meters, 6.7°C. Beginning in the fall, the lake temperature starts to equalize and by winter comes to equilibrium at a much lower temperature. This is brought about by the annual "turnover" of water temperature during the period from December to March. Thus, in mid-February the temperature range is only 5.8°C from water surface to the bottom 60 meters down.

When Victor Scheffer, with Rex Robinson, published the baseline study of the 1930s, Lake Washington came close to having the attributes of an oligotrophic lake; its biological productivity was relatively poor (1939). Scheffer fitted the general characteristics of an oligotrophic lake to Lake Washington in several particulars: (1) Lake Washington, like other oligotrophic lakes, is deep, with shallower shoal areas narrow or absent; thus its hypolimnion is greater in volume than the epilimnion. (2) At that time its transparency was high; the water was blue to green in color, and the amount of suspended detritus was low. (3) The lake was relatively low in nitrogen and phosphorus; and organic (humic) materials were absent, and calcium content was variable. (4) The lake's oxygen content was relatively uniform; even the bottom layer of water had oxygen at 51.7 percent of saturation, an indication that putrefactive activities in the absence of oxygen were not appreciable at that level. (5) The numbers of planktonic organisms were low and fairly uniformly distributed; population outbursts (water blooms) of algae were rare and more often consisted of green algae than blue-green algae. (6) The biology of the shoreline versus the deeper offshore zones was largely the same except for scanty vegetation rooted in the littoral or shoreline zone.

The quantity and variety of planktonic organisms also reveal the nutrient status of a lake. In the 1930s, the plankton population of the lake was found to be uniformly distributed and stable from year to year. "The [plankton] population is typical of a large, deep fresh water habitat and strikingly resembles that of Lake Michigan" (Scheffer and Robinson 1939). Lake plankton showed a strong seasonality. Blue-green algae appeared in summer and fall; diatoms were common throughout the year, except in summer. Green algae peaked in late spring and to a lesser extent in the fall. Protozoa were not found in great variety, but the few species came on in great numbers for brief periods in the summer. These are the signs of a lake ecosystem whose foodweb is still oligotrophic and not yet changed by added nutrients.

The dramatic changes in the lake from its earlier oligotrophic status (low nutrient levels) to its alarming deterioration through eutrophication occurred in the 1950 to 1963 period. Prior to the 1930s, some raw sewage entered the lake from sewer outfalls. This primitive practice was abandoned when it became an evident health hazard; the raw sewage was then simply diverted at that time to Puget Sound, a less reactive reservoir. For a time after 1930, the lake was relatively free of sewage. The next round of eutrophication came in the 1940s when new sewage treatment plants were built to accommodate the growing metropolis in the lake's drainage basin. Treated effluent now entered the lake in an increasing volume; ten such plants were pouring the highly nutrient stuff into the lake. Though it may reduce the health hazards of raw sewage, adding treated sewage accelerates change in a lake's biology. Nutrients are rapidly made available to other organisms in the food chain when they have been released by decomposition. Both the ready accessibility of nutrients in treated sewage and the greatly increased volumes of sewage-derived nutrients could turn the lake into a gigantic, fertilized aquaculture reservoir. It was in 1955 that the prominence of *Oscillatoria rubescens*, the critical algal indicator of eutrophication and lake deterioration, was noted by Edmondson and his coworkers. At that time, 6.4 million gallons per day of treated sewage were being discharged into the lake. The algae were thriving on two of the nutrients in the effluent; 56 percent of the phosphate and 11 percent of the nitrogen income of the lake originated from sewage effluent.

As the volume of nutrient effluent was bound to increase with the increase in human population in the lake basin, the lake biology was headed for drastic change. More effluent could mean only more algae . . . up to a point. Then, the dominant "bloom" of blue-green algae, composed of both living and dead masses of planktonic plants, would begin to limit oxygen supply to other organisms in the lake. The overall catastrophic result would be a severe reduction in the biological diversity of phytoplankton, zooplankton, and the larger herbivores and carnivores (mostly fish) in the ecosystem.

The gloomy prognosis for Lake Washington would have become a sad reality in a few short years had not the political "know-how" teamed up with scientific knowledge. James Ellis, an attorney working with several of the sewer districts bordering the lake, saw that adding more sewage-treatment plants with effluent going into the lake would only aggravate the eutrophic trend. Yet to divert sewage away from the lake and to treat it at centralized facilities would require the cooperation of several communities, each of which cherished its own autonomy. From every standpoint—scientific, sanitary, and political—the situation called for the pooling of resources and ingenuity of all local governmental units to develop a unified sewage disposal system; a system that would have the sustained cooperation of all communities, large and small, in the drainage basin. Out of this realization was born the "Metro" plan. "Metro," or the Municipality of Metropolitan Seattle, would be a regional body with the authority to deal not only with sewage but with other multicommunity problems such as transportation and land-use planning.

The first phase of this visionary scheme was to be the development of a regional network of sewage diversions and treatment plants that would put only treated effluent in Puget Sound. The Sound, because of its size, tidal flushing, and other marine water attributes, might be expected to resist any significant efforts of eutrophication. Such was the conventional wisdom in the 1960s on using the Sound as the ultimate sink for effluent. We need to re-examine that premise in light of findings of the 1980s. Eutrophication and pollution of the Sound are discussed in chapters 4 and 9.

From visionary plan to accomplished project turned out to be a thorny political path. The first attempt in 1958 to launch "Metro" failed at the ballot box; even though the measure won a majority of votes (101,947 to 85,950), it failed through a system of weighted voting. During the campaign, both Ellis and Edmondson were the prime targets for vituperative and usually irrelevant criticism; one public opponent ridiculed Edmondson's efforts on the grounds that anyone attached to a zoology department should stick to his business of tending to animals in zoos! However, the next try at the polls succeeded and "Metro" finally came into being. From the groundbreaking ceremony in 1961 to substantial completion in 1967, the vast engineering project began diverting effluent in steadily increasing amounts. By March 1967, 99 percent of the treated sewage had been diverted. The biological response of the lake has been dramatic. The simple but effective transparency readings of lake-water depth with the Secchi disk is a good measure of the retreat from disastrous eutrophication. In 1963, the transparency reading was to a depth of only 1.0 meter; by 1969 it had increased to 2.8 meters. This change is a direct expression of the decrease in nuisance algae which is in turn an indicator of the decrease in nutrient input.

Recovery of the lake and the attendant decrease in undesirable phytoplankton can be directly traced to the reduction in phosphorus input. Phosphates and eutrophication have been hand in

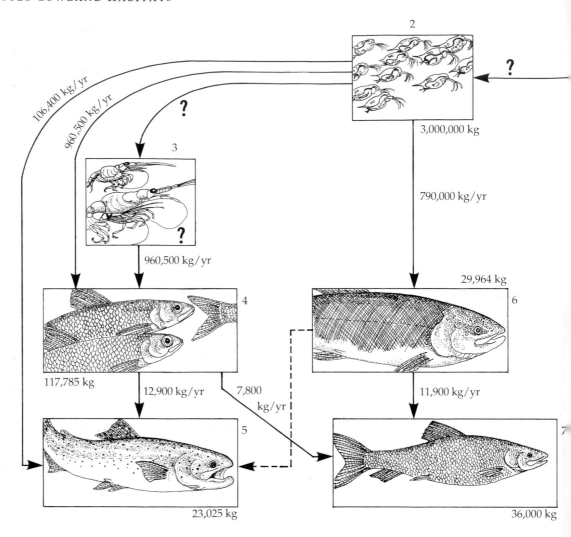

hand in many lowland lakes in North America; in Lake Washington phosphorus appears to be the limiting factor in the nutrition of the lake ecosystem. Clearly much of the phosphorus entering the lake in pre-Metro days was of human origin. And of all the human sources, roughly half the phosphates came from detergents. Edmondson estimated that removal of *all* phosphate detergents in the effluent would have had the same effect as that of removing half the total effluent input into the lake.

Fixing the blame on phosphate detergents for eutrophication of lakes raised a hornet's nest of controversy nationally. A pseudo-scientific retaliation to the limnological evidence tended to raise doubts in the public's mind about the effects of phosphate detergents on lake quality. Edmondson's prediction, based on his long study of nutrient enrichment and phytoplankton densities, still stands. Eliminate phosphate detergent loads in effluent reach-

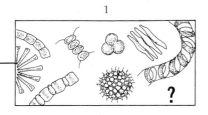

1

A Lake Washington limnetic (open-water) food web. Phytoplankton (1), the primary producers, are consumed by the tiny water flea (Daphnia, 2), which in turn is food for the freshwater shrimp (Neomysis, 3). Four fish species are the vertebrate consumers in this food web: longfin smelt (4), rainbow trout (5), sockeye salmon (6), and northern squawfish (7). Amounts of biomass next to "boxes" (in kilograms) are estimates of summer biomass; annual estimates of consumption rates (kilograms/year) are located next to arrows. "?" means values not known. (Rendering by Sandra Noel of sketch by Dave Beauchamp.)

ing a lake, and a large source of phosphorus nutrient disappears.

Since the major reversal in eutrophication of the late 1960s, further improvement in Lake Washington's water quality has occurred. Transparency has further increased from 2.8 meters to a depth of 3.4 meters in 1975, and again to 7.0 meters by the early 1980s. These further dramatic improvements are, in part, the outcome of a fascinating biological drama involving algae, minute crustaceans, and fish—a classical food chain in action. The minute crustacean, *Daphnia* or water flea, itself harmless, began to increase when the noxious blue-green alga, *Oscillatoria*, decreased. Although *Daphnia* is an efficient consumer of some phytoplankton, it cannot cope with masses of *Oscillatoria*. With the *Oscillatoria* drastically reduced by the Metro diversion, *Daphnia* could increase to feed on other algae and, in so doing, further aid the increase in transparency. But *Daphnia* had been prey to another crustacean, a small, freshwater shrimp, *Neomysis*. Only when long-fin smelt, a consumer of the shrimp, became abundant, could *Daphnia* populations rebound. With optimum levels of *Daphnia* in the lake, high water transparency should continue, that is, unless the ecological truism that *we can never merely do one thing* is inevitably enacted. The yearly introduction of rainbow trout into the lake for sport fishing may affect water clarity. The trout find *Daphnia* a favored source of food.

Arresting the rapid eutrophic trend on Lake Washington has been a many-sided success story. The joining of sound political efforts with scientific knowledge has made the Edmondson-Ellis-Metro triumph a challenging and yet realizable model for communities all over the world. Good science and good politics proved to be eminently compatible.

Metro's automated control of flows of sewage (effluent) to treatment plants. Map on wall shows Lake Washington Ship Canal connection to Puget Sound in the west (above), and Lake Sammamish to the east (below).

Lake Sammamish has been slower to respond to diversion of phosphate in effluent than has its sister Lake Washington just to the west. Photo taken October 2, 1989.

Studying Change in Lake Ecosystems. The management of a lake's biology is not always a simple matter of controlling nutrient inputs. Nearby Lake Sammamish appeared to be foundering on too much nutrient a few years ago. Yet this large lake, only a few miles east of Lake Washington, has been less responsive to sewage diversion than has Lake Washington. In 1968, one-third of the phosphorus income to Lake Sammamish was diverted, but with no significant improvement in water quality. Apparently phosphorus, bound to the tiny particles of the lake sediment, goes into solution in the lake as free phosphate decreases. Thus, even with reduced phosphate income to the lake, it will take time for the accumulated phosphate bound to lake sediments (much of which came from prediversion human sources) to find its way out of the lake. Only from the late 1970s on, has Lake Sammamish shown substantial recovery. Gain in transparency, reduction in phosphate concentration, and other indicators of improvement in water quality had been the eventual consequence of a change in lake chemistry. The root cause was a decrease in the release of phosphate from that bound in the lake-bottom sediments.

There is hardly any low elevation lake in the Puget Sound basin that could serve as the pristine baseline comparison for lakes now

undergoing rapid modification due to human enterprise. Essentially all lowland lakes have been disturbed by humans to some degree, if only to the extent of having been stocked with fish or having received inputs of nutrient-laden runoff from logging, agriculture, et cetera, from their upland drainages. Yet such a comparison should provide a critical yardstick for measuring quality of a disturbed lake against the "control" or undisturbed lake. The ecologist, just as any other scientist, requires as experimental control the inclusion of baseline or "benchmark" habitats in the study of change in a given ecosystem. Ideally, such a lake should have features that match those of the lake in which experimental modification, planned or unplanned, is occurring. The next best thing is to find a near-pristine lake at higher elevations, along the upper contours of the west slope of the Cascade Range. Findley Lake, at the headwaters of the Cedar River drainage, turned out to be a particularly choice selection for baseline comparisons. It is situated in the City of Seattle watershed where rigid control over disturbance is practiced in at least the upper reaches of the drainage. The lake is at 3,701 feet just west of the Cascade crest and lies in a clearly defined basin. The undisturbed basin contains a mixture of upper montane forest, talus, meadow, and avalanche slope.

Streams, from rivulets and creeks to major rivers, feed into the lakes and Puget Sound. Below left: Nisqually River just below Nisqually Glacier on Mount Rainier runs "milky" with its load of glacial "flour." (Photo by A. H. Barnes.) Below right: Rivers on the west side of the Olympic Peninsula have broader stream beds than those entering Puget Sound: here the Queets River with exposed gravel bed in late summer. (Photo by the author.)

According to Roger del Moral, who has described the vegetation of the basin in detail, there has been no severe fire in the basin for at least two hundred years. He writes: "The lake itself is oligotrophic and lacks fish. Soils weather slowly and are infertile. The major herbivores [as sources of nutrient input to the lake] are native ungulates, presumably deer and elk. No introduced weedy plant species were found. . . . Air pollution from Tacoma [about thirty airline miles to the west] is the only major source of potential perturbation to the system" (1973:26–27). Findley Lake thus nicely meets the specifications of several scientists who seek reference points in undisturbed habitats to gauge the effects of human activity. Findley Lake was chosen by the Northwest Coniferous Biome team of the International Biological Program just for its rare virginity.

What makes Findley Lake oligotrophic? Though the strands of a lake ecosystem will be intricately interwoven, it should be possible to determine which factor or factors are in such short supply that

Left: Panoramic view of Findley Lake (foreground), looking southwest to Mount Rainier.

Above right: Findley Lake shoreline, a mosaic of talus, forest (Pacific silver fir and mountain hemlock), and upper montane shrubs. This near-pristine lake in the upper Cedar River watershed serves as a referent (baseline) ecosystem for other such environments modified by human disturbance. (Photo by Bob Gonyea.)

the whole web is limited in its processing resources. Limnologists with the International Biological Program found the limiting resource to be low available phosphorus. Primary productivity in the lake and hence the dependent activities of consumers and decomposers is limited by the annual depletion of phosphorus. Quantity and kinds of phytoplankton, like diatoms and other floating algae, remain low throughout the growing season. Zooplankton that feed on the algae are limited by the algal production, as would be fish that feed on the zooplankters—if the lake were stocked. Why the low phosphorus income to the lake? Remember that the lake basin supports a stable, undisturbed upper montane vegetation; nutrient runoff is expected to be minimal under such stability.

The steady state is only relative. By probing into the past history of Findley Lake basin, we would find periods of instability, following fire or other natural disturbance. In turn, these would set in motion land-based shifts in nutrients and sediments that would alter the biological status of the lake. An ingenious methodology has been developed to reconstruct the past histories of lakes and their immediate surroundings; since no television camera was trained on the lake continuously since the end of the last Ice Age, indirect methods of unraveling a lake's past must be resorted to. Two subdisciplines of ecology—paleolimnology and palynology—team up to provide some intriguing insights on these past events.

Such stratagems reconstruct the past history of the lake and adjacent land vegetation. The approach is like that of the historical geologist who uses fossils trapped in sedimentary rocks to reveal sequences of events in the more remote past. In the present instance, however, the fossils are pollen grains of conifers and flowering plants and skeletons of diatoms, as well as fossil chlorophyll from phytoplankton and the tiny exoskeletons of crustacean zooplanton in the sediments, only a few hundred years old.

Dan Adams, working with a University of Washington palynologist, Matsuo Tsukada, put together an account of some postglacial history of Findley Lake (1973). Just getting in position to sample remote Findley Lake was no small feat. Equipment, including rubber raft and sampling gear, had to be packed in on the backs of the research team. And because of the lake's pristine quality and its location in the Seattle watershed, special care had to be taken to minimize human disturbance in the lake and its surrounding basin. Sampling lake sediments utilizes special equipment, since it is necessary that an undisturbed sequence of sediments be withdrawn from the lake bottom for analysis. Adams, afloat on his rubber raft, would lower a device called a Davis-Doyle piston sampler into the lake and with it recover thin continuous cores of lake sediments, up to one meter long. Imagine trying to obtain a "plug" of watermelon by remote control and you can visualize the intricacies inherent in getting intact cores from the bottom of the lake, ten meters below the water surface. Seven such cores were taken from the northeast corner of the lake. These were packed back to Seattle and stored at 5°C for later analysis. Cores were then extruded from the stored core sample tubes in small (five millimeter) increments for the first thirty centimeters, and then at five-centimeter intervals to the end of the core. Each increment in sequence, when analyzed for its particular signs of past life, becomes a chapter of lake history in which is revealed the biological and chemical composition of the lake (and its surroundings) at a particular segment of time. Absolute time can be more closely determined by getting a "fix" with radiocarbon dates on one sector of the core.

What do these thin slices from the slender core of Time reveal? The word "basin" connotes the idea of catchment. All things, whether living, dead, or inanimate, may gravitate to the lowest level of the lake basin. Of all such materials, pollen is uniquely revealing of a basin's past. The study of pollen grains and other microscopic vestiges of life is the domain of the palynologist. See diagrams, pages 24 and 25.

The palynologist simply counts the different kinds of pollen grains in the slices of a one-meter core from a lake's bottom sediments. The result, when pollen number and kind are arranged in the vertical sequence of their appearance, is a chronology of change in the character of vegetation in the vicinity of the lake. And since change in species composition of plant communities reflects physical changes, especially climatic events, as well as more abrupt perturbations like fire or a rain of volcanic ash, the pollen record can be deeply revealing of what took place in past times. The one-meter cores that Dan Adams retrieved from Findley Lake encompassed roughly four thousand years of vegetational (and environmental) history, accumulated bit by bit. When synthesized in the typical pollen diagram of the palynologist (see p. 268) the most striking feature for Findley Lake is the stability of dominant arboreal vegetation through this span of forty centuries. Neither conifers nor the dominant hardwood, alder, have changed abundance in the four thousand-year stretch. Only when the top few centimeters of sediment are scrutinized, is a perceptible shift in pollen composition noted. Conifer pollen decreases slightly while alder pollen increases. Since there has been no significant alteration of the tree composition of the basin, Adams suggests that the alder pollen came from outside the basin. Intensive logging, fire, and other disturbance in adjacent west slope drainages have brought successional alder into prominence in place of coniferous forest in many places.

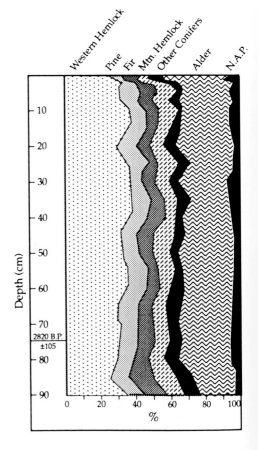

Not only does the pollen record reveal the shift in alder frequency; it also provides an example of the subtle bias that can enter the interpretation of a pollen sequence. Adams, like most other palynologists, recognized that the pollen record of any lake bottom is composed of both pollen fallout from vegetation within the drainage basin together with a lighter rain of pollen grains airborne from beyond the basin. In fact the presence of pollen grains of one weedy introduced plant, *Plantago lanceolata* (narrow-leaved plantain), at the top three-centimeter level of lake sediments is explained as having come from outside the basin, probably blown in from some habitat altered by human activity. At present, there is no plantain in the near-pristine habitat of the lake. Weed pollen gives the palynologist sure evidence of human disturbance in an area. In other parts of the world, the appearance of one or more of man's weedy associates in lake sediments helps triangulate the time when nearby land was cleared and planted to cultivated crops.

If the sediments of a lake contain a faithful history of what was present in past land-based plant communities, surely they also could be a museum of the lake's own aquatic life sequences. The dead husks of tiny planktonic life constantly settle out to the bottom sediments. Diatoms make perfect fossils since their tiny exteriors are made of silica (glass) and each species has its own "shell" pattern. Adams used the changes in proportion of two kinds of diatoms to assess past changes in planktonic composition of Findley Lake. Three distinct shifts in diatom populations occurred in the last 900 to 950 years. The cause of the change can be interpreted in terms of change in nutrient status of the lake. And to get increase in nutrient input inevitably depends on change somewhere in the basin. Adams suggests that following natural fire in the basin, nutrient runoff increased, only to slowly decline as regrowth of vegetation healed the scarred landscape. Here, only a slight eutrophication (nutrient enrichment) triggered the shift in diatom composition. That shift was, though, a response to change on land.

Though it is possible to extract still more information from the record in a lake's sediments, I want to single out only one revealing imprint in the sedimentary measures of time. Nearly every lake in western Washington has at least one ashy gray, inorganic layer in its sediments and each gray layer is nearly always in the same relative position. So suggestive was this simultaneous occurrence that early palynologists proposed that it was volcanic ash from some prehistoric eruption in the Cascades. The next question was, which of the several now extinct (or at least quiescent) volcanoes had its ash embalmed so consistently? Microscopic comparison of the crystal and chemical structure of ash from each of the major

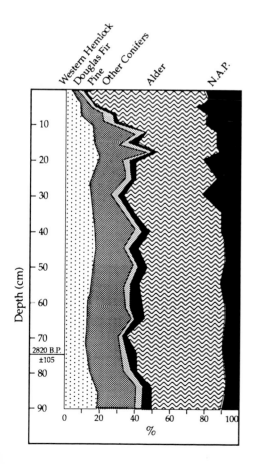

Pollen diagrams contrast past environments for Findley Lake (left) (3,666 feet) and Angle Lake (right) (367 feet, near sea level). Conifer forests remain dominant at Findley Lake, while alder increased dramatically at Angle Lake (presumably following logging). Depth signifies age from present to more than 2,000 years ago. (Rendering by April McCoy.)

volcanoes clinched the issue. Mount Mazama, the volcano that became Crater Lake, Oregon, was the prehistoric "polluter." And then radiocarbon dating of organic fragments next to the ash zeroed in on the date of the event: around 6,600 B.P. (Before Present, in the language of paleoecology). Palls of ash beclouded the Puget Sound area more than once, leaving their mark ultimately in the bog and lake "libraries" of sediments. Other ash layers can be traced to yet other volcanic eruptions. Glacier Peak and Mount St. Helens have left more than one tell-tale ash layer in peat bogs and lakes.

The reconstruction of the past life and times of the Findley Lake basin serves as an example of a worldwide effort among paleoecologists. The methodologies of the discipline permit a close reading of the biological, climatic, and geological events of the past. The time frame for this historical reconstruction is much more modest than that of the sedimentary geologist or paleontologist. While the latter detectives can roam back through several hundred million years of time, the effective limits for the kind of palynology we have described here is essentially post-Pleistocene, or what is now called the Holocene or Recent, not more than 25,000 years B.P. If the "time machine" of Holocene paleoecologists is limited in span, it makes up by having a fine-grained capacity to read changes of short duration. Such paleoecological techniques have even been used to detect the first presence of agricultural society in an area or even to unearth the time at which lead was first put in gasoline.

It has taken a bit less than 11,000 years to reforest lowland Puget Sound from the raw beginnings left by the retreating glaciers. Yet in so short a span of time, the natural etching in of the landscape by forest seems to have reached a climactic steady state, forest replacing forest, apparently predictably so, for endless time to come. Even without human intervention, some change is still inevitable.

There is one rapid natural change to the living landscape that we can see or at least reconstruct from contemporary observation. The thousands of lakes in our area are the epitome of impermanence. Nothing could be more inexorable than the gradual erasure of fresh-water ponds and lakes by the very processes that sustain their aquatic life today. The moment a lake begins to receive runoff from its lowlying terrestrial drainage basin, the filling-in process begins. Visits at random to a dozen or so lakes in the Puget Sound region are sure to bring out the lesson of dynamic change. Some lake basins will have been nearly completely filled by sediments, organic matter, and living semiaquatic vegetation. Others not so far down the successional path will have tongues of encroachment entering the remaining body of water. (See diagram, page 250.)

Although the 11,000-year baseline is the same for all lake basins, some have yielded to landmaking processes more rapidly than others. Conditions nurturing such successional change differ in kind and intensity. Size of the initial basin, the steepness of the surrounding runoff drainages, volume of water input-outgo in relation to volume of sediment input, acidity-alkalinity of water as an influence on the kind of life that can be supported, and character of surrounding vegetation, all such physical and biological factors must be integrated in particular proportions to account for the fate of a given lake. But in time, most lakes cannot outlast the steady increment of animal, vegetable, and mineral accumulation. The replacement of lake water by land is inevitable.

Habitats at the Land-Water Margin

Distinctive aggregations of plants and animals occur in and around our lowland lakes. In primeval times forest often marched right up to the edge of lakes; even today second-growth forest, when allowed to regenerate, may tower over the border of a lake. In those lakes where terrestrial life is relentlessly closing in on the water, a kind of amphibian existence holds sway. Bogs, swamps, marshes, and fens are the largely treeless, semiterrestrial transition zones between forest and lake proper. Of these habitats at the land-water margin, the bog stands out as the most distinctive microcosm with its own climate, lifeform pattern, and aggregation of bog-adapted organisms. In the making of a bog, a fragile fringe of living sphagnum moss first edges out into the open water. As more sphagnum, sedges, and other bog plants grow to overtop the older dead strata of the moss, a more solid peat border is built up. And all the while, the thin fringe of floating sphagnum nearest the water's edge is inching out to encroach further on the open water. The older, deeper, and firmer peat terrain becomes the seedbed for a special assemblage of plants, dominant among which are members of the acid-loving heath family, Ericaceae. Among the more usual ericoids are Labrador tea (*Ledum groenlandicum*), wild cranberry (*Vaccinium oxycoccus*), bog blueberry (*Vaccinium uliginosum*), and bog laurel (*Kalmia polifolia*).

In some bogs, other shrubs may assume a waist-high dominance; especially common near the coast is bog wax-myrtle (*Myrica gale*). Growing in the shelter of bog shrubbery and nestled in the shallow depressions of hummocks of sphagnum moss, one is sure to find that most curious insect-digesting plant, the sundew (*Drosera rotundifolia*). Its tiny spoon-shaped leaves are covered with sticky, stalked glands that ensnare tiny insects and digest them, to add the animal juices to the barest nutrition from the impoverished bog

Peat bogs, common in Puget Sound, are impermanent stages in lake succession. These glacial kettles inevitably fill in with the bodies of plants, mostly sphagnum moss and grasslike sedges. Kings Lake and its associated bog in eastern King County still have open water, though the floating mat of sphagnum (below) is slowly encroaching. (Photo by the author.)

substratum. Table 21 adds other woody and herbaceous plants that may occur more generally across the bog in sequence from forest border to the unstable water's edge.

A virgin peat bog in midstage of development would appear to have arrested the creep of succession. The peat substratum is so sterile that it accommodates only the progeny of its own acid-tolerant bog flora. So it would seem. But visits to several bogs can change that impression. On some bogs, often not more than a few feet from open water and the edge of the floating sphagnum mat, one can find isolated individuals or even dense strands of pygmy conifers. Often they are the same species that figure prominently in the climax forest farther back on "dry" land. I have seen dense stands of stunted western hemlock growing on peat hummocks—

This older sphagnum "peninsula" at Kings Lake is being colonized by hemlocks and acid-tolerant shrubs. (Photo by G. Pirzio-Biroli.)

Far right: The distinctive texture of sphagnum moss living at the surface of its peaty morgue. (Photo by G. Pirzio-Biroli.)

fifty-year-old trees not more than five or six feet tall. Lodgepole pine and western white pine are two other conifers that can hang on as aged dwarfs. The annual rain of tree seed from nearby forest is unrelenting. Only a few of the millions of seedlings persist to join the pioneering hemlock and pine. They become established more readily in the hospitable microclimate of the earlier tree pioneers. In this way the forest tree zone advances, inching toward the inner treeless bog, plant succession on the march.

New life on the advancing bog surface gains a roothold on the bodies of dead plants. Underneath the living bog surface lie many vertical feet of accumulated organic matter. Depending on the type of vegetable matter to expire in place, the accumulated peat, as it is called, may be classified as moss or sphagnum peat, fibrous or sedge peat, sedimentary peat, and so on. By far the most common peats are the first two, moss and fibrous peat. One of the great men of Puget Sound botany, Professor George B. Rigg, made the study of peat bogs his special passion during his long and active professional life at the University of Washington. In 1958, at the age of eighty-six, he brought this lifetime's devotion together in *The Peat Resources of Washington,* culminating a study that had begun in 1909. This work, published by the State Division of Mines and Geology (as Bulletin 44), is mostly a compilation of a statewide field and laboratory study of samples from 327 peat deposits. For each deposit, Rigg provides a map and a vertical profile and description of the deposit. These concise summaries fail, through Rigg's own modesty and scientific detachment, to depict the long, backbreaking hours in hot or wet and cold weather to extract the raw samples, the basic data for each summary. A hand-operated peat borer was used to take samples at intervals across a bog. The peat borer is essentially a very long and thin vegetable corer that can extract three-

Table 21. Woody and Herbaceous Plants Common in Bogs

Shrubs	*Herbs, grasslike plants, etc.*
Hardhack (*Spiraea douglasii*)	Bog cinquefoil (*Potentilla palustris*)
Twinberry (*Lonicera involucrata*)	Bog buckbean (*Menyanthes trifoliata*)
Rustyleaf or fool's huckleberry (*Menziesia ferruginea*)	Sedge (*Carex,* various species)
Willow (*Salix,* various species)	Cotton-grass (*Eriophorum vaginatum*)
Red alder (*Alnus rubra*)	Mosses other than sphagnum
Cascara (*Rhamnus purshiana*)	Reindeer "moss" (*Cladonia rangiferina,* lichen)
Creek or osier dogwood (*Cornus stolonifera*)	

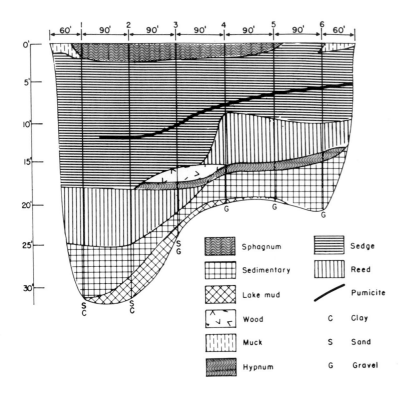

sec. 2, T. 21 N., R. 6 E.

Sphagnum	Sedge
Sedimentary	Reed
Lake mud	Pumicite
Wood	C Clay
Muck	S Sand
Hypnum	G Gravel

300'   0'   600'

Peat area

Sphagnum peat area

quarter-inch wide and foot-long cores of peat or other semisolid sediment. With brute force and the maximum feasible number of four-foot lengths of borer, it is possible to bring up samples at depths up to forty feet.

As the sample profiles show, typical western Washington peat bogs will have an upper layer of sphagnum or fibrous peat that overtops any one of several kinds of deeper strata; these may be sedge peat, lake sediments, lake mud, or other strata. Like lake sediments, most bog profiles have a thin layer of volcanic ash (pumicite) sandwiched in between the lower peat horizons. It was Rigg and his coworkers who first determined that the ash layer was deposited approximately 6,600 years ago from an eruption of Mount Mazama in the southern Cascades of Oregon.

Of the several kinds of peat that accumulate in postglacial depressions around Puget Sound, none is so distinctive as that formed by sphagnum moss. Bryologists, those botanists who specialize in mosses, assign the species of genus *Sphagnum* to their own unique family. Though there are about 150 species worldwide, only a few species live in Northwest bogs. The remarkable water-holding capacity of sphagnum moss plants comes about through the peculiar architecture of the tiny, filmy leaves. The leaf of a sphagnum plant, only one-cell layer thick, is a symmetrical mosaic

Profiles of two peat bogs in King County. The Black Diamond profile (above) has a large sphagnum peat layer, while the Bow Lake profile (opposite) has only fibrous (sedge) peat. The band of pumicite in both profiles is from the deposition of volcanic ash (tephra).

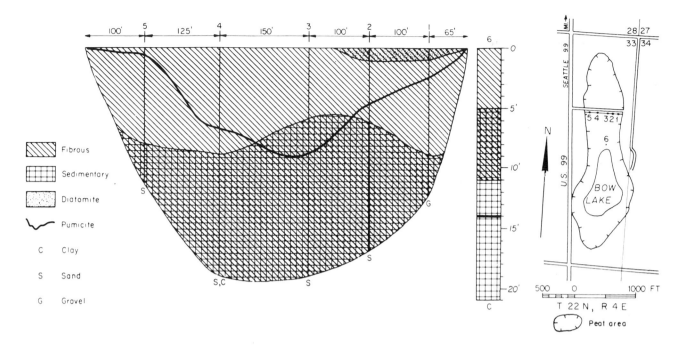

of dead and live cells. The dead cells are not only larger than the adjacent living cells; each one has a tiny pore that opens into the empty cell, now a water-retentive chamber. Thus, alive or dead, peat moss can take in and store large quantities of water in proportion to its dry weight. Moreover, it is particularly resistant to decay. No wonder that sphagnum peat is treated as a valuable resource. Tons have been mined from western Washington bogs for nearly a hundred years. Unlike Douglas fir, though, sphagnum is not quickly renewable. Mining for peat is hardly different from coal mining. The replacement rate is extremely slow and requires the undisturbed conditions of the bog-and-lake ecosystem progressing slowly toward bog-and-forest.

With seemingly unlimited water supply and the benign regional climate of the Pacific Northwest, one would hardly expect life in a Puget Sound bog to be stressful. But of all our local nonforested habitats, bog existence is the most rigorous for organisms. While temperature fluctuations in the nearby forest are moderate, the microclimate of the bog can undergo drastic oscillations. Years ago, when George Rigg first started poking around in bogs, he sensed that temperature could be a limiting factor to plant growth. He found that bogs usually have much lower temperatures at night or during cold periods of the year than do the forests just beyond on higher ground. Cold air slides into low-lying places such as bogs to depress air temperatures.

A closer look at bog microclimate was taken by Betty Jo Fitzgerald, a graduate student at the University of Washington during the mid-1960s. By using thermocouple thermometers that sensed ground-level temperatures, she found that temperatures on the bog could climb to over 100 degrees Fahrenheit on days when the adjacent forest temperatures were in the mid-70s. Though sphagnum seems to stand such temperatures, aided no doubt by its high water-holding capacity, seedlings from the adjacent forest vegetation would be killed by such temperatures. No doubt this range of temperature extremes, plus the sterile, acid substrate and other features of the bog habitat, slow down plant succession. Conifer seedlings do get a toehold on the bog, but a great many cooked or frozen seedlings are expended to get a few pioneers established.

Wetlands

"Wetlands" is another ecological buzzword of the 1990s. Like old-growth temperate forest and tropical rain forest, the wetland habitat has become a cause célèbre. Their surprisingly high productivity, their many values to humans, and their alarming disappearance put wetlands near the top of the environmentalist's agenda. Yet the word "wetland" scarcely appeared in the early literature on the environment or in the textbooks of ecology. Nonetheless, wetlands were there, annually performing a host of invaluable ecological functions, and annually losing ground to development, pollution, and other assaults. Ecologists had been studying wetlands for years under other names: marshes, swamps, estuaries, riparian habitats (lake and river shorelines), bogs, and the like. Nowadays, the collective term "wetland" comes to embrace all these land habitats liberally saturated with water.[2]

The essence of the wetland's key role in lowland ecosystems is summed up tellingly by Anne and Paul Ehrlich:

> . . . Marshes, swamps and [other saturated soil] are among Earth's most productive ecosystems. These wetlands are important providers of ecosystem services, especially in the cycling of nutrients. They also protect shore areas against severe storms, function as storage areas for excess water, thereby alleviating flood problems, and as natural reservoirs in time of drought. Wetlands, moreover, serve as nurseries for many important fish species and as way stations for migrating wildfowl, while harbouring an abundance of permanent plant and animal residents. (1987:54)

2. The definition of wetlands from King County's Sensitive Areas Ordinance (1981): "those areas that are inundated or saturated by surface or ground water at a frequency and duration to support, and that under normal circumstances do support, a prevalence of vegetation typically adapted for life in saturated soil conditions" (p. 2).

Land and water join to make a semi-aquatic ecosystem, one of many highly productive wetlands in the Puget basin. Nisqually delta. (Photo by Mary Randlett.)

Wetlands are common and widespread in lowland Puget country. Major saline wetlands occur on the shores of Puget Sound, especially in estuaries, where rivers meet the salt water. Salt marshes and tidelands with eelgrass beds are typical saline wetland types. Freshwater wetlands are no less common, given the post-Pleistocene topography that produced lakes, ponds, and streams studding the lowland landscape. Elsewhere in this chapter we explored some freshwater wetlands: lake margins, stream borders (riparian habitats), and bogs. The local inventory adds other freshwater wetlands: seasonally flooded basins or flats, wet meadows, marshes (deep or shallow), and swamps with tree or shrub cover. It all adds up to habitat types, distinctive in the organisms they harbor and yet most vulnerable to human intrusion.

Left: Depressions made by the retreating continental glacier often become bogs, unique wetland types with characteristic plant and animal life. (Photo by Mary Randlett.)

Besides peat bogs, other wetlands abound in the lowlands: Facing page, top: Saltmarsh at Sequim Bay on Olympic Peninsula. (Photo by Ron Vanbianchi.) Below left: This water-lily pond with wetland grasses and sedges at its margin is on the North Fork Snoqualmie River, east of Snoqualmie Falls. (Photo by Mark Sheehan.) Below right: This variant of wetlands is dominated by grasslike sedges (species of Carex*) and can be found in the lower reaches of broad river valleys in the Cascade foothills. (Photo by Mark Sheehan.)*

Coniferous Trees

Deciduous Trees

Right: A common wetland habitat is between forest and stream, called the riparian zone. Deciduous hardwood trees and shrubs predominate.

Shrubs

Sedges, Rushes and Grasses

Water

AQUATIC ZONE

RIPARIAN ZONE

UPLAND ZONE

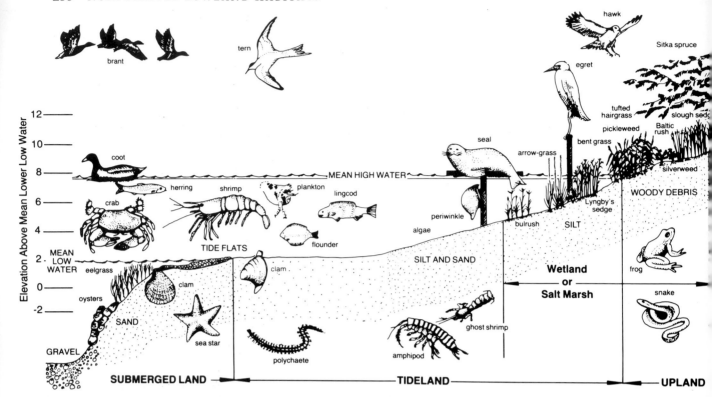

The most telling and dramatic attribute of many wetlands, especially estuarine habitats, is their exceptionally high productivity. Annual plant biomass production of these well-watered lands compares favorably with tropical rain forests and can surpass that of agricultural land (see Table 22).

Amateur bird watchers or professional ornithologists will extoll the rich variety and overwhelming numbers of waterfowl and land birds that use wetlands for food, nesting sites, and the like. Some birds occupy as permanent residents the freshwater or saline wetlands; more may use them as vital way-stations on their migratory journeys. Major waterfowl habitats in Puget Sound include the deltas of the Nisqually, Stillaguamish, Nooksack, Skagit, and Fraser rivers, major lakes with marsh vegetation, as well as innumerable lesser streams throughout the Puget Sound drainage basin. Spectacular sightings of snow geese, trumpeter swans, Canada geese, bald eagles, and a host of other water-loving birds are recorded for local wetlands (see Angell and Balcomb 1982 for a full account of Puget Sound wetland wildlife). These wetland inhabitants and transients all partake directly or indirectly of the rich and productive bounty of Puget Sound wetlands. The pyramids of biomass and of numbers, illustrated on p. 225, are dramatically exemplified by the producer-to-consumer network of wildlife in wetlands.

The highly productive estuarine ecosystem with its diversity of plant and animal life.

Table 22. Primary Productivity in Wetlands

Habitat Type
Wetlands
Tropical forests
Temperate forests
Temperate grasslands
Cultivated land

Note: From R. H. Whittaker 1975.

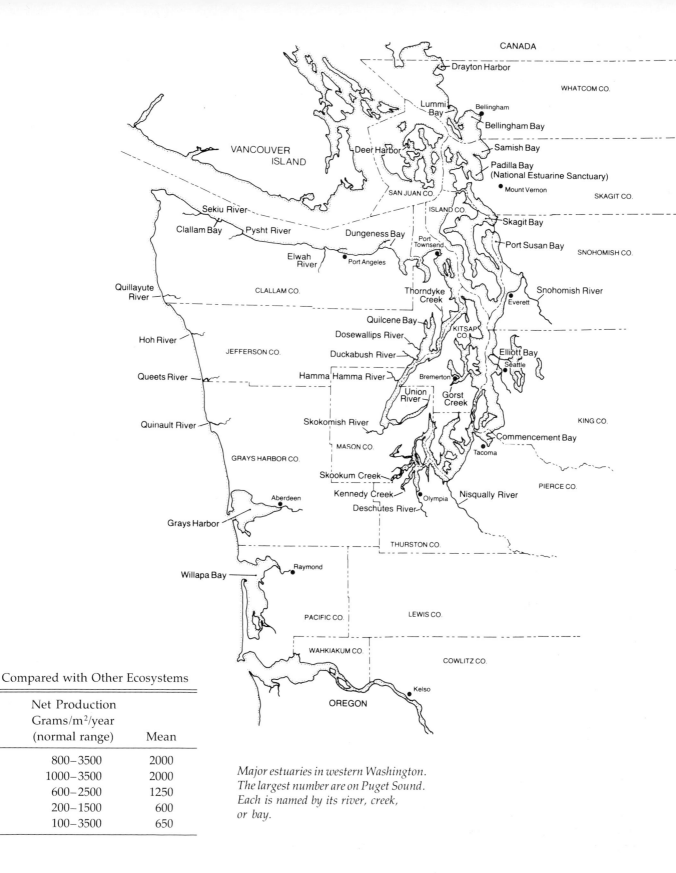

CANADA

Drayton Harbor

WHATCOM CO.

Lummi Bay

Bellingham

Bellingham Bay

Samish Bay

VANCOUVER ISLAND

Deer Harbor

Padilla Bay (National Estuarine Sanctuary)

Mount Vernon

SAN JUAN CO.

SKAGIT CO.

ISLAND CO.

Skagit Bay

Sekiu River

Clallam Bay

Pysht River

Dungeness Bay

Port Townsend

Port Susan Bay

SNOHOMISH CO.

Elwah River

Port Angeles

Snohomish River

Quillayute River

CLALLAM CO.

Thorndyke Creek

Everett

Hoh River

Quilcene Bay

Dosewallips River

KITSAP CO.

Elliott Bay

JEFFERSON CO.

Duckabush River

Seattle

Queets River

Hamma Hamma River

Bremerton

Union River

Gorst Creek

Quinault River

Skokomish River

KING CO.

Commencement Bay

GRAYS HARBOR CO.

MASON CO.

Tacoma

Skookum Creek

Kennedy Creek

Olympia

Nisqually River

PIERCE CO.

Aberdeen

Deschutes River

Grays Harbor

THURSTON CO.

Willapa Bay

Raymond

PACIFIC CO.

LEWIS CO.

WAHKIAKUM CO.

COWLITZ CO.

Kelso

OREGON

Compared with Other Ecosystems

Net Production Grams/m²/year (normal range)	Mean
800–3500	2000
1000–3500	2000
600–2500	1250
200–1500	600
100–3500	650

Major estuaries in western Washington. The largest number are on Puget Sound. Each is named by its river, creek, or bay.

Ronald Bog, just north of the Seattle city limits, was on its way to extinction—just another landfill (dumping in a wetland is so easy!). Near right: Ronald Bog in 1968, giving way to inundation by rubble. Far right: Twenty years later, after a citizens' campaign to save the bog, native vegetation reappeared, with its small lake still intact. (Photos by the author.)

Also significant is the wetland's function as a nursery for fish populations. From nongame fish like sticklebacks and sculpins to the highly prized salmonid fishes, whether spawning here or simply passing through, all enter into watery feasting in wetland habitats.

Still another vital function of wetlands is controlling water levels of drainage basins by storage and streamflow regulation, thus alleviating flooding of lowlands. These natural check dams are invaluable in times of excess runoff, and in dry periods as well. A local case makes the point. A small lake and bog in north King County, Ronald Bog, was close to extermination; plans for filling it as a building site were the last affront to a rich freshwater wetland that had already suffered from peat extraction, land fill, and sundry other assaults. The neighborhood's citizenry mounted a campaign to save and restore Ronald Bog. Now it is a well-manicured county park with lake, shoreline vegetation, and waterfowl. But it was saved because it could also serve as storage for seasonal storm water runoff.

Attempts to preserve remaining wetlands in lowland Puget Sound country have met with mixed success. A few saltwater wetlands have come under protection in recent years: the Nisqually Delta (a National Wildlife Refuge) and parts of the Skagit River flats and Padilla Bay salt marshes (state refuges) are notable examples. Freshwater wetlands have fared even less well. Unless concerted

Right: The Nisqually Delta, just north of Olympia, is a major wildlife habitat, especially for birds. The delta is mostly preserved as a National Wildlife Refuge.

actions are taken, the remaining freshwater wetlands, either in private or public ownership, will disappear by the year 2000. Thus, it is in the remaining years of this century that we will witness major campaigns to preserve wetlands.

The Nature Conservancy and Audubon societies have put wetland preservation high on their agendas. County, state, and federal government agencies are also giving wetlands a high priority. Witness the efforts and accomplishments of the Washington Natural Heritage Program (Department of Natural Resources), state departments of Fisheries, Wildlife, and Ecology, as well as various county planning units (e.g., King County Planning Division). Since a large portion of lowland wetlands are in private hands, their secure future is both costly and chancy.

Recognition of wetlands' preservation in urban Puget country has taken the form of an "environmentally sensitive areas" ordinance (No. 9614), passed by the King County Council in August of 1990. The ordinance, recognizing the need to preserve not only wetlands, streams, and floodplains, but other sensitive landscapes in King County, thus comes to grip with the dangers of loss of natural environments caused by development and other human intrusions in the environment.

The "Prairies" of Lowland Puget Sound Country

The shores of Puget Sound were once rimmed with a nearly unbroken wall of lofty virgin timber. Yet the venturesome explorer of the late eighteenth century need only have headed south from the lower reaches of the Sound at Olympia or Fort Nisqually to leave continuous forest. Here towering forest gave way within a few short miles to vast parklands and prairie, some utterly flat, others terraced, and still others with a bizarre, mounded landscape. What is now popularly called the "Tacoma prairies" is a mosaic of open land and forest that fans out southward from the southern borders of Tacoma into the Fort Lewis country and radiates through Yelm, Rainier, Rochester, and Tenino. The greatest stretches of this prehistorically more open country fit into lowland sectors of Pierce and Thurston counties, with a southward finger into Lewis County and intermittently reappearing in Clark County right down to the shores of the Columbia River. The northern portion of this patchwork of prairie, oak woodland, and open forest is best called a *gravelly outwash plain*, a name that hints of the way that this singular landscape was created: gravelly, because of the coarse, cobbly texture of its soil and substratum, and outwash, to epitomize the rush of gravel-laden glacial meltwater that formed channels and morainal banks in the country just beyond the southern limit of the last continental ice sheet.

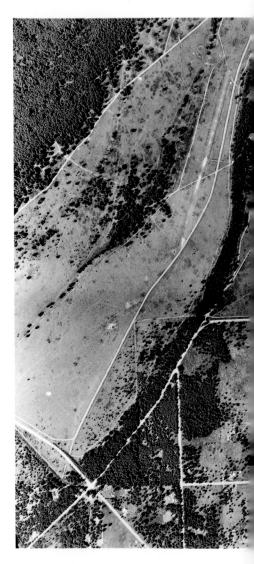

Prairie and forest, in some places having sharp borders, in others showing invasion of Douglas fir. This vertical aerial of June 18, 1985, looks down on Tenalquat Prairie just southwest of Yelm.

Ecologists quibble over the use of the word "prairie" as appropriate to these lowlying, flat openings in Northwest forest. The word came west with the pioneers who had spanned mile after level mile of tall- and short-grass prairie in middle America. There, the vast treeless plains between rivers displayed a rich sea of grass on a deep and fertile soil blown out of the perimeter of the old Wisconsin ice sheet. The deep black soil of the midwest prairies contrasts with the shallow stony soils of western Washington. (See Appendix 5.) Yet an on-the-ground view of a Puget Sound prairie does bring the midwestern landform to mind. And so ingrained is this usage of the term that the purists need not try to change it.

The word prairie came into local use from the earliest description of the unusual landform. Dr. William Frasier Tolmie, in residence at Fort Nisqually where he was in the employ of the Hudson's Bay Company, wrote in his diary of a day on the prairie in August 1833: "Had a long walk on the prairie in the afternoon and came upon a portion new to me where winding elevations carpeted with young oaks and brake [= bracken fern], and clothed with pines are not infrequent. Marshy hollows were also formed of small extent." Tolmie doubled as company medical officer, a not uncommon practice for naturalists in the early days of far western exploration. As a student of the celebrated English botanist, Sir William Jackson Hooker, Tolmie had been schooled in the careful observation of plants and landscapes. His further observations on the prairie merit quoting. "The shade of a lofty pine beautifully interspersed and surrounded with oaks and through the gaps in the arch we see the broad plain extending southward to the Nisqually." And further on in his walk he notes that "the point of wood now became broader and the intervening plain degenerated into prairie." Incidentally, Tolmie was the first botanist to explore Mount Rainier. Although he did not get to the summit, he collected plants on the slopes of the mountain.

The name "prairie" is further engraved on maps of this landscape by the place names given to many of these open flat expanses of land (see page 31). A gazetteer of the country below Puget Sound makes colorful reading for the seeker of prairies. Feast on this place-name sampler: Mima Prairie, Weir Prairie, Tehalquat Prairie, Chambers Prairie, Bernards Prairie, Smith Prairie, 90th Division Prairie, Neats Prairie, to pick a few at random. In nearly every sample of prairie, the pattern assumes a predictable form. Flat or mounded expanses of treeless land are densely covered with grass, moss, lichens and other low herbaceous plants; indeed, so densely interspersed is the moss-lichen layer (or turf) that no further encroachment by plants seems possible. But unlike midwestern prairies, Puget Sound prairies are shaped and rimmed at their perimeters by trees, either at the same topographic level or more often by a change from level to sloping land. Where prairie gives way to forest, the zone of transition may take on the character of a park or open woodland. Though we may hold a vision of a park as a humanly contrived array of trees adrift on a sea of well-kept grass, the word park has been used as well to describe natural openings in dense forest. Our only native oak, *Quercus garryana*, commonly occupies this parkland border between open prairie and dense coniferous forest. But the same landscape can be produced by Douglas fir. No treescape in our woods is more graceful and stately than the open, prairie-grown firs, widely spaced, with their huge downarched lower limbs often touching the ground.

Where the gravelly prairies occur on outwash terraces, the contact between treeless flat prairie and forested slope of the adjoining lower terrace can be exceedingly abrupt. Old aerial photos of the region show a prairie-forest border so sharp that one wants to invoke human intervention as the maker of the contact. That sense of human influence is supported by the history of the prairies. In most recent times, these abrupt contacts have become somewhat more fuzzy, due to the inching into the prairie by Douglas fir, now protected from wildfires. Early reports tell of intentional burning of the prairies by Indians, which would prevent the encroachment of fir onto the prairie. It is now believed that the Indians had at least a twofold purpose in burning: one, to drive game into hunting range, and the other, to keep the camas thriving in the open prairie. (Camas, or *Camassia quamash*, that beautiful blue lilylike plant of the Northwest, was dug by the Indians for its edible bulbs.) I will return later to the encroachment of forest onto prairie when pondering over that most mysterious of prairie landscapes, the Mima mounds.

It is no accident that the gravelly outwash prairies coincide in position with the southern terminus of the last continental ice sheet. Prairie landscape and gravelly outwash soils take their character from the hydraulically devastating events associated with the Vashon glaciation. Recall from chapter 1 that continental ice, hemmed in by the resistant flanks of the Cascades and Olympics, squeezed southward down the Puget trough to just below Olympia. Here the massive ice flow separated into two lobes, with the resistant volcanic rocks of the Black Hills (southwest of Olympia) as the separating wedge. Both east and west lobes were nearly played out as the viscous mass of ice came to rest, a scant 15,000 years ago, along an irregular border stretching through southern Thurston County.

The towns and villages of Eatonville, Vail, Rainier, Tenino, Little Rock, and Mima ring the border of the glacial drama, some within and some just beyond the maximum limit of that last (or latest?)

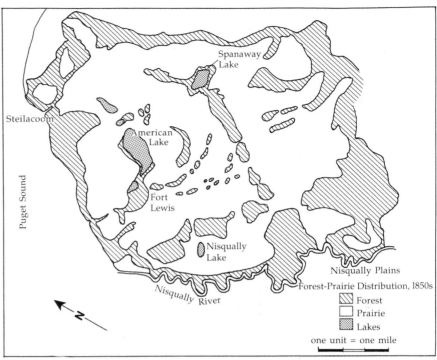

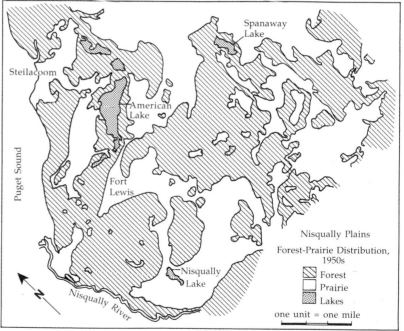

Washington's only oak (Quercus garryana, *Oregon post oak or Garry oak) is a common associate of prairie vegetation. Above: Garry oak on prairie. (Photo by James McDermott.) Left: Mature oaks in comely colonies bordering Fort Lewis. (Photo by the author.)*

Right: Change in areal extent of prairies over the last 150 years. Top: The prairies of 1850, reconstructed from land use and other historical records. Bottom: Shrinking of prairie area by the late twentieth century. (Rendering by Sandra Noel.)

tongue of ice to pour out of British Columbia. The Vashon ice sheet, though possibly 6,000 feet thick at the United States–Canada border, 4,000 feet thick at Seattle, and 1,800 feet thick at Tacoma, tapered down to nearly sea level at the southern border of its maximum advance. Though destined to remain in the Puget trough only fifteen hundred years or so, the impress of its presence was felt everywhere in the basin. And at the southern terminus, the ice and its meltwaters engineered unique changes on the land.

During melting and consequent recession of the glacier, three major land-shaping actions took place. Initially, much glacial debris, mostly ice-rafted rock and gravel, was deposited as a thin veneer on the preexisting glacial till. Then, major drainage channels were formed to carry off gravel and silt-laden waters. Because of the hilly terrain below the receding ice front, the water escaped, not to the south, but to the west. The meltwater drainageways of Deschutes Creek, Skookumchuck River, Scatter Creek, and the Black River found outlets into the ever-widening channel of the Chehalis River.

The third element of the ice-influenced processes to shape the

Above: Douglas fir has long since moved onto prairies that were once free of trees. (Photo by James McDermott.)

Right: Retreat of continental ice in late Pleistocene, forming glacial Lake Russell in its wake. Maximum extent of Puget lobe of continental glacier also shown. (Rendering by Sandra Noel.)

The Douglas fir invasion of a prairie in all stages, from tiny saplings (foreground) and young trees to dead older trees. (Photo by the author.)

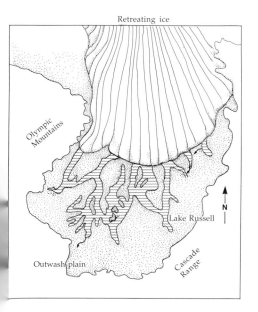

prairies was the creation of ice-fed lakes along the retreating border of the continental ice flow. The channeling of meltwater was dictated by the mountainous perimeter of the southern Puget Sound basin. Water was thus diverted into the Chehalis River, its drainage channel vastly larger than is now needed. To the geologist, such "underfit" water courses with outsized channels are sure indicators of postglacial runoff and overflow from glacial lakes. At one time, one such lake (named Lake Russell by J. Harlen Bretz, pioneer glacial geologist of the area) extended from Olympia north to Everett, the new terminus of the retreating ice sheet. Many feeder streams in the prairie area carried meltwater eventually into the Chehalis. The magnitude of their burden of water, silt, and gravel varied as the ice sheet ebbed to the north. Thus, when Lake Russell reached its maximum size, it was the Black River that served as its outlet to the Chehalis. At Little Rock, southwest of Olympia, the exceptional width of the Black River tells the story of the dramatic shift from a turbulent water-gouged channel for ever-filling Lake Russell, to the quiet stream of today. The Black River is another prime example of an "underfit" stream.

At other times during the period from glacial maximum to ultimate recession, other causeways funneled off meltwater. Scatter Creek, Skookumchuck River, Ohop Creek, Spurgeon Creek, and others are now only trickles compared to their earlier torrential outpourings. Channeled into the drainage of the Chehalis River, as was the water from Lake Russell and from the melting glacial front, the trending of gravel and silt deposits in terraces and drainageways was to the southwest. For roughly fifteen hundred years the southern fringe of the Vashon ice sheet was feeding the prairie-to-be with sterile cobble, gravel, and silt. The tailings of this gigantic earth-moving project formed the present landscapes of the prairies of Tacoma, Olympia, and Tenino. The pattern is one of flat, water-cut terraces that once rimmed the causeways serving to carry meltwater out to sea.

The Mima Mounds: Pimpled Plains of Southern Puget Country

For the early explorer-naturalists, one surprise followed another in their wanderings south of Fort Nisqually. First, there were the unexpected openings in forest leading onto stretches of prairie. But the ultimate in the unexpected were those prairie openings with mounded topography. Nothing so captured the imagination and whetted the curiosity of explorers and pioneer settlers as that unusual and enigmatic landscape, the Mima mounds. Were they ancient Indian burial grounds or the humped-up nests of sucker fish from an earlier marine seascape? Were they the ancient eroded remains of frozen ground during the last Ice Age? The mounds of the gravelly outwash prairie challenged the inventive minds of the first visitors to the land, and the controversy over their origin has simmered on into the late twentieth century.

Here and there on the prairies of Thurston County, the open land is dominated by a topography of nearly evenly spaced, circular mounds, large and plentiful enough easily to command the attention of the traveler. A nearly pristine display of mounded prairies is at Mima Prairie, just southwest of Little Rock in Thurston County. The highway to Rochester suddenly breaks out of dense fir forest into open land where mound after mound dominates the scene. Mima Prairie epitomized the mound phenomenon and in fact is the "type locality" for all such singular microrelief wherever such mounds occur in other parts of the world.

The geographer encountering similar pimpled plains in the Altiplano of the Andes or the "hogwallow" country of the Great Valley of California would categorize them as Mima mounds. On Mima Prairie, the well-rounded mounds average six to eight feet in height and are about thirty-five to fifty feet in diameter at their base. These earthen, grass-covered "haycocks" are so closely spaced that it is the mound, not the intermound trough, that dominates the scene. At first sight they appear evenly distributed, but when mapped, some variation in their spacing became evident. What appears to be the exposed half of a huge buried sphere loses that character on closer inspection. Where mounds have been sliced vertically in two, the above-ground portion is seen to be nearly hemispheric; the below-ground section is a shallower concave lens. The sectioned mound in profile consists of a blackish gritty soil and subsoil from convex top to concave bottom. A coarse gravel, the primary resource of mounded prairies, underlies the base of the mound. Unfortunately, some of the finest samples of this remarkable landform are still being destroyed to get at the accessible gravel. While the mound itself is exceptionally free of the larger rock and cobble underneath, the lowlying intermound areas harbor a dense concentration of rock just beneath a thin mossy turf. This highly nonrandom distribution of gravel and cobble will bear further scrutiny when we assess the various hypotheses as to the origin of the mounds.

Areas with mounded topography are local and apparently randomly distributed through the outwash prairie country. J. Harlen Bretz, in his 1913 pioneering study of post-Pleistocene landforms in Puget Sound, mapped the major occurrences of Mima-type relief. He showed the mounds to be predominantly within the perimeter of the maximum southern extent of the Vashon glacier, though some mounded prairies are distinctly outside and south of the glacial front. For example, while Mima Prairie, most of Rocky Prairie, and Offut Lake Prairie are mounded prairies that once were covered with Vashon ice, others at Cedarville, Oakville, and Gate were not. This distribution of mounds surely must be another piece of the fabric from which to weave a credible theory of mound origin. Further, some Mima-type mounds in other parts of the world have no connection with ice-age events: witness the mounds in the Great Valley of California that were never in contact with glacial activity.

Origin of the Mima Mounds. Popular accounts of the mounds cloak the problem of origin in mystery. The reason for such dramatic tactics is not hard to find. Ever since their discovery by Europeans in the early 1800s, conjecture and imagination have run unchecked in trying to account for the genesis of the mounds. There is blessed little that meets the casual eye to provide a ready and unequivocal explanation of their origin. The gross physical qualities of the

Mima mounds, a remarkable topographic variant within the prairie-in-forest landscape. Mima Prairie, the "type locality" of Mima-type mounds worldwide, about four miles west of Little Rock, Thurston County. Indistinct remnants of Mima mounds on left just beyond farm buildings. Douglas fir encroaching in distant upper right. (Photo by Victor Scheffer.)

mounds both external and subterranean hardly provide the answer. Bereft then of easy scientific explanation, like those for volcanoes or river valleys, the void has been filled with all manner of hypotheses, wild and tame—and largely untested. Bretz, in his characteristically thorough presentation of postglacial events in Puget Sound, devotes a whole chapter to the mounds, together with fine turn-of-the-century photographs of them (1913). A section on "hypotheses" in his chapter on the mounds is of special interest to us here.

The first sightings on record piqued the imagination of the viewer. Commodore Charles Wilkes, controversial leader of a major United States exploring expedition, spent a portion of the year 1841 in the Puget Sound area. On May 20, Wilkes had his first encounter with the mounds. So impressed was he with the phenomenon that he returned in July of that year to take a closer look. He writes:

> We soon reached the Bute Prairies, which are extensive, and covered with tumuli or small mounds, at regular distances asunder. As far as I could learn there is no tradition among the natives relative to them. They are conical mounds, 30 feet in diameter, about 6 to 7 feet high above level, and many thousands in number. Being anxious to ascertain if they contained any relics, I subsequently [around 11 July, 1841] visited these prairies and opened three of the mounds, but nothing was found in them but a pavement of round stones.

He expands on his return to the mounds in July with a party of soldiers to investigate the interior of the mounds.

> The men began their digging early in the morning. These mounds have been formed by scraping the surface earth together in a heap. The soil, therefore, is very rich, and they have a rank growth of vegetation on them. Much of this rich earth or mould must have been brought from a distance. The regularity of their construction and shape, as well as the space over which they are scattered, are surprising. Although I could obtain no direct information respecting them, I was one day told that the medicine-man gathered his herbs from them, to make the decoctions with which he effects his cures.

These conjectures led Wilkes to the crux of his theory:

> Although all tradition concerning them may be lost, yet the custom of these medicine men may have survived and taking into consideration the influence they have had and still have over the tribes, it is possible that their predecessors might have had something to do with the formation of these monuments. They certainly are not places of burial. They bear the mark of savage labor and are such an undertaking as would require the united efforts of a whole tribe.

Ground views of the mounds at Mima Prairie. Top: In the 1980s, the mounds still look like Commodore Wilkes's grassy "haycocks." Bottom: Cutaway view of a mound with black topsoil (unstratified profile) and cobble subsoil.

After his search for artifacts proved fruitless, Wilkes concluded: "I heard it suggested that they had been formed by water-courses, but this I view as impossible, for they are situated on a level prairie and are at least a thousand in number."

The Wilkes hypothesis of a human origin of the mounds is one of several in that vein. As expected, other observers have thought the mounds to be Indian burial grounds; still another idea is that the mounds are hillocks created by Indians for the cultivation of camas bulbs, a common Indian edible. Two other major contexts for speculation and hypothesizing accommodate all the rest of the proposed causes. There is the group of hypotheses that relate to various physical factors and processes associated with glaciation and postglacial events. And then there is the final category of propositions that exploits the activities of animals other than humans, and plants. We shall examine examples of these three basic modes of origin—human, physical, animal—in pursuing a chronological account of man-meets-mounds.

Barely two years after Wilkes encountered them, Canadian Paul Kane came upon the mounds. As a prodigious and skillful artist of the North American frontier, Kane left a far more vivid record than Wilkes' paltry diagrams and general descriptions. During the year 1847, Kane traveled overland from Fort Vancouver to Fort Nisqually and on to Vancouver Island. It was on April 6 of this lone artist's tour of Indians and landscapes that Kane saw and recorded so vividly his impressions of the mounds. The oil painting shown here, based on his original sketches, is now in the collection of the Royal Ontario Museum, Department of Archaeology in Toronto, Canada.

His fascination with the mounds led to a long detour among them. Of his encounter, he writes:

> This evening we encamped in the Prairie de Bute. This is remarkable for having innumerable round elevations, touching each other like so many hemispheres, of 10 or 12 yards in circumference, and 4 or 5 feet in height. I dug one of them open, but found nothing in it but loose stones, although I went 4 or 5 feet down. The whole surface is thickly covered with coarse grass. I travelled 22 miles through this extraordinary looking prairie. (1925:142)

In the interval of over a hundred years, from Wilkes and Kane to the present, the procession of ideas on the mounds has both widened and gotten complex. Easily dismissed is the idea of the celebrated nineteenth-century naturalist, Louis Agassiz, who "unhesitatingly" concluded that the mounds were the nests of a species of sucker fish; this unsupportable assertion was based on second-hand descriptions and sketches he had seen.

Theories that resorted to the activities of ice, water, sedimentation, and postglacial thawing were drawn into the drama well before the turn of the century. Their first clearest statement was by the indefatigable glacial geologist, J. Harlen Bretz. After reviewing all the known hypotheses and evaluating their strengths and weaknesses, he had the courage of his convictions to provide a hypothesis: the workings of ice and water. In great modesty he writes:

> It may be suggested tentatively that if a sheet of ice several feet thick could be formed over the surface of an outwash gravel plain and could subsequently be flooded so that stream-carried debris would be deposited on its surface, it might, on melting, develop pits into which the surficial debris would gravitate. Since water is densest at 39°F, the lower interstices of the gravel in the pits of the postulated sheet of ice would become filled with water at this temperature. Since such water would be 7° warmer than the adjacent ice, it would cause deepening and enlarging of the pits after the earthy accumulation had become so thick that warming of the gravel by the sun ceased to be a direct factor in formation of the pits. Sliding and washing of the surface debris into these pits would expose interpit areas, and the melting of such areas would then proceed more slowly than when rock fragments strewed it, and absorbed the sun's heat . . . Some such set of conditions might give rise, on final melting of the ice, to mounds; these being without structure, without assortment and superposed on current-bedded gravels as are the Mima type mounds. (1913:105)

Thus appeared the first in a series of "ice-and-water" hypotheses to account for the mounds that were to reach their fullest expression many years later.

By the 1930s, enough glaciologists had seen the vast areas of polygonally patterned frozen ground of arctic Alaska to be smit-

Paul Kane, early Canadian artist, preserved this view of Mima mounds on April 6, 1847.

ten by the germ of an idea. They saw in the frost-polygons of the far North the first stages of what could have produced the Mima mounds, the by-products of glacial and postglacial physical processes. The first modern explanation in 1940 by R. C. Newcomb using these ingredients was further refined by Arthur M. Ritchie (1953), geologist for the Washington State Highway Commission. Both Newcomb and Ritchie agreed on the polygonal patterning in frozen ground as a starting point. Newcomb deduced that frost-buckling at the perimeter of the large permafrost polygons forced blocks of earth upward at the edges of the polygon. Where the ice melted, the earthen bulges remained as mounds.

Ritchie substituted thawing followed by erosion as sculptors of the ice-age polygons to form the final postglacial mounds. After the frozen polygonal cores melted at their edges, leaving still-frozen cores, postglacial flooding rounded off these cones to leave the conical cores of thawing silt we now call Mima mounds.

Until recent years, this complex explanation served to satisfy most scientists, especially if they were too far away to consult the mounds firsthand in order to check out the theory. By 1965, however, when the International Association for Quaternary Research (INQUA) held its field conference in the Pacific Northwest, geologist Stephen Porter could point out shortcomings in both Newcomb and Ritchie proposals. Porter (1965:65) states: "A possible objection to Newcomb's theory is the question of whether or not the thrusting action of ice wedges can force silt into mounds 7 feet high. Also, there is no additional convincing evidence of permafrost conditions near the close of Vashon time." Likewise, Porter saw a defect in the Ritchie version of the altered frost polygon theory. To have eroded the polygons into mounds would have required a vast inundation of mound country now on terraces at several levels. Such an ice-dammed "head" of water would have had to be nearly three miles long and at least four hundred feet deep.

Where uncertainty exists, science never rests; inscrutable phenomena continue to challenge and provoke investigation. Another theory on how the mounds might have been formed took shape in the writings of two highly respected biologists, Walter W. Dahlquest and Victor B. Scheffer, just about the time the ice-and-water theories were beginning to congeal. As a radical antidote to the frost polygon-erosion theory, these two vertebrate zoologists offered what has now been pithily called "the gopher theory."

The mere linking of the words gopher and mounds evokes an image of how the mounds might be built. Given enough time and the energies of enough gophers, the earthen "haycocks" could come into being. But so startling an idea of small fossorial rodents, the size of squirrels, building thousands of huge mounds boggles the mind. And so the gopher theory for many years was considered too fanciful and bizarre to be worthy of serious consideration. However, Scheffer has persisted and by that persistence has induced others to examine the hypothesis. We would do well to give it a proper hearing.

It all started in 1941 when Dahlquest was undertaking a survey of the mammals of Washington. As he worked through the state, he came upon the mounded prairies near Mima. He was enrolled in a geology course at the University of Washington about that time, and he knew that geologists still felt that the origin of the mounds was something of a mystery. His mammal survey of the prairies and the unexplained mounds kindled the spark of an idea. Could the mounds be the handiwork of the pocket gopher (*Thomomys talpoides*)? Dahlquest's idea quickly caught the interest of a fellow naturalist and vertebrate zoologist, Victor Scheffer, then working on marine mammals for the U.S. Fish and Wildlife Service. After considerable field investigation and search of the literature on both gophers and mounded relief in western North America, the two scientists published the "gopher theory" in 1942. It and a later article by Scheffer (in *Scientific Monthly* for 1947) set forth in cautious detail the support for the novel hypothesis. I quote from this paper at length:

> Our theory of the origin of the Mima Mounds by gopher activity may be summed up as follows: A few tens of thousands of years ago, the Puget Sound prairie was laid down by rivers draining from the Vashon Ice Sheet. At first, the rivers were powerful and were able to carry the large boulders now found in the substratum of the prairie. Later, the rivers were quieter and were able to carry only the fine silt that, richened and darkened by the addition of grass-root humus, now composes the topsoil.
>
> As soon as vegetation captured the raw new soil, we suppose that pocket gophers came in from the unglaciated country to the southward, advancing perhaps a few hundred feet in a gopher generation. By the time they reached the southern end of Puget Sound they encountered a barrier, the evergreen forest that had been racing against them to occupy the new land. There they were stopped, and, to the present day, no gophers are found on the lowlands of the Pacific coast north of southern Puget Sound. . . .
>
> We can picture, then, thousands of years ago, gophers rooting through the thin silt of the Puget Sound outwash in search of plant roots. At certain places they dug deeply into the gravelly subsoil in order to make nest chambers well protected from prowling bear, wolf, or wildcat. Areal spacing of the nest chambers corresponded to the size of the "territory" of each animal. The center of an old territory now marks, we believe, the center of a modern mound.
>
> In excavating for its nest chamber, the gopher was instinctively led to dig deep into the bedded gravel, regardless of the effort involved. When the animal ran into a large boulder it undermined the obstruc-

tion and allowed it to settle. Thus, we now find, at the base of most mounds, a concentration of coarser materials. On the other hand, in foraging daily for food over its home range, the gopher was driven by less powerful instincts. When it encountered a bothersome rock in its path, it simply passed around it, shoving dirt along as it went. Thus, we find plainly exposed in the intermound hollows large boulders that were doubtless at one time buried in the topsoil.

Where the mound and its bed are in contact, there are found "mound roots," long a puzzle to geologists, which are simply abandoned gopher tunnels now filled with black silt contrasting in color with the yellow gravel around it. . . . We can imagine that, in cases where a gopher mound was abandoned by its owner for some reason or other, the nesting chamber collapsed and caused a depression at the crest of the mound, a characteristic feature of many of the mounds on Mima Prairie.

In fancy, it is easy to picture the start of a Mima Mound. It is less easy to account for its growth. For reasons that may never be known, the gophers carried more dirt toward the nest than away from it. Perhaps some biologist will suggest an experiment whereby the growth of a Mima-type mound can be studied from start to finish. At present, we do not know whether the mounds on the Puget Sound and other prairies are still growing, whether they are in equilibrium with the forces tending to reduce them, or whether they are shrinking. (1947:290–93)

As with much of scientific explanation for events of the remote past, Scheffer and Dahlquest had to rely on indirect evidence, yet their theory is marshalled with convincing thoroughness.

In the twenty or so years following the publication of the Dahlquest-Scheffer interpretation, the two prevailing and contending ideas—frost polygon–erosion theory versus the gopher theory—have had about equal time in the arena of debate and discussion. The apparent stalemate seems now nearer to being broken, for wholly new firsthand evidence adds support to the gopher theory. The new information comes from painstaking microscopic analysis of the pattern of organic accumulation in the profiles of mounded and unmounded prairie soils. Matsuo Tsukada, botanist at the Quaternary Research Center at the University of Washington, has found that pollen grains and other plant fragments are not stratified in mounds as they are in soils or lake sediments. His findings reveal that mound soils have been mixed, as though some biological agent, possibly gophers, has kept these soils churned up (Washburn 1988:8). So the gopher theory, once ridiculed by cartoons of giant prehistoric gophers even wielding shovels, has gained further support. And although active mound-building by gophers is not now evident on Mima Prairie, the phenomenon has been seen elsewhere in the West.

Scheffer would like to see one more test of the hypothesis. He reasons that the introduction of a colony of pocket gophers onto a

The postglacial history of the Mima prairie area as revealed by the pollen record for 4,500 years. Douglas fir is dominant and non-arboreal pollen (NAP) from plants other than trees shows an increase. (Rendering by Michael Emerson and Robert Hutchins.)

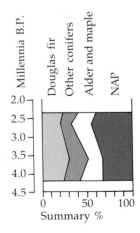

section of shallow unmounded prairie would be a useful experiment. He predicts that substantial mounds would appear in a matter of decades, rather than taking great stretches of geological time.

Another account of the origin of the mounds appeared in *Natural History* (spring 1984). The author, George W. Cox, a mammalogist, has clearly linked fossorial rodent activity to mound building: the Mima mounds of Puget Sound are but one of several such displays worldwide and all are associated with particular species of burrowing rodents.

On the other hand, a compelling account of the Mima mounds problem by A. Lincoln Washburn, an internationally respected authority on periglacial (near-to-glaciers) phenomena, has recently appeared (Washburn 1988). The author gives a full account of the Puget lowland's Mima mounds, with special attention to the several leading hypotheses on their origin. He finds the fossorial rodent hypothesis "subject to a number of serious objections." Washburn prefers an explanation that combines post-Pleistocene runoff of glacial meltwater with the anchoring effect of vegetation. Thus, the top of a mound would have been occupied by vegetation (clumps of woody or herbaceous plants or by trees). Post-glacial runoff would have differentially removed earth from the non-vegetated sectors. This runoff-erosion/vegetation-anchoring hypothesis has been invoked for mounds elsewhere. It merits serious consideration.

A serendipitous series of events involving a doghouse and the eruption of Mount St. Helens has led geologist Andrew Berg to propose earthquakes as the cause of the mounds. While constructing a doghouse in 1980, Berg happened to hammer on a piece of plywood covered by a fine coat of volcanic ash from the Mount St. Helen's eruption that spring. Berg, who works for the U.S. Bureau of Mines in Spokane, noticed that the pounding produced a pattern of bumps in the ash that looked suspiciously like miniature versions of the Mima mounds. Berg repeated the experiment under more controlled conditions. He observed (1990) that the vibrations from several hammer blows sorted the material, causing soft sediments to form mounds separated by coarser-grained material—a feature on the mounded prairies.

Berg believes the experimental mounds arise because vibrational waves traveling through the plywood interfere with each other, causing certain locations to vibrate heavily while others remain still. A similar interference patten of earthquake waves, he reasoned, could create Mima mounds in areas where a thin layer of loose soil rests on a flat section of rock or hard soil. Berg is of the opinion that mounds formed in this way are stable once formed and would not fall apart during repeated earthquakes.

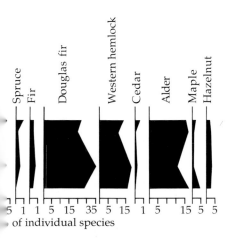

Spruce
Fir
Douglas fir
Western hemlock
Cedar
Alder
Maple
Hazelnut

5 1 1 5 15 35 5 15 1 5 15 5 5
of individual species

The reviewer of Berg's paper in *Geology* (March 1990), C. G. Higgins, observes that Mima mounds "may have generated a greater variety of hypotheses than any other geologic feature." Berg does not claim that his hammer experiments prove the earthquake hypothesis; but he calls the evidence "extremely compelling." His theory would explain why Mima mounds form in many earthquake-prone areas around the world that have markedly different climates.[3]

Mima Mounds and Vegetation. The mounds serve as a choice example of the effect of small-scale topography (microrelief) on the distribution of plant species. Let the imagination take flat prairie terrain and heap it into mounds. By so doing one creates small-scale habitat differences defined by compass direction, which controls the pattern of the distribution of plants. With the prevailing weather coming from the southwest, there is a different exposure for each of the four quadrants of the circular mound. Moreover, the intermound sites with their concentration of gravel and rock add another dimension to habitat diversity.

Change in the composition of plant communities as a manifestation of differences in mound topography was investigated by Lawrence Giles, graduate student in botany at the University of Washington. He did a thorough hands-and-knees study of mound vegetation (1970). The most clearly defined difference is in density of the grassy prairie vegetation on different quadrants of the mounds. South-facing slopes of the mounds have a noticeably less dense cover than do the north-facing slopes; though fog and rain come from the southwest, so does the intensity of the parching summer sun. The stressful time of year on the prairie is from July to September when these gravelly, well-drained soils lose moisture rapidly. The south-facing exposure of a mound is an arid microcosm at such times, while 180 degrees to the northeast, the leeside of the mound microhabitat is less severe. Not only is the density of total vegetation different on these two opposing sectors of a mound, but some sorting of plant species also occurs. Thus, the two native bunch grasses, a violet, a buttercup, and *Prunella*, occur with greater frequency and abundance in the northeast and northwest quadrants of the mound. The intermound area is decidedly less luxuriant both in absolute density of vegetation and in numbers of species represented. Two known drought-tolerant species, the annual grass (*Aira praecox*) and the pigeon-wheat moss (*Polytrichum*

3. While recording this latest hypothesis, I remain a firm adherent of the fossorial rodent theory. Note my uses of *hypothesis* for the seismic causation and *theory* for the gopher causation. The agency of gophers in making mounds worldwide has withstood rigorous observation and testing; it is a wholly tenable theory. Further, George Cox has rejected the seismic idea after critical scrutiny (Cox, personal communication, 1990).

juniperinum), comprise the bulk of the cover in the intermound sectors. Though it might be expected that the intermound troughs would support a more luxuriant vegetation, it should be recalled that the soil and subsoil here is thin and underlain by a porous and coarse gravel. Water never stands in these lowlying intermound areas.

Mima mounds are the scene of yet another drama of nature. Far from being frozen in time, to live on eternally as grassy treeless hillocks, the mounds are a transient embossing on the geomorphic landscape. Even now in the span of one human lifetime, change can be witnessed. Aerial photos highlight a profound change: the advancing encroachment of Douglas fir. From the air, a wave of evergreens seems to be rolling across the treeless, mounded prairie. The advancing front of the wave is occupied by scattered outliers, while farther back in a northeasterly direction, the crest of the wave is a solid rank of young firs that have overwhelmed the mounded prairie. No doubt this invasion has been going on for years, possibly even before the coming of western settlers to Puget country. Bretz, the thorough chronicler of postglacial history, was struck by the magnitude of the encroachment on the mounds by fir, already well underway in 1913. He writes:

> It is stated that the Indians formerly burned over these prairies annually, and destroyed the trees growing on them. It is certain that today the forest is encroaching. In retracing surveyor's lines run 50 years ago, the limits of forest growth were found to have advanced on the prairies. The western part of Rocky Prairie bears many scattered firs. These were found to possess from eight to ten annual rings at the base, though some were ten feet high and some hardly ten inches. Evidently a wet season a few years ago allowed the seedlings to send their roots deep enough to survive the drought of ordinary summers. The older residents all testify to the former great extent of the prairies. Many gnarled skeletons of the broad-spreading prairie oaks are found mouldering in a dense growth of young fir which has killed them in the last half century. Though much prairie land thus is being invaded by the forest, there are large mound-bearing areas where the dry soil probably never can support tree growth and probably never has. (1913:101–2)

Bretz's early observation on encroachment and its possible cause can be sustained right down to the present time. There is no more spectacular example of plant succession in our area than this dynamic replacement of prairie by forest. Clearly an analysis of the conditions that would favor encroaching succession was called for. The title of a study by Giles (1970) poses the problem succinctly— "The Ecology of the Mounds on Mima Prairie with Special Reference to Douglas Fir Invasion."

Dramatic invasion of mounded prairies by Douglas fir. (Photo by Victor Scheffer.)

Giles realized that Douglas fir must gamble in its attempt to establish itself on mounded prairies. In most summers, soil moisture becomes perilously depleted on the mounds, especially on the south and west quadrants. Seeds are shed in the fall, finding their way onto a dry cushion of parched moss, lichen, and grass herbage. With the fall rains and on through winter, the whole mound microcosm wicks up to reach optimal water-holding capacity. If germination is delayed until spring, as is the usual case in Douglas fir, then the tiny seedling must extend its roots down through the closed mat of living and dead moss to reach mineral soil. The initial disadvantage of germinating above mineral soil can be further aggravated by the not infrequent spring dry spells on the prairie. Even if the seedling Douglas fir roots reach mineral soil, their slow start may not keep pace with the progressive drying out of the soil in the mound as summer's drought progresses. The precariousness of germination and establishment results in the death of Douglas fir seedlings. The rare individual that persists through the drastic elimination period during the growing season can be expected to live on through many such years to come. Giles found that initial survival of the few successful pioneers was greatest on the less severe microenvironment on north-facing quadrants of the mounds. Moreover, as these initial emigrants grew to small sapling size, other seedlings tended to aggregate around the older tree. Such gregariousness or clumped distribution of individuals of a species is not uncommon in plant communities. In this case Giles suspected that the initial Douglas fir invader can create, by the time it is a sapling, a microclimate favorable to the establishment of additional seedlings.

Though the advance of Douglas fir onto the mounded prairies is a slow and chancy business, it is nonetheless inevitable. To preserve for posterity a sample of this remarkable treeless, mounded topography, a concerted effort to keep Douglas fir out has been made. Approximately five hundred acres of Mima Prairie have been designated as a natural area preserve. With the clear evidence of Douglas fir invasion, The Nature Conservancy, in cooperation with the Department of Natural Resources, instituted a management plan for a part of the prairie. On one sector, Douglas firs of sapling size and larger, as well as any other woody species, are to be regularly eliminated; on another sector the invasion of conifers will not be interfered with. By this two-way treatment of the tract, we have the opportunity of watching the dynamics of succession as Douglas fir replaces treeless mounded prairie, and the assurance of keeping a portion of the mounds treeless, just as they appeared to the Indians and to explorers in the early nineteenth century.

Prairies are now dominated in many places by introduced herbs and even shrubs. Here herbaceous weeds and Scot's broom are conspicuous invaders. (Photo by James McDermott.)

Preservation of the Mounds. Once Europeans began in earnest to settle into the land, their chief preoccupation with topography and its living skin was to tame it. Mounds were leveled for farming, or else suffered more gradual defacing from animals grazing, invasion of alien weed plants, or encroachment by forest now "protected" from fire. Thus, in the interval of a hundred years between the first explorers' wonderment and the twentieth century human tenants' obsession with exploiting the land, the mounds and kindred landforms—unique and irreplaceable—have suffered from abuse and apathy. The accounts in the popular press of recent years, telling of the "mystery" of the Mima mounds, helped sustain the hopes of local conservationists. Their goal, to ensure that a representative example of the mounds be preserved, was realized in 1981, after years of effort. In the 1960s the Washington State chapter of The Nature Conservancy took over a grazing lease on over eight hundred acres of mounded Mima Prairie. The lease, held by the State Department of Natural Resources, afforded only stopgap protection of the mounds. It is an ironic twist in state constitutional law that requires the citizens of the state to pay the state to preserve one of its own unique natural heritages. Presently such state lands must provide revenue for public schools.

Additional recognition of the mounds came when The Nature Conservancy secured the interest of Bennett Gale, a geologist in the National Park Service. He was convinced that the mounds merited National Landmark status, and now a large wooden, framed plaque commemorates this event on the west border of the "preserve." Yet neither the efforts of The Nature Conservancy nor those of the Park Service gave permanent protection to the mounds. That could come only from the concerted efforts of citizens working out a preservation plan with their state government.

In 1981, preservation of a sample of the mound topography was consummated. At the request of a citizen's advisory committee on natural areas for the state, the Department of Natural Resources negotiated purchase of a portion of Mima Prairie. Once purchased, the fair market value requirement for the school lands trust is satisfied and the department can manage the property as a natural area preserve. The 470 acres of the Mima Mounds Natural Area Preserve provide partial access to the public. At the northeast perimeter of the preserve, the Department of Natural Resources has developed a fine interpretive center. A self-guiding nature trail through the mounds gives the visitor an intimate view of this classic natural phenomenon.

Unusual rock formations can dramatically alter vegetation occasionally in the lowlands, as in the eastern San Juan Islands and here on Twin Sisters Mountain, southwest of Mount Baker. Iron and magnesium silicate rock, like dunite and serpentine, makes a soil that stunts forest vegetation. Here, dunite on steep, unstable slopes creates a "barren." (Photo by the author.)

Serpentine Rock—A Hard Life!

By the end of this chapter, we should have created the impression that life in Puget country is influenced not only by variations in climate, but by the changes in habitat wrought by variations in geology. In a nutshell, within a region's uniform climate, variety in habitat is created by discontinuous changes in landform, rock, and soil type. Already we have noted the effect of topography on vegetation. Yet another geological influence has been glaciation, producing topographic variety and, in the case of the prairies, unusual soil types. One other conditioner of habitat needs to be mentioned. Bedrock geology, though not as common as glacial sediments in the Puget trough, does outcrop here and there. And if that bedrock has some unusual chemistry, then the soil it yields by weathering can be distinct. It then follows that unusual soils can promote exceptional habitats for floras and vegetation.

Soils from the more usual bedrock-like lavas or granites may not harbor exceptional plant life. But here and there in Puget country, one particular bedrock demands the most out of plant life, often yielding species that occur only on that rock. Its name is serpentine, a rock composed of silicates of iron and magnesium, often with inclusions of toxic nickel, cobalt, and chromium. When serpentine weathers to a soil, it is deficient in the normal nutrients, especially calcium. And then because of its innate chemical composition, the serpentine soil harbors a sparse vegetation and thus little else of nutrient value gets recycled; deficiencies in nitrogen and phosphorus result. Soil scientist Hans Jenny calls the phenomenon the "serpentine syndrome."

Serpentine rock and its derived soils occur in the Puget lowland west of Anacortes in Skagit County, easily found at Fidalgo Head, and with a bit more effort, on Cypress Island and Sumas Mountain. Some telltale plants, such as the little rock fern (*Aspidotis densa*), indicate the presence of these sterile soils. Other species of plants, found on normal soils, may also make it on serpentines. But their trick is to have evolved races of their species tolerant of sterile soils (Kruckeberg 1969).

The "serpentine syndrome" in Washington can be found on a variety of rocks in the iron–magnesium silicate family: dunite, as in the Twin Sisters Mountain of eastern Skagit County; peridotite and serpentine, east of the Cascades in Kittitas County. This "fix" between plants and rocks is a worldwide phenomenon, and the serpentine case is its most spectacular manifestation. I portray its biological uniqueness with one other example: the high montane display of the serpentine syndrome in the Twin Sisters Mountain southwest of Mount Baker (see chapter 8).

The grand sweep of montane topography along the eastern border of Puget Sound. Glacier Peak (right) along the rugged crest of the Cascade Range, viewed from the Olympics, across the Sound and nearby foothills. (Photo by Josef Scaylea.)

8 Montane Natural History of the Puget Sound Basin

"Wood is a luxury in the alpine."—Ola Edwards

Our focus on the ecology and natural history of lowland Puget Sound was both intentional and inevitable. It is here in the lowlands, where the inland sea meets the land, that the drama between humans and primeval nature has been played out. Moreover, it is here that the vast majority of humans encounter the remaining fragments of the natural ecosystem that once covered all of sealevel Puget country. Curiosities are whetted by this daily contact with lowland nature and consciences are prodded to see that some of it is conserved or restored before it is all gobbled up by "progress."

But given easy mobility and the panoramic views that lowlanders have of the basin's setting, it is inescapable that we see the lowland as the footing and catch-basin for the mountainous land that rims the Sound area. A regional natural history cannot be complete without an account of the mountainous borders of the lowland and its inland sea.

The Montane Setting: Geology and Major Environments

The land bordering central Puget Sound dramatically portrays the basin's topography. From Everett to Olympia the lowland trough is contained on east and west by the Cascade Range and the Olympic Mountains. The jagged snow-capped rim seen from vantage points near sea level is not a simple one like the sides of a bathtub. Not only is the crest of the ranges a sinuous and jagged border, the flanks of the mountains do not simply and smoothly slope into the basin. Any west-to-east traverse of the Olympics or Cascades drives home the real picture of depth and intricate contour along the route traveled. The skirts of the two great ranges billow out east and west for many miles and are pleated into folds that define major drainage patterns. The mountains are intricate systems of ridges and valleys acting as catchments for life-giving precipitation. The broad eastern and western flanks of the ranges have acquired their unique pattern of river valleys and ridge tops through the workings of several land-shaping processes. First, there was mountain-building by vulcanism, igneous intrusion, folding and faulting of ancient sediments, and other uplift actions; then, ice, water, and wind have chipped and worn away the uplifted terrain (see chap. 1). The ceaseless runoff in the streams and great rivers of the two mountain ranges, with the products of montane erosion, bears witness to the eternal wearing away of the mountains.

The lay of this ridge-and-valley pattern for both Cascades and Olympics has profound influences on the living fabric that clothes the mountains. The main trend of the two ranges is, of course, north to south. The lofty crests of the two ranges trap moisture-laden air from the Pacific. The two immense watersheds and their vast entrapment of precipitation dominate the processes that promote the life of the region. Besides holding moisture-yielding clouds over Puget Sound, the mountains return to the basin the water that is shed in their upper reaches. All drainages run westward from the west-facing crest of the Cascades, even though the course of their westerly paths may take short spurts along other compass directions. The runoff of the east-facing side of the Olympics heads east into the Sound via Hood Canal. Compared to the Cascades, the shorter downhill run of Olympic rivers is also a less sinuous one. Olympic drainages like the Dosewallips, Hamma Hamma, Duckabush, and Quilcene run almost due east to Hood Canal.

Near right: The upper montane forest with open parkland of meadows, streams, and tree clumps is a landscape unrivaled in western North America. Paradise River, Mount Rainier National Park. (Photo by Bob and Ira Spring.)

Far right: Timberline in the Cascade and Olympic mountains makes its statement with krummholz (crooked-wood) trees; here, dwarfed whitebark pine. (See also page 343.) (Photo by the author.)

Lowland forest of hemlock, cedar and Douglas fir gives way upward to the unique mid-montane Pacific silver fir forests, then upward to the spectacular subalpine parkland, just below timberline and topped by the alpine zone.

Below: Mid-montane view up the South Fork Stillaguamish River valley, with Big Four Mountain on right skyline. Lowland forest and Pacific silver fir stands meet on the lower slopes of the valley. (Photo by Bob and Ira Spring.)

Left: The alpine zone (a land above the trees) expresses itself mostly when the highest peaks become so steep as to keep trees from gaining a toe-hold.

Below: Less often, only on the major volcanoes, does more gentle terrain get high enough to become alpine, as on Mount Fremont, just north of Mount Rainier. (Photo by the author.)

Armed with these elementary facts of geomorphology, we can better appreciate the habitat differences created by the trend of the ridge-and-valley topography of both ranges. Regardless of size, each of the countless drainageways that ultimately feed the major valley, generates a local setting with differences in slope and exposure. A profile of a section of any such drainage shows the rich potential for different places that vegetation can establish. Valley bottoms may have broad floors like the lower Skagit or Skykomish, or the major drainage may be wedged into the narrow defile of a V-shaped canyon or gorge such as in the upper reaches and tributaries of most major rivers. Both the presence of cold air and the proximity of water in the channels of drainage systems evoke a particular set of responses in the vegetation.

Then, as one leaves the bottoms to work along the slopes of the canyon or valley, two topographic features, slope (steep or gradual) and exposure (north-facing, south-facing, or in any other compass direction), create particular environments that further define the character of the plant cover. Other intricacies of plant response to local topography and climate are encountered as one goes up the slope toward the ridge. Composition of vegetation almost inevitably changes with some species dropping out, others persisting to the ridge and still others appearing at the upper contours of the slope. On south- and west-facing slopes, local change in vegetation with elevation can be abrupt. Such changes in plant cover are the results of complex changes in depth of soil, steepness of slope, change in moisture and temperature, and often more exposed parent rock. Once gaining the ridge after the steep traverse of a valley wall, one can expect the most extreme manifestation of the moisture-temperature gradient along such a transect. Ridge tops are often the driest habitats along the traverse of ridge-and-valley landforms. Major climatic features as they change along the montane traverse from sea level to alpine are given in Tables 23 and 24 and the graphs below.

Opposite: Two representations of the effects of topography on montane forests. (Drawings by Sandra Noel.) Top: Forests "track" solar intensity as it varies from cool, shaded north-facing slopes to dry and sunny south-facing slopes. Bottom: Subalpine forest type moves downward in canyons (vertical arrows), but is confined upwardly on ridges. Solid wavy lines are boundaries of vegetation zones; dotted wavy line is the 3,500-foot contour line.

Below: Annual trends of temperature and precipitation for three montane weather stations: Snoqualmie Pass, Stevens Pass, and Stampede Pass. Summer drought periods (shaded area) in mountains are less severe than for lowland Puget Sound (see graph, page 39).

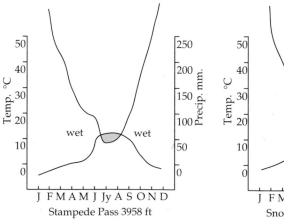

Stampede Pass 3958 ft

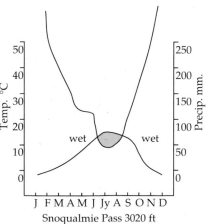

Snoqualmie Pass 3020 ft

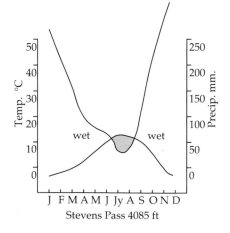

Stevens Pass 4085 ft

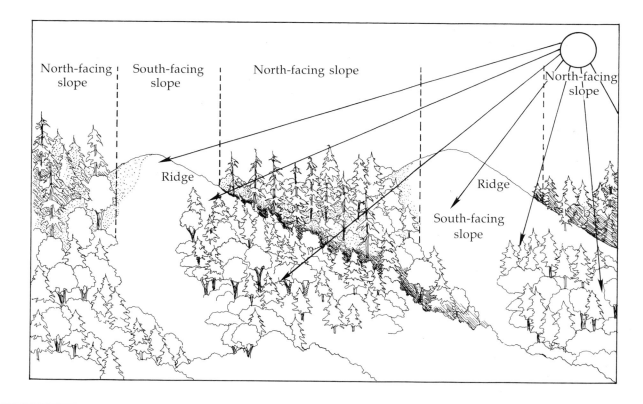

North-facing slope South-facing slope North-facing slope North-facing slope

Ridge

Ridge

South-facing slope

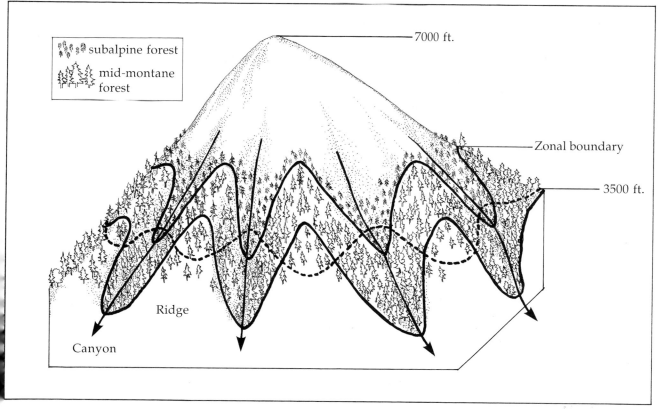

subalpine forest

mid-montane forest

7000 ft.

Zonal boundary

3500 ft.

Ridge

Canyon

Table 23. Climate at Stations from Sea Level to the High Country

Station	Elevation (feet)	Annual Precipitation (inches)	Average Monthly Temperatures, °F		Environmental Features
			January	July	
Transect from Sea-Tac Airport to Stevens Pass					
Sea-Tac Airport	386	38.94	38.3	64.9	Level, treeless terrace just above Puget Sound
Bothell	100	39.28	37.5	61.9	Near valley bottom of Sammamish River
Duvall	814	60.29			In broad valley of Skykomish River
Monroe	120	46.76	38.0	64.0	In broad valley of Skykomish River
Startup	170	64.15	38.6	63.6	Flat valley bottom bordered with low Cascade foothills
Skykomish	933	80.00	31.9	62.9	In canyon bordered by steep montane slopes
Scenic	2224	83.08			Same
Stevens Pass	4085	75.55	23.4	56.3	Crest of Cascade Range (northern sector)
Transect from Tacoma to Snoqualmie Pass					
Tacoma	127	37.06	39.9	64.4	'Built' environment on Puget Sound
Snoqualmie Falls	440	60.30	37.7	63.0	Broad river valley, just above large falls
Snoqualmie Pass	3020	107.60	26.3	57.8	Crest of Cascade Range (central sector)

Table 24. Climate for Upper Montane Areas of the Cascade Range, Washington

Locality	Elevation (feet)	Temperature (degrees Fahrenheit)				
		Average Annual	Average January	Average January Minimum	Average July	Average July Maximum
Mt. Baker Lodge	4467	40.8	27.3	21.7	53.7	63.5
Stevens Pass	4085	39.3	23.4	18.0	56.3	67.9
Snoqualmie Pass	3020	41.8	26.3	20.4	57.8	69.9
Stampede Pass	3958	39.5	23.5	19.5	56.2	65.4
Paradise Ranger Station	5550	38.3	26.0	19.4	53.0	62.9

Note: Data from Franklin and Dyrness 1973 and Phillips 1968.

With increasing altitude in the Cascades, average temperatures in both January and July are lower and precipitation substantially increases. But averages of weather station data hardly reveal the nature of intimate climate on slopes and ridge tops and in canyons where plants and their associated animals are directly sensing their environments. It is here that daily and seasonal fluctuations in temperature, as well as moisture input/loss, sort plants and animals into recognizable communities. More than the National Weather Service data, the technical reports of foresters, ecologists, and microclimatologists contain data on the local climate near the ground. Ideally, microclimatic data should be sensed from a wide variety of local natural environments, from lowland river bank to alpine talus. A place to start is with descriptions of microclimate along an imaginary trail—with plenty of switchbacks—that traverses several major microclimates from river bank to ridge top.

Such an imaginary transect of microclimatic variations can be traced in the North Cascades, north of Snoqualmie Pass. Here the ridge-and-valley mosaic of the Cascade Range is so precipitous that it is possible to go from lowland river bottom to subalpine habitats by traversing one steep slope. In so doing, one passes through several plant communities, each responding to a unique combination of local microenvironmental conditions. The drainages of the Stillaguamish, Skykomish, or Snoqualmie rivers afford superlative examples of this range of microhabitats over minimal "horizontal" distances. From Table 25, two features of the microenvironmental mosaic emerge. Life conditions shift from the optimal to the stressful as one goes from river bottom to ridge top; moreover, the change is more abrupt and extreme on south- and west-facing slopes. When the slope traverses several hundreds of feet of elevation it is possible to go from the lowland forest of western hemlock and western red cedar to the subalpine forest of mountain hemlock, subalpine fir, and Alaska cedar. And on the highest and most exposed ridges, one could emerge from forest onto an alpine, treeless landscape. At least one other major vegetation zone occurs between the lowland forest at the foot of the slope and the highest ridge summit. This zone is characterized by one dominant conifer, Pacific silver fir (*Abies amabilis*).

The elevational traverse through different types of vegetation reveals major microenvironmental differences along the gradient. Steepness of slope, soil, bedrock geology, and exposure to the daily and seasonal march of the sun interact to produce local microclimatic differences. Unique regimes of temperature and moisture are the result. And the local differences in microclimates are further sharpened by the character of the plant life on particular sites. The vegetational response is a continuum of change in species composition, abundance of dominant and subordinate plants. From nature's continuum, the ecologist abstracts four or five dominant vegetation types: lowland forest (western hemlock with western red cedar and Douglas fir) (chap. 5), mid-montane forest (Pacific silver fir with Alaska cedar), upper-montane or subalpine forest (mountain hemlock with subalpine fir and Alaska cedar), and alpine tundra or treeless meadow above timberline.

Precipitation (inches)		
Average Annual	June thru August	Average Annual Snowfall
111.06	12.32	550.4
75.55	5.67	466.9
107.60	8.56	420.2
92.19	7.59	457.6
104.97	7.96	582.1

Table 25. Microenvironmental Mosaic from River Bottom to Ridge Top

Habitat Type and Slope	Exposure	Forest Cover and Site Quality*	Diurnal Temperature (Summer)
Streamside; none	—	Riparian broadleaf trees, mixed conifer; medium	Continued cool
River terrace; none	Base of N-facing slope	Mixed conifer; highest	Continued cool
River terrace; none	Base of S-facing slope	Mixed conifer; high	Cool to moderate
Lower slope; moderate	N- and E-facing	Dense conifer; high	Cool to moderate
Lower slope; moderate	S- and W-facing	Fairly dense conifer; medium	Moderate
Middle slope; often steep	N- and E-facing	Fairly dense conifer; medium	Moderate
Middle slope; often steep	S- and W-facing	Fairly open; medium	Fluctuating: moderate to high
Upper slope; steep	N- and E-facing	Dense to fairly open; medium	Fluctuating: moderate to high
Upper slope; steep	S- and W-facing	Open to nonforested; low	Extreme fluctuations from low to high
Ridgetop: rock outcrop, flats, swales, cliffs	—	Variable: from open, parklike subalpine conifer to meadows, to "krummholz" and rock outcrop herb flora	Extremes of hot and cold

*Site quality: estimate of productivity (biomass production).

Left: Topography of a single drainage basin, the South Fork of the Snoqualmie River, with the characteristic U-shaped valley and steep side walls and ridges, shows signs of past glacial ice workings. (Photo by Austin Post.)

Right: An exceptionally open stand of Pacific silver fir, with mature trees and saplings of the same species.

The Pacific Silver Fir Zone: Mid-montane Crossroads

Somewhere along the traverse from sea level to timberline, one is sure to encounter the forest type dominated by Pacific silver fir (*Abies amabilis*). Notice my use of the vague "somewhere" to fix the position of the Pacific Silver Fir Zone (PSF) in the ascent to timberline. This mid-elevation zone is delimited only imprecisely, at least at its lower and upper limits. Since tree species and many of the associated shrubs and herbs overlap one another in their elevational distributions, zonal boundaries are inevitably fuzzy. Yet, roughly midway along the climb from typical hemlock–cedar–Douglas fir forest in the lowlands to the mountain hemlock–subalpine fir forests of the subalpine, one enters pure stands of Pacific silver fir, or at least forests where it is the dominant species. In western Washington, the zone can occur from as low as 2,000 feet upward to 4,300 feet.

Where it is the dominant tree, Pacific silver fir forms the lead species in several communities that differ in species composition under the influence of differences in moisture. The wettest PSF community has devil's club (*Oplopanax horridum*) as the most frequent understory component, along with two or three species of huckleberry-blueberry (*Vaccinium*). As moisture decreases, mostly in response to local topography (slope and exposure), the subordinate species change. Besides the phase dominated by devil's club, Franklin and Dyrness (1973) recognize the PSF/rosy twisted-stalk, PSF/blueberry, PSF/salal, and PSF/beargrass communities, with the latter at the drier end of the sequence. The moist-to-dry trend in the PSF forest is highly relative, however. As expected, the altitudinally higher PSF forest receives more precipitation than the lowland hemlock zone and its moisture comes more in the form of snow (the snow pack from one to ten feet deep). (See Table 26.)

But what about the dominant tree itself? Pacific silver fir, or amabilis fir,[1] is one of four species of true fir in the Pacific Northwest. In the most favorable habitats, it is a symmetrical conifer, ranging from 150 to 180 feet in height, and from 3 to 5 feet in diameter at breast height. Such giants have straight, clean boles, free of lower limbs, and a smooth, ashy-gray, unbroken bark, often splotched with large chalk-white patches. The crown is broadly conical, rounded at the top; lower branches have a pronounced downward sweep. The foliage of lower branches and of saplings is a dark lustrous green, with a distinctive leaf arrangement. The lower two ranks of linear needle are attached at right angles to the

---

1. *Amabilis* means lovely or beautiful. David Douglas used superlatives for other firs as well: *grandis*, *magnifica*, and *nobilis*.

Microenvironmental Features

Cold air drainage; cooling effect of stream

Some cold air drainage; late-lying snow; alluvial soils

Some effect of cold air drainage; alluvial soils

Slope moderated by alluvial accumulation from above

Same as preceding

Soils formed in place, fairly shallow and rocky

Same as preceding; often herb and shrub understory

Forest usually continuous to ridge; persistent snow pack

Forest open and discontinuous; talus or rock outcrop frequent; shallow residual soils

Direction and topography of ridge may afford great variety of microhabitats

twig, spreading stiffly out to form a flat two-ranked background pattern. Superimposed on this flat spray of foliage is a "ruff" of needles that arch forward on the twig, like the hair on an aroused dog's back. Pacific silver fir cones are perched erect on branches high in the crown (as on all other true firs) and are two by five inches in size.

Caught in the middle of the environmental traverse, the Pacific Silver Fir Zone is a meeting ground for most other western Washington conifers. They may reach their upper as well as lower limits in the zone. Expect to find western hemlock, western red cedar, Douglas fir, and western white pine reaching their upper limits in this mid-montane forest type. And throughout the upper reaches of the PSF forest, one commonly encounters Alaska cedar, mountain hemlock, and even subalpine fir. A further clue for finding a sample of typical PSF Zone is the presence of seedlings and saplings of the fir under its own species or under the canopy of a mixed conifer forest.

Pacific silver fir (Abies amabilis) branches with telltale "ruff" of needles on top of twigs, and the upright cone. (Drawings by Ramona Hammerly.)

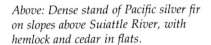

Above: Dense stand of Pacific silver fir on slopes above Suiattle River, with hemlock and cedar in flats.

Right: Noble fir (Abies procera) is a frequent associate of Pacific silver fir in mid-montane Mount Rainier National Park. Cone from near top of tree.

Table 26. Common Understory Associates of the Pacific Silver Fir Forest

Shrubs	Herbs
Vine maple (*Acer circinatum*)	Bear grass (*Xerophyllum tenax*)
Salal (*Gaultheria shallon, G. ovatifolia*)	Twin flower (*Linnaea borealis*)
	Pipsissiwa (*Chimaphila umbellata*)
Cascade Oregon grape (*Berberis nervosa*)	Dwarf dogwood or bunchberry (*Cornus canadensis*)
Blueberry (*Vaccinium alaskense*)	Bead lily (*Clintonia uniflora*)
Mountain huckleberry (*Vaccinium membranaceum*)	Trailing blackberry (*Rubus pedatus, R. lasiococcus*)
Devil's club (*Oplopanax horridum*)	Low false Solomon's seal (*Smilacina stellata*)
Fool's huckleberry, or rustyleaf (*Menziesia ferruginea*)	Foam flower (*Tiarella trifoliata*)
	Trillium (*Trillium ovatum*)
	Oak fern (*Gymnocarpium dryopteris*)
	Lady fern (*Athyrium filix-femina*)

Treeless Vegetation within the Pacific Silver Zone

The terrain occupied by Pacific silver fir often has the steepest topography along the entire forest profile. Steep slopes and deep snowpack make for a wintertime instability familiarly known as the avalanche track. In every major drainage along the western slopes of the Cascades, the steep upper forested zone is broken by vertical gashes of nonforested vegetation. Here, snow avalanches run with high predictability. The tracks made by these violent downhill surges of snow have created their own vegetation types which contrast with the PSF forests nearby. Coniferous evergreens are usually conspicuously absent, or are scattered and stunted on avalanche tracks. In their place, dense thickets of the shrubby mountain alder (*Alnus sinuata*) or other deciduous shrubs and herbaceous plants predominate in the tracks. Unlike the lowland red alder (*Alnus rubra*), mountain alder appears to be singularly adapted to yielding to periodic avalanches. Its short, tough but flexuous stems are devoid of foliage in the winter and thus bend unharmed to the creep or downrush of the snow. As a result, mountain alder and other shrub species have strongly bowed stems. Mountain alder communities may have a rich understory of perennial herbs such as bracken, montia, false Solomon's seal, bead lily, and trailing blackberry. Other deciduous shrubs occur in the community, especially vine maple, huckleberry, serviceberry, thimbleberry, willow, and mountain ash. When scattered conifers occur in old tracks, they are usually shrubby individuals of western red cedar, Alaska cedar, subalpine fir, and mountain hemlock.

Closer study of avalanche tracks reveals that their vegetation is not the same on every track. This observation has led ecologists to expect that frequency of avalanche occurrence can be correlated with vegetation composition. The argument is made that the vegetation of the track is in a state of flux, but trending toward a stable coniferous forest. Avalanche tracks that run every year or so can be expected to have a vegetation cover in an earlier stage of succession than those that run less frequently. Martha Cushman (1981) made estimates of avalanche frequency from a quantitative analysis of vegetation composition and the physical attributes of the slope. Were it possible to tell how frequently any track will run, by the quality of its vegetation, the predictions could be of practical value to forest managers, highway departments, and the operators of winter sports areas. Cushman has come up with a list of plant indicators of avalanche periodicity (see Table 27).

Cushman reminds us that plant responses to environmental variables are seldom simple and direct. Elevation, slope, exposure, history of the avalanche track, and the flora of the adjacent forested slope, all make for a heterogeneous vegetation. The simple use of indicator species to predict avalanche frequency must be done with caution.

Besides the more spectacular avalanche track, the PSF forest-type contains other nonforested plant communities. Along seeps

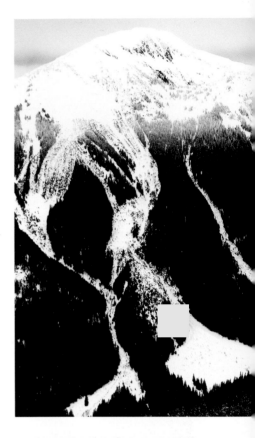

Table 27. Vegetation Cover and Frequency of Avalanches

Frequency, in years	Vegetation and species
0–1	Oregon box (*Pachystima myrsinites*), a low growing evergreen shrub, and white hawkweed (*Hieracium albiflorum*)
2–6	Mountain alder, vine maple, red elderberry, bead lily (*Clintonia uniflora*), hedge nettle (*Stachys cooleyi*), and vanilla leaf (*Achlys triphylla*)
10–20	Mountain alder, vine maple and a few scattered conifers (western red cedar, Alaska cedar); rich herb cover
25-, 30-, 50-year intervals	Mountain alder and vine maple; conifers more frequent; Alaska cedar and mountain hemlock at higher elevations, bigleaf maple and red alder at lower elevations

and streams, mountain alder, willow, and vine maple replace the coniferous forest just at the water's edge. Water-loving herbs like saxifrage, yellow willow-herb (*Epilobium luteum*), monkey flowers (*Mimulus guttatus* and *M. lewisii*), rein orchid (*Habenaria* spp.), and bluebells (*Mertensia*) are common. Mid-montane lakes are plentiful throughout the zone. Though their basins appear to be forested to the water's edge when seen from afar, a zone of treeless vegetation often occurs along their shores. Again, mountain alder and vine maple may form the shrubby perimeter of the lake. But when the lake shoreline is flat or only gently sloping, a bog or marsh habitat can develop. Sedges (species of *Carex*), grasses and low shrubs like *Salix* (willow), *Ledum* (Labrador tea), or *Kalmia* (bog laurel), as well as a scattering of showy flowering herbs like marsh marigold, arnica, groundsel, pedicularis, etc., can be found on the peaty soils.

Back on drier land, openings in the forest can be expected where the country rock outcrops at the surface in locally steep exposures, or forms talus stripes. Oregon box, mountain huckleberry, or mountain ash may form a shrubby backdrop for rock-inhabiting plants like the parsley fern, penstemons, sedums, cinquefoil (*Potentilla glandulosa*), strawberries (*Fragaria vesca* and *F. virginiana*), phlox, kinnikinnik, alum root (*Heuchera micrantha*), lomatiums, yarrow, and pearly everlasting. Annuals such as blue-eyed Mary (*Col-*

Occasional gaps in Pacific silver fir stands caused by rock and snow slides or unusually wet places:

Left: Avalanche tracks, a common treeless landscape in the Pacific silver fir zone. (Photo by Edward LaChappelle.)

Below left: Moist talus, rock covered with hardwood "brush," mostly vine maple and Douglas maple, upper Perry Creek, South Fork Stillaguamish River drainage. (Photo by the author.)

Below right: Marsh and bog with sedges and bog buckbean. (Photo by Jerry Franklin.)

A

B

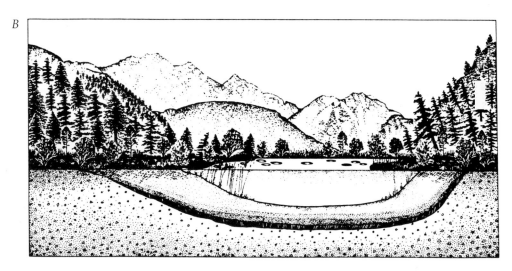

C

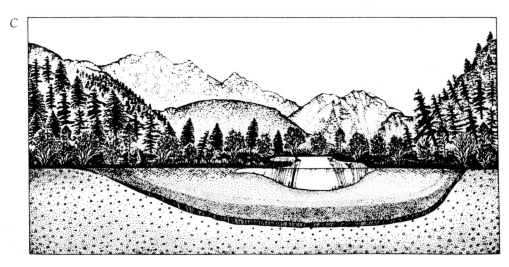

Montane lake succession.
A. Early stage: mostly open water.
B. Mid-stage: sediments and aquatic
vegetation encroaching on open water.
C. Bottom sediments and vegetation
substantially replace open water.
(Drawing by Lilla Samson.)

Mountain hemlock (Tsuga
mertensiana), the grandest of
montane conifers, occurs in either
continuous forests or upwards in
isolated groves as subalpine parkland.
Below: Lone mountain hemlock near
timberline.

linsia parviflora), and two phloxes (*Collomia linearis* and *Microsteris gracilis*) can be common, though briefly visible, in these rocky openings.

The restless volcanoes of the Cascades have had a particular impact on the Pacific Silver Fir Zone. Nearly everywhere, airborne volcanic ash, not bedrock, became the raw material for making soils. Jerry Franklin surmises that the ash fallout has shaped montane landscapes. Without it, we might have a "bonier," more angular range like the Sierras of California. The omnipresence of the ash is most noticeable along powder dry (dusty) trails in the late summer. I remember being ankle-deep in the stuff, hiking up to Miner's Ridge, east of Glacier Peak.

Trails through the PSF zone are frequent all along the midmontane flanks of the Puget basin, in the Olympics and in the Cascades. Of easiest access for study are the mixed forest stands around Snoqualmie Pass (such as the Commonwealth Basin, Snow Lake, and Denny Creek trails). Pacific silver fir here is mostly associated with western hemlock. But, whatever drainage you choose to visit, don't delay. Many fine stands of PSF are being logged in patch or clear cuts, for the tree is valued as a source of pulpwood. Eventually it may be only in national parks or natural area preserves that one can stand in awe of montane forests dominated by this species.

The Upper Montane (Mountain Hemlock) Forest Type

The anticipation of panoramic vistas, of flowery mountain meadows, and of wandering free in the high country is whetted by the time the traveler reaches the mountain hemlock zone, the last forested zone before the ridge top is reached. At its best the zone can be an unbroken forest of mountain hemlock (*Tsuga mertensiana*), accompanied by isolated trees of Alaska cedar and Pacific silver fir. More frequently along the western slope of the Cascades, the traveler's path ascends through the upper Pacific Silver Fir Zone to reach the open parkland of the subalpine, without any appreciable occurrence of continuous mountain hemlock forest. Both the closed mountain hemlock forest and the open parkland are in fact recognized as the two dominant phases of this upper montane forest. After some background on the subalpine environment, we can turn to the natural history of this, the most spectacular zone of all, where rocky peaks meet the forest.

Intensive monitoring of microclimate in the subalpine environment has been done by ecologists in the Mount Seymour–Garibaldi Park high country just northeast of Vancouver, British Columbia. Their results are applicable to the Mountain Hemlock Zone for the North Cascades of Washington. The climate of this high montane forest type can be described as "snowy microthermal," a climate in which snow cover allows little heat to be generated for plant growth during the relatively short growing season. The cool, short summer of the subalpine is followed by wet winters, when snow and the snow cover is of several months' duration. Moreover, these coastal subalpine areas suffer less from dessicating winds than do similar subalpine areas in more continental areas (as in the Rocky Mountains). Using a variety of microclimatic instrumentation, the British Columbia ecologists (Brooke et al. 1970) found significant differences in the microclimate of the two major vegetation types—parkland and forest.

Parkland habitats consist of communities where trees are either absent or are sparse and scattered to form open parklike stands. Often parkland is at the upper boundary of the Mountain Hemlock Zone as it meets the completely treeless Alpine Zone. In contrast with the forested sector of the Mountain Hemlock Zone, the parkland habitat experiences "larger annual, seasonal and daily temperature ranges, higher absolute maxima and minima (of temperature) and greater evaporation rates. Moreover, the open parkland habitats have greater accumulation of snow, longer periods of complete and continuous snow cover and shorter snow-free periods" than in the nearby forest (Brooke et al. 1970:199). Several microclimatic variables act singly and in concert to shape the environment of a particular piece of upper montane forest, as we shall now see.

Solar radiation. At our northern latitude, the amount and quality of incoming radiation from the sun on the mountain hemlock forest type is conditioned by slope, exposure, season, time of day, cloud cover, and vegetation type. Thus, incoming solar radiation will be highly variable from place to place and at different times and seasons. Some local habitats are permanently shaded, while others will receive the maximum available solar input. The quality of vegetation is intimately tied to this variable.

Air and surface temperatures. Given the wide range in solar radiation, temperatures at or near the ground are bound to be correspondingly variable. In the more open parkland habitats, temperatures can range from 20° to 50°F (−7 to +10°C) during a single day in the summer months under cloudless skies. Yet beneath the canopy of mountain hemlock and associated conifers, the effect of shading markedly reduces the ranges of daily temperatures, seldom exceeding fluctuations of 20°F. In the open ground of parkland habitats, there is still another temperature phenomenon of direct influence on plant life. "With clear summer skies, dew is common and relative humidities reach their maximum" (Brooke et al. 1970:179). Nighttime cooling of surface air is rapid under these conditions and the cold air drains into basins or depressions often producing sharp temperature differences over short distances from the basin to the open slope or flat. During winter, however, with overcast conditions common, the daily temperature ranges are much reduced, hardly more than 1° to 3°F. Even under cloudless skies in winter, the angle of incidence for incoming radiation is so low that little warming of surfaces occurs. The strong reflectivity of the snow reinforces this reduced surface heating during winter.

Unusual local temperature conditions may occur during fall to spring when warm subtropical air slides over the cool maritime air of lower elevations. The result is a temperature inversion, where subalpine temperatures can be 20°F higher than at sea level and humidity can drop to an unseasonable low of 10 percent, while fog and high relative humidities blanket the lowlands. At such exceptional times the vegetation exposed above the snowpack is under severe physiological stress since root systems under snowpack are at near-freezing temperature, and the plants cannot take up moisture. Winter dessication of exposed twigs and leaves is the major adverse result.

Soil temperature. The intensity of biological activity in a terrestrial ecosystem is intimately tied to temperature of soils, particularly those temperatures affecting roots, soil animals, and soil microorganisms. Soil temperatures are dependent on the conduction of heat at ground level down through the soil profile. Thus, daily and seasonal changes in the climate near the ground greatly influence heat gain and loss to and from the soil mass. The snowpack acts as an insulating buffer against temperature changes—"during periods of snow cover, monthly soil temperatures near the surface were very uniform but showed a slow and definite decline until late spring" (Brooke et al. 1970:185). Following snow melt, the soils gain heat rapidly. Brooke found instances of 10° to 15°F rise in soil temperature in early summer. There are only two seasons in the soils of the upper montane—summers with temperatures at 46° to 52°F and fall-winter-spring with temperatures at 34° to 40°F. Though soil temperatures in winter hover just above 32°F, soils rarely freeze. The microclimate of soil gives security to life's persistence throughout the year in the subalpine.

Vegetation of the Mountain Hemlock Forest Type

Recall that there are three major vegetation zones above the Puget lowland forest (the Western Hemlock Zone): the Pacific Silver Fir

Zone at mid-elevations, then the Mountain Hemlock Zone ranging upward to timberline, and finally the treeless Alpine Zone. Having just examined the climatic setting of mountain hemlock ecosystems, we can now better understand how such a rigorous environment influences groupings of organisms.

Continuous forest cover at the highest elevations in the Cascades and Olympics ideally will be represented by stands of that most magnificent conifer, mountain hemlock (*Tsuga mertensiana*). This species typifies a forest zone clothing the crest and upper western slopes of the Cascades at elevations between 4,000 and 5,400 feet. Mountain hemlocks mature to a ripe old age and impressive stature. Trees from 500 to 700 years old can be 30 to 80 inches in diameter and 100 to 125 feet tall.

When the hemlocks are in pure stands, there is no mistaking the zone. Mountain hemlock is easily distinguished from all other native conifers: it has short greyish-green needles that densely clothe the twigs in bottle-brush fashion, rather than in flat sprays; its branches and leader are stiffly graceful yet not so formally symmetrical as they are firs and pines; its cones are large for hemlocks (2 to 3 inches long) and are borne at the ends of the branches.

The zone is not always pristine mountain hemlock in composition. Other conifers may be frequent tò even codominant. Alaska cedar (*Chamaecyparis nootkatensis*) and Pacific silver fir (*Abies amabilis*) often cohabit with the hemlock on the western slopes of the Cascades, while subalpine fir (*Abies lasiocarpa*) and western white pine (*Pinus monticola*) are companions of the hemlock on and just east of the Cascade Crest. The shrub and herb understory will be dominated by members of the heather, rose, and sunflower families. Prominent heather allies would be two huckleberry species (tall mountain huckleberry, *Vaccinium membranaceum*, and low blue mountain huckleberry, *V. deliciosum*). Our only high mountain rhododendron (*Rhododendron albiflorum*) is a common shrub associate of this predominantly ericaceous (heather family) understory. The plant is readily recognized by its shiny green deciduous leaves (often mottled white, presumably by a pathogen) and creamy white flowers clustered just below the leafy twigs. And that most spectacular member of the zone, Indian basket grass or bear grass (*Xerophyllum tenax*), may often form conspicuous clumps or pure stands in the shrub and herb understory. In bloom, bear grass would never be taken for a grass, even though its leaves are grasslike; the tall flowering stalks bear a huge plume of pure white flowers, individually tiny, but strikingly handsome *en masse*.

Forest ecologists Jerry Franklin and Ted Dyrness recognize the following communities in the Mountain Hemlock Zone of western Washington (Franklin and Dyrness 1973):

1. The Hemlock/Fir/Huckleberry (*Tsuga/Abies/Vaccinium membranaceum*) Community. Mountain hemlock and Pacific silver fir are codominant in the overstory and the tall mountain huckleberry predominates in the shrub understory.

2. The Cedar/Rhododendron (*Chamaecyparis nootkatensis/Rhododendron albiflorum*) Community. In wetter habitats (often on north slopes), mountain hemlock and Pacific silver fir give way in abundance to Alaska cedar in the tree layer. A dense thicket of rhododendron, huckleberry, rusty-leaf or fool's huckleberry (*Menziesia ferruginea*), and mountain ash (*Sorbus*) forms the shrub layer.

Where fire has destroyed the forest, a near-permanent shrub community may take over. This treeless vegetation is the familiar huckleberry thicket of our western Cascade slopes; fields of *Vaccinium membranaceum* persist for many years, particularly when forest regeneration is inhibited by natural or human causes. Other shrub and herb members of the prefire forest may continue on after fire in the huckleberry brushfields. Bear grass, mountain ash, and the low mountain spirea (*Spiraea densiflora*) are familiar companions of huckleberry.

Where drainage is impeded, especially in depressions, flats, or on gentle slopes, a boggy meadow habitat may replace forest; sedges (*Carex* species), cotton grass (*Eriophorum*), and sphagnum moss form a green but soggy carpet. These wet habitats are usually bordered by a shrub thicket of mountain alder (*Alnus sinuata*), willows (*Salix* species), hardhack spiraea (*Spiraea douglasii*), and twinberry (*Lonicera involucrata*).

Not far from Snoqualmie Pass, a half day's hike can put you in the midst of a prime example of the Mountain Hemlock Zone: the spectacular country to the north of the Pass at Snow Lake. And just to the west, the zone, as seen after severe fire, is clearly defined on the upper slopes of Granite Mountain.

If you were brought up on the now-classic Merriam Life-Zone system of classifying vegetation in the Pacific Northwest, you would probably recognize our Mountain Hemlock Zone as the very similar Hudsonian Zone. By whatever name it may be called, the zone has singular environmental character: it is the wettest and coolest of the forested zones, with annual precipitation of from 64 to 112 inches. Snowfall is heavy (160 to 500 inches), with persistent snowpack up to 21 feet deep. The multitude of vegetation variations on the zonal theme of mountain hemlock is an inevitable outcome of the intricate interplay between topography, elevation, and microclimate.

In its upper elevational limits, the Mountain Hemlock Zone ceases as continuous forest to become a landscape of shrub-herb

Opposite page: Top: Branches and cones of mountain hemlock. (Drawings by Ramona Hammerly.)

*Bottom: Alaska cedar (*Chamaecyparis nootkatensis*) is a frequent associate of mountain hemlock in closed stands and in parkland. (Photo by Mary Randlett.)*

An upper branch of subalpine fir laden with cones. (Photo by W. Marten.)

meadows studded with isolated patches of trees. To any high-country backpacker, this parkland landscape is the most familiar and spectacular of all montane habitats. It dominates the scene along and just west of the crest of the Cascade Range and in the high Olympics. Mile after breath-taking mile of this incredibly beautiful mosaic of forest and meadow stretch from Snoqualmie Pass to beyond the Canadian border. South of the Pass, parkland appears again in the drainages of Puget country mainly on Mount Rainier. A bit more glamour touches the spectacular meadow-parkland landscapes. Ecologists contend that this montane parkland is unique on the planet, both for the impressive area it covers and for its gradual (or "deep") transition between the forest and the open meadows. Though the Rocky Mountains have their share of high-country parkland, the forest-meadow boundary there is often abrupt.

The parkland subzone of the Mountain Hemlock Zone derives its singular character from topography and climate. In the North Cascades, subalpine landforms take on an entirely different character from the ridge-and-valley pattern at lower elevations on the western slope. The almost continual action of snow, ice, and wind has plucked away at the summits to produce jagged peaks, knife-like ridges, cliffs, talus and scree, cirques, and other depressions. The heavy snowpack persists into late summer in selected places within the topographic mosaic. Rugged topography and a heavy snowpack then probably control the destinies of the several plant communities that decorate the high-country scene. The "islands" of forest in the subalpine parkland can consist of three conifers, in pure or mixed stands: mountain hemlock, subalpine fir, and Alaska cedar. In the Cascades, all three may coexist in any one habitat, while in the northeastern Olympics a drier parkland mosaic has subalpine fir as its sole tree component. The Olympic version of parkland is superbly displayed in the area of Hurricane Ridge, especially on the trail to Mount Angeles and at Obstruction Point.

Heather meadows are the most representative of the shrub-herb communities that interfinger among the scattered clumps of subalpine trees. The "heather" is really a blend of three dominant species, none of which qualifies as a heather in the botanical sense since true heathers are Old World plants. Even so, the term heather for these subalpine shrublets is appropriate. The two phyllodoces (*Phyllodoce empetriformis*) with purple flowers, *P. glanduliflora* with yellow flowers, and the white-flowered *Cassiope* (*C. mertensiana*) bear a strong resemblance to certain European heathers and are relatives of the two European heather genera, *Erica* and *Calluna*. Along with the mountain huckleberry (*Vaccinium deliciosum*), these two mountain heathers form a distinct community of species that dominates the gentler slopes of the subalpine. Many a mile of Cas-

Subalpine meadows can be loved to death. "Social trails" destroy meadow vegetation at Sunrise, Mount Rainier National Park, and have to be healed with matting and transplants. (Photos by the author.)

TRAIL CLOSED FOR MEADOW RESTORATION

cade Crest Trail wanders through heather meadows. Most striking is the impact on these fragile heather meadows by humans, even though people may seem to be least intrusive here, away from their machines and built environment. The steady use of trails in heather meadows year after year degrades or destroys the plant cover. The ribbon of trail cuts deeper and deeper, following loss of protective vegetation and subsequent erosion, and finally becomes a knee-high ditch, only to be abandoned for another track alongside.

Because the topographic and climatic mosaic changes so quickly from place to place in the subalpine, heather meadow communities are never continuous. Some Cascadian heatherlands are exclusively *Phyllodoce-Vaccinium,* others pure huckleberry, and so on. A particularly beautiful associate of the heather meadows is the foamy cream-on-green mats of the groundcover shrublet, *Luetkea pectinata,* called Alaska spiraea or partridge-foot.

The mosaic subalpine landscape is decorated with still other meadow communities, particularly those where showy herbaceous species dominate. The most lush meadow community, developing on steep and wet slopes, is dominated by the white-flowered valerian or mountain heliotrope (*Valeriana sitchensis*) and *Veratrum viride,* a tall false hellebore or corn lily with drooping tassels of greenish flowers.

One group of dominants blends gradually into another in a parkland landscape. From the valerian-false hellebore community on wetter slopes, a trail through the parkland could lead quickly into a sedge-dominated community of herbaceous species. Sedges are grasslike plants of great diversity in form and habitat; yet all possess common features: triangular stems topped with tight tassels, each bearing male or female florets. The upper montane is richer in sedge species than in grasses. One sedge, *Carex spectabilis,* is abundant in this drier meadow habitat. The sedge shares dominance with two most familiar montane plants, a lupin (*Lupinus latifolius*) and the alpine bistort (*Polygonum bistortoides*). The latter plant is unique in sight as well as smell: tall spiky heads of tiny white florets whose odor is an unmistakable blend of sweet and sour. Many other familiar mountain meadow plants luxuriate here: cinquefoil (*Potentilla flabellifolia*), Indian paint brush (*Castilleja* species in variety), the boldly handsome pasque flower (*Anemone occidentalis*), and the subalpine daisy or fleabane (*Erigeron peregrinus*).

Two species of the lowlands reach the subalpine to constitute the dominant plants of still another community in the parkland meadow habitat. More often on steep, south-facing slopes that are the freest of snow during the growing season are the ubiquitous thimbleberry (*Rubus parviflorus*) and fireweed (*Epilobium angustifolium*). Their presence in the parkland of the subalpine is not a simple upward extension of these two plants, so at home around sea level in the Puget Sound basin. Like other plants with wide altitudinal and habitat ranges, thimbleberry and fireweed in the parkland are undoubtedly subalpine races, hereditarily distinct from their lowland counterparts. Evolutionary accommodation to a diversity of habitats is common among plant and animal species that superficially appear to be broadly tolerant of a variety of habitats. Rare indeed is the organism equipped with a "general purpose" heredity. Rather, most wide-ranging species develop races, genetically altered to suit new and different habitats.

Besides the dominance of subalpine forms of thimbleberry and fireweed, other beauties add to the floral display in this community type. Early in the season fawn lily (also called avalanche lily, glacier lily, or dog's tooth violet, *Erythronium grandiflorum*) and spring beauty (*Claytonia lanceolata*) command the hiker's attention. Late summer finds such members of the sunflower family (Compositae) as goldenrod and mountain artemisias, in full bloom.

One other plant community of the parkland bears special mention, particularly because of its precarious appearance from year to year. In long-persisting snow beds and snowmelt basins in the upper subalpine and on into the timberline, a threadbare community of a low sedge, *Carex nigricans* (black alpine sedge), lives wholly at the mercy of late-persisting snows. The scruffy sparse turf of the sedge appears late in summer with barely time to flower and fruit. Other species like the heathers, huckleberry, and a few herbs may share this spartan habitat, but make a much poorer showing here than elsewhere in the parkland. The black alpine sedge community is surely the poorest in numbers of species and in production of biomass and least colorful of the subalpine meadow communities. But the very existence of this bleak plant association, living under such spartan conditions, speaks eloquently of the tenacity of life under stress.

The breathtaking landscape of subalpine meadows and isolated "islands" of trees is far from static. The most spectacular change took place in the early 1900s when tree species (mostly subalpine fir and mountain hemlock) began to invade the meadows. The massive invasion could be seen at many places in the parkland setting, and reached its peak in the 1930s. The invasion was short-lived, and now only remnants of sapling stands in meadows tell of the dramatic shift in vegetation. Ecologists believe that a warmer, drier climate persisted only for forty to fifty years, long enough to promote the invasion. Since the mid-1940s, a cooler, moister climatic regime put an end to the invasion. But it could happen again; all it would take is a slight shift in climate.

The subalpine parkland meadows are rich with showy shrubs and herbaceous perennials in summer flower. A field of avalanche lilies is the showpiece of any mountain meadow, either in full bloom (right, photo by Asahel Curtis), or singly, just emerging from the receding snowbank (below, photo by Ruth and Louis Kirk.)

The "Serpentine Syndrome" in the High Country

In chapter 7, the unusual habitats created by serpentine rock and its derived soil were portrayed. Besides the occurrences of the serpentine syndrome near sea level, its unique character at high elevation also can be witnessed in the Puget basin. Just southwest of Mount Baker, in southern Whatcom County, lies a lofty, westerly outlier range of the Cascades. Called the Twin Sisters Mountain because of its two prominent peaks, North and South Sister, the nearly 7,000-feet high range is all of one rock type, dunite. Indeed this is the largest single outcrop of dunite (with the mineral, olivine) rock in all North America. Like its metamorphic counterpart (serpentine), dunite is an iron-magnesium silicate, blended with "impurities" of nickel and chromium minerals. Soils weathered from dunite support a sparse and often distinctive vegetation (see photo, page 343).

In the montane to alpine regions of the Twin Sisters, one finds unusual plant responses (Kruckeberg 1969). First is the exclusion (or avoidance) of some species that are content growing nearby on normal soils. Then there are some species that thrive mainly on dunite soils; two ferns, *Aspidotis densa* and *Polystichum lemmonii* (the Shasta holly fern), frequent the barren rocky slopes. But the most remarkable plant response occurs at timberline. Instead of the usual timberline species, subalpine fir and mountain hemlock, the highest woody plants on the Twin Sisters are dwarfed (krumm-holz) specimens of lodgepole pine (*Pinus contorta*). On the North Twin Sister, one encounters a waist-high impenetrable thicket of this pine. So, once again, geology can determine the pattern of life.

Animals of the Mountain Hemlock Zone

Larger mammals and birds are much less narrowly confined than most plants to the Mountain Hemlock Zone. Deer, elk, bear, cougar, and many bird species, though encountered in both forested and parkland phases of the zone, wander freely downward beyond the limits of the subalpine. Distributions of common mammals, compiled by Franklin and Bishop (n.d.) for the four life zones of Mount Rainier National Park, reveal only one mammal, the hoary or whistling marmot as restricted to the subalpine and alpine environments. Those mammals with a wide altitudinal distribution usually migrate from one zone to another during the course of a season to search for food, to avoid winter snowpack and to breed.

The marmot best typifies the close fit to the upper subalpine habitats. Over and over again, in both the Cascades and the Olympics, the moment one passes from forest into parkland, the sharp, metallic whistles of marmots are sure to greet the hiker. With their piercing call, these furry sentinels announce to their kin (and to other animals) the approach of an intruder. Three species of marmot reside in the Puget Sound area: the Olympic marmot (*Marmota olympus*) occurs throughout the parkland and timberline country of the Olympic Mountains; the hoary marmot (*Marmota caligata*), a close relative, occupies similar habitats in the Cascades; the yellow-bellied marmot (*Marmota flaviventris*), is widespread in the Pacific Northwest, where it reaches the subalpine only in the North Cascades.

Marmot colonies are found most often at or near the base of rock talus slopes and adjacent parkland meadows. Their burrows are made beneath the protective cover of the massive boulders near the

Large mammals are not uncommon in upper montane forests and openings.

Far right: Mountain goat (Oreamnos americanus) in the high Olympics is an intruder at any elevation, increasing in numbers since its introduction in the early 1900s. It is rarely sighted in the Cascades where it is a native herbivore.

Near right: Columbian black-tailed deer are summer residents in the high country. (Photo by Mary Randlett.)

Most animals move in and out of the subalpine, but marmots stay put and are the characteristic mammal of the mountain meadow slopes. Near right: Marmot outside its burrow (den) in a rocky heather meadow. (Photo by Victor Scheffer.)

Far right: A black bear making a rare appearance in the subalpine, Paradise, Mount Rainier National Park. (Photo by Bob and Ira Spring.)

toe of the talus; well-worn paths both interconnect burrows and run out into the nearby meadowy feeding grounds. Naturalists find that the marmot runways are used by other mammals such as chipmunks, conies, and mice. Peaceful coexistence marks this rodent segment of the mammalian world.

Marmots are the largest of our indigenous "squirrels," in the Family Sciuridae, and thus kin of ground and tree squirrels as well as chipmunks. But marmots have not adopted ground squirrel behavior; they neither have cheek pouches nor do they store food for winter. Instead this voracious vegetarian piles on layer after layer of fat, up to one-half its body weight, as metabolic insurance for waiting out the deep winter in hibernation. By midsummer, the marmot colony is a thriving nursery of young animals learning survival from their parents and close relatives. Breeding takes place in March soon after the winter sleep is over; litters of six young on the average are born in May and soon join in harvesting vegetation in the nearby meadows.

Marmots show some degree of food preferences among the plants available in the high country, though they may take parts of most available herbs. They prefer young, tender plant parts and seek out the nutrient-rich seeds. The high dependence of marmots on the nearby vegetable larder is easily demonstrated. But should we not expect a reciprocal consequence? Do marmots shape the

Bare zone around a marmot burrow, Olympic Mountains. Marmot activity locally modifies herbaceous vegetation near burrows. (Photo by Roger del Moral.)

structure of the surrounding vegetation? Ecologist Roger del Moral (1984) and his student Alan Watson have convincingly shown that these industrious and voracious foragers alter their habitats in telling ways. Marmots can alter species composition and productivity of the plant community, and as well can change the look of nearby landscapes. Like larger foragers—elk and deer—marmots put their stamp on their surroundings. Indeed, the shaping of most "pristine" vegetation usually has an animal component.

Not infrequently, they may take animals for food. Stomach contents may reveal residues of insect larvae, especially caterpillars, and even chipmunks. Inevitably, those who eat are also eaten. Marmots are taken by predatory birds such as eagles and hawks; the coyote, the badger and bears are the principal mammals—besides humans—that prey on marmots.

The conspicuous colonial existence of marmots in our subalpine country strongly suggests an integration of behavior into a distinguishable social system. Though we know most of such animal societies in primates such as apes, chimpanzees, and monkeys, a new breed of ecologist—the sociobiologist—is turning to other groups of animals where social order also appears to prevail. David Barash (1974) found the social world of marmots a fascinating arena for the study of behavioral traits so essential for survival. Marmot species and their close relatives, the woodchucks, are descendants from a probable common ancestor. Yet, as the different species live in very different habitats, Barash has hypothesized that social behavior is strongly linked to the character of the particular environment of each marmot or woodchuck species. Thus, the eastern relative of the high-mountain marmot, the woodchuck (*Marmota monax*), enjoys the longest season for foraging in habitats at low elevations. In such favorable environments, the animals of this species are hardly social at all. In fact, they are largely solitary and aggressive, linked to each other only during mating and the rearing of young. In contrast, the three high montane species of the west, which have to feed and reproduce in a much shorter growing season, have become highly social.

The Olympic marmot (*Marmota olympus*) shows best among the members of the genus *Marmota* the kind of integrated social behavior that can be related to survival. In this species, Barash finds discrete colonies, each closely knit with an extended family of several adults (usually one male and two females), two-year olds, yearlings, and the young of the year. No distinct dominance hierarchy (that is, one "top-dog" animal with subordinates) or well-defined territory and its defense seems to exist in the Olympic marmot. Barash elaborates:

This species is highly tolerant and playful, commonly feeding in social groups of three to six individuals. No territories or even home ranges are maintained; all parts of the colony are equally available to all colony members. Dominance relationships are generally indistinct and nonpunitive. Olympic marmot social life is characterized by a high frequency of active "greeting" behavior . . . and apparently associated with individual recognition. . . . During the early-morning "visiting period" the inhabitants of each colony enter all occupied burrows and exchange numerous greetings with the other colony residents. (1974:415)

The very different rigors of life and habitat for eastern woodchucks and the Olympic marmot are thus suspect as being at the roots of the great behavioral differences in the two species. A fortuitous circumstance provides additional evidence for the hypothesis that the evolution of behavioral differences is keyed to different environments. The yellow-bellied marmot (*Marmota flaviventris*) happens to live at intermediate elevations and thus enjoys a growing season (70–100 days) roughly midway between that of the woodchuck and the Olympic marmot. The yellow-bellied marmot, Barash writes,

. . . lives in recognizable colonies composed of numerous adults, and is thus considerably less solitary than the woodchuck; but individually distinct home ranges are maintained, physical spacing between individuals is relatively great, and infrequent social interactions are overlain with considerable aggressiveness, indicating that [the yellow-bellied marmot] has a less highly socialized behavioral system than the Olympic marmot. The highly social Olympic marmots average about one greeting per animal per hour, while greetings in the yellow-bellied marmots average about one tenth of this number and among the relatively asocial woodchucks, the behavior has not even been described. (1974:416)

As further support to the hypothesis that behavior is linked to environment, Barash finds that the third species in the Pacific Northwest, the hoary marmot, is a close match for the Olympic marmot in *both* behavior and restriction to the same kind of high montane habitat.

A key question then is urged upon us by this close linkage between social behavior and habitat. What adaptive function is served by progressively less aggressive behavior in the more severe subalpine environments? Barash proposes that the key motivation is the urge of the young to disperse and set up housekeeping in new sites. The degree of sociability apparently relates in a not unexpected way to the urge to disperse. Dispersion of young is earliest in the woodchuck and progressively later in higher altitude populations of marmots. Early dispersal in lowland woodchucks with a long growing season can occur since the young have acquired

*Left: Clark's nutcracker (*Nucifraga columbiana*), along with the gray jay (*Perisoreus canadensis*), both well known as "camp robbers," are faithful indicators of the upper montane conifer forests. (Photo by Victor Scheffer.)*

Below left: The ruffed grouse, with the spruce and blue grouse (species of Dendragapus*), can be heard (if not always seen) by their unique wing-drumming sound, in upper montane brushy areas. (Photo by Bob and Ira Spring.)*

*Below: Shooting star (*Dodecatheon jeffreyi*), an herb of wet meadows. (Drawing by Libby Mills.)*

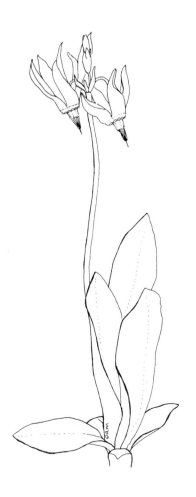

ample energy reserves in their first year. No strong social bonds need hold the young in a colony much past the period of maternal care of the first season. But dispersal of marmot young must be delayed in the rigorous and short season of the subalpine. Such delay allows for accumulation of bodily reserves critical to successful dispersal and reproduction. A social, nonaggressive life in colonies can give time for this crucial preparation for future independence.

Insects and Flowers of Subalpine Meadows

Those who visit the subalpine parkland at the peak of summer flowering are at first overwhelmed by the grand panoramic sweep of lofty snow-flecked mountains, rimming colorful meadowy basins dotted with the isolated groves of the upper montane trees. But after the impact of the immense landscape is assimilated, the alert mountaineer can discover other wonders, much smaller in magnitude. The parkland meadows at the height of flowering become colorful mosaics of yellows, purples, reds, and blues, a floral display advertised in a multitude of sizes, shapes, and clusterings. Almost instinctively one looks for the connection between the riotous exhibition of flowers and a "purpose." The subalpine floral world is richly matched by a world of insects, and thus the issue of purpose is joined.

No matter how biologists may discount "plan and purpose" in nature and thus shun seeking out the "why" of structure and function, the one world of flowers and insects proclaims *purpose* at every turn. We can clothe the evident purposefulness of the matter with respectability by putting it in ecosystem terms. The meadows of the parkland subzone are exquisite arrays of plants, animals, and microorganisms attuned to each other and to the physical necessities for life-giving heat, light, water, and soil. If we view each insect and flower species as part of a complex network in the subalpine meadow ecosystem, we would create an intricate "wiring diagram" of many cross-connections. Yet to simplify that network is to gain at least partial understanding. The insect-flower association is a pairing of trophic (feeding) dependence of insects on flowers with the reciprocal dependence of flowers on insects to pollinate and thus produce seed.

Flower- and insect-watching have come of age in recent years, after having been eclipsed by laboratory biology in the long interval since Darwin's time. Field biologists nowadays are finding fascinating, vital connections that have coevolved between plants and animals, above and beyond plants as food. Pollination ecology is an important chapter in the plant-animal story of reciprocity.

Bees, butterflies, moths, beetles, and flies are the principal classes of insects that carry on commerce with flowers. But before examining more closely some of the remarkable cases of insect behavior and floral contrivance, we must not overlook the one, and highly visible, vertebrate pollinator. Hummingbirds find richly colored sources of nutritious nectar in our high meadows, to amply supplement their insect diet. The gorgeous red columbine (*Aquilegia formosa*) is the flower most avidly sought by hummingbirds, although the tall, purple-flowered horse thistle (*Cirsium edule*) and the monkshood (*Aconitum columbianum*) of wetter meadows are also eagerly visited.

Floral biologists have long been curious about the strong correlation between the red flowers and hummingbird visitors. The simplest explanation—that hummers prefer red flowers—appears to be inadequate. The tiny birds do "home in" on flowers of different colors and will sample different-colored sugar solutions in feeding experiments. The bond between hummingbirds and red flowers appears to be built around the migratory and nomadic behavior of the birds. The few native temperate North American species of hummingbirds, unlike the many more tropical species, migrate over vast distances from Mexico to Alaska. Their local forays in a flora are fleeting and of short duration. One can hypothesize a "need" for a strong visual signal for optimal foraging while on their immense journeys. Red flowers in the Northwest native flora are peculiarly modified for visits by hummingbirds. In addition to being red, they are characteristically odorless and have long and broad floral tubes bearing richer-than-usual nectar as the reward for hummingbird visits. Flowers of this form are usually borne aloft either singly or in loose clusters at the ends of long and flexuous stalks. It is precisely this suite of traits that tends to exclude most insect visitors: insect pollinators usually require flowers that give off odors; they often utilize narrow tubular flowers; and they cannot easily "clue in" on red. Karen Grant (1966), working with the California flora and hummingbird visitors, proposes a testable hypothesis to account for the red flower-hummingbird affinity. Red coloration is significant in hummingbird pollination only in that red serves as a signal for the migrant birds to home in on a particular patch of flowers, thence to feed not only on red flowers but on those of other colors but similarly adapted to the behavior of hummers.

An embellishment on the hypothesis of red as lure is the suggestion by Peter Raven of the Missouri Botanical Garden, a careful student of floral biology. Raven (1972) sees the high caloric energy values of nectar in red to orange flowers as critical in the association of flower with bird. He finds that hummingbird flowers produce copious and nutritious nectar far in excess of that produced by insect-

Above: The moutain pasque flower (Anemone occidentalis) in its shaggy seed stage in late summer after a brief but showy floral display. (Photo by Ruth and Louis Kirk.)

Right: The showiest displays of bear grass (Xerophyllum tenax) are in open meadows, often after fire. (Photo by Asahel Curtis.)

pollinated flowers. As expected, the nutritional requirement of hummingbirds greatly exceeds that of insects. It is probably no coincidence then that red-orange flowers that are visited by hummingbirds are odorless and thus not attractive to insects.

Learning more about our subalpine flowers and their insect cohabitants will have to be somewhat of a letdown. Scarcely any comprehensive investigation has been published—or even undertaken—on flower-insect interactions for the subalpine-alpine habitats of our region. To start with, we could use a tabulation of just what insects live in the upper montane parkland habitat and accurate information on which ones make their living from the products of flowers. Case histories are needed for particular associations between insect and plant species. Even though a working library of published information is lacking, we can sketch out a reasonable outline of the relationship of the subalpine insect fauna to the parkland flora. The summary in Table 28 should indicate what kinds of more specific information would be needed to make a "wiring diagram" for this aspect of the subalpine ecosystem. Applying to Northwest subalpine country the findings from other similar regions of the temperate world is wholly justified. The insects and flowers are of the same common stock, and most genera are the same, even though species may be unique to a particular habitat. We can draw upon knowledge gained in the Rocky Mountains of North America and the Alps of Europe for similarities in the plant-herbivore interface of our own subalpine.

The foraging of insects on plants is a huge subject, as all manner of plant parts are consumed by insects. Here we restrict ourselves to those insects that utilize flowers and their products. Form and function are nowhere more beautifully illustrated than by the various floral contrivances and the structural and behavioral specializations of the insect consumers. So closely tied to one another are certain flowers and their insect visitors, that explanation of one without simultaneous attention to the other loses the essence of the intimacy. Floral adaptation to insects and the accommodation of insects to flowers can best be understood in the context of coevolution—the reciprocal hereditary response of insect to flower and of flower to insect over long stretches of evolutionary time. One stimulus for such close partnership between flowers and insects is the high premium placed on outbreeding or cross-fertilization by the plant partner. Though by no means universal and consistent, outbreeding by cross-pollination between different individual plants promotes evolutionary survival. Offspring from outbreeders are more variable than those from inbred or self-pollinated plants. Variant offspring are the raw materials from which natural selection can mold a successful, more adaptive race.

The idea of coevolving systems of the pollinator and the pollinated as a functioning and self-perfecting unit avoids simple-minded botany and closed-circuit entomology. Yet we are forced by sequential patterns of language to deal one at a time with the pieces of the whole mosaic. Only in the mind's eye can the coevolutionary dynamics of plant-animal interactions knit together the pieces of the total fabric. So, then, to flowers we turn first. The catalogue of floral structure consists of devices for attraction, landing platforms, and food for insects. These devices are made in variety from flower parts—petals and sepals that support the pollen-bearing stamens and seed cases or pistils. Attraction of insects by flowers is accomplished by scent, color, and form. Floral lures are built out of flower parts or clusters of flowers, the inflorescences. Food, the primary target for insect visitations, is furnished in the form of nectar and pollen, although almost all other flower parts can be eaten by certain more omnivorous insect visitors. (See Table 28 for the plant-animal connection.)

The simpler types of insect-pollinated flowers, like the buttercup or wild rose, do not have their sets of outer floral organs (sepals and petals) fused into tubes. Rather, the organs are separate and alike in size and shape, with the members of each set having the same coloring or markings. Moreover, this basic (and probably ancestral) flower type commonly has many pollen-producing stamens and seed-producing pistils. A wide variety of insect types visits flowers of this low grade of specialization: short-tongued species of flies, bees, wasps; voraciously chewing beetles; some butterflies and moths; and species of true bugs (Hemiptera). Not all flowers of the buttercup level of organization may produce nectar; the nectarless types are sought for their pollen only. In most cases, the pollen- or nectar-seeking insect visitors tend to wander from one plant species to the next, rather than remain constant to a given plant host.

Fusion of petals and sepals to form flowers in the shapes of saucers, bells, or funnels comes next in the evolutionary trend toward increasing specialization. Correlated with union of parts is the reduction in stamens and pistils (pollen- and seed-producing organs) to a low and constant number. Many subalpine flowers have attained this ensemble of floral characters, for example, phlox, Jacob's ladder (*Polemonium*), mountain heather (*Phyllodoce* and *Cassiope*), mountain bluebell (*Mertensia*), and the common bellflower (*Campanula*). Such tubular flowers foster a greater selectivity among potential insect visitors, since nectar and/or pollen may be concealed within the short or long tube. Bees (both solitary and social types), butterflies, and moths are the common visitors, while only highly specialized flies (hover flies and bee-mimics) and certain beetles have adjusted to tubular flowers.

*Below: Jacob's ladder (*Polemonium pulcherrimum*). Right: Alaska harebell (*Campanula lasiocarpa*). (Drawings by Libby Mills.)*

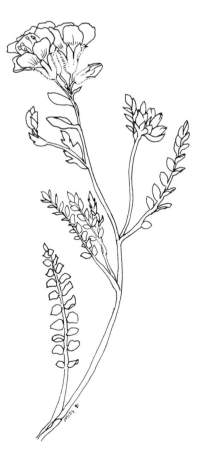

A further floral specialization is the conversion of a radially symmetrical flower (like buttercup or phlox) into one with a two-lipped or other bilaterally symmetrical form. In the subalpine flora, the most eye-catching examples of this type are the penstemons (e.g., *Penstemon tolmiei, P. davidsonii, P. rupicola*), the louseworts (*Pedicularis groenlandica* and other species),[2] the paintbrushes (*Castilleja*), and the showy, bright pink monkey flower (*Mimulus lewisii*). Not only are the kinds of floral visitors reduced by the intricate construction of bilabiate (two-lipped) tubes, the fidelity of the fewer pollinators is markedly increased. Bumblebees and solitary bees show strong preferences and a high degree of constancy to flowers of this type.

This sketch of the major grades of coevolutionary partnerships between flowers and their insect pollinators will goad the inquisitive reader to delve further into this fascinating corner of natural history. A good place to start is the delightful *Story of Pollination* by Bastiaan J. D. Meeuse (1961). From this introduction to floral biology, you may be led to the early classics by Darwin and Hermann Muller, then on to two modern books, *The Pollination of Flowers* by Proctor and Yeo (1972), and *The Sex Life of Flowers* by Meeuse and Morris (1984).

2. Why lousewort, you may ask? In olden times the plant was supposed to cause lice on sheep feeding on it. The generic name, *Pedicularis,* originates from the common root *pediculus,* meaning louse.

Table 28. Feeding Preferences of Insects in the Subalpine Vegetation

Plant Feeders (herbivores)	Detritus Feeders (saprovores)	Animal Feeders (carnivores)

1. Feed on nonfloral parts:
  a. Sucking insects: aphids, Hemiptera (bugs)
  b. Chewing insects: grasshoppers, leaf cutters, leaf miners, larvae of butterflies and moths, beetles
2. Feed on floral parts:
  a. Nectar seekers: bees, flies, adult butterflies, and moths
  b. Pollen seekers: social bees, hover flies, beetles
  c. Seekers of both pollen and nectar: bees and certain flies
  d. Eaters of fruit and seed (ripe and unripe): beetles, larvae of beetles
	1. Feed on dead and decaying plant matter: beetles and flies (larvae and adults)
	2. Feed on dead animals: beetles and flies (larvae and adults)
	3. Feed on feces: flies and beetles (larvae and adults)
		1. Parasites
		  a. Feed on other insects
		  b. Feed on animals other than insects
		    Some flies; many beetles, wasps
		2. Nonparasites
		  a. Feed on other insects
		  b. Feed on animals other than insects; beetles, wasps

Before leaving the subject to your own further reading and patient observation in some subalpine meadow, I must share with you the discoveries of Walter Macior, who has applied some modern observational tools to flower- and bee-watching. Six different species of the colorful louseworts occur on the subalpine slopes of Mount Rainier. Macior (1973) finds these species of *Pedicularis* to be exquisite examples of the coevolutionary interplay between flowers and pollinators. Their floral structure shows amazing variation on the two-lipped floral shape, each major variant linked with a particular type of insect "behavior." All are herbaceous perennials, growing in distinctive habitats, from wet or dry meadows to the understory of the open subalpine forest.

The least modified floral structure is that of a two-lipped flower where the upper lip will extend well beyond the lower to form a grooved hood that encloses the pollen-producing stamens and the upper stylar and stigmatic portion of the seed-producing pistil. Two species in the Mount Rainier area have this least specialized floral form—*Pedicularis bracteosa* and *P. rainierensis.* The floral pattern of the extended upper lip or hood takes on bizarre and elegant elaboration in the other four species on Mount Rainier. In each, the galea (the hood or beak) enclosing the stamens is elongated and twisted into distinctive shapes. The common names of these four louseworts call attention to the intriguing floral forms assumed by the eye-catching galea. Thus, *Pedicularis racemosa* takes the vernacular name of "sickletop lousewort"; *P. contorta* is the "white coiled-beak lousewort"; the common widespread *P. groenlandica* is tellingly known as "elephant's head"; and *P. ornithorhyncha* becomes in translation the "bird's beak lousewort." These same four louseworts are visited by bumblebees seeking pollen; they produce no nectar but promote in their structure the gathering of pollen by worker bees of the bumblebee colonies. The other two species, *P. bracteosa* and *P. rainierensis,* are also visited by bumblebees, but the rewards are both pollen and nectar. Recall that the species *bracteosa* and *rainierensis* have a simple hooded corolla, not at all twisted into a beak. The beaked species provide only pollen, while the simple hooded flowers of the other two species yield pollen and nectar.

Is there any meaning to this scheme of things? Macior believes that the nectarless species are evolved as bumblebee specialists, presumably as an adaptive response to the efficient pollen-gathering habits of bumblebees. And the reward to the plants is assured cross-pollination!

The two nectar-producing species are visited by hummingbirds and carpenter bees as well as by bumblebees, while the four nectarless species are exclusively pollinated by the bumblebees. The

Each of these six species of Pedicularis *(louseworts) has a distinctive floral form and is visited by bumblebees in singular ways. All can be found often in the same high montane setting. Three species of the forest border are (above) P. racemosa (sickletop lousewort) and (opposite page, left) two similar tall louseworts, P. bracteosa and P. rainierensis. The elephant's head, P. groenlandica (page 342) is in the wettest sites, while P. ornithorhyncha (bird's beak lousewort) (top right) and P. contorta (coiled-beak lousewort) (bottom right) are in drier sites of open meadows. (Photos by Walter Macior.)*

most specialized of the pollen-feeding bumblebees work in the up-side-down position. Pollen-gathering is aided by rapid wing vibrations against the floral "beak," for hidden within the elongate and curved beak are the pollen-laden anthers. Agitation of the beak forces pollen out through the beak tip. Once forcibly extruded, the pollen is packed into pollen baskets on the bee's legs. During this precise pollen-extracting exercise, the bumblebee will deposit pollen from a previously visited flower (on the same or different plant) on the tip (stigma) of the seed-producing organ (pistil). Thus cross-pollination can be effected, although if the pollen deposited on the stigma comes from another flower on the same plant, the result is self-pollination. Most insect-pollinated plants that have several to many flowers per plant have this mixed type of breeding system, some outbreeding and some inbreeding. Only where one plant produces one flower is cross-pollination assured; likewise, it is as-

sured when self-pollinations are unsuccessful owing to a functional incompatibility of a plant's own pollen on the stigma.

With five species of bumblebee known to pollinate one or more of the six species of *Pedicularis* in the Mount Rainier area, one would expect some "illegitimate" pollinations. Such crosses between species could result in the formation of interspecies hybrid plants. Macior has yet to find hybrids in the field. Apparently two factors ensure against such illegitimacy. In the first place, all six species do not really coexist closely in the same habitat or in the same local area. The range of habitats for the six is sufficiently varied so that each species tends to be isolated within its particular microenvironment. In addition, there is some innate behavioral isolation between species. Since particular bumblebee species show some degree of fidelity to a particular species of lousewort, illegitimate pollinations are kept to a minimum. But nature is no perfectionist in these matters. Macior has observed the same *Bombus* species working alternately between two different species of *Pedicularis*. Yet no hybrids have been found. Either they are so rare as to have been overlooked, or the hybrid is unsuccessful because of some malfunction beyond the initial step of transfer of pollen.

Much of this fascinating story of pollination in subalpine louseworts has been compiled from the results of good old-fashioned observation in the field, where the investigator watches and records, while fighting off mosquitoes, getting sunburned, and yet reveling in the beauty of the subalpine setting. But Macior has added sophisticated instrumentation to visual astuteness. He uses both movie and still camera, the latter in stereo pairs. The film can then later be analyzed frame by frame for the complex sequence of events in insect behavior as the bumblebees probe the structure of the flower. We can hope for further painstakingly careful work like this to illuminate in fine detail the rich array of pollination devices in our high parkland meadows.

The dazzling colors of the flowers in open subalpine meadows proclaim a strong Darwinian "purpose"—pollination. But close by the meadows, in continuous forest, flowers of a more subdued hue prevail. Whites are common, with a sprinkling of yellows and lavenders. Is there a different set of pollinators for the flowers of the forest floor? Though not studied adequately, some woodland flowers, for example, baneberry (*Actaea*), are known to be visited by beetles and flies, the generalists among insect visitors of flowers. Yet some forest floor wildflowers such as bugbane (*Cimicifuga*) are serviced by bumblebees.

The Alpine Rim of the Puget Sound Basin

The summit of the Puget Sound basin is only a few hundred rock-strewn feet above the timbered subalpine. While so close, one must venture upward, yielding to the urge to see what is on top and beyond. The subalpine mosaic of parkland and mountain hemlock forest grades quickly into the highest zone of all, the treeless Alpine Zone. On the higher mountains—usually above 5,000 to 6,000 feet, and only on those peaks which provide more *Lebensraum* than the forbidding vertical surfaces of knifelike ridges and spires thrusting above the subalpine—the transition between subalpine and alpine is detected with ease. In such high elevation habitats, where topography does not run to extreme vertical slopes, subalpine forest and meadow grade into timberline, and above timberline a zone of vegetation devoid of any tree species can be recognized. Timberlines are best seen on the higher slopes of the tapered volcanic peaks like Mount Baker, Glacier Peak, and Mount Rainier. Often the same tree species of the subalpine reach their upper limit here. Other tree species, commonly whitebark pine (*Pinus albicaulis*) and Lyall's larch (*Larix lyallii*), may instead serve as the occupants of the narrow undulating band of scrub forest we designate as treeline or timberline. The impact of a rigorous environment is most dramatically portrayed as timberline. The rigors of cold temperatures, high winds, and pelting snow and ice, as well as a deep and persisting snowpack, all conspire to frustrate attempts of trees to gain a sure foothold. The most vivid manifestation of this struggle between the valiantly persisting trees and the demanding physical environment is the dwarfed nature of the "forest" at timberline. So apt is the German word for this standoff struggle for survival that the elfin and gnarled treeline forest is widely called *krummholz* ("bent or crooked wood"). Though ecologists have invented terms like "wind timber" or "alpine scrub" to identify the dwarfed treeline timber, krummholz is the word most commonly used.

Krummholz is defined as a vegetation type "occurring in the transition between the alpine and subalpine zones characterized by dwarfed deformed tree species which tend to sprawl along the mountainside in the direction of the prevailing wind" (Cox 1933, quoted in Habeck 1968). At Sunrise on Mount Rainier or in the high country above the lodge at Mount Baker, displays of fine examples of krummholz are easily spotted. As uppermost extensions of the subalpine, timberline areas can be expected to support much the same parkland and forest associates. Especially common in the understory of timberline forest are the mountain heather species, Alaska spiraea (*Luetkea pectinata*), and herbaceous lupines, pen-

Opposite: Pedicularis groenlandica *(see caption, page 340).*

Timberline's most telling feature is the dwarfing of conifers that were good-sized, erect trees in the parkland just below. The krummholz growth form of lodgepole pine appears on higher slopes and ridges of dunite rock on Twin Sisters Mountain (see page 330), while subalpine fir is dwarfed in other timberline habitats.

stemons, species of *Pedicularis,* grasses, and sedges. To stand in the midst of timberline, where the elements bend and trim the pliant trees to streamlined hedges, is to be in the midst of a silent drama. The intent of trees to grow erect is curtailed by strong and bitter cold winds. Growing tips are sandblasted by blown sand, ice, and snow, and lower branches exposed by minimal protective snow cover. The few erect stems that arise above the krummholz skirts of trees are dissected "flags" of foliage swept leeward under the force of prevailing winds, giving further evidence of the struggle.[3]

Heather meadows of *Phyllodoce* and *Cassiope* can be expected in the wetter treeless places in the alpine. Other common dominants of the subalpine such as mountain heliotrope (*Valeriana sitchensis*), black sedge (*Carex nigricans*), or Alaska spiraea (*Luetkea pectinata*) also reach well into the alpine. But where topography and exposure permit, one encounters communities with truly alpine species. Here and there in the Sunrise area of Mount Rainier National Park one can find good examples of alpine vegetation. Burroughs Mountain, above Sunrise, is a favorite of botanists for exploring what little truly alpine tundra vegetation there is in western Washington. Parts of Burroughs Mountain are nearly flat with a cover of pumice deposited in geologically recent times. Here the vegetation appears to be in a pioneer stage with much open ground between the low herbaceous cushion plants. Sandworts (*Arenaria* species), alpine lupine (*Lupinus lepidus lobbii*), phlox (*Phlox diffusa*), alpine grasses, and sedges are the most common species. From the vantage point of high and treeless Burroughs Mountain, one can see other alpine landscapes, sandwiched between permanent snowline and treeline. On these adjacent slopes the herbaceous and low woody cover is highlighted by a characteristic topographic feature of many alpine areas of the world. The loose rock of the slopes has become patterned into long vertical stripes. Cycles of freeze-thaw from ground level into the shallow mantle of soil is presumed to be the shaping force of this telltale *patterned ground.*

On gentle slopes and flats where the country rock has been broken loose, again by the wedging action of expanding ice, or where the outcrops of rock are exposed, the plant cover is sparse, finding foothold only in shallow soil between the rocks or in rock crevices.[4] Cushion-forming species of sandworts (species of *Are-*

Only rarely in the Cascades does the alpine occur on gentle terrain, as here at Burroughs Mountain (immediately below, in the middle distance) on the

3. The peculiar form of *krummholz*—isolated upright "flag" (stem) on a cushion of low-spreading branches—is so characteristic of this tree formation that ecologists have yielded to the temptation to give terms to the phenomenon. The flags are called "supranivational flags" (erect stems above the snow pack) and the springy mass of more or less horizontal branches fully protected by the persistent snow are called "infranival cushions."

4. Stony terrain in the alpine zone is called a "fellfield" in many parts of the world.

flanks of Mount Rainier. (Photo by the author.) Bottom: The flat, treeless summit of Burroughs Mountain is reminiscent of Arctic tundra.

naria), asters and fleabanes (*Erigeron* species), saxifrages (species of *Saxifraga* and *Heuchera*), wild buckwheats (*Eriogonum* species), and campions or catchflies (*Silene* species) are the conspicuous plants in such demanding habitats. One catchfly (*Silene acaulis*) of our alpine country is just as much at home in the Rockies, the European Alps, or the north polar regions of the world. Until in bloom, it could be mistaken for a moss, so tiny and tightly clustered are its leaves. But when in bloom, the "moss campion" shows its true colors: a gorgeous pink-flowered species of the Carnation or Pink Family (Caryophyllaceae). Geobotanists believe that the moss campion once had a more continuous distribution in past geological times, only to be carved up into isolated populations by Pleistocene ice.

Though truly arboreal species are left behind at lower elevations, the alpine does support woody species of small shrubs or even creeping ground cover plants with woody stems. The common juniper (*Juniperus communis* var. *montana*), with its steely blue-gray and prickly foliage in ground-hugging dense mats, is perhaps the most characteristic alpine shrub. Not infrequently, though, the careful observer finds other woody species, such as kinnikinnik (*Arctostaphylos uva-ursi*), shrubby cinquefoil (*Potentilla fruticosa*), and even dwarf willows (species of *Salix*). Dwarf willows are a real surprise in the alpine and yet so easily overlooked except when in flower. Both "pussy" and "tom" willow flowers appear in short stalked catkins often covering the dense prostrate mats. This remarkable growth form is common for some willow species throughout the high north temperate regions of the world. The course of willow adaptation to increasingly severe conditions with altitude or latitude is from tree or shrub to prostrate shrublet. The change in stature (or life form) is not simply racial accommodation within a single species. The dwarf willows of the alpine (and Arctic regions) are reckoned as clearly distinct species by botanists.

There is no mystery about the forces behind the alpine way of life. Temperature, light, wind, and snowpack are easily identified as the major life-determining variables that in stressful measure govern life above the treeline. But "quantifying the obvious," a cardinal preoccupation of the ecologist, discloses close tracking between the physical environment and the responsive plant cover. Temperature, more than any other controlling function, tailors the alpine vegetation to its characteristic expression. The growing season is only two to three months and even in summer ambient air temperatures drop almost daily to barely above freezing. Plant processes of growth and metabolism are pushed to their lower threshold under such conditions. Moreover, it is just when temperatures ease upward from zero degrees Celsius (32°F) that physiological processes take on their most significant acceleration. Thus, near zero degrees, metabolism is retarded, but at low temperatures just above freezing alpine plants can rapidly metabolize their reserves. Given the short growing season under low average temperatures but with great diurnal fluctuations, the alpine flora adjusts in many ways. Physiological ecology now has some answers.

American ecologist Dwight Billings and his students have been probing the mysteries of plant physiological tolerances to the alpine way of life over the past twenty years. Billings and Mooney (1968) pose a fundamental problem: "The key to successful adaptation to tundra or alpine environments is the development and operation of a metabolic system which can capture, store, and utilize energy at low temperatures and in a short period of time" (p. 508). The source of metabolic capital is of course the solar energy-trapping process of photosynthesis. Experiments with alpine plants, both in the field and under simulated alpine conditions in controlled environment chambers, do substantiate the expected: alpine plants reach optimum photosynthesis at lower temperatures than do lowland plants. The products of photosynthesis (sugars, starches, and other energy-rich substances) are made available to the living plant by the near reverse of photosynthesis—the universal cellular activity of respiration. It too runs at higher rates at lower temperatures, unlike lowland species.

The alpine rim of Puget country is at once an exhilarating yet forbidding world. In summer it dazzles the eye and restores the soul. But its long winter demands the utmost of life for its sheer survival. Why then has plant life ventured upward into the forbidding alpine? Like a human alpinist seeking to conquer an unclimbed summit, "just because it is there," so plants seek new habitats. They adapt to new rigors as long as there is a place to put down roots.

The rich mosaic of environments from sea level to eternal snow provides neverending wonder and pleasure for all who live in and around the Puget basin. A person can draw upon the magic of altitudinally changing landscapes by traveling up through the transformations in life and things inanimate. The traverse through the several life zones demonstrates a pattern of worldwide occurrence. The stature of vegetation gets smaller, the space between trees and other woody species widens, affording habitat for a rich herb and shrub cover, and finally, at the upper reaches of the living transect where the now treeless landscape is dominated by the inanimate pattern of rock, snow and ice prevail. As a subject for postcards, bank checks, calendars, and coffee table picture books, the high montane panorama is unparalleled. But far more than an aesthetic delight for those who live close to such grandeur, the montane arena is charged with self-sustaining vitality—not only for its own immediate environmental well-being, but for the singular influ-

The impress of glaciers, past and present, on high country terrain is seen everywhere in the Cascades and Olympics.

Left: On retreating, Coleman Glacier on Mount Baker leaves a bare zone devoid of vegetation. (Photo by the author.)

Right: Alpine glaciers once overrode this high plateau leaving smoothed rock and glacial ponds (tarns), Rampart Ridge, Cascade Range. (Photo by Bob and Ira Spring.)

Below: The dramatic "trimline" (edge left by the furthest advance of a glacier into a forested area), below Coleman Glacier, Mount Baker. (Photo by the author.)

ences it has on the lowland basin skirting the mountain perimeter.

The Cascade and Olympic mountains govern the life in the basin with both subtle and overt accent. The power of the mountains to guide the destiny of the lowlands has gone on incessantly in the past, much as it does now. In Pleistocene times, the mountainous walls of the Puget Sound corridor channeled the course of the great tongues of continental ice that so thoroughly etched and scraped our sea-level landscapes. And during each stay of continental ice in the lowlands, alpine glaciers in the mountains lost some of their massive stores of ice. The great U-shaped valleys gouged by the alpine glaciers serve as today's causeways for runoff, bearing waters back to the sea from the mountains. The north-to-south thrust of the mountains assures Puget Sound of a reliable, maritime weather. Pacific storms meet the mountains and are relieved of some of their moisture-laden air. Our mountains influence weather in yet another way. During inversions of the normal altitudinal decrease in temperature, the warmer upper layers of air put a lid on the air between the mountain borders of the basin. Entrapped and contained, this stable air mass stagnates until the inversion is broken. It has only been in recent decades that stagnating air trapped in the basin has taken on a noxious flavor, thanks to the polluting automobile, factory, and the general fallout from concentrating humans and their multifarious activities in the basin. A short-sighted view of an air-pollution alert in Puget Sound would be to find the mountains guilty because they trap the befouled air that otherwise would disperse to "innocuous" levels. But surely we all know who is to blame.

9 Water and the Quality of Life

"Water is the driver of Nature."—Leonardo da Vinci

Life-giving water, as melting ice, makes its reentry into the ecosystem. (Photo by Josef Scaylea.)

Water, when delivered in adequate amounts as snow, rain, mist, or humid air, when released at the right times and at optimal temperatures, and when channeled onto deltas and flood plains by converging watersheds, becomes the most critical determinant of the quality of all life for any part of our planet. The coastal areas of the Pacific Northwest are singularly blessed with an optimal delivery and distribution system for this life-sustaining molecule, H_2O.

Water, whether liquid, solid, or gas, is a sparkling example of the old adage, "what goes up must come down." In fact, the water (or hydrologic) cycle is simply a series of local to worldwide ascents and descents of water, with some horizontal movement when aloft in the air and when flowing on, or seeping under, the ground.

Water begins its journey along the hydrologic cycle by evaporation. The oceans are by far the greatest source for this evaporative return to the atmosphere, although terrestrial evaporation, including evapotranspiration from vegetation, is not insignificant. Once airborne, water vapor is moved by winds usually in predictable directions. Each year, the Pacific Ocean sends aloft and landward 6.8×10^{11} metric tons[1] of water. In the atmosphere, water vapor may be transported anywhere from a few feet to thousands of miles, to be released as rain or snow. The average time in the air is about ten days.

What makes water so precious? The obvious, though incomplete, reply is that water is an essential ingredient for living systems, from molecule and cell to ecosystem. As life first evolved, it adapted to the available resources of the environment and hence to water. The fitness of water to life—and life to water—is a reciprocity born out of evolutionary adaptation of organisms to an aqueous habitat, and in particular to the remarkable properties of water. H. L. Penman (1970:39) says it well: "In nearly all its physical properties water is either unique or at the extreme end of the range of a prop-

---

1. Equal to 680 billion, a lot of water in metric tons. One metric ton contains 1,000 kilograms or about 2,200 pounds of water, or 264.3 gallons of water. And for those not yet thinking in metric, the grand total is 1.797×10^{14} in gallons.

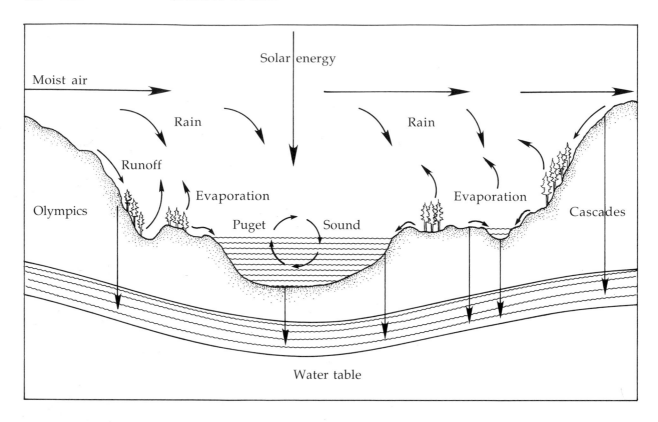

erty. Its extraordinary physical properties, in turn, endow it with a unique chemistry. From these physical and chemical characteristics flows the biological importance of water."

One property of water, so critical for life beyond the tropics, is the unique way it freezes, so as to sustain (not congeal) life at cold temperatures. Freezing starts at the surface of a body of water and proceeds downward. But a total freezing of the water column does not occur. While cooling, water contracts, but only to 4°C above freezing; from there down to freezing, it expands. The cooler and less dense (expanded) water then rises to the surface, buoying up with it the similarly less-dense ice. A pond frozen at the surface is in reality a watery aquarium with an ice lid.

Further remarkable attributes of water also have to do with its relation to heat energy. First, water has the greatest capacity of all common liquids to store heat, hence to withstand change in temperature. Also it takes more heat to vaporize water than other liquids. Both these heat-related properties significantly affect living things. The water-primed bodies of plants and animals are securely buffered against sudden changes in temperature, owing to water's singular stubbornness when heated.

Hydrologic (water) cycle for the Puget Sound basin. Moist Pacific air moves eastward. Precipitation and runoff charge soils, the water table, and bodies of water with moisture. Water is returned to the atmosphere by evaporation and by transpiration (vegetation). (Drawing by Sandra Noel.)

Meltwater from snowpack enters streams along the west slope of the Cascades, a vital link in the hydrologic cycle. (Photo by Josef Scaylea.)

Water: Input and Runoff

The water cycle for the Puget Sound basin is a regional version of the evaporation, transport, and release of water anywhere on the globe. The Pacific Ocean north of the equator is the source of the basin's water. Solar energy evaporates and sends aloft billions of tons of water each year. Though much of that water falls back into the ocean before it is moved over land surfaces, enough water (9 percent of the total evaporated) makes it into the airstream overland to serve in many life-giving and landscape-making ways along its continental journey.

If we take 100 units as the total amount of water vapor entering western Washington in one year from the North Pacific, then we should expect release of predictable portions of that water as precipitation along its eastward journey (Church and Fritschen 1968). Thirteen units of the 100-unit total are precipitated before the crest of the Cascades is reached; 4 of these 13 units will be returned to the air by evaporation. This leaves 9 units on and in the ground, eventually to trickle back to the Sound and Pacific Ocean as runoff. The remaining 91 units are still airborne and in transit to eastern Washington. Although the mountains ringing the Puget basin aid in extracting water before it moves eastward, a surprisingly large amount of water vapor stays aloft. In eastern Washington, 5 more units of vapor join the eastbound stream, having come across the state borders undetected, probably at high elevations, and 5 units are released as precipitation. But before the air mass leaves the state, still 4 more units return to the air by evaporation and only one unit remains as the runoff from precipitation. In sum, just 10 units of the 105 stay in Washington temporarily in the form of liquid water; the other 95 leave the state in the form of vapor. Despite the astonishingly low figure of only 9.5 percent (10/105) of the total airborne water staying here, we can be comforted by the fact that in acre-feet, or gallons or tons of water, the delivery of moisture to Puget Sound is amply sufficient. To some who deplore the wet climate, it is even an annoying superabundance.

The Olympic and Cascade mountains extract, store, and channel a significant portion of the water that stays on the west side. How do mountains lay claim to moisture from the eastward-moving air mass? A mountain range athwart the prevailing storm tracks causes warm, moist air from the Pacific to rise and to cool to a point where precipitation occurs. And with increase in altitude, the amount of precipitation increases. At the higher altitudes, the bulk of the water is shed as snow. About 80 percent of the total precipitation enters a downhill trek either directly or with varying durations of storage. Surface runoff immediately begins its journey to the sea. Water that percolates down through the soil may return to the soil surface by capillarity, be drawn up by plants and transpired (evaporated through leaf pores), or may enter the ground water. Ground water is the subsurface reservoir of water with ill-defined limits, but usually below the upper layers of the soil mantle. The common denominator of ground water is its state of full saturation. Any subsurface layer of the earth's mantle with sufficient porosity can become saturated with water to form a spongelike meshwork of water and particulate matter (soil, sand, clay, porous rock, etc.). In sloping terrain, ground water migrates by gravity. It too eventually reaches sea level and discharges into salt water. Ground water usually surfaces along a slope as springs, or it may directly trickle into

The water budget on a regional scale: precipitation, runoff, and evaporation for the Puget Sound region. Given 100 units of water rising from the Pacific Ocean, their fate can be followed across the mountains and the Puget Trough to the interior of Washington. (Drawing by Sandra Noel.)

Influences of mountains on rainfall. Though rainfall is high on outer coast (Aberdeen area), note increase with elevation in Olympics (orographic precipitation). Sequim's low rainfall is also caused by mountains (the "rainshadow" effect). Orographic precipitation also occurs over the Cascades. Points from left (west) to right (east); Aberdeen area, 80 inches; Sequim, 16 inches; Seattle, 32 inches; Snoqualmie Pass, 96 inches; Cle Elum, 23 inches. (Drawing by Michael Emerson.)

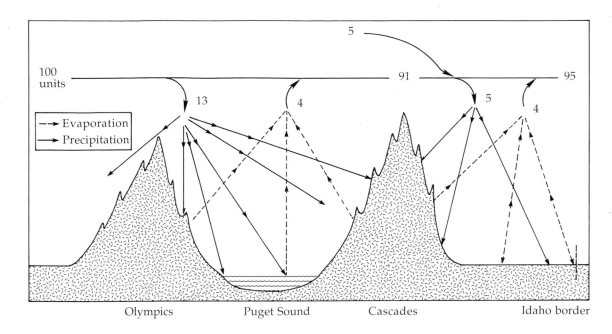

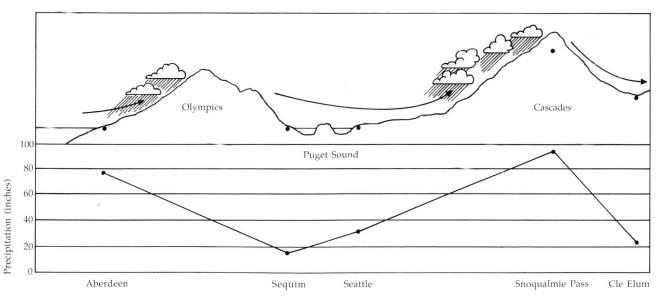

creeks and streams. It is, of course, the ground water, roughly de-limited by the "water table" at the uppermost layer of saturated earth, that is trapped for wells and serves as the greatest supply of stored water on land, usually far more than the volume of water stored in reservoirs and lakes. In this region of glacier-made to-pography, water catchment basins are plentiful and come in all shapes and sizes, so that storage of runoff in lakes as well as its transport in streams runs a close second to groundwater storage.

Water is continually at work plucking at the land, dissecting the Puget Sound basin into countless minor and major ridges, hillocks, and drainageways. It is a sample of the most massive earth-moving force known. The annual work of landscape-modeling by precipitation and runoff is estimated to be equivalent to the work of one horse-drawn scraper kept busy day and night on every ten acres of land surface.

With precipitation and runoff, erosion is inevitable. Every cupful of water in the runoff phase of the hydrologic cycle carries some of the land with it, even when that water runs pristine and clear off of virgin forestland. The purest of runoff still is "contaminated" with the weathered particles of rock (molecules and charged particles, or ions, of earth elements like calcium, magnesium, sodium, potassium, and iron) and the soluble remains of life (organic matter in molecular or colloidal form like nitrate, phosphate ions, humic

Only the dikes outline the Snohomish River during the November 1990 flooding east of Everett. (Photo by Pedro Perez.)

Aerial view of flooded farmland.

acids, etc.). Where runoff is severe, following storms or on watersheds disturbed by fire, logging, or road building, the murky discharge is laden with a visible increment of the earth's mantle: clay, silt, sand, gravel, rock, and even large pieces of detached life, bodies of animals and plants.

As I write on a soggy day early in January, all signs outside my window point to another rash of floods in western Washington. During the past week a cold front moved into the Puget Sound basin to bring fresh increments of wet snow which fell from near sea level on up to the crest of the mountains. Then, overnight, a rapid warming trend set in, accompanied by continuous rain. Snow at lower elevations has now become meltwater, joining the rain in the vast runoff network descending to the inland sea. When the waters of swollen creeks and rivers reach the flood plain of the Skagit, Snohomish, Nisqually, Nooksack, and all the other major rivers, their banks will strain at the added flow (see Table 29 for rates of river flow). The fresh surge of water will overtop confining channels and spread out over farmland and lowlying suburbia, heralding the annual drama of flooding.

Year after year we can expect two sharply defined periods of flood danger, brought on by maximum stream flow. From October to March, the winter runoff is fed by the highest precipitation of the year, amplified by the brief flushes of snowmelt at the lower

Table 29. Principal Rivers of the Puget Sound Area: Drainage Areas and Rates of Discharge (cubic feet/second = cfs).*

| Basin-River | Drainage Area Sq. Miles | Discharge (cfs) | | |
		Min. Daily**	Max. Daily	Average Annual
Nooksack-Sumas				
Nooksack River near Lynden	648	595	46,200	3,699
Skagit-Samish				
Skagit River nr. Mt. Vernon	3,093	2,740	144,000	16,490
Stillaguamish				
South Fork, Stillaguamish River				
nr. Granite Falls	119	55	32,400	1,064
Snohomish				
Snohomish River nr. Snohomish	1,714	—	136,000	9,500†
Cedar-Green				
Cedar River at Renton	186	56	6,640	711
Cedar-Green				
Green River at Tukwila	440	195	12,100	1,462
Puyallup				
Puyallup River at Puyallup	948	306	57,000	3,364
Nisqually-Deschutes				
Nisqually at McKenna	517	20	25,700	1,415
Nisqually-Deschutes				
Deschutes River nr. Rainier	90	16	5,620	263
West Sound				
Skokomish River nr. Potlatch	227	125	27,000	1,188
Elwha-Dungeness				
Elwha River nr. Port Angeles	269	10	41,600	1,487
Elwha-Dungeness				
Dungeness River nr. Sequim	156	77	8,400	373

*From Puget Sound and Adjacent Waters, App. XIII-Water Quality Control. Puget Sound Task Force-Pacific Northwest River Basins Commission.
**Discharge below 10,000 cfs not generally computed due to large tidal fluctuations.
†Accurate continuous streamflow records in the Snohomish River have not been possible because river stages are affected by tidal fluctuations. Projection of upstream records, however, suggests that the mean annual discharge of the entire Snohomish River system is probably about 9,500 cfs.

borders of the winter snow levels. This winter high-water period is characterized by brief but massive surges in water discharge, followed by return to low levels of runoff. Rapid rise and fall of discharge occurs in a matter of hours and usually is repeated several times during the winter high-water period. The graph on p. 358 shows the discharge pattern for the Sauk River as gauged near Darrington in 1950. Later on, from March to June, the Sauk and all other rivers rising high in the mountains take on a different discharge character. Volumes of water measured in cubic feet per second increase to a maximum in June. But the pattern is one of steady increase, not as in winter with its wild surges followed by quiet intervals. Further, the flood waters of the spring high-water period are largely of snowmelt origin, water released from the high mountain snowpack gradually and steadily as spring and early summer temperatures increase. Again the mountains irrigate and feed the lowlands; in flood times, however, the downhill run of water is excessive (see graphs, below).

The annual flooding is just as much a part of the hydrologic cycle as is the much less spectacular and continual delivery of moisture

Maximum, mean, and minimum monthly stream volumes for Skykomish River near Gold Bar, Snohomish County (1931–60), and Snoqualmie River near Carnation, King County (1931–60).

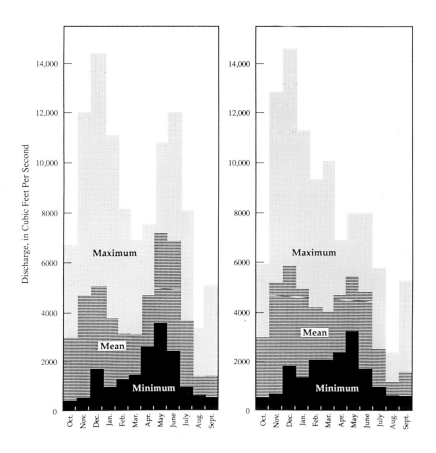

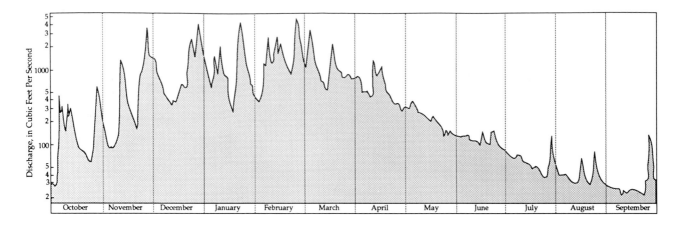

Graph of mean daily stream volumes in Sauk River (above Whitechuck River) near Darrington, Snohomish County. Peak discharges in winter due to sudden snow melt.

by precipitation. The flood plain and delta country of Puget Sound have been receiving flushes of river discharge for centuries, stretching far back beyond the Pleistocene. The periods of flooding, though they appear to do violence to the landscape, are in truth part of the life-restoring function of the water cycle. Flood-quickened waters are laden with sediments that blanket the land with a new film of nutrient soil. Those rivers that rise from the meltwater of glaciers, like the Nisqually, Nooksack, and White, carry perpetually a load of milky sediment, the whitish suspension of glacial "flour," milled at the headwaters by glacial action. Other sources of particulates are the dissolved soils torn loose from stream banks, silt- and clay-laden waters in the runoff from sloping terrain, disturbed naturally or by humans, and the movement of solid material (silt to boulder in size) dislodged and carried downstream in the streambed itself. A river like the Nisqually carries tons of suspended matter annually. At McKenna, near sea level, the Nisqually moves 250,000 to 300,000 tons annually in its suspended-sediment load. Though both the Alder and La Grande dams in southeastern Pierce County trap a good portion of the suspended load, a heavy burden of particulates escapes westward to fertilize and augment the delta in southern Puget Sound.

Interpreting the dynamics of water movement—input, storage, and output—for a typical drainage basin or watershed, though by no means simple, has been done by a research team of the Coniferous Biome, U.S. International Biological Program (USIBP Symposium 1972:54). First, a model of all the interacting elements of the hydrologic system is developed. Then reference data to fit several of the "subroutines" in the model are gathered in the field and in the lab. The model and the control data can be adjusted to a particular watershed and questions of prediction can be asked of the model. For example, what is the expected outflow from the water-

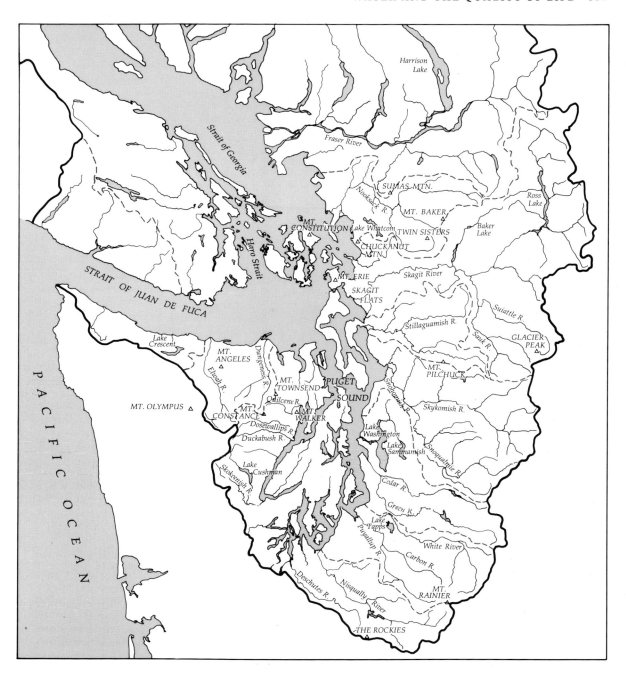

The entire, grand drainage basin for Puget Sound and adjacent maritime waters to the north and west is a function of topography. The high country bordering the lowlands funnels water downhill to the inland seas. (Map by Nancy Eberle.)

shed, given particular figures for precipitation, snowmelt, temperature, water loss by vegetation (evapotranspiration), etc.? The input data can be fed into a programmed computer, and the printout will be a simulation of a specific hydrologic episode.

Two ingredients of the hydrologic model in montane watersheds are of particular interest. They are snowpack as a water reservoir,

and evapotranspiration, the perpetual dissipator of water at ground and vegetation levels; both figure prominently in the water economy of upland habitats and contribute much to the aesthetics of our mountainous country.

Atmospheric moisture enters the downhill precipitation phase of the water cycle as rain or snow, depending on air temperature. Just above freezing, around 34° Fahrenheit (1.5°C), there will be a 50 percent chance that the precipitation will fall as snow. Since temperatures decrease with elevation, this transition of rain-to-snow occurs at elevations from 1,500 to 2,500 feet in mountains of the Northwest. In winter, almost all precipitation above 2,500 feet will be in the form of snow. As long as temperatures remain near freezing, the snow persists to become the seasonal snowpack. In forested terrain, some of the snow intercepted by trees eventually falls to the ground to accumulate as snow storage. Annual pre-

Winter floods and water-soaked terrain make slides frequent in winter, here along the Great Northern (now Burlington Northern) Railroad between Edmonds and Mukilteo (near Picnic Point). Landslide above railroad destroyed the house.

Headwaters of the Nisqually River at Nisqually Glacier, Mount Rainier. The downhill run of water starts high up off the winter snow pack. The change in snow pack from spring to midsummer is dramatically shown by these two pictures of the same site by Arthur Harrison, long-time observer of Cascade glaciers.

cipitation as snow (snowfall) and the annual amounts that accumulate on the ground differ. Seasonal snowfall[2] ranges from 10 to 30 inches throughout the lowlands, 75 to 100 inches on the foothills, and 300 to 500 inches in the mountains. Maximum accumulation as snowpack shows a corresponding trend, with maximum depths of 15 to 30 inches in valleys near the mountains and on the foothills, 150 to 200 inches at 3,000 feet, and 200 to 350 inches above the 5,000-foot level. Equivalent volumes of snowpack change in density dramatically from winter to spring. This change is measured by increase in water content, from 30 percent water in early winter to 45 percent in April. In exceptional years snowfall and snowpack can be phenomenal. During the 1955–56 snow season, Paradise Ranger Station at 5,550 feet elevation on the west side of

2. A ten-inch snowfall is equivalent to one inch of rain.

Mount Rainier recorded a seasonal total snowfall of 1,000 inches, the greatest snowfall in the lower forty-eight United States. The maximum snow depth at Paradise of 357 inches (about 30 feet deep) was reached in March of that year.

The Snowpack

The snowpack in the Upper Montane (mountain hemlock) Zone shows distinctive variations in pattern, crucial for plant life. The greatest depths of snowpack are in treeless meadow habitats. In situations with scattered trees or unbroken forest canopy, the ever-green overstory deflects snow in various ways. Some snow exposed on branches melts before reaching the ground. The "black body" (heat absorbing and reradiating) effect of trees dissipates additional snow by evaporation. As trees modify local wind patterns, snow is piled into drifts in openings within the forest by eddying wind currents. Heavy, wet snowpack on forested slopes inevitably responds to gravity; the creep of snow bows sapling trees downhill, leaving a permanent bend near the base of the trunk.

The winter skier touring in the high country is sure to encounter the "craters" in the snowpack around trees, each a special microcosm of the interplay between inanimate and living nature. These snow craters are deepest just next to the tree trunk, becoming shallower in a concentric pattern outwards. The craters are caused by trees and snowfall in two ways. First, the "through-fall" and accumulation of snow is least right next to the trunk. Second, the black body effect of trees further reduces the accumulation of snowpack. Both these effects vary gradually with distance outward from the trunk, thus causing the cone-shaped crater.

The annual accumulated snowpack in the mountains ringing Puget Sound is a massive water storage reservoir. No one knows how many millions of acre-feet of water are held in place as snow in the mountains. And each year the great bulk of the storage is released as snowmelt into the tributaries of our fast-running river system. Since snow is such an excellent reflector of light, it is a wonder that it ever melts to release its life-giving water as runoff. The measure of reflecting power of any object, called the albedo, is highly variable. Bare ground and green forest have an albedo of 3 to 20 percent, while fresh snow, a most efficient reflector, has an albedo of 80 to 85 percent. This means that vastly more light is reflected (not absorbed and turned into heat) by snow than by vegetation or soil. Yet snow *does* melt.

No sooner do the elegantly shaped snowflakes reach the ground or the gathering snowfield than they begin a metamorphosis. The exquisite hexagonal plates, star-shaped crystals, or needles of fall-

Above: Midwinter snow pack in the Cascades. (Photo by Josef Scaylea.)

Right: Snow and ice turning to water and starting the downhill run to Puget Sound. (Photo by Ruth Kirk.) Top: Water cascades off a snow bank and gushes out of an ice tunnel. Bottom: Snow melt temporarily impounded in Picture Lake near Mt. Shuksan. (Photos by Bob and Ira Spring.)

ing snow begin an alteration to the stable form in the snowpack, becoming round grains of ice. This storage form of snow persists until the heat budget of the snow column is sufficient to bring about evaporation or melting. Much more of the moisture in the snowpack is melted than is given off as vapor. It takes only 90 calories of heat to melt one gram of snow, while 657 calories are required to evaporate the same weight of snow.

Though fresh snow reflects most of the incoming shortwave (visible) radiation, it reacts in a crucially different way to another component of radiant energy from the sun. Longwave (infrared) radiation from the red end of the visible light spectrum is readily absorbed by snow. In fact, snow reacts to infrared radiation as though it were black. It is quite unexpected that snow approaches the ideal "black-body" state for the absorption of energy in the longwave end of the spectrum. The additive effect of the small amount of absorbed shortwave radiation and the larger amount of longwave radiation makes up the net heat input to the snowpack. When the heat gained by the snow column exceeds heat lost, melting will occur. Warm rain and the surrounding black-body absorption of heat by forest vegetation accelerates melting. As the snowpack accumulates dust and debris from surrounding soil, rock, and vegetation, its albedo decreases, from the 80 to 85 percent figure for new snow to a low of 40 percent. Thus, old snow with a lower reflecting power should melt more rapidly. The effect of particulate matter on snow is especially noticeable after a few days of intense insolation in our subalpine. Every conifer needle, twig, or cone, as well as any stray soil or rock particle, acts as a minute black body to increase the heat input on a microscale around the piece of debris. The result is the pockmarked surface of old and dirty snow.

The annual cycle of the snowpack can be more than the dynamics of additions, subtractions, and internal change to the aqueous column of ice and snow. The solar heat engine causes melting, a rather simple inanimate transformation. Besides this physical action, there is organic life in snow as well. In midsummer the visitor

Debris on the surface of snow creates "black body" effect—local melting around heated black body. (Photo by Mary Randlett.)

to the high country can witness color effects in snow, some of which are due to the presence of microscopic plants. The so-called snow algae are tiny unicellular plants which may contain a red pigment, besides the green chlorophyll. When these unicells are abundant in the snowpack, they can give the snow a conspicuous pinkish or reddish color. Of the 110 or so species of algae that are associated with snow around the world, several have been isolated from snow fields in the Pacific Northwest. Although some form green or brown patches where they colonize snow, the most common alga, *Chlamydomonas nivalis*, is red. Ron Hoham, a student of snow algae, believes that the predominance of red has a functional significance (Hoham 1971). High altitude snow fields receive high intensities of light during the long days of summer. The red pigment may serve as a protective "mask," shielding the green photosynthetic apparatus from intense radiation. Though they are photosynthetic and therefore able to make sugars, etc., from simple atmospheric molecules, these algae (like all other plants) require inorganic nutrients. Since pure snow is nutritionally sterile, where does the fertilizer come from? Hoham finds that such supplemental nutrient arrives as dust, atmospheric fallout.

The presence of tiny animals completes a simple snowbank ecosystem. In the mountains of the Northwest, as in other parts of the world, snow fields above timberline receive a continual supply of insects that are blown in from surrounding forest and from lower altitudes. Other animals, mostly invertebrates like spiders, mites, etc., forage on the living airborne flotsam. Some of this windblown food serves hungry vertebrates, especially birds, as well.

Most every alpinist has heard of ice worms as succulent morsels in a cocktail mixed with melted snow. If the source was said to be fresh snow then the tale was garbled. Austin Post and Ed LaChapelle, in *Glacier Ice,* assure us that "the life-cycle [of the ice worm] can occur only in permanent snow and ice, and thus the ice-worm is never found in transient winter snow fields. In fact, its presence or absence on a particular part of the glacier surface can clearly delineate the margin separating glacier ice from annual snow fields." (Moral: If you want ice-worm *hors-d'oeuvres* with your "mountaineer's gimlet," use old snow, called firn or névé, from a nearby glacier.)

Avalanches

Each winter, along with the floods from the warm rains and precociously melting snow, the Cascade passes and high country are beset with another danger—avalanches. Any snow perched on an inclined plane is subject to the forces of gravity and thus may slide.

Precipitous gashes in the forest tell of repeated runnings of avalanches in the upper montane.

Top left: Avalanche tracks in summer, mostly with pliant shrubs in the runs. (Photo by Mary Randlett.)
Bottom: Avalanche tracks in winter, North Cascades Highway. (Photo by Edward LaChapelle.)

But special conditions, common and recurrent in our mountains, aggravate the problem of slippage, from minuscule snow creep to dangerous avalanche proportions. In his pocketsized booklet, *The ABC of Avalanche Safety,* LaChapelle recognizes two types of avalanches. An amorphous mass of uncompacted snow characterizes the *loose snow avalanche.* Its movement may start from a small nucleus of snow set in motion, but may gather great size and momentum in transit. Wet snow of spring or summer can produce the most dangerous loose snow avalanches; their burden of wet snow, gathering weight and mass on a steep slope, gives them tremendous destructive power. Everywhere in the mid to upper montane valleys, one can find evidence of such avalanches. The streaks of nonforested slopes flanked by forest are the tracks, old and new, of avalanches. Following the devastation of masses of timber, bent or snapped off in rude downhill chaos, a characteristic vegetation begins. For many years after an avalanche, a plant community of shrubby mountain alder or vine maple, with a certain herbaceous flora, marks the track of the original avalanche, and persists through subsequent inundations of snow on the move (see chapter 8).

The other type, the *slab avalanche,* gives the alpinist and skier the greatest cause for concern. These great cohesive masses of snow are the most frequent cause of accidents in the mountains. Although the conditions of the snow, the atmosphere, and the substratum which nurture the slab avalanche may vary greatly, the end product is much the same: a large area of snow begins to slide all at once, cleaving away in irregular fracture from the snowpack from which it is calved. The most trivial impulse may trigger a juggernauting slab avalanche. In fact, most avalanche accidents are set off by the victims themselves as they attempt to pass across the sensitively poised and unstable mass of snow. Slab avalanches, pulsed by some disturbance, begin to slide as a cohesive layer, either over an underlying bed of snow or directly over the ground surface. The extreme sensitivity with which a potential snow slab may respond to triggering is a major factor in their danger. It is this responsiveness to shock that is utilized by avalanche-control people, who set off explosive charges or fire cannons to trigger avalanches artificially in dangerous areas.

Many conditions of both the internal properties of the snowpack, the nature of the slope and underlying substrate (rock, soil, vegetation, etc.), as well as the prevailing and prior weather conditions, may foster avalanche conditions. Hence there is no single way to predict avalanche danger. The common theme that threads its way through the various forces that produce snow avalanches is change in or to the snowpack: new and substantial increments of

Mountain alder (Alnus sinuata) copes well with repeated avalanches, here in early spring showing its pliant, bent stems.

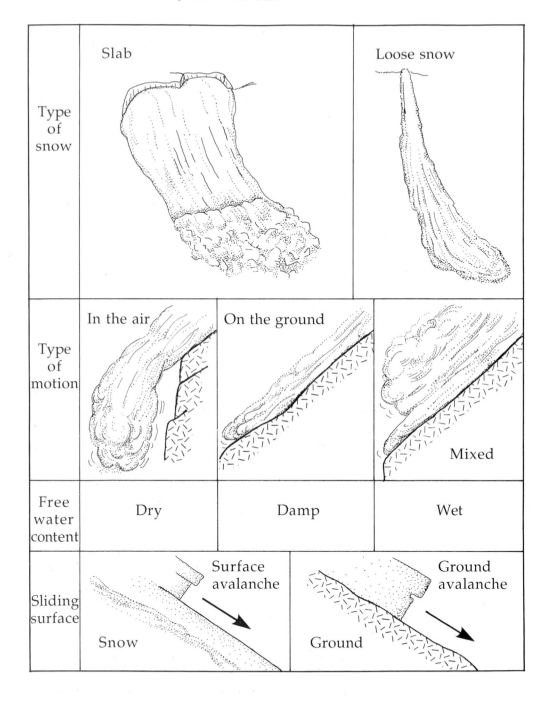

The types of avalanches encountered in the mountainous border of Puget Sound are created by four variables: type of snow, type of motion, water content of snow, and nature of the avalanche surface. (Rendering by Sandra Noel.)

snow to the old snowpack, changes in temperature and wind, changes on the surface of old snow, all produce instability in the inclined snow fields. LaChapelle's warning bears repeating here: *"Beware of avalanche danger during and after winter storms."*

A detached view of the snowpack as a natural ingredient in the montane environment may not come easily to us. Humans are in the montane scene more and more, physically and spiritually. Its dangers, its great reserve of water, and its aesthetic embellishment of the mountains make it very close to the human orbit. But a detached view, as an intellectual exercise, requires only an inclined plane (that is, a mountain range), a source of kinetic energy (solar evaporation and wind power), and then the partial release of the energy of atmospheric uplift by the seasonal deposition of snow across the endless mountain landscapes. That energy is then stopped in its further surge, and held as the energy-charged potential in the poised snowpack. Avalanches, snowmelt, and evaporation eventually transform stored energy into action and the kinetic downhill surge turns the wheel of the hydrologic cycle yet another giant turn.

Vegetation and Evapotranspiration

The green mantle of forest, meadow, and parkland is a colossal contributor to the water budget of the Puget Sound watershed. Water is intercepted, stored, and released by every last stitch of vegetation. Of the vast amount of water trapped by plants, only one-fifth stays in the bodies of plants. The remaining four-fifths, ever on the move, is called the water of evapotranspiration. Water lost to the atmosphere from plants and adjacent soil is transformed by the energy of the sun into its gaseous form, water vapor. Of the solar energy reaching vegetation, 40 percent effectively enters the machinery of the plant body, there to be unevenly divided between a minuscule allotment of energy to photosynthesis and a lion's share of the energy to speed water on its way from soil through the plant, back to the atmosphere.

The initial phase of evapotranspiration is simply the loss of water vapor from leaf and other porous plant surfaces. For every volume of water lost to the atmosphere by plant surfaces, an equivalent volume is replaced in the so-called transpirational stream: countless capillary threads of liquid water in the tubular conducting system (xylem cells) of roots, trunks, twigs, and leaves, as well as in the porous microscopic meshwork of cellulose cell walls of the entire plant. In effect, a Douglas fir, a salal shrub, or the trailing twinflower of forest floor, each is both a sponge and a living "wick." The analogy to a wick must be temporized by the fact that the living plant has some control over amounts of water given off, while the inanimate wick is helpless in the face of evaporation.

The major control is by the leaf, a marvelously contrived "sandwich" of photosynthetic, conductive, storage, protective, *and* ventilating tissues. Ventilation is the prime function of the lower epidermis of a leaf, with its many regularly spaced pores (stomates). Though the number varies widely from species to species, typically the leaves of plants have from 1,000 to 4,000 stomates per square centimeter of lower epidermal surface. The stomates are far from passive holes in the leafy skin. Each slitlike pore is between two living cells, the guard cells. These can open or close the pore by changing their shape. At ten A.M. on a bright summer day, the stomates are likely to be open, especially if the rest of the plant has been charged with transpirational water from the soil during the previous night. Stomates will be closed at night and at certain other times, especially on days of high humidity or extreme drought. It would seem a curious miscalculation of nature to have "invented" a living system that is so elaborately contrived, simply to lose four-fifths of all the water it imbibes. At a loss to account for the exorbitant output of water, botanists have often labeled the transpirational loss of water a "necessary evil." By this argument, the great uptake and output of transpirational water is tolerated only to allow for adequate water supply for all vital processes in the plant: growth of new tissue, flexuous support of the leafy shoots, photosynthesis, and mineral uptake from the soil. Necessary evil or not, the water-saturated living wick is a tremendously successful invention.

We need now to look at the way vegetation and its transpired water figure in the hydrologic cycle.

> Fully 71 percent of the precipitation received by the United States disappears through evapotranspiration from nonirrigated pastures, meadows, cultivated fields, forests, and noneconomic stands of plants. Further, about five times as much water is expended in irrigation as in industry. Part of the 1 million-billion gallons which escape each year through evapotranspiration escapes directly from the soil. But much—perhaps most—is transpired through leaf stomata or pores no larger than 35 by 15 microns [0.035 by 0.015 inches]. In other terms, evapotranspiration consumed 28 to 40 inches of the 75 to 80 inches of rain that fell on one North Carolina hardwood forest. (Waggoner and Zelitch 1965:1413)

How much water does a Douglas fir tree consume in a day, or a season? Until quite recently we could only guess at the amounts of water lost by a tree in its natural habitat. But in the Cedar River watershed near Seattle, a most remarkable technology was put to use for getting our answer. One group of the Coniferous

Water uptake and loss (transpiration) by vegetation traced in a single stylized tree. Evaporation from the porous surface of the leaf initiates the upward movement of water from roots and soil. Inset: Cell structure of a tiny piece of leaf in cross-section. Water exits through pores (stomates) of lower epidermis. (Rendering by Sandra Noel.)

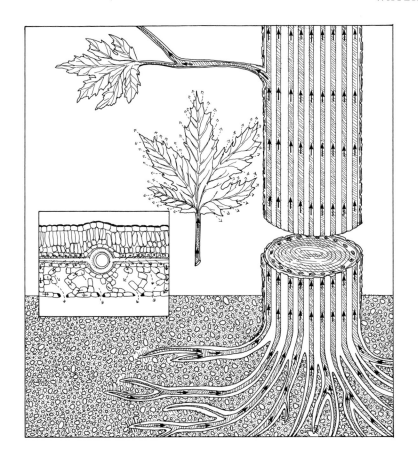

Biome's research team, under the leadership of Leo Fritschen and Richard B. Walker, reasoned that one tree could be manipulated in such a way as to monitor transpirational water loss. They chose a thirty-five-year-old Douglas fir, 92 feet tall, and "potted" it so it could be weighed at will. Short-term weight changes would reflect water flux in the tree. Now, potting a 92-foot Douglas fir was no ordinary task! The container was actually two huge metal cylinders, one nested within the other, both approximately 12 feet in diameter and 4 feet deep. The massive rootball was enclosed in the inner cylinder. The potted tree, resting on a rubber hydraulic transducer, sensitive to changes in weight, was replaced in its hole in the ground. The whole system, tree and container (called a lysimeter), weighed 29,000 kilograms (65,979 pounds), yet could detect small changes in moisture. (The lysimeter's sensitivity of 630 grams is equivalent to 0.06 millimeters of water.) With this ingenious device, it was possible to record accurately water loss by transpiration in the lysimeter tree.

Data from this Douglas fir were converted to an area basis to give

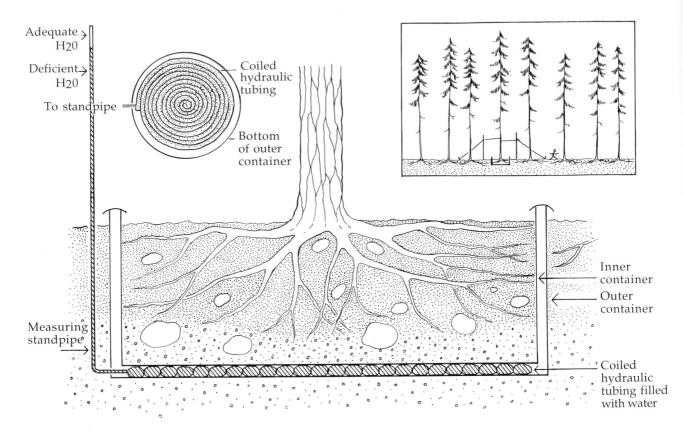

the annual loss of water in a typical second-growth forest in Puget Sound. Fritschen's team made that calculation, based on an average water loss of 1.4 millimeters per day by the potted tree. For an acre of second-growth Douglas fir, the annual water loss by evapotranspiration is 546,405 gallons.

The significance of vegetation for the retention and release of water in the hydrologic cycle varies widely from dry (xeric) desert to wet (mesic) tropics anywhere in the world. The mesic vegetation of the Puget Sound basin intercepts and releases vast amounts of moisture, midway in capacity between desert and tropics. How does this plant-related moisture enter into the region's water cycle? First of all, the return of water to the atmosphere is accomplished by evapotranspiration, but in much more protracted, smaller increments than by flooding of deforested watersheds. Note the emphasis on the *quality* of moisture returned to the atmosphere. A clearcut watershed will return precipitation to the sea in greater volumes and at faster rates, but at a price. The environmental costs of erosion, flooding, and attendant destruction or alteration of upland as well as lowland landscapes is avoided when vegetation stands between soil and atmosphere to release water gradually.

The "lysimeter tree" in the Cedar River watershed. The "potted" Douglas fir rests on a sensitive system of coiled tubing. Gain or loss of water by the tree can thus be accurately measured. Water level in the glass-tube standpipe is the measuring device. (Drawing by Linda Wilkinson.)

Foresters now reckon with yet another way that water enters the forest ecosystem. On a foggy or cloudy day, the drip, from conifer foliage, of water condensed from the atmosphere can be felt (and heard) on its way to the forest floor. Fog drip from vegetation significantly compensates for some of the loss of water by evapotranspiration. It has been estimated that fog drip can account for 25 percent of the annual precipitation in a mid-montane forested watershed.

The question of what makes a forest cool in summertime can be answered in terms of the transpirational return of water to the air. Part of the cooling effect results from the reflection and absorption by trees of the incoming radiation. But the tree is also a leafy wick, losing water by evaporation; the air next to the evaporative surfaces of leaves is thus cooled. Air currents in the forest waft this cooled air about to further depress air temperatures. So, when hiking in the mountains, by all means, *do* thank a tree the next time you leave a hot and dry clearcut, avalanche slope, or scree and enter the nearby cooler forest.

Erosion and Eutrophication

"We treat our soil like dirt."—National Geographic, *March 1987*

Precipitation and its runoff ceaselessly eat away at familiar landforms. Rugged mountains, rolling hills, and deep-cut valleys all spark in us awe for these seemingly changeless horizons in our environment. Yet so short is the human vision that scarcely seen are the workings of unending change on the land. The wearing down of mountains by erosion and the consequent build-up of sediments have been transforming Puget Sound topography throughout geologic history. Normal erosion is a fundamental geologic process whereby land surfaces are gradually worn away by natural mechanisms, called base-leveling. Depending on environmental conditions—slope, plant cover, climate, bedrock geology, etc.—the normal erosion may be so gradual as to escape detection, or so devastating as to excite suspicion that the gods are wreaking some sort of vengeance. But whatever the magnitude, trickle or flood, of sediment runoff, normal erosional change is an integral part of the continual remaking of the earth's surfaces.

Accelerated erosion, on the other hand, is chiefly caused by the hand of man. Besides normal erosion, rapid removal of the surface materials of the land adds enormous burdens to the runoff. Disturbance of any landscape above sea level by whatever activity (mostly human) renders the soil mantle more susceptible to removal by runoff. To normal runoff of the season's precipitation, disturbed landscapes will add more sediment from accelerated erosion. Then under conditions of unusually heavy runoff, such as times of cy-

clically recurring flood conditions, the runoff burden assumes awesome and destructive proportions.

The problem of erosion should be cast in terms of its opposing process, soil formation, in order to appreciate the great disequilibrium—more erosion than soil formation—that can occur under conditions of accelerated erosion. Soil formation proceeds at slow rates. One figure for Northwest soils is two to four centimeters (about one inch) per 1,000 years. Normal erosion may account for almost an equivalent removal. The effects of accelerated erosion produce massive imbalances in the soil-forming and erosion cycles; vastly more soil disappears than is generated by natural processes. These effects have continued in the Mediterranean basin now for over 1,000 years. From archeological evidence in Christian and pre-Christian habitats in Italy, it is possible to approximate the rate of accelerated erosion in areas where there has been continued and intensive human activity. Beginning about the second century B.C., the rate of erosion rose to an average of twenty to forty centimeters per 1,000 years. Natural soil-forming processes cannot possibly overtake such a rate of erosional removal of the land.

Another factor mitigates against the steady, predictable replace-

Erosion caused by excessive water (and associated debris) run-off has both natural and man-induced causes.

Left: The Kautz Creek mud (slurry) flow, of November 1947, on the slopes of Mt. Rainier, was due to natural causes. Heavy overburden of mud and rock killed trees along the stream. (Photo by Ruth and Louis Kirk.)

Above: A road maintenance crew working to improve the road above the Nestucca River, Oregon, dumps mud into the river, helping to degrade this once fine fishing stream.

Right: A creek badly eroded from mud and debris coming from an upstream logging operation, Skagit County.

ment of eroded soil by natural weathering processes. Many deeper soils are the result of short-term pulses of massive deposition. Yet volcanic ash from an episode of eruption or massive mud flows of the past cannot always be counted on to replenish soils.

In the Puget Sound basin the rates of erosion can be greatly accelerated by the removal of forest. This loss of the soil mantle is particularly acute when logging is associated with a network of roads. The erosion takes two forms, gullying and mass wasting. While gullying is a surface effect involving sediment transport by running water, mass wasting has a more deep-seated effect. Under unstable conditions, following the removal of vegetation, rock and soil are transported *en masse* downslope by gravity. Mass wasting is an ever-present process on bare areas in most landscapes, only it is accelerated by disturbance of vegetated slopes. Often the effect is delayed after logging until the roots of the dead tree stumps have decayed sufficiently. See Appendix 5.

Intensive studies of erosional effects on an experimental forest in western Oregon give a graphic picture of the impact of logging on erosion. The sediment runoff was measured on three different but adjacent watersheds. In one, all trees were cut down and removed

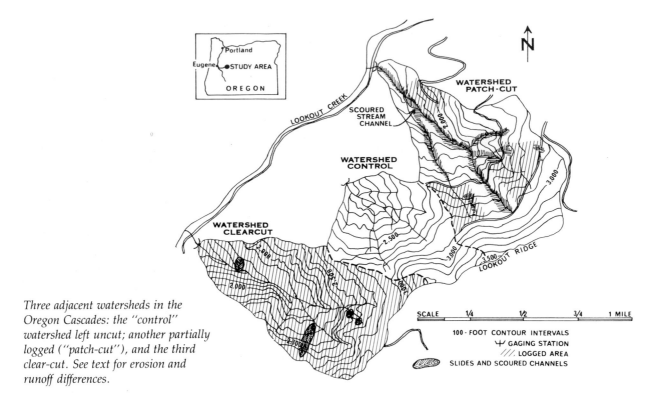

Three adjacent watersheds in the Oregon Cascades: the "control" watershed left uncut; another partially logged ("patch-cut"), and the third clear-cut. See text for erosion and runoff differences.

by skyline logging, a system requiring *no* roads. In the second watershed, 25 percent of the trees were cut ("patch-cut" system) and removed over the 1.65 miles of newly constructed logging roads. The third, "control," watershed, used for comparison with the other two watersheds, was left in its natural state. Measured sediment runoff from the patch-cut site was 109 times greater than the uncut control area over the same time span. Mass wasting was the cause of 99 percent of the soil erosion. The researchers claim that the major portion of this sediment burden came from the road system. Loss of soil on the skyline-logged site was 3.3 times greater than on the control area (see Rothacher et al. 1967).

It should be evident that the differences between the gradual growth of the soil mantle of 3 to 8 centimeters per 1,000 years and the loss under disturbance could be devastatingly large. In fact, the same Oregon study provides the figures on loss per 1,000 years in the three different watersheds. The patch-cut (with logging roads) lost soil at the rate of 280 centimeters per 1,000 years. In the clear-cut (skyline, roadless) logged area, soil loss was 10 centimeters per 1,000 years, while the control plot with no disturbance had a rate of 3 centimeters per 1,000 years. It is evident by these telling figures that intact vegetation impedes markedly the rate of erosional runoff. Plants *do* preserve the soil.

Erosion means an irreplaceable loss to the upland ecosystem. Part of the erosional burden in runoff waters is the life-giving natural fertilizers in soils. Either in dissolved form or in larger particles, the elements and compounds of nutritional value to the ecosystem are carried from the upland to the basin below. Some of this nutrient reaches terrestrial vegetation in the lowlands, especially in times of floods. In fact, the flood-plain soils adjacent to stream deltas and estuaries depend on periodic natural enrichment when runoff exceeds their confining banks. A particularly good example of the vital role of flood-plain nutrient recharge in maintaining a specific type of vegetation is to be found in the coast redwood belt of northern California. Where it occurs on alluvial flats, the redwood is supreme, but only if those alluvial flats are periodically flooded. Only redwoods thrive on periodic flooding, with its attendant silt and nutrient load. Flooding effectively eliminates three prime competitors: Douglas fir, grand fir, and tan oak. It is feared that with expanded flood control measures, the redwoods of alluvial flats may lose the race for survival in the face of these three competing species. In the Puget Sound basin, flood-plain species like Oregon ash, bigleaf maple, black cottonwood, and associates are, like the redwoods, dependent on enrichment by silt and nutrient deposited in the normal erosional runoff at flood stage.

Runoff from the Cascades reaches Puget Sound through lowland flood plains and estuaries. Left: A typical flood plain.

The Skagit River delta, the largest of the Puget Sound flood plains. (Photo by Bob and Ira Spring.)

The effect of accelerated erosion following upland disturbance on the rate of nutrient removal can be much more severe. Nutrient elements like nitrogen, potassium, phosphorus, calcium, and others, as well as complex organometallic particles may be carried all the way to water impoundments (lakes, estuaries, and the Sound). The consequences are twofold. The loss of upland soils through mass wasting and gully erosion includes nutrients removed in the eroded soils. Also, the addition of the nutrients and the sediments can seriously affect downstream sites where they are deposited. Not only are lowland impoundment basins greatly altered by siltation, etc., but their waters are excessively enriched.

The transformation of an oligotrophic (slow producing) lake into a eutrophic (fast producing) one is now a familiar story. Here the polluter is the devegetated upland, not suburbia, but humans are still the key agents in perturbing the environment.

Unintentional and indirect fertilization of lakes, deltas, and estuaries by logging, fire, etc., has the same effect as if one were deliberately to add nutrients to the waters. The extra nutrients can trigger increased growth of algae and set off a chain of processes that can change water quality. Data on the amounts and quality of nutrient discharge during accelerated erosion coupled with excessive runoff are conflicting. Prior to disturbance, upland forests appear to show a net gain in nitrogen while moderate losses of other nutrients occur. Gains in nitrogen are largely the result of biological activity, while the losses of other nutrients due to biological or physical processes are compensated for by further weathering of the parent rock. It is following disturbance that the observed results vary so widely. On an eastern Washington watershed following burning (the 1970 fire in the Entiat River drainage), increases in nitrogen and other elements were detected in runoff waters but not in as large amounts as expected. It is possible that the lower-than-expected rate of nutrient loss is the wrong measure. Since burned or logged watersheds are bound to lose much greater volumes of runoff water, the absolute amounts of dissolved nutrient in the runoff are diluted by the extra volume of water descending the slopes. If we looked at the total amount of nutrient in the runoff for a season, the amount should be significantly higher. The Entiat burn study shows just that; four major inorganic nutrients (calcium, potassium, magnesium, and sodium) increased in the runoff from 1.3 to 60.6 kilograms per hectare per year.

A now classic study in New England gives us a good yardstick of comparison. Within the watershed of the Hubbard Brook Experimental Forest (central New Hampshire), one plot of beech-maple-birch forest was completely leveled, but nothing was removed from the clearcut. Monitoring the quantities of nutrient export in runoff revealed that the cutover ecosystem suffered increased losses of nutrients. Nitrogen loss was equivalent to the amount naturally recycled each year in the undisturbed ecosystem; losses of other nutrients ranged from three to twenty times greater than from comparable undisturbed ecosystems. It is tempting to use these values of nutrient losses in the Hubbard Brook forest in estimating what to expect in other ecosystems similarly treated. To paraphrase a well-known utterance, "When you've seen one ecosystem, you've seen 'em all." But that simple view just won't work for ecosystems. Each watershed of each ecosystem has different physical and biological attributes and variables. Until there is a comparable study for Puget Sound involving clearcutting without removal of the cut biomass, data from the New Hampshire study or from logged-over land must suffice as indications of what could happen here.

Recall the erosional runoff studies for the experimental forest site in western Oregon. Chemical water quality was also monitored on the three experimental plots. The results are applicable to similar old growth and logged lands in western Washington. After clearcut logging and slash burning, chemical nutrients increased in the water runoff. The loss of nutrient cations from the logged area was 1.6 to 3.0 times the loss from an old-growth Douglas fir forest. The greatest surge of nutrient runoff occurred for twelve days after slash burning, and the concentrations of ammonia and manganese exceeded federal water-quality standards during this period. Loss of nitrogen was monitored closely, as this element is so critical to the nutritional well-being of plants and all other life. Following burning, loss of nitrogen annually averages 4.6 pounds per acre. About one-half of this was organic nitrogen contained in the sediment runoff; inorganic nitrogen, dissolved in the stream, accounted for the remainder. In contrast, annual loss of nitrogen from the undisturbed forest was only 0.16 pounds per acre.

The evaluation of water quality is a critical index measure for the health of the forest habitat. Knowing the amounts and kinds of nutrients, sediments, and organic matter in runoff waters makes it possible to predict the effects of change on the ecosystem. Loss of nutrient by the disturbed ecosystem and excessive inputs to downstream lakes, estuaries, and flood plains are the two most significant effects.

So direct and far-reaching is the measure of chemical nutrient runoff that land managers cannot help but get the message. Minimizing losses of nutrient capital from manipulated lands turns out to be good business in the long run. And, federal, state, and local water-quality standards help enforce better land use practices.

Contaminated Waters

Human-induced changes in water quality often involve more than increases (or decreases) in nutrients. Toxic wastes and pathogenic microorganisms are two kinds of contamination in Puget basin waters that we must cope with. Toxic wastes—both domestic and industrial in origin—can be detected in our freshwater and marine habitats, and their biological consequences determined. The contaminants include inorganics (especially heavy metals) as well as a Pandora's box of organics (from petroleum byproducts to pesticides and industrial residues). We reap the products of past careless community "toilet-training" in the form of diseased fish and

Flood plain and delta vegetation in Puget Sound brackish wetlands. Discovery Bay on Olympic Peninsula. (Photo by Ron Vanbianchi.)

shellfish. The sad consequence of releasing toxic substances is told in greater detail on page 69. Local, state, and federal agencies are committed to stemming the flow of toxic wastes, but past excesses will haunt us and our biological kin for years to come.

Disease microorganisms, too, have entered the hydrologic cycle. Certain pathogenic bacteria, protozoa, and viruses are out there in the waters of Puget basin, kept at bay only by water purification. Those who revel in the very accessible out-of-doors of Puget country know of one such pathogen that has diminished the delights of a wilderness experience. *Giardia,* and its excruciating affliction, giardiasis, is known to hikers, hunters, and fishermen as a new menace in the woods.

Years ago, the one sure thing in the mountains was the purity of the water; it could be drunk with complete confidence. Indeed, drinking out of a cold mountain stream was one of the joys of being in the back country. But no more. Giardiasis is a serious gastrointestinal infection that is caused by a microscopic protozoan animal, *Giardia lamblia.* It first came to the attention of Washingtonians in a big way in 1976, when 4 percent of the population of Camas, Washington, came down with giardiasis-like symptoms (diarrhea lasting ten days or longer). The Camas water supply had become inoculated with *Giardia* cysts, the resistant stage of the parasite. The source of the contamination was beavers near the intake of the city's water supply. How the beavers got it is unknown, but probably they became infected from a human *Giardia* carrier who left fecal material in the habitat. From this early outbreak in the state, many additional cases have been identified. Giardia is now widely distributed in the Puget basin, from lowlands to the alpine. Other animals, besides beaver and muskrat, can be sources of water contamination. Water voles, elk, deer, bear, and other terrestrial vertebrates, all can carry *Giardia.* To date no native birds, including waterfowl, are known to have the parasite.

It is known that the incidence of giardiasis infections decreases with increasing altitude. But even snowfields or springs at high elevations could be contaminated as animals do leave "scat" on snowfields.

Northwesterners can tolerate a clearcut or two enroute to the trail head, or even an untidy horsepacker's camp in a high mountain meadow. But veteran outdoorspeople have become thoroughly disgusted by the need to purify the once-pure high mountain drinking water. The pest *Giardia* is almost too much to bear. The mountain experience is forever diminished, tarnished by this microbial virulence, so recently a sad part of the Northwest wilderness experience. Once again, we see a poignant examples of the ecological dictum at work: "We can never merely do one thing."

Skokomish Indians at a temporary camp, ca. 1912. (Photo by Edward S. Curtis.)

10 Aboriginal Indians in the Puget Sound Basin

"Every part of this earth is sacred to my people."—Chief Seattle

Long before the arrival of Europeans, the Pacific Northwest had been discovered by aboriginal peoples. By the time European voyagers ventured into Puget Sound, a series of elaborate and rich cultures had been flourishing for millennia along its inland waters and the outer ocean coast, christening the Northwest with a distinctive human touch.

The first people were nomadic hunters, fishers, and gatherers. The ones who succeeded them lived much of the year in large villages, alternating this settled life with seasonal expeditions for food and materials. The latest cultural variant to the Northwest implanted the European life style here. Each of these culturally distinct waves of human settlement has had its impact on the land and water habitats, and as one culture replaced another, the impact on environments profoundly increased.

My reason for bringing humans into the picture is ecological. The dominant theme of this book has been the natural processes that have shaped this land and seascape with their teeming plant and animal life. Though I have already touched on the influence of humans upon Puget Sound ecosystems, I want here to look at how the first Americans, as well as those arriving later, reacted to the bountiful habitats of the Puget Sound basin, and reciprocally, how those Indian predecessors of Europeans modified the land and waters by their very presence.

First, the shadowy, mysterious beginnings. Before the last two major surges of Pleistocene ice, the North American continent had never felt the hand of any hominid. The entire continent had evolved complex ecosystems of great variety and biological richness, yet with no human element. Then, as continental ice sheets began to retreat, humans arrived, as revealed by evidence in the subsurface layers of the land. The timing is no mere coincidence, for all over the world humans were profoundly conditioned by the events of the Pleistocene. Their routes from Siberia to America formed when a broad land bridge emerged between the two continents as sea level dropped during the last glacial periods. Archeological evidence suggests that a nomadic hunting culture in northeastern Asia migrated eastward at the time the land bridge became habitable for game and small parties of human predators. Though substantial areas on either side of the Bering land bridge were more or less free of ice, the potential pathways for the first trickle of human migration to the south were blocked by the pent-up frozen waters of the late Pleistocene. The hunting cultures could move southward only when the retreat of the ice was well underway, or after a Yukon corridor had opened up. Yet, at intervals between 12,500 to 3,500 years B.P. (Before Present), Stone Age Paleo-Americans were south of the retreating ice border, well within the present lower forty-eight United States. Though a fuller story of our current knowledge of these early migrations is outside my objective, it is tempting to ponder the amazing feats of survival and exploration presumed to have been achieved by this early hunting culture.

Some believe that the first human wave onto North America was one of skilled big-game hunters from Siberia. In a few generations of wandering in a new land, these hunters dramatically increased their numbers at the expense of game animals whose extinction they directly may have caused. Some paleoecologists think of this earliest epoch of Paleo-Americans as an ecological disaster because of the game they slaughtered and the eventual population crash the slaughter caused. The nearly simultaneous appearance of Stone Age hunters in North America and the disappearance of native American mammoths, mastodons, ground sloths, horses, and camels is argued as more than just coincidence. Paul Martin, respected paleoecologist, is convinced that early humans rode the crest of an unprecedented wave of predation, and in 350 years felt the backlash of their big-game "overkill" (Martin and Wright 1967). It should not be thought that the "overkill" idea is fully accepted by all archeologists and paleoecologists. To some authorities, the arrival of early Americans and large animal extinctions is more coincidence than correlation. This opposing view sees post-Pleistocene decimations of certain mammals as a product of more complexly related changes in the environment.

Early recovery from the presumed post-Pleistocene overkill may have been made possible by turning to a new way of life. Certainly by 7,000 years B.P., adaptive accommodation by early humans to a vanishing big-game supply had succeeded. The forager's way of life supplemented a predominantly hunting existence in most North American Indian groups. Food could be counted on from sources other than large animals; not only small game but the nutritious parts of plants were gathered. By foraging locally for fish, meat, berries, roots, and fiber, a less nomadic life replaced that

Women digging clams along Puget Sound, early 1900s. (Photo by Edward S. Curtis.)

of the restless big-game hunter. A truly sedentary existence demanded by a primitive agriculture had yet to come, at least in the West. Perhaps the first Indians of Washington were from the foraging cultures, which were thinly and widely spaced throughout the Great Plains. At this same time (7,000 to 9,000 years B.P.), there may not have been as yet a definable coastal Indian culture. In fact, the origin of the coastal Indians seems more deeply shrouded in mystery than the much earlier arrival of humans in North America.

The maritime Eden that was to spawn the audaciously rich cultures of the North Pacific Coast was virgin territory at a time when the Plains peoples may have shifted from hunting to foraging cultures. The earliest artifacts of inhabitants in the Puget Sound country date to around 8,000 years ago. These cultural remains were unearthed in two separate archeological sites, one on the lower Columbia River and the other just above the mouth of the Fraser River. From very sketchy beginnings, this coastal culture came into extravagant bloom not more than 1,000 years B.C. It was in full

manifestation 2,800 years later when the first Europeans came on the Indian scene. The Northwest Coast Indian cultures capitalized on the natural bounty of the area with a full repertory of maritime industry and life style. This very preoccupation with the harvest from the sea may give a partial clue to a separate and unique origin of the coastal cultures.

Between the hazy and speculative beginnings and the full, rich flowering of the unique, isolated coastal Indian cultures, the archeological record runs disappointingly thin. The influence of environment on culture provides reasons for the scarcity of artifacts. First, peoples of the past employed mostly perishable materials; wood, reeds, and fiber materials are subject to rapid decay in a coastal environment. The absence of pottery and a scarcity of stone tools further widens the information gap for early cultures. And there is blessed little compensation in the way of useful artifacts when one sifts through the many massive kitchen middens of shellfish left by coastal Indians in the past. Second, intervals of exposure or inundation of coastal habitats caused by fluctuations in sea level further complicate the archeologist's work. Late glacial and post-Pleistocene shorelines were either drowned or became ex-

Baskets and canoe fabricated from Nature's bounty. Puget Sound, still life. (Photo by Edward S. Curtis.)

posed for colonization as the level of the ocean changed with shifts in regional climate.

Despite these limitations, work in northern Puget Sound, as at Birch Bay and Deception Pass, has yielded traces of the earliest Puget Sound cultures. The oldest recorded food-gathering life style emphasized hunting on land, though in the immediate coastal surroundings. The next buried level or horizon reveals a distinct maritime flair to the culture, possibly introduced from the Fraser River delta to the north; hunting of sea mammals (seals and otters) became the economic focus. Following the maritime interval, the Indians hunted both on land and in coastal waters.

In late prehistory another period of maritime (or littoral, the shallow coastal waters and shoreline bordering the land) preoccupation is recognized, followed in most recent (protohistoric and historic) times with a reemphasis on land hunting and a decrease in harvest of food from the sea. This sequence of shifts in cultures can be inferred from the archeological remains of only one Puget Sound sequence of horizons.

By the time the first Europeans wandered into Puget Sound, the coastal Indian cultures had changed to a remarkable degree. Although the most richly diversified cultures were to the north of us on Vancouver Island, along the coast of British Columbia and into southeastern Alaska, the Puget Sound tribes were not far behind in attaining an economy of natural abundance in a society where arts and customs flourished.

Puget Sound Indian tribes are of the Salish or Salishan language

Ruth Kirk, sensitive observer of nature and writer on Northwest Native Americans, here in a favorite haunt along the beach. (Photo by Mary Randlett.)

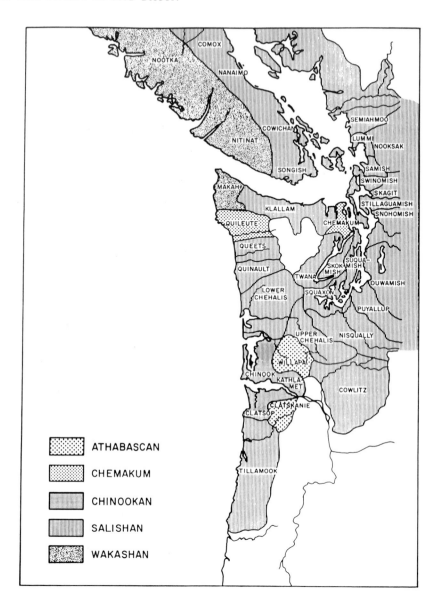

Tribal and linguistic distribution on the lower Pacific Northwest coast, during the period 1820–50. Legend refers to different linguistic groups.

family. Lest this suggest a social cohesiveness to the groups of Indians scattered around the Sound, it is well to remark that the idea of the tribe stems from the attempts of Europeans to confer a political unity on local Indian groups. In the Indians' view of social order, the cluster of permanent plank houses that defined a village was their "nation." Those beyond the village were outsiders, even though intermarriage was frequent. And certainly there were language barriers between some tribes or groups. Though Nisqually and Skagit peoples could understand each other, Puget Sound groups could not converse with Hood Canal or San Juan Island peoples. Only neighboring villages engaged in economic and social intercourse to any degree. Hence, given the insularity of villages, the recognition of larger groupings as tribes is an artifact, a latter-day device, of non-Indians. The tribal names do serve to help locate the various peoples on a Puget Sound map.

The majority of settlements were near salt water, especially at the mouths of the major rivers emptying into the Sound. Working downward along the eastern shore of Puget Sound from north to south, anthropologists locate the following coastal tribes or clusters of settlements. In what is now Whatcom, Skagit, and San Juan counties, there were the Semiahmoo, Nooksack, Lummi, Samish, Swallah, Swinomish, and Skagit tribes. Then, in central Puget Sound, the essentially maritime groups were the Snohomish, Suquamish, and Duwamish. At the southern extremity of the Sound, the rich estuarine waters supported the Puyallup and Nisqually tribes. On the west shore of Puget Sound there were two or three tribes: the Skokomish lived on the lower reaches of their namesake river as it rushes southeastward out of the Olympics into Hood Canal; another name for roughly the same ethnic group seems to be Twana.[1] Still on the west side, but up north where Puget Sound opens into the Strait of Juan de Fuca, early Europeans encountered a "tribe," the Chemakum, whose language had closer affinity to that of the Hoh and Quileute Indians on the Pacific Coast side of the Olympic Peninsula.

Bearing in mind that the tribal names connote a tenuous grouping of similar but local communities, we would expect only the most general attributes of these tribes to be consistent around Puget Sound. Though true for the coastal groups, this proviso is even more necessary when we enumerate the few upland tribes of Puget Sound, whose foraging extended from near sea level to the upper reaches of the Cascades and even to east of the crest of the range.

Simply enumerating the upland peoples, we begin at the northeast perimeter. The Skagit were spread out beyond the estuarine shores, from the lowland well into the interior of that river's great drainage. Southward, other interior tribes have been identified: the Stillaguamish, Skykomish, Snuqualmi (Snoqualmie), and Muckleshoot. All but the last can be located geographically in the drainages of the major rivers they occupied. The Muckleshoot, the origin of whose name is obscure, occupied the middle to upper reaches of the White River, coming swift and milk-water white off the slopes of Mount Rainier. Though the Nisqually and Puyallup tribes are placed in the maritime grouping above, their activities

---

1. Compare with current place name, Twanoh (State Park) on Hood Canal.

took them into the interior, especially in the summers, for hunting and trading. In fact, the vast territory used by the Nisqually extended from the head of the lower Sound to east of Mount Rainier. Again, one must guard against the white man's view of the boundaries of occupied "real estate." All that can be said about these Indian territories is that late nineteenth- and twentieth-century Indian informants have provided ethnographers with information about areas used in various ways by a particular tribe. "Ownership" of a tract of land by an Indian group probably applied only to land where there were permanent winter communities, mostly on the coast, or commonly frequented summer camps inland.

Ecological Insights

Nature's abundance at the border between lowland forest and inland sea served generously as the larder and storehouse for the saltwater Indians along Puget Sound. The timber and fiber resource of the near sealevel forest, along with food and fiber from nearby meadow, prairie, and marsh habitats, formed one set of pillars of the Indian economy. The rich yield of fresh- and saltwater animals provided the other major support to the coastal way of life. How were the products of land and sea woven into the cultures of the saltwater tribes?

From the land came the shelter, the tools, and the wherewithal to harvest the sea. One tree, the giant cedar (*Thuja plicata*), was exploited for all manner of uses. Besides furnishing the timbers for the large and impressive shedlike winter longhouses, cedar was fashioned into a whole array of domestic implements and fiber for making serviceable textiles. Cedar was also fashioned into dugout canoes, dipnets, and a variety of gear for gathering food from the rivers and saltwater reaches of the Sound.

How did the Indians harvest and transport the huge cedar logs, using only simple hand tools? The story of Indian logging is a revelation of human ingenuity. Though the Indian craftsman might often take advantage of the natural harvest of drift logs coming his way after winter storms, live trees were often harvested away from water. Those males of a community with special woodsmen's skills and endowed with singular spiritual powers, searched for the right tree in the right place, not too far from water and aligned for easy maneuverability after felling. With a small band of helpers, the woodsman set about with simple tools and consummate skill to bring the giant down and snake it down to water's edge for further manipulation. Sometimes a tree was tightly wound with native cordage well in advance of harvest to make cutting down the girdled tree easier. The giant was felled by a combination of simple

Western red cedar, described as "the tree of life" for North Coast Indians, was a mainstay product of nature for coastal tribes around Puget Sound. Above: One mode of harvesting planks was called a "begged-from" tree. (Photo by Edward S. Curtis.)

Left: Ada Markiston, Makah basket maker, continues the ancient craft of preparing cedar bark for domestic uses and weaving cedar strips into a basket.

stone hammers, wooden or horn wedges, and skillfully applied fire. Planks for houses were easily split along the clean, straight grain of the cedar with wooden wedges. The rough boards, two to three inches thick, two feet wide, and ten or more feet long, were then tied together and rafted by canoe back to the village for fashioning into planking for houses.

For making the famed and indispensable canoes, the felled logs were maneuvered down to the nearby beach where handcrafting began. On the beach, the craftsman could use the drifts of seaweed for dampening the hull as it was being fashioned. Hand adzes, wedges, and bone augers, coupled with carefully controlled heat—akin to the hot rock cookery back in the village—were united by the canoemaker's skill to fashion a variety of boats, some long, large, and seaworthy, others smaller for less demanding use in nearby rivers and estuaries. Perhaps only one or two men in a village had the spiritual gift and manual skills to convert a cedar log into one of the several versions of seaworthy craft.

Other natural bounty from the forest and sea gave service in the

Makah Indian fashioning a canoe out of cedar. (Photo by Norman Edson.)

making of shelter, fishing gear, and domestic utensils, not to mention the more artistic possessions that conferred prestige and rank in the community. Besides cedar, every other major tree species, from the mighty hemlock and Douglas fir to the infrequent understory evergreen, western yew, were fashioned into objects of use or ceremony. And among the hardwoods of the lowland forest, red alder and bigleaf maple found favor in a variety of ways, especially in fashioning utensils and ritualistic carvings.

The intimate dependence of coastal Indians on the prodigal richness of the forest seems hardly unexpected in retrospect. Survival of any animal—human, deer, or mouse—depends on the evolutionary adjustment of animal to its surroundings, adaptation by Darwinian selection. But humans can quickly adapt over the short run by cultural selection, a non-Darwinian acquisition of cultural implements and social traits. Indian cultures in their intimate fitness to the coastal locale can be looked upon as outgrowths of an hereditary and cultural adjustment of an unusually adaptable, omnivorous animal to its surroundings. In Indians there evolved all the ingredients for a highly viable niche in the coastal forest ecosystem.

Was this land-and-water economy self-sustaining, with a capacity for balanced perpetuity? That is the critical question we could ask of any animal, elk, grasshopper, seal, or person. In other words, was the ecological niche of the coastal Northwest Indian buffered by its own processes (cultural and biological) to keep from exhausting the resource base of its existence? To get a clear answer to that question would take more information on the dynamics of Indian populations—birth and death rates—as well as the rate of resource utilization and replenishment, than we probably ever will have. Yet we are impelled to ask such a question as a means of comparing the success and lasting quality of our own European ecological niche with that of the Indian. Despite the inadequate archeological record for sustained Indian economies, one thought supports the idea that the Indian way of life was in fair balance with the resource potential of the Puget Sound coastal ecosystem. After all, with 10,000 to 12,000 years of growing occupancy of the Puget trough, Indian cultures had *not* decimated the forest, had *not* fished out the nearby waters.

Early white explorers found a vast primeval forest and water wilderness that seemed to have the capacity for perpetual renewal and continuity. The Indians within this ecosystem formed a pattern of sparse populations fringing the Sound, kept that way by the technological limits of their culture. Accommodation, not overkill, was a way of life. Even the much debated periodic excesses of the status-seeking potlatch, the gambling sprees, the ritualistic use of cedar canoes as burial sites, the periodic abandonment of the plank-board villages, and sporadic intentional burning of forest made little dent on the natural abundance of the region. Natural events such as spontaneous fire, periodic vulcanism, and the shifting of postglacial climate caused greater changes in the natural abundance than did the activities of the Indians themselves. Indeed, it seems that the Indian way of life had the potential for self-perpetuation in a land of natural self-restoring abundance, requiring little husbandry of that resource by its human users. Had not a vastly more exploitative and technologically sophisticated culture superseded Indian culture, the Puget Sound ecosystem, in its stable pre-nineteenth-century state, might have continued long into the future. But more on this uncertain matter later on.

If the land seemed to have an inexhaustible supply of wood, fiber, and plant food, the adjacent waters kept pace with equal prodigality. Nowhere else in North America but in Northwest Coast Indian country had the bounty of the rivers and sea served up such a rich and seemingly unlimited supply of food. The blessings of cedar plus salmon assured the thinly populated coastal cultures of dependable superabundance. A few months of midyear fishing and gathering provided coastal Indians with the mainstays of their diet for the year. Besides salmon, other fish, such as halibut, sturgeon, flounder, smelt, cod, candlefish, and even skate, diversified the diets of the coastal peoples. The other prized animal of the sea was the seal; its oil was used as food and in other domestic activities. There is no record of Puget Sound Indians harvesting whales, though whales did appear sporadically in the Sound. Only certain of the outer coast tribes—the Makah, Quileute, Quinault on the Pacific Ocean, and the Klallam on the Strait of Juan de Fuca—developed the courageous and status-giving skills for hunting whales.

Besides fish and sea-going mammals, many other foods from the waters of coastal habitats entered into the year-round dietary variety of the saltwater Indians. Clams, barnacles, small rock oysters, and crabs were taken in quantity. The evidence of shellfish intake by Indians is in the great shell mounds or kitchen middens found still today here and there around Puget Sound. One such midden near Everett in the Snohomish River delta had the astounding dimensions of six feet in height and nearly a quarter of a mile long.

The saltwater tribes left hunting on land pretty much up to chance, or they acquired game by trading. When deer or elk ventured close to the winter villages, special effort was made to take them. In addition, the seagoing Indians might spot a deer swimming between the mainland and one of the nearby islands in the Sound, and these deer were probably easier to kill than the wilier seals. To most saltwater villagers, the forest deep beyond the village was an intimidating unknown. Only one or two individuals in the village might have acquired the right spirit helper, endowing them with the bravery and skill of the hunter. Besides, the saltwater tribes could come by the rewards of hunting for game through a flourishing traffic in barter with upland tribes. Rather permanent intertribal relationships existed, wherein specific tribes maintained friendly exchange. For example, the coastal Snohomish had social and economic intercourse with the upper Skagit, the Snuqualmi, and certain other upland groups. And trade usually included contact with east-of-the-mountain Indians like the Klikitat. Such access to the hunting efforts of upland tribes surely was reinforced by the strong tendency for intertribal marriages (exogamy) practiced throughout the Salish peoples of the Pacific Northwest. In return, the upland tribes received in trade the harvest of the inland sea and lower reaches of the rivers. The shell money of the coastal peoples often was the currency of this barter.

Big game like elk, deer, and bear furnished not only meat but skins for clothing. Mountain goats provided horn for making tools and wool for weaving. A variety of hunting techniques were used to harvest game. Bows and arrows, as well as traps, were employed by Puget Indians with practiced skill. A more fatiguing

Edibles from the seemingly inexhaustible inland sea ranged from salmon and other fish to a variety of shellfish.

Left: Old man smoking salmon on a Puget Sound beach. (Photo by Norman Edson.)

Below left: Native Americans in Western dress at a fish trap, early 1900s.

Right: Harvesting shellfish (probably mussels) and spearing octopus. (Photos by Edward S. Curtis.)

method was to chase an animal until it was exhausted, then kill it. Early white settlers in the Nisqually prairie country claimed that Indians used fire to drive game for ease of kill. It was this practice that supposedly perpetuated the grassy prairie openings so prevalent just south of the Sound.

If fish and big game were taken, why not birds? The versatility and ingenuity in food-gathering of the saltwater tribes included spearing or netting ducks. Often permanent structures were maintained near winter villages where nets could be strung for taking waterfowl.

A tantalizing dichotomy seemed to exist among the various tribes in the Puget basin—tantalizing because the differences between saltwater and upriver Indians have not been extensively documented by ethnographers. From scattered writings, mostly accounts from twentieth-century Indian informants, it appears that tribes like the upper Skagit, Skykomish, and Snuqualmi were just as adept at hunting game as the saltwater peoples were at harvesting the inland sea. The upriver tribes might have up to thirty dogs kept mainly for hunting. These dogs were of different but unknown breed from the equally mysterious small Pomeranian-like breed that the lowland peoples kept for their wool. Using dogs, bows and arrows, traps, or the endurance chase, the upland hunters drew on the plentiful supply of big game animals, especially deer and elk. After stockpiling the harvest for their own needs, the surplus went downriver to serve as exchange for coastal products.

Birds were harvested by stretching nets on these "four remarkable, supported poles, in Port Townshend, Gulph of Georgia."

Indian villages were close to water, much as were later settlements of Western man. Here, a view of "the village of the Friendly Indians at the entrance of Bute's Canal, Vancouver Island," about 1792.

Skill in hunting might then be the major difference between the upland and saltwater tribes of Puget Sound.

Many historians of Indian lore suggest that the coastal people were wary of the forests at their backs. Only those especially endowed with a spirit helper sought game in the nearby woods. In contrast, we are led to believe that the upriver peoples used the forested habitat with ease. Perhaps this is only conjecture. After all, inland living on the Skagit or Snohomish rivers, where the valleys of these great drainages were broad and flat and the streams easily navigable by canoe, could have provided riverside village sites not much different from those downstream on the Sound. For example, the permanent winter village for the Snuqualmi tribe was at Tolt, only a few airline miles from the Sound, where the Snoqualmie River passes through a broad river valley.

While the sea was the prime larder, lowlands bordering the Sound did furnish Indian peoples a variety of plant foods. In forests, salal, huckleberries, salmon berries, and bracken fern were harvested. And in more open habitats of prairie, marsh, and meadow, a variety of plant foods were gathered: camas bulbs, acorns, and a variety of herbs were of major importance to Puget Sound Indians.

Indians and Ecological Balance: Real or Apparent?

It seems apparent that the quantum changes wrought by European newcomers in scarcely more than one hundred years of assault on the land greatly surpassed those made by the Indian populations. Since the first European ships touched shore in the eighteenth century, vast tracts of lowland Puget country have been irrevocably altered from an earlier more pliant and restorable state. In contrast, the inroads of Indian cultures on the lowland ecosystems appear to have been of such a slight and superficial nature as to have allowed for easy and quick recovery of land and water habitats. This difference between Indian and white ways of life inevitably leads to judgments regarding each culture's effects on its environment. Inescapable is the view that Indians dealt lightly with their surroundings and that whites wielded a heavy and destructive hand. This self-evident truth usually leads to a sentimental contrast of the two cultures: the wishful thought claims that Indians had an intuitive ecological conscience, compelling them to be gentle to their surroundings, whereas Europeans, steeped in the Judeo-Christian tradition, were compelled to exact the utmost from the surrounding natural abundance. We want to believe in these Indians as benign, enlightened husbanders of natural resources, while viewing the Europeans as rapacious exploiters, indifferent to or challenged by nature.

That the two cultures made vastly different inroads on their surroundings is a simple truth. But are we justified in reading into the difference a moral judgment that one culture was more conserving and ecologically gentle than the other? All living things modify their surroundings, and humans everywhere on the planet bear witness to this ecological truism, especially in post-Pleistocene times. In Puget Sound country, it is evident that human activity since the beginnings of cultural intrusion on the coastal ecosystem has left its mark. Europeans have done most things that Indians did, but on a vastly more massive scale. Both have lived in villages and both have sought shelter, food, clothing, and other trappings necessary to social existence—mostly taken from surrounding nature. How then do we account for the great difference in the quantity of natural resources taken by the two cultures? Surely, the sheer difference in numbers peopling the two cultures accounts for differences in impact on natural resources; there are over *one hundred times* as many humans here now as were here around 1770. Yet, I believe a case can be made for psychic as well as technologic differences as the keys for distinguishing the two ways of life.

Why did the coastal Indians turn their backs on the forest and look to the waters for primary sustenance? It would be easy to claim that an aversion to the forbidding vastness of the unknown forest provided a spiritual barrier against substantial exploitation of the forest. Though this may be a part of the truth, it must be set in the context of the abundant source of food from the sea. The tools for the aquatic harvest were simple though elegant; a modest technology met the demand for sustaining life, and a not too difficult life at that. So I would suppose that the psychic and technological biases developed hand in hand, one reinforcing the other. A reasonably secure existence could be had with minimal intrusion on the land—some hunting, some timber harvest, some gathering of terrestrial plant foods. The bulk of Indian economy, however, centered around the seemingly inexhaustible waters. Two elements of human technology were conspicuously absent in the Puget Sound Indian economy. There was no true agriculture, and scarcely any tools were fabricated from metal (prior to latter-day contact with non-Indians). Thus, neither the motive nor the means (other than fire) to clear the lowland forest existed in the life of the Indian.

Domestic scene in a longhouse; the dog, breed unknown, was a source of wool.

Just think of the great contrast in cultures that existed in Europe during the few centuries before, and right up to, the confrontation

between Northwest Indians and whites. With a sophisticated agriculture, metallurgy, and the compulsion for progress fed by the Christian faith, Europeans had altered vast areas of forest, savannah, and grassland from the Mediterranean to the spruce forests of northern Europe. And from these ingredients came communication via the written and printed word, transportation, towns and cities with their ingenious artifacts of metal, wood, stone, and fiber. The world's resources were furbishing a complex civilization at a time when the Northwest coastal Indians maintained a seemingly steady-state economy. The really hard question surfaces again: Can any of this vast technological disparity be traced to a fundamental difference in the way the two cultures viewed their worlds? Much has been written in recent times of the presumed crucial role that the Christian ethic has played in moulding the minds and actions of European peoples. Historian Lynn White, Jr., develops a persuasive argument that links the Judeo-Christian belief in the primal position of man in nature to our present ecological crisis (1967). Thus, humans become the supreme overlord of the forests and the sea with the God-given power to exploit nature for "man's proper ends." Moreover, Lynn White argues that the unique Judeo-Christian faith that perpetual progress is inevitable and desirable eases the way to draw upon nature's finite stores without thought to exhaustibility. If this be the mental framework of Christian cultures—in, but apart from, nature—then what do we find in the Northwest Indian psyche for contrast?

A culture that has no written legacy of its history retains an aura of mystery and conjecture for its students. The ethnographer must rely on the stories and accounts rendered by those survivors of a culture which had already been tainted by outside influence. The archeologist has to draw inferences from the fragments of a vanished, buried culture to piece together even mundane information on how the people fed, clothed, and housed themselves. One can hardly expect such kinds of raw data on a vanished culture to reveal the subtleties of psychic reaction to nature or the elements of a land ethic. The substantial data from informants and from buried artifacts distilled by nineteenth- and twentieth-century anthropologists do reveal societies with a complex hierarchy and a governing religious code. Yet in these writings there is little mention of the problem we pose here: How did the coastal tribes psychically and ethically coexist with their habitat at the meeting of land and sea?

Although I may not have probed deeply enough into the scattered anthropological writings on coastal Indians, what I have found, besides a wealth of information on customs, social systems, daily life, and religious ceremonies, is a singular *lack* of information on what might be called an Indian environmental ethic. This is not to say that other Indian peoples had not developed some sense of an environmental conscience. Interior Indians like the Athapaskan and Cree may well have evolved an "ethic of environmental morality." Since no such evidence exists for Puget Sound Indians, this lack might be explained in two ways. First, perhaps something so subtle as an ecological conscience could not be accurately recorded, no matter what means for doing so may have existed. Or, more perversely, we may be freer to develop our own hypothesis (largely untestable) on the matter of an Indian "eco-ethic."

Taking the second alternative, I am emboldened to offer the following ideas. My first premise is that it was the *absence* of several biological and cultural ingredients that served to promote a reasonably balanced, steady-state interplay between coastal Indians and nature. The coastal Indians did not indulge in agriculture in the sense of seed-planting, but ethnobotanist Nancy Turner does record a kind of plant husbandry. These Indians cared for beds of camas, silverweed, and other foods. They also practiced periodic burning, selection of larger bulbs/roots and replanting of smaller ones, clearing of larger rocks, and year after year "cultivating" of

Temporary shelter of mats woven from cattail leaves, Skokomish River, ca. 1912. (Photo by Edward S. Curtis.)

the same areas. This care allowed in many locations sustained yields that went on for generations. Yet there was no extensive clearing of the land nor was there any technology for raising and harvesting crops. The difference between their way of life and ours suggests my conclusion. The sentimental view that coastal Indians were kind to the land, I would reject. In its place I would advance the view that they had no need to disturb in any substantial way their surroundings on land. In this view, their failure to overexploit the forest ecosystem was effortless and without intent. With no need to till the land, there was no motivation to evolve any ethic of land conservation—only a "detente" existed, between the Indians and the impenetrable vastness of forest at their backs.

But what of their exploitation of the aquatic environment? Was this seemingly unlimited resource ever strained by the Indian harvesters? If the great piles and windrows of mussel and clam shells in the "kitchen-middens" scattered rather plentifully about Puget Sound are any clue, the answer may be yes. Robert C. Dunnell, an archeologist at the University of Washington, has evidence that at certain sites a shellfish resource could be so overharvested that the fishery had to be relocated. Remember, though, that data on the economics of Indian tribes in prehistoric times are very meager. And as soon as Europeans intruded on the coastal scene, the Indian way of life was abruptly altered. In fact, early Europeans' views of Indian cultures may already have been drastically distorted by the catastrophic diseases that overwhelmed the Indians soon after the first Spanish came to the Pacific Northwest in the late eighteenth century. Dunnell and Fuller reveal the dramatic impact of this event:

> The earliest descriptions of the aboriginal occupants of the region date from the late 18th-century explorations of Captain Vancouver. Unfortunately, these descriptions were apparently preceded by massive disruption and depopulation associated with the spread of exotic epidemic disease. Vancouver's journals themselves provide convincing evidence of this catastrophe in noting that the ground in some areas was littered with human skeletons and that many of the living inhabitants bore the scars of smallpox [Menzies' journal of Vancouver's voyage]. Consequently there is little reason to believe that the recorded ethnographic observations can be extended back in the past more than a few years before Vancouver's visit. Not only political and territorial limits, but also social organization, settlement pattern and subsistence systems can be expected to have been greatly altered by this kind of catastrophic event. (1975:9–10)

Thus, without a good record of harvest practices in prehistoric times, untainted by European intrusions, we are left with an unsolved problem. We may never know whether coastal Indians

Plants of the lowlands were harvested for food and fiber. Two Native American women return to their canoe from foraging ashore. (Photo by Edward S. Curtis.)

"managed" their resource wisely or overexploited it, only to be put out of business locally. Probably both occurred.

Perhaps the only safe course is to apply the rather unsentimental ecological rule of supply-and-demand as conditioned by the carrying capacity of the habitat. In this view, humans, as all other animals, will expand their populations until they overshoot the sustaining power of the environment and its resources. The population then is often drastically reduced and the system—users and resources—begin a slow recovery. Only if the culture fortuitously adapts to meet the inevitable crash phase of the population-resource cycle can an approximation to steady-state conditions emerge.

There is little sign that any culture evolved a truly successful land ethic as the outcome of natural selection for cultural survival. Some primitive cultures, like the Kalahari Bushmen and the Australian aborigines, devised effective control over their populations. But others seem to have suffered at the hands of the Malthusian demon of overpopulation. The environmental impact of prehistoric human enterprise was undoubtedly relatively local and minor in magnitude as compared to our global influence in modern times. The population size and the technological know-how of primitive peoples were of such low level that large-scale effects did not occur. In this view, then, our species, much like other animals, is at the mercy of its heterotrophic nature: we must "parasitize" the environment to survive. Populations grow, overshoot the resource, and crash (at least in some situations) and have probably done so throughout the entire human lineage.

Those who feed on other living things cannot afford a wholly nonexploitative conservation ethic. But, what about Saint Francis of Assisi, Thoreau, Aldo Leopold, the ancient Chinese philosophers, and all those exceptional individual humans down through the ages that have seen the necessity and espoused the hope that humans must live with nature and not against it? Surely might not we, the uniquely thinking animal, devise a strategy for survival, developed from past experience, present rational considerations of ecological principles, and a predictive look at the future? The answer to this question has to be a *very* guarded yes. Only the *enforcement* of an elaborate ecological ethic on a global scale could achieve some sort of regulated steady state for us, as we husband the life-support system on which we and all other organisms depend. The instituting of worldwide sanctions on population growth, energy and resource utilization, etc., would have to overcome the massive impediments of nationalism, prejudice, and all the other cultural deterrents that have trapped us into grossly nonecological behavior. Past human responses to the environment, usually exploitative, only serve as negative lessons for the future.

This 1990 view of freeway gridlock just east of Lake Union, Seattle, was the site of old-growth hemlock-cedar forest less than two hundred years ago. (Photo by Greg Gilbert.)

11 The European Impact on Puget Country

"Give me enough Swedes and enough whiskey and I'll build a railroad through Hell."—James J. Hill

The search for any intentional environmental ethic in the Indian way of life around Puget Sound may have seemed disappointingly inconclusive. In contrast, for the next act of the human drama in the region, there is a wealth of evidence to support a firm statement regarding Europeans. From the very first, their attitude toward Puget Sound was exploitative.

The history of early exploration and settlement of the Pacific Northwest and the Puget basin has been told and retold in textbooks, novels, and firsthand diary accounts. Europeans do leave a record of their thoughts and actions. For good summaries of the period from the late eighteenth to the early nineteenth centuries, the reader will want to consult histories of Washington State: *Washington, the Evergreen State,* by Avery (1961); *Washington State,* by LeWarne (1986); or the latest history by Ficken and LeWarne, *Washington: A Centennial History* (1988). But, in assessing the ecological impact of Europeans on Puget country, I propose something other than a conventional history. Is it possible to find, in the great wealth of writings by early explorers, pioneers, missionaries, and settlers, any signs of a concern for environmental preservation?

There is little doubt that the primary motive for Europeans' journeys to the Northwest Coast country was to find wealth. They sought wealth from furs, precious metals, and other raw materials to support a sophisticated culture already steeped in a tradition of subduing wilderness and harvesting its substance. Given such non-ecological preoccupations, is there any hope of unearthing vestiges of an ecological conscience among those individuals swept into the excitement of exploration and the prospect of material reward? I embark on a dual purpose: to recount the major steps in the ego-centric business of taking material abundance from the land and sea, all the while searching for a glimmer of individual wonder, and possibly feeling remorse at what fellow Europeans were doing to the landscape. (See Appendix 4, "Chronology of Events.")

The Writers' Record

Spaniards were the first white people to become acquainted with the Northwest Coast country. Once settled in the New World, they were eager to find way-stations along the lucrative but arduous Pacific trade routes between Mexico, the Philippines, and the Orient. Intermittently from the mid-sixteenth to the late-eighteenth century, they tried to probe the coast for suitable havens to break the perilous voyage eastward back across the Pacific. None of these first attempts was successful. Even if the legendary Greek-turned-Spaniard, Juan de Fuca, actually did discover the strait that bears his name, the event made no impress on the landscape. Only when the exploring and fur-seeking activities of the Russians gained momentum in the mid-1700s, did the Spanish quicken their concern for planting their flag on the threatened domain. Though the Russians had not yet moved south of what is now the Alaskan coast, the Spanish acted quickly, sending Juan Pérez in 1774 to the north. He got as far as the Queen Charlotte Islands, just north of Vancouver Island. It was at Nootka on Vancouver Island, however, that he and subsequent Spaniards eventually founded a settlement.

José Mariano Moziño. The Spanish interlude in the Northwest was shortlived and gained barely a toehold on the land. One episode is of significance to our search for attitudes evoked in Europeans by the wild landscape they encountered. Owing to disputed claims on the Nootka settlement between the Spanish and British, a veteran navigator and explorer, Juan Francisco de Bodega y Quadra, was sent north in 1792 to seek agreement with Captain Vancouver on British territorial claims in accordance with the Nootka Convention. Although he failed in this mission, Bodega y Quadra engaged in friendly exchanges with Vancouver who had begun the British survey of Puget Sound waters. On the Bodega y Quadra expedition was a remarkable young naturalist, José Mariano Moziño. Moziño's detailed chronicle of the Nootka area gives us the first real insight on the way the Northwest environment impressed Europeans.

Moziño, born and educated in Mexico, had become a favorite botanical protégé of Martín Sessé, director of the Royal Scientific Expedition to New Spain. Through Sessé, Moziño was named to be the naturalist on the Bodega y Quadra expedition to Nootka. With his classmate, José Maldonado, and the accomplished artist Atanasio Echeverría, Moziño spent several months making collections of plants and animals, and compiling observations on the land, including the rich Indian culture at Nootka Sound. Moziño's natural history of the area was published a century later as *Noticias de Nutka: An Account of Nootka Sound in 1792.* Its English translation of 1970 by Iris Higbie Wilson makes fascinating reading.

As was the tradition among early naturalists, Moziño's coverage of the natural phenomena observed at Nootka is extremely broad, ranging from identification of the flora and fauna to detailed descriptions of the Indians and even of the political and economic future of Spain's ill-starred claim at Nootka. Despite his naturalist's background and curiosity about the novel surroundings, Moziño looked at the Northwest scene in the rather typical "What's in it for us?" point of view. In so doing he is rather pessimistic about the prospects for developing a successful agricultural base at Nootka Sound. He predicts that:

Possibly a new fertilization of these lands, debilitating its vegetative force a little in some parts and augmenting it in others, would provide nearly a mile of planted fields from the lagoon to the Maquinna River on a strip not less than thirty feet across at its narrowest. It is obvious that a successful harvest of a crop of grain on such a plot would sustain a small garrison, which in turn could maintain this establishment. But how many trees would have to be rooted out? How many rocks would have to be removed? And how much tenacity would be necessary to clear out the roots and burn out the seeds of the many wild plants that occupy this terrain? Among them one finds many grasses, several brushwoods, andromedas, and berry bushes whose present luxuriance, it seems to me, does not forecast failure for the more useful plants that might be cultivated later. (1970:7)

He goes on to throw cold water on the naive vision of his compatriots who see riches in furs.

Up to now this establishment has not produced any advantage in favor of the crown, but, on the contrary, the enormous expenses it has had to pay out are notorious. Even private individuals have achieved nothing more than a miserable trade in furs, and the hopes of making it absolutely lucrative, besides being extremely remote, could be realized just as well, as the Bostonmen have done and are still doing, if the port were independent. Nootka is a place where one finds very few furs, and these come from the Nuchimanes, Calyoquot, and Tutusi [Indians]. (P. 91)

From this written account at least, we derive little sense of the wonder and grandeur of the landscape. Moziño, though excelling in his appointed position as naturalist, ventures not at all into the realm of appreciation of nature.

Archibald Menzies. The year 1792 was a busy one for exploration of coastal waters in the Northwest. While Moziño was preoccupied with closely observing Indian life as well as flora and fauna at Nootka, Captain Vancouver was making his historic survey of Puget Sound and adjacent waters. With him, serving as medical officer and naturalist was Archibald Menzies—he of the madrone (*Arbutus menziesii*), of the fool's huckleberry, (*Menziesia ferruginea*), and a host of other discoveries. A protégé of the renowned patron of natural history, Sir Joseph Banks, Menzies had already made one voyage to the Pacific before he joined the Vancouver expedition.

Might we expect from another naturalist some sense of wonderment for the strange and new landscape he saw? The detailed Menzies journal, published in 1923, should reveal any such sentiment. A search of its pages is of slim reward. The journal is mainly a prosaic account of daily observations of Indians, plants, and animals, as though each were an item of acquisition for a museum. Only here and there are passages suggesting that Menzies was

Of the early naturalists to witness and record the rich life of the lowland land-and-water scene, two of the most notable were Archibald Menzies (top) and David Douglas. Archibald Menzies (1754–1842) was surgeon-naturalist on the Vancouver Expedition. His narrative of the natural history of Puget Sound records the earliest collection of plants, animals, and Indian artifacts for the region. Scotsman David Douglas (1799–1834) made extensive plant collections for the Royal Horticultural Society in his two visits to the Pacific Northwest (1825–27 and 1830–32).

touched by the beauty and grandeur of the vast Northwest scene. Most such fragments of aesthetic appreciation are flavored with the European conception of human-centered landscapes. Menzies sees the grand scenes as though he were in the midst of a great park, floridly designed by man for human pleasure. What is more, given the presentiment that the new land would one day become settled, and to the eminent advantage of the settlers, he voices no apprehension or warning against the inevitable assault on the vast tracts of virgin land.

Perhaps we should judge Menzies in light of the fixed and predetermined mission of the Vancouver expedition: discover and lay claim to the land for the Crown. Menzies' own particular tasks were explicitly set out by a set of formal instructions from Sir Joseph Banks. Surely his official journal would have to reflect a dutiful compliance with the strict stipulations. The written mandate from the British Admiralty reveals the motives so prevalent in European explorations of the New World. The details of the mission are set out in John Forsyth's biographical note on Menzies, published with the journal in 1923.

> He was to investigate the whole of the natural history of the countries visited, paying attention to the nature of the soil, and in view of the prospect of sending out settlers from England, whether grains, fruits, etc., cultivated in Europe are likely to thrive. All trees, shrubs, plants, grasses, ferns, and mosses were to be enumerated by their scientific names as well as those used in the language of the natives. He was to dry specimens of all that were worthy of being brought home and all that could be procured, either living plants or seeds, so that their names and qualities could be ascertained at His Majesty's gardens at Kew. Any curious or valuable plants that could not be propagated from seeds were to be dug up and planted in the glass frame provided for the purpose. He was also to examine beds of brooks, sides of cliffs, and other places in a search for ores or metals and mineral substances. He was also to note what sort of beasts, birds, and fishes were likely to prove useful either for food or in commerce. Particular attention was to be paid to the natural history of the sea-otter and (he was to) obtain information concerning the wild sheep, and (to) note particularly all places where whales or seals are found in abundance. Inquiry was to be made into the manners, customs, language, and religion of the natives and information obtained concerning their manufactures, particularly the art of dyeing. He was to keep a regular journal of all occurrences, which journal, together with a complete collection of specimens of the animals, vegetables, and minerals obtained, as well as articles of the cloths, arms, implements, and manufactures of the Indians, were to be delivered to His Majesty's Secretary of State or to such person as he shall appoint to receive them. (1923:ix)

Such a binding commission would scarcely have allowed for free expression of wonder and thrill at the grand landscapes that Menzies came upon in the Northwest. Yet the very magnetism of the newness and beauty of the country did occasion flowery words of rapture here and there in his journal. Of a chance visit to an unnamed San Juan Island, he writes:

> On ascending the bank to the summit of the island, a rich lawn beautified with nature's luxuriant bounties burst at once on our view and impressed us with no less pleasure than novelty—it was abundantly cropped with a variety of grass, clover and wild flowers, here and there adorned by aged pines with widespreading horizontal boughs and well sheltered by a slip [sic] of them densely copsed with underwood stretching along the summit of the steep sandy cliff, the whole seeming as if it had been laid out from the premeditated plan of a judicious designer. (P. 18)

Later on he gives a more practical judgment of the assets of Puget Sound for eventual settlement.

> We cannot quit Admiralty Inlet without observing that its beautiful Canals & wandering navigable branches traverse through a low flat country . . . thus diffusing utility & ornament to a rich Country by affording a commodious and ready comunication through every part of it, to the termination of the most distant branches. Its short distance from the Ocean . . . & easy access by the streights [sic] of Juan de Fuca is likewise much in its favour, should its fertile banks be hereafter settled by any civilized nation. Its shores are for the most part sandy intermixed with pebbles & a variety of small silicious stones abounding with Iron Ore in various forms, for we hardly met with a Rock or Stone that was not evidently less or more impregnated with this useful Metal which the benevolent hand of Nature has so liberally dispersed throughout almost every part of the world but perhaps no where so apparently abundant as along the shores of this great Inlet. . . . Between us & the above Ridge [the Cascade Range] & to the Southward of us between the two Mountains already Mentioned [Mount Baker and Mount Rainier] a fine level Country intervened chiefly covard [sic] with pine forests abounding here & there with clear spots of considerable extent [gravelly prairie?] & intersected with the various winding branches of Admiralty Inlet as already mentioned. These clear spots or lawns are clothed with a rich carpet of Verdure & adorned with clumps of Trees & a surrounding verge of scattered Pines which with their advantageous situation on the Banks of these inland Arms of the Sea give them a beauty of prospect equal to the most admired Parks in England. (P. 47)

And in the next paragraph, Menzies waxes eloquent on the great charm of the country.

> A Traveller wandering over these unfrequented Plains is regaled with a salubrious & vivifying air impregnated with the balsamic fragrance of the surrounding Pines, while his mind is eagerly occupied every moment on the new objects & his senses rivetted on the enchanting variety of the surrounding scenery where the softer beauties of Land-

This early watercolor (1859) by J. P. Alden depicts a small settlement at water's edge on San Juan Island, with Lopez Island and Mount Baker in distance.

scape are harmoniously blended in majestic grandeur with the wild & romantic to form an interesting & picturesque prospect on every side. (P. 48)

Though such glimpses of Menzies' fascination and pleasure in encountering an utterly new land are occasional in the mundane prose of the journal, there is no sign of a concern for the fate of the land. He seems to see it waiting there to be used by the waves of settlers yet to come.

David Douglas. While Moziño, Vancouver, and Menzies made brief sorties into the wilderness from the comparative security of settlement or ship, another naturalist, David Douglas, became totally immersed in the country. Douglas (of the fir) arrived at Fort Vancouver in 1825, eager to fulfill his charge as explorer-botanist. He had been commissioned by the Horticultural Society of London to collect specimens and harvest seeds of all plants of garden potential. Though Douglas's botanical pursuits were of the highest quality, from his lengthy journal and letters to colleagues and friends in England, we might believe him indifferent to the sights around him. Douglas traveled mostly by foot or by canoe with scarcely any companionship of fellow Europeans, though his shipboard friend, Dr. John Scouler, did make a few forays with him out of Fort Vancouver. Otherwise he went either with his dog or with an Indian guide. Obsessed with his botany, he wrote of little else, except when misfortune descended on him whereupon he spoke eloquently about his distressed state. When traveling under great physical adversity, it is understandable that even the most sublime scenes would not stimulate appreciative prose. Between illnesses, injuries, difficulties with the terrain and with Indian guides, it was all Douglas could do to keep account of his itinerary, his botanical observations, and his worldly possessions.

Just after he landed at Fort Vancouver in the flowery month of April, when he had not yet been bruised and harassed by the rugged country, he could spare a sentence of eulogy for the beauty of his surroundings: "The scenery round this place is sublimely grand—lofty, well-wooded hills, mountains covered with perpetual snow, extensive natural meadows, and plains of deep, fertile, alluvial deposit, covered with a rich sward of grass, and a profusion of flowering plants." Later, when occupied by his passionate quest for the unusual, Douglas does break away from his Scottish taciturnity. With an Indian guide he had set off into the forests of the upper Umpqua River in Oregon in search of the elusive sugar pine (*Pinus lambertiana*). Having been shown a sketch of cone and tree, his guide was able to lead him to a stand of the much-coveted sugar pine. Of this encounter Douglas writes:

At midday I reached my long-wished-for pines, and lost no time in examining them and endeavouring to collect specimens and seeds. New and strange things seldom fail to make strong impressions, and are therefore frequently overrated; so that lest I should never again see my friends in England to inform them verbally of this most beautiful and immensely grand tree, I shall here state the dimensions of the largest that I could find among several that had blown down by the wind. (1904:89)

After noting the record measurements of the mammoth trees, Douglas proceeded to shoot down specimens of the large and symmetrical cones of the tree. The sound of his gun provoked another of the hair-raising episodes so commonplace in his Northwest travels. He immediately became surrounded by hostile Indians who were intent on ending his life. Only by ingenious bluff with guns, tobacco, and diversion did he escape. His own account of this adventure (pages 89 and 90 of his published journal, 1904) is well worth reading.

Douglas's only excursion into Puget Sound country was a painfully exhausting trip in constant rain, and attendant discomfort, to Grays Harbor by way of the Cowlitz and Chehalis rivers. He could accomplish little botanically while he was preoccupied with survival and with nursing an infected knee. Never eloquent about his surroundings, Douglas on this journey could only complain. Thus another potential Thoreau leaves us unrequited!

James Swan. The supreme chronicle of western Washington in the 1850s was written by James G. Swan, adventurer, scholar, seaman, and, above all, promoter and entrepreneur. Although he stayed close to his home base at Shoalwater Bay (now Willapa Harbor), he was surrounded by a wilderness much like that of Puget Sound. In his fascinating book, *The Northwest Coast, or, Three Years' Residence in Washington Territory,* Swan dwells mostly on his contacts with the local Indians and with the nearby white settlements, and on the comings and goings of the embryonic maritime commerce. "The enormous growth of the timber trees" impressed him repeatedly; the quaint sketch of a man with outstretched arms at the base of one mammoth dramatizes his wonderment. Yet in the next utterance he reverts to the pioneer attitude about the benefit that the great land and water resources can bring to enterprising settlers.

We soon, with the aid of some of the settlers, made a havoc among the trees, and in a few days most of them were cut down. . . .
Joe and the captain now went to work to cut the trees into logs, which we then blew open with powder, and then with beetle and wedges reduced to blocks small enough to handle, and then piled them round the stumps and set fire to them. We usually kept these

James Swan illustrated his narrative on the Northwest Coast ([1857] 1972) with this charming drawing of members of the earlier Wilkes Expedition, measuring a huge evergreen.

fires going all night, and the light these tremendous bonfires made could be seen for miles. The Indians enjoyed the fun of piling on logs and making a blaze, and every evening were sure to gather round and have a frolic. (1972:53–54)

So much for Swan's ambivalent appreciation for the great trees of the forest!

Later on, in extolling the great untapped wealth of Washington Territory, he finishes with a tribute to "the beauty and fertility" of the country. Words to match the natural grandeur of his surroundings seem to fail him; instead he lets Captain Vancouver speak for him:

> "To describe the beauties of this region will on some future occasion be a very grateful task to the pen of the skillful panegyrist. The serenity of the climate, the innumerable pleasing landscapes, and the abundant fertility that unassisted nature puts forth, require only to be enriched by the industry of man with villages, mansions, cottages, and other buildings, to render it the most lovely country that can be imagined, while the labor of the inhabitants must be rewarded in the bounties which Nature seems ready to bestow on cultivation." (P. 67)

Below: Clearcuts in the Cascades may harvest a renewable resource, but at a cost. This lowland clearcut in Lewis County has only a local visual impact. (Photo by Michael Wooton.)

Elsewhere in his charming account of pioneer life in western Washington, Swan turns again to describing the natural beauty and richness of the lowland country. As ever, the narrative is slanted toward the possibilities of exploiting the land. Swan was an unabashed emissary of the progress-and-development syndrome that prevailed in the early West. And like developers of much later times, he exaggerates—even misleads— in his account of the fertility of the soil in the forested as well as treeless prairie lands nearby. The truth of the matter is that despite the luxuriance of the native vegetation, most western Washington soils are something less than fertile by agricultural standards (see Appendix 5). Exaggerated or not, Swan's words would surely beckon emigrants from the East.

> The soil of all the prairie lands, with the exception of those directly around Puget Sound, is exceedingly fertile. Those of the Sound are of a sandy, gravelly nature, not readily cultivated, but producing enormous fir and cedar trees. The soil on the mountains, wherever I have seen any attempt at a clearing, is generally very rich; but the dense growth of forest deters the emigrant from attempting clearings on a large extent, as the fine, fertile plains and prairie offer far greater inducements. Fruit of various kinds, particularly apples, can be cultivated very readily, and in the greatest perfection. Indian-corn does not thrive well, as the seasons are not hot enough; but wheat, barley, oats, and potatoes yield the most abundant crops, of the finest quality. The potatoes, in particular, are the best I have ever met with in any part of the world. (P. 397)

Despite this glowing picture of an agricultural Garden of Eden, he perceives the true value of the land, as ever, in terms of human commerce:

> "the staple of the land must continue to be the one which Nature herself has planted, in the inexhaustible forests of fir, of spruce, and of cedar. Either in furnishing manufactured timber, or spars of the first description for vessels, Washington Territory is unsurpassed by any portion of the Pacific coast" [Gov. I. I. Stevens]. Washington Territory abounds in fine timber, and the enormous growth of its spruce and fir excites the admiration of every one who sees them. The trees in the region about Puget Sound are especially large, comprising the spruce, hemlock, yew, cedar, fir, oak, ash, maple, and alder. (P. 398)

And what to make of Nature's forested extravaganza? The answer had already been given to Swan: the saw mill. He follows directly his enumeration of the trees with this statment of fact: "There are now about thirty-seven saw-mills in the Territory, the largest of which is that of Pope, Talbot & Co., . . . at Teekalet (Port Gamble), on Hood's Canal."

Paul Kane. If neither naturalist nor settler-scholar were moved to utter some word of concern for staying the execution of the forests, then who would? I turn to the memoirs of another kind of intellectual, the lone traveling artist. Surely he who is schooled to read nature and render it on canvas or in sketch book would have grasped the urgency and portent of a wilderness soon to be forever changed. It is in the writings of Paul Kane, itinerant Canadian artist, that I looked for manifestations of even an embryonic ecological conscience. Kane came west in the 1850s, attaching himself to one of the Hudson's Bay Company's overland parties. After arriving on the Pacific Coast of Canada he ventured south as far as Oregon, passing through Puget Sound. He noted with great curiosity and wonderment the strange Mima mounds.

Kane, however, was thoroughly preoccupied with recording in sketches and diary the ways of local Indians along his itinerary and scarcely ever wrote about the landscape, even though some of his well-fashioned sketches and paintings of wilderness scenes, which still exist, speak for themselves. Perhaps we should simply be thankful for Paul Kane's sensitive renditions of what he saw. Even from his artist's eye we can scarcely probe for a personal meaning. We can only infer that he did see beauty and grandeur in this western country, and perhaps even felt an urge to see it all perpetuated for an eternity.

Tim Egan, in his delightful book *The Good Rain* (1990), eulogizes one early gentleman-explorer who did see Puget country with an uncommon eye. Theodore Winthrop visited Puget Sound and the

Northwest in 1853, to find that already assaults on the land by pioneering whites were under way. Winthrop both decried these invasions of pristine nature and wrote eloquently about the natural beauty of the land. His "By Canoe and Saddle" (1913) needs to be restored to a prominent place among writings on the Pacific Northwest.

Search for a Land Ethic

On the other side of the continent, another artist did reveal his inner thoughts about the fate of the yet untrammeled land. During a journey into the Ohio country, the great naturalist painter John James Audubon reflected on alterations to the land at human hands.

When I think of these times, and call back to my mind the grandeur and beauty of those almost uninhabited shores; when I picture to myself the dense and lofty summits of the forests, that everywhere spread among the hills and overhung the margins of the stream, unmolested by the axe or the settler; when I know how dearly purchased the safe navigation of that river has been, by the blood of many worthy Virginians; when I see that no longer any aborigines are to be found there, and that the vast herds of Elk, Deer, and Buffaloes which once pastured on these hills, and in these valleys, making for themselves great roads to the several salt-springs, have ceased to exist; when I reflect that all this grand portion of our Union, instead of being in a state of nature, is now more or less covered with villages, farms, and towns, where the din of hammers and machinery is constantly heard; that the woods are fast disappearing under the axe by day, and the fire by night; that hundreds of steamboats are gliding to and fro, over the whole length of the majestic river, forcing commerce

Around the turn of the century, "the forest by the sea" was fast becoming a forest of masts and a horizontal forest of logs in holding ponds. Above: Photographers frequently focused on the men who battled the giant Douglas firs. Right: Lumber ships tied up at Port Blakely circa 1900. (Photo by Wilhelm Hester.)

to take root and to prosper at every spot; when I see the surplus population of Europe coming to assist in the destruction of the forest, and transplanting civilization into its darkest recesses; when I remember that these extraordinary changes have all taken place in the short period of twenty years, I pause, wonder, and although I know all to be fact, can scarcely believe its reality. (Audubon 1969:26)

We sense in Audubon's words a yearning to stay the axe, turn back the plow, and silence the steamboat. Yet, he is asking only that someone record the grandeur of the scenes before they all vanish. "Whether these changes are for the better or for the worst, I shall not pretend to say; but in whatever way my conclusion may incline, I feel with regret that there are on record no satisfactory accounts of the state of that portion of the country, from the time when our people first settled in it." Indeed, Audubon could have been the country's first Thoreau.

Puget Sound country after the period of the 1850s was so cataclysmically altered and with such unanimity of purpose that no single voice of conscience could have effectively stemmed the onslaught on the land. Timber, agriculture, mining, and attendant urbanization rolled back the wilderness frontiers[1] to a few remnants now sanctified in parks and other paltry preserves. And now in the twentieth century the juggernaut of exploitation and development continues its careening path across our land. Despite a tremendous upsurge in ecological awareness, despite countless organizations devoted to preservation of this or that piece of nature, despite legal restraints and citizen protests, the spoilation continues. To be sure, some victories can be pointed to in praise of the conservation efforts made in midcentury. The Wilderness Bill, the North Cascades National Park, the successful resistance to paring down the size of Olympic and Mount Rainier National Parks—these and other accomplishments are tributes to the perseverance of people in the conservation movement and their many unnamed citizen friends. But still there is *no* land ethic amongst us. We who espouse freedom, justice, equality, and all those other enlightened social verities, have yet to "give Earth a chance."

Aldo Leopold, in his classic ecological primer, *A Sand County Almanac,* planted the germ of an ethic based on an ecologically sensitized conscience. The essence of Leopold's meditations on a land ethic must be thoughtfully read and reread. His chapter "The Land Ethic" begins this theme with the statement: "There is as yet no ethic dealing with man's relation to land and to the animals and plants which grow upon it. Land, like Odysseus's slave-girls, is still property. The land-relation is still strictly economic, entailing privi-

---

1. Someone has facetiously defined frontier as simply "the edge of the unused."

What was once the scene of unobtrusive Native tenancy now is the massively altered landscape at Olympia. Industrial activity bordering Budd Inlet, south Puget Sound.

leges but not obligations." Enlarging on the attributes of a land ethic, he maintains that "all ethics so far evolved rest upon a single premise: that the individual is a member of a community of interdependent parts. His instincts prompt him to compete for his place in the community, but his ethics prompt him also to cooperate (perhaps in order that there may be a place to compete for). The land ethic simply enlarges the boundaries of the community to include soils, waters, plants, and animals, or collectively: the land." Leopold's most succinct statement on the land ethic then follows:

> An ethic, ecologically, is a limitation on freedom of action in the struggle for existence. An ethic, philosophically, is a differentiation of social from antisocial conduct. These are two definitions of one thing. . . . In short, a land ethic changes the role of *Homo sapiens* from conqueror of the land-community to plain member and citizen of it. It implies respect for his fellow members, and also respect for the community, as such. (1987:202–4)

Right: Subdividing the forest for vacation homes in south Puget Sound, Oakland Bay and Hammersley Inlet, Mason County.

Below: Further assaults on the land: Gravel quarry, Tacoma.

How then to remake the mind, spirit, and attitudes of humans toward their environment? Can a new ethic, fabricated from Aldo Leopold's beginning, save as well as restore a portion of the great natural fabric of Puget Sound country?

To convert the modern, evolved product of countless human generations from self-centered exploiter to enlightened steward of nature, there must be a thorough rewiring of our behavioral circuitry. Even the most dedicated behavioral "engineer," heady with Madison Avenue success in thought-control, might despair of achieving any success in retooling fundamental attitudes on nature. Even if a land ethic of the kind advocated by Leopold were universally adopted, voluntary support of the ethic would not be enough. Though many "programmed" persons might behave in the desired way, others might seize the opportunity for continued despoliation. For an ethic to be effective, certain accustomed freedoms will have to be abridged. Garrett Hardin, noted biological philosopher, says it persuasively in "Tragedy of the Commons" (1968). Just as freedom to rob banks is severely curtailed by society, so can other presently accepted freedoms be abridged. Freedom to reproduce and to indulge in self-interested exploitation of the environment must be severely curbed, too. When an ethic is thus linked to abridgment of laissez-faire actions on the environment, we will have given our planet a chance. Restriction of action, mutually shared and mutually agreed upon, is in the realm of law; ethics is in the realm of conscience. When effectively wed, these two aspects of behavior can serve to extend the life of all organisms on the Earth.

Epilogue: An Ecological Imperative for Puget Sound

The enjoyment of nature has been in and out of fashion over the years. Those living in the twentieth century, perhaps more than any other human generation, have had the leisure time, the material wherewithal, and the urge to seek enjoyment from natural environments. Witness the weekend exodus of people from the built

Roadside gravel pile and rural dump, Whidbey Island. (Photo by the author.)

The evolution of an urban landscape—
Bellevue transformed: 1936 to 1974.

environment of cities to camp, ski, hike, mountain climb, fish, hunt, and just relax in wild nature. Though most who partake of outdoor life might equate the experience with other leisure pursuits like chess, wine-making, or music, the outdoor experience could have far more significance than simple diversion from day-to-day toil. The trip to the ocean, the desert, or the mountains can serve to affirm the inseparability of humans and the rest of the natural world. That has been the central theme of my book.

The pursuit of natural history can be a source of great personal enjoyment. And from it, the lively mind can perceive, by simple observations in forests, on beaches, or in a tide pool, the vital inter-

connectedness of things. An appreciation of natural processes and phenomena in Puget Sound country can lead to wiser, more peaceful coexistence between people and the elements of their natural environments. From such appreciation, there comes a sense of belonging to, and deriving both material and spiritual sustenance from, the natural world. Only then, when those living in a region develop an awareness of their natural heritage, will they be in a position to preserve it. Conservation on a national or global scale may be too intangible a goal for the individual. Rather, we can begin with our own spectacular Puget Sound setting: to understand it, to appreciate it, and to preserve it from further degradation.

Appendix 1   *The Naming of Plants and Animals*

The use of Latin names in this book for native plants and animals has not been simply a display of erudition; common names have been used, too. But the Latin name is the "lingua franca," the universal mode of communication among peoples of all tongues when dealing with the catalogues of life on our planet. Common names turn out to be unreliable in several ways. Over and over again we find cases where one organism may have many different common names, often in different languages. Common names may give rise to erroneous ideas about the affinity of organisms; for example, several unrelated plants have the word "cedar" in their common name. Then, common names are unusable on a worldwide basis. Or, they may not exist for a large number of organisms; countless obscure flies, worms, locoweeds, and sunflowers have no particular ("specific") common name.

The twin functions of the Latin name—a paired term or binomial like *Gaultheria shallon*—are *stability* and *universality* of nomenclature. According to the International Code of Botanical Nomenclature (applying equally to Latin names of animals):

> Botany requires a precise and simple system of nomenclature used by botanists in all countries, dealing on the one hand with the terms which denote the ranks of taxonomic groups or units, and on the other hand with the scientific names which are applied to the individual taxonomic groups of plants. The purpose of giving a name to a taxonomic group is not to indicate its characters or history, but to supply a means of referring to it and to indicate its taxonomic rank. This Code aims at the provision of a stable method of naming taxonomic groups, avoiding and rejecting the use of names which may cause error or ambiguity or throw science into confusion. Next in importance is the avoidance of the useless creation of names. Other considerations, such as absolute grammatical correctness, regularity or euphony of names, more or less prevailing custom, regard for persons, etc., notwithstanding their undeniable importance, are relatively accessory. . . .
>
> The only proper reasons for changing a name are either a more profound knowledge of the facts resulting from adequate taxonomic study or the necessity of giving up a nomenclature that is contrary to the rules."

The impressive body of stabilized nomenclature and its eminently workable machinery for keeping the names of several million kinds of organisms in order, is a tribute to the several generations of taxonomists who have brought order and system to Nature's diversity.

Common versus Latin Names

Initial encounters with Latin names are usually painfully unrewarding. To confront the Latin name, *Gaultheria shallon*, for the first time is bad enough, but if you are an easterner, the common name, "salal," is not much better. It is simply that a strange name has no inherent informational content. But being shown a specimen with its name-tag fulfills the information gap. Both names now have meaning. Then why not use common names exclusively? If each kind of plant were unique—without a sign of kinship to any other kind—then a simple common name might do. But within Nature's array of diversity there is also the strong element of relatedness. Thus, two kinds of *Gaultheria* when called by their common names, "salal" and "wintergreen," are forever separated. But their Latin names, *Gaultheria shallon* and *Gaultheria procumbens*, reflect their bond of kinship in *Gaultheria*.

Common names are relegated to subordinate usage for other reasons. First, they lack universality. Common names are usually indigenous to a single country, or even only to one part of a country (in Europe the inhabitants of a single village or valley may have passed on a local name for generations). The bipolar shrublet, *Empetrum nigrum*, is a simple case: Americans call it "crowberry," Russians, "vodyanika," and Germans, "Krahenbeere" or "Tauschbeere." For more aggravating and picturesque examples, we can turn to the flora of rural England, where we find lavish use of common names for one and the same plant. In that delightful work by Geoffrey Grigson, *The Englishman's Flora*, I counted nearly a hundred different, common (and often very local) names for *Caltha palustris:* Marsh marigold, bachelor's buttons, cups and saucers, water goggles, to name a few. Sometimes the same common name may apply to several very different plants. The name "may flower" has been given to *Podophyllum* in the Midwest, to a member of the Heath family in New England, to the hawthorn, marsh marigold, and cuckoo flower in England, and to a legume in the West Indies. Though such examples could be repeated endlessly, I cannot resist just two more to further the proof of confusion in common names. A handsome member of the sunflower family was called "Venus's paint brush" when it first appeared in America; later, as it proved to be an aggressive noxious weed, it became known as the "Devil's paint brush." Finally, there is the case of corrupted meaning through centuries of usage. Plants of the genus *Cornus* were once called "dagwood," because "dags" were made of its wood for use as skewers. To be historically correct, you would call our native "dogwood," the skewerwood. The use of common names often becomes ludicrous when they are "manufactured." "Tweedy's rattleweed" does not add much to the binomial, *Astragalus tweedyi*. Are you any better off knowing that *Tropicarpum capparideum* can also be called "caper-fruited tropicarpum"? Enough said of common names—established as well as contrived—except to say that when in wide popular use they should be retained, while Latin names should be used for conducting the international business of scientific botany and zoology.

The Binomial or Latin Name

There is really nothing scientific about the so-called "scientific name" in biological nomenclature. It is derived neither by experiment nor by observation, and only what it stands for—systems of populations of organisms—can be tested like a hypothesis. Yet it is the only valid "handle" that can be attached to organisms. The scientific name is a compound of two Latin or Latinized words, the generic and the specific: this double epithet is the species name. Thus, the binomial, *Pinus ponderosa,* is applied to a particular kind of pine, one with a distinctive ensemble of structural features and one which occurs in self-reproducing populations throughout a wide but delimited geographic and ecological range.

Other species of pines, each with their distinct attributes, are given particular species names: *Pinus monticola* for the western white pine, *P. contorta** for the lodgepole or beach pine, *P. albicaulis* for white bark pine, and so on. (These species and the eighty or so others of pine reveal their kinship in the genus name, *Pinus,* the collective name for all the major pine variants.)

The Taxonomic System

Our discussion of the binomial suggests that the two categories of plant names—genus and species—are collective terms. The species category[†] collects unto itself individuals, while the genus contains one to many species. Both categories are levels of inclusiveness; one (the genus) more inclusive than the other. In fact, the whole vast array of biological diversity—all the species worldwide—can be "nested" in successively more inclusive categories. This hierarchy of categories constitutes the taxonomic system. Though the lowest level is logically the individual, the species is actually the lowest formal rank; the variety or subspecies often is subordinate to the species. The catalog of categories does not stop here, however. When looked at from above, the most inclusive category would gather together all plants—the Kingdom Plantae. Looking downward from maximum to minimum inclusiveness we find the following array of categories:

Category	*Example*
Kingdom	Plantae
Division	Magnoliophyta
Class	Magnoliopsida
Subclass	Dilleniidae
Order	Ericales
Family	Ericaceae
Genus	*Gaultheria*
Species	*shallon*

As the categories become less and less inclusive, there will be more kinds of each of them at successively lower levels. Thus, while there are only three kingdoms, within one, the Kingdom Plantae, there are at least twenty-eight divisions, many classes, orders, and families, and over a quarter of a million species of plants.

What variations on plant names do we encounter within the framework of the binomial? There are essentially four classes of generic and specific names. Take, for example, *Gaultheria,* a commemorative genus epithet

*Note that we can abbreviate the generic name when using it later in the same text, if no other binomial is interposed. Binomials are underscored or printed in italics.

†Remembering one sequence or hierarchy of taxonomic categories can be aided with this cute phrase: "Kings Play Chess On Finely Ground Sand" (for Kingdom, Phylum, Class, Order, Family, Genus, Species).

honoring a little-known, French-Canadian physician and botanist, Jean Pierre Gaultier. Kings, rogues, botanists, patrons, and lovers, all have been memorialized in this way. The addition of "-ia" to a personal name is a sure route to immortality: *Linnaea, Kalmia, Lewisia, Kolkwitzia, Magnolia, Jepsonia, Jeffersonia,* and so on through floras and faunas of the world. *Linnaea,* the delightful trailing twin-flower of our woods, is named for Carolus Linnaeus, the father of systematic botany. *Kalmia,* the mountain laurel, is named for one of Linnaeus' students, Peter Kalm. You would be certain to recognize that *Lewisia* is named for Meriwether Lewis of the Lewis and Clark expedition; William Clark is commemorated in the genus *Clarkia,* a delightful group of annuals common in the spring floras of the Pacific Coast.

A more "academic" class of generic epithets is the classical descriptive name. Here, Greek or Latin, or sometimes a mismatch of both ancient tongues, is used to depict some characteristic of the genus in question. Thus, the genus *Liriodendron* is translated from the classic language as "lily tree"; *Xanthorhiza* means "yellow root"; *Oxydendron* means "sour tree"; *Cladothamnus* means "branched shrub"; *Enkianthus* means "pregnant flower"; etc. Occasionally, generic names have been derived from the original native word. A botanist in the tropics would find that many of the genera he finds there are Latinized versions of the original native name. Two examples from the Asiatic flora are *Tsuga,* which is the Japanese name for hemlock, and *Gingko,* the Chinese name for that famous and sacred tree of temple gardens. The last category of generic names is both an amusing and intriguing one, the so-called fanciful, poetical, or mythological name. Here are five names which typify this kind of generic epithet: *Dodecatheon* means "twelve gods"; *Theobroma,* the generic name for the cocoa plant, means "god's food"; *Phyllodoce* means "sea-nymph; *Calypso* and *Narcissus* are characters in Greek mythology.

Of the four categories of species names, the descriptive and commemorative are the most common. *Rubra* (red), *nana* (dwarf), *repens* (prostrate growth), *saxatilis* (growing in rocks), etc., are descriptive adjectives. Sometimes the descriptive adjective is compound, as in *angustifolia* ("narrow" and "leaf"), *cordifolia* ("heart-shaped leaf"), *racemiflora,* (flowers in a racemose inflorescence). Occasionally, a specific name is taken from the generic name in another group; thus, we find the specific name *bignonioides,* which means "like bignonia," or *acerifolia* ("leaves like the maple"). A great many of the more recent specific epithets are simply commemorative. Thus, you would find on almost any page of Hitchcock and Cronquist's *Flora of the Pacific Northwest,* plants with proper names as the specific epithet, such *douglasii, menziesii, lyallii, thompsonii, piperi, barrettiae.* Whereas in the past, commemorative specific names have been capitalized, the current recommendation of the International Rules is to use lowercase for both commemorative and place names (although this is largely left to the discretion of the user). The last group consists of species names which indeed are nouns, such as the binomials, *Pyrus Malus* and *Prunus Laurocerasus.* Usually such names were formerly generic; thus the species in question, which was once placed in another genus, now uses the former genus name as a specific epithet.

Appendix 2

Place Names and Kindred Matters for the Puget Sound Basin

Puget Sound

Two problems arise in seeking a precise definition of Puget Sound. The first has to do with its extent and boundaries; the second with the origin and priority of the name, "Puget."

First its several *geographic definitions:* "Nautical charts label the main basin, extending from Point No Point on the Kitsap Peninsula to Tacoma, as "Puget Sound," while the individual inlets of the original "Puget's Sound" (see below) south of the Tacoma Narrows have all been given their own names (like Budd Inlet, Carr Inlet, etc.). The charts also designate the body of water connecting Puget Sound with the Strait of Juan de Fuca as "Admiralty Inlet."

A broader definition is given the Sound by the U.S. Board on Geographic Names. Puget Sound is that body of water "extending 90 miles south from the Strait of Juan de Fuca to Olympia; the northern boundary is formed, at its main entrance, by a line between Point Wilson on the Olympic Peninsula and Point Partridge on Whidbey Island; at a second entrance, between West Point on Whidbey Island, Deception Island and Rosario Head on Fidalgo Island; at a third entrance, at the south end of Swinomish Channel between Fidalgo Island and McGlinn Island." Thus, Puget Sound is officially understood to include the waters of Admiralty Inlet, Hood Canal, Possession Sound, and Saratoga Passage, among others. It does not include Rosario Strait, Haro Strait, the Strait of Georgia (in B.C. waters), Bellingham Bay, Padilla Bay, or Samish Bay.

Agencies concerned with water quality expand the limits of Puget Sound, since pollution can spread over the wider region. Thus the Puget Sound Water Quality Act defines Puget sound as "all salt waters of the state of Washington inside the international boundary line between the state of Washington and the province of British Columbia, lying east of Ediz Hook at Port Angeles."

So, take your pick. Each of the definitions of the Sound's perimeters has merit. Now that we have "clarified" the geographic limits, we look at the matter of origin and priority of the name, "Puget." According to Washington State Place Names (1971), the waters now commonly referred to as Puget Sound were called "Whulge" by the Native Americans here before the arrival of the explorers. In 1792, Captain George Vancouver, aboard the ship *Discovery,* anchored in Discovery Bay, sent Lt. Peter Puget with the ship's launch and cutter into the waters south of what is now known as the Tacoma Narrows. Upon Lieutenant Puget's return, Vancouver gave the name "Puget's Sound" to those waters he had explored. In later years, common usage and legal decisions resulted in the extension of the name (without the apostrophe) to the waters north or the Tacoma Narrows. (Excerpted from Puget Sound Notes, Spring 1989).

"Whulge," then, is the original name of the inland sea. It is variously rendered from the Indian language, Lushootseed (or "Puget Salish"). It is less a place name than the word for sea, ocean, sound, salt water: "any and all salt water where Lushootseed speakers live" (fide, Harvey Manning, pers. corres.). Manning would like to "right an ancient wrong, correct a geographical corruption," by restoring the Indian name, Whulge, to Puget Sound. He would "restore imperialistic Puget Sound where it belongs, south of the tip of Whidbey Island." Manning recognizes that Vancouver put it south of Point Defiance (Tacoma area), but adds, "I'm a reasonable man, and I'll compromise."

Origins of Place Names

Learning the origins of place names in one's home country can add a richer meaning to the familiar. Two source books can be consulted for the derivations of place names in Puget (a.k.a., Whulge) country. Robert Hitchman, *Place Names of Washington* (Tacoma: Washington State Historical Society, 1985); James W. Phillips, *Washington State Place Names* (Seattle: University of Washington Press, 1971).

It will become apparent to those seeking the origins of place names that they fall into more than one category:

1. Aboriginal Indian names, or their Europeanized versions. Examples: Puyallup, Tacoma, Seattle, Swinomish, Snohomish, Snoqualmie, etc.

2. Place names awarded by early explorers. First, the Spanish explorers, with names like Fidalgo, Rosario, Guemes, San Juan, etc.; then, the Vancouver Expedition bequeathed to us Mount Rainier, Puget Sound, Mount Baker, etc. In the 1840s, the Commodore Wilkes Exploring Expedition added to the map with Shaw, Waldron, Maury, and Decatur islands in the San Juans. It was not unusual to find that an earlier named place was given a later name; Wilkes is guilty of this redundancy.

3. Names were plentifully attached to places by later-arriving Europeans. Places were christened by early settlers, farmers, founders of villages, shopkeepers, builders of railroads, miners and timber harvesters.

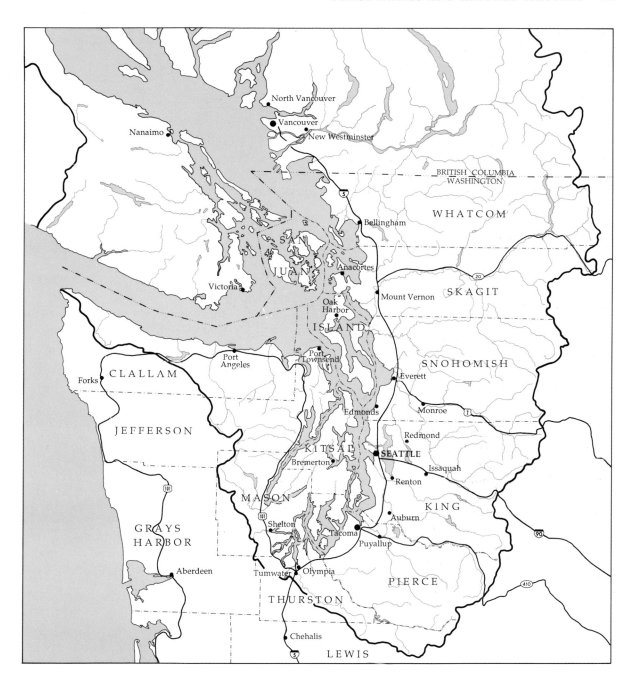

A political map of Puget country, while perhaps less intriguing for the naturalist than would be geological and vegetation maps, will help the reader locate major towns and cities, counties, and main highways. (Map by Nancy Eberle.)

Appendix 3   *Chronology of Happenings in the Puget Sound Basin and the Pacific Northwest*

Geologic and Biological Events

50 million years B.P.*	Puget Sound basin covered by marine waters.
10 million years B.P.	Puget Sound basin at or above sea level.
13,000–15,000 years B.P.	Glacial ice covered Puget lowland from Olympia to Canada; Seattle area under 2,000 feet of ice.
12,000 B.P.	Eruption of Glacier Peak, its ash widely dispersed.
11,000 B.P.	Retreat of last (Vashon) ice sheet begins.
8,500–3,000 B.P.	Hypsithermal climatic interval: climate warmer and drier than present.
6,750 B.P.	Volcanic ash from Mt. Mazama (Oregon) eruption deposited in western Washington.
4,800 B.P.	Osceola mud-flow, from Mt. Rainier to Enumclaw; 2.5 billion cubic yards of mud and rubble.
1,000 B.P.	Creation of modern volcano of Mount St. Helens.
600 B.P.	Electron mudflow down Puyallup River valley to Orting; last significant eruptions on Mt. Rainier.
A.D. 1792	In May-June, Archibald Menzies, with Vancouver expedition, records sightings of native trees: madrone, bigleaf maple, red alder, Douglas fir, western red cedar, western hemlock and other forest trees of Puget Sound basin.
1825	In April-May, David Douglas begins botanical survey of Northwest from Fort Vancouver under auspices of British horticultural sponsors.
1825	In July-September, Dr. John Scouler botanizes along outer coast from mouth of Columbia River to Straits of Juan de Fuca.
1830	David Douglas begins second botanical survey of Northwest.
1835	Thomas Nuttall, naturalist with Nathaniel Wyeth expedition, collects plants and animals in vicinity of Columbia River.
1837	Dr. W. F. Tolmie botanizes on slopes of Mt. Rainier.
1841	Dr. Charles Pickering and Mr. W. D. Brackenridge, botanists with the Wilkes Expedition, explore Puget Sound basin; collect at Port Discovery, Port Madison, and Fort Nisqually.
1842–43	Eruptions of Mount St. Helens witnessed by early settlers.
1840s	Much steam and ash vented from Mt. Baker.

1920–1960	Retreat of several glaciers in Cascades and Olympics
1930s	Beginning of invasion of subalpine meadows by trees during a warm-dry climatic phase
1947	Kautz Creek mud flow on Mt. Rainier.
1963	Massive rock falls from Little Tahoma Peak onto Emmons Glacier on Mt. Rainier.
1975	Renewed steam venting on Mt. Baker
1980	Massive eruption of Mount St. Helens (May 18)

Environmental Events, Natural and Human-caused:

Earthquakes

1833	Early major quake.
1946	Worst Seattle quake.
1949	Worst quake in Pacific Northwest history.
1959	Quake centered north of Seattle.
1960	Strong quake, felt from Bellingham to Olympia and Aberdeen.
1965	Second worst quake since 1833.

Severe Freezes and Heavy Snows

1916	Crippling snowfall in Seattle and environs; 26 inches total.
1950	Blizzard in western Washington.
1955	Statewide cold snap, November 11–15.
1989	Record cold spell, February and March.
1990–91	Severe freeze, December 18 to early January

Windstorms

| 1921 | The great Olympic "blow-down" |
| 1962 | The Columbus Day storm: timber blow-downs and other severe damage. |

Other notable windstorms: 1891, 1894, 1964, 1965, 1966, 1967, 1969, 1971, 1973, 1974.

Floods (though flood conditions occur nearly every year, only the more damaging are listed): 1892, 1906, 1933, 1955, 1959, 1971, 1990

Fire and Insect Outbreaks in Forests

1826–30	David Douglas reports sighting of fires in Northwest; mentions disappearance of forest around Fort Vancouver.
pre–1847	Little record of fires sighted by whites.
1847–on	Following influx of white settlers, reports of great fires appear.
1868	St. Helens fires; 300,000 acres.
1902	In September, disastrous Yacolt (or Cispus or Lewis

River or Cowlitz) fire burned off 600,000 acres; 18 people killed. Downtown Seattle "as dark as night."

1910	Bad fire year in Pacific Northwest.
1930	Bad fire year in Washington; 131,475 acres burned.
1931	Outbreak of hemlock looper (moth larva) in Pacific County.
1933	Tillamook burn in Oregon; smoke reached Puget Sound area.
1974	Severe outbreak of tussock moth in eastern Washington.
1975	Spruce budworm epidemic rages along east slope of Cascades.

Forest Modification in Puget Sound Basin (logging, fire protection, conservation efforts, etc.)

1788	First timber extracted by Captain John Mears, who left Puget Sound for China with cargo of ship spars.
1827	First lumber mill in Washington (and first west of Mississippi) started by Hudson's Bay Company at Fort Vancouver; whipsaw mill operated by Hawaiians.
1840	Original (pre-white) timber stand for all of Washington estimated at 578 billion board-feet.
1853	Henry Yesler built first steam-powered mill on Puget Sound.
1864	U.S. Congress grants odd-numbered sections in a 40-mile strip to Northern Pacific Railway. Much timbered land then sold at $2.00 per acre.
1880's	Donkey engine and railroad first used in local logging.
1899	Mt. Rainier National Park created.
1900s	Major logging in progress in Puget lowland. Beginnings of patch-cut, clear-cut methods of logging.
1905	Beginnings of private fire protection associations. Creation by Congress of national forests and U.S. Forest Service to administer forests.
1924	Clark-McNary Act creates cooperative fire protection: private, state, and federal.
1936	Four billion board-feet of lumber produced in western Washington.
1938	President F. D. Roosevelt signs bill to create Olympic National Park.
1940	Inventory of western Washington forest resources: 12 million acres of forest land; 245.5 billion board-feet of timber.
1940–on	Intensive logging during WW II period and on into present decade in virgin and the regrowth areas of lowland and montane Puget country.

1964	Congress passes Wilderness Act.
1968	Congress establishes North Cascades National Park.
1973	Inventory of western Washington forest resources: old growth, 60 billion board-feet; second growth, etc. 100 billion board-feet (approximate, Scribner scale).
1976	Congress establishes Alpine Lakes Wilderness Area.

Other Environmental Events

1778–1805	Ruthless exploitation of sea otter by Europeans.
1825	Europeans begin commercial exploitation of fish resource.
1850	Native oysters discovered in local waters; shipped in quantity to California.
1850	Introduction of quail at Fort Vancouver.
1853	First Washington game laws passed by Territorial legislature.
1891	Introduction of freshwater fish to area (large-mouthed bass, crappie, yellow perch, sunfish).
1895	First salmon hatcheries constructed.
1900 and later	European rabbits introduced to San Juan Island.
1916	Lowering of Lake Washington 10 feet for ship canal to Puget Sound.
1918	Cedar Reservoir breakthrough floods lower Cedar River drainage.
1933	Washington State Game Department established.
1937	Nutria, introduced mammal, escapes from fur farms.
1941	Grand Coulee Dam on the Columbia is completed.
1942	Introduced opossum first trapped in western Washington.
1947	European starling first reported in western Washington.
1957	State Department of Natural Resources established.
1961	Bounty payments halted on cougar.
1965	Pacific hake, a fish abundant in outer coastal waters, introduced into Puget Sound.
1966	Cougar classed as a game animal.
1969	Congress establishes National Environmental Protection Agency.
1970	State Department of Ecology established.
1971	Washington state adopts statewide environmental protection laws.
1971	State adopts Shoreline Protection Act measures.
1972	State legislature passes Natural Area Preserves bill, administered by Department of Natural Resources.
1973	Federal legislation on rare and endangered animal

species (plant species added in 1976); State Game Department and Department of Natural Resources (in 1975) designated state authorities or agencies.

Human Events (Indians and Europeans):

9,000 B.P.	Earliest evidence of Indians in eastern Washington.
8,000 B.P.	Earliest evidence of Indians in Puget Sound.
2,000 B.P.	Coastal Indian cultures well represented in Puget Sound area.
A.D. 1592	Juan de Fuca (Apostolos Valerianos) alleged to have discovered strait later given his name.
1774	Spanish begin to probe Russian settlements in Pacific Northwest; Juan Pérez sights Mt. Olympus, naming it Santa Rosalia.
1775	First white contact with Indians of coastal Washington: Spanish (Bodega y Quadra's) landing party at Hoh River were killed.
1775–92	Catastrophic reduction of Indian populations, probably due to smallpox and other European diseases.
1778	Captain James Cook sighted Cape Flattery on his third attempt to find the Northwest Passage (the Strait of Anian).
1787	Captain Charles W. Barkley locates Strait of Juan de Fuca.
1792	Captain George Vancouver's expedition explores Puget Sound; natural history recorded by expedition's surgeon-naturalist, Archibald Menzies.
1792	American Captain Robert Gray discovers Columbia River and Gray's Harbor.
1805	Lewis and Clark expedition reaches mouth of Columbia River and stays the winter at site of Fort Vancouver.
1811	Fur-trading station established at Astoria, near mouth of Columbia River.
1825	Hudson's Bay Company establishes Fort Vancouver on north bank of Columbia River.
1825–26, 1830–34	David Douglas makes major plant collections in Pacific Northwest.
1833	Hudson's Bay trading post established at Fort Nisqually on southern Puget Sound.
1845	First American settlement on Puget Sound, at Tumwater.
1846	Establishment of 49th Parallel as boundary between Canada and United States.
1848–49	Admission of Oregon Territory to Union; included Oregon, Washington, Idaho, and portions of Wyoming and Montana.
1849	Snoqualmie Indians, resenting white influx to Puget Sound, attack Fort Nisqually.

1849	Founding of Fort Steilacoom, south of Tacoma.
1851	Settlement of Elliot Bay sites begins, eventually to become Seattle.
1853	Congress creates the Territory of Washington.
1854	Governor of Washington Territory, Isaac I. Stevens, concludes the Medicine Creek treaties with Indians of Puget Sound basin: fishing/hunting rights to be protected, lost land to be paid for, land for reservations to be set aside, etc.
1855–56	Recurrent Indian attacks on white settlements in Puget Sound, including attack on Seattle.
1859	Indian treaties negotiated by Governor Stevens are ratified by Congress.
1861	Opening of Territorial University at Seattle.
1887	First transcontinental railroad (Northern Pacific) direct to Puget Sound completed.
1889	Washington State admitted to the Union; white population, 3,965.
1889	Great fire razes much of city of Seattle.
1897	Discovery of gold in Alaska promotes a boom in Puget Sound economy.
1909	Alaska-Yukon-Pacific Exposition opens in Seattle.
1941	Indian population of Washington State estimated at 14,000; 6,500 in western Washington.
1974	Indian fishing rights of 1855 treaties upheld by Judge Boldt.
1990	Listing of northern spotted owl as endangered creates "window of opportunity" for rethinking the ecological values of old-growth forests.

Appendix 4

Threatened and Endangered Wildlife in Washington

Washington State Endangered Species

American white pelican, *Pelecanus erythrorhynchos*
Brown pelican, *Pelecanus occidentalis*
Aleutian Canada goose, *Branta canadensis leucopareia*
Peregrine falcon, *Falco peregrinus*
Sandhill crane, *Grus canadensis*
Snowy plover, *Charadrius alexandrinus*
Upland sandpiper, *Bartramia longicauda*
Sperm whale, *Physeter macrocephalus*
Gray whale, *Eschrichtius robustus*
Fin whale, *Balaenoptera physalus*
Sei whale, *Balaenoptera borealis*
Blue whale, *Balaenoptera musculus*
Hump-backed whale, *Megaptera novaeangliae*
Right whale, *Balaena glacialis*
Wolf, *Canis lupus*
Grizzly bear, *Ursus arctos horribilis*
Sea otter, *Enhydra lutris*
Columbian white-tailed deer, *Odocoileus virginianus leucurus*
Woodland caribou, *Rangifer tarandus caribou*

Washington Threatened Species

Oregon silverspot butterfly, *Speyeria zerene hippolyta*
Western pond turtle, *Clemmys marmorata*
Ferruginous hawk, *Buteo regalis*
Bald eagle, *Haliaeetus leucocephalus*
Spotted owl, *Strix occidentalis (caurina)*
Pygmy rabbit, *Sylvilagus idahoensis*

Note: All federally listed threatened and endangered species that are found in Washington are automatically included on these lists. Compiled from "Threatened and Endangered Wildlife in Washington," a publication of Washington Department of Wildlife, Olympia, Washington, 1987. For lists of endangered plants in Washington, consult *Washington Natural Heritage Program*, 1990. "Endangered, threatened and sensitive vascular plants of Washington," Department of Natural Resources, Olympia. 52p.

Appendix 5   *Soils of the Puget Basin*

Humankind treats soil like dirt. Yet, that seemingly inert stuff enmeshed in tree roots and underfoot in gravelly prairies or alpine meadows is alive. Soil is seldom recognized as an ecosystem in its own right. Everywhere vegetation and soil are dynamically interactive. But being underfoot and dirty to boot, it is the most neglected component of any terrestrial ecosystem.

Soils are complex, structured systems where the living and the non-living are intricately intertwined. Initially they are the products of the conversion of rocks or other substrates in a transformation called weathering. Soils have both gross and microscale structure. Dig a soil pit in a Douglas fir forest floor and find a vertical array of layers, or horizons, from litter and organic duff at the soil surface through twelve or more inches of textured, weathered material down to bedrock. Such a vertical sequence is called a soil profile, with from but one to several distinct layers, called horizons. The weathering of rock or other parent materials to soil involves dramatic physical and chemical changes. The crystalline rock is physically broken down into gravel, sand, and silt, and, as well, is chemically altered to a new mineral, clay. Soil formation, a process of slowed-down chemical alteration, is a function of five independently acting environmental factors: climate, topography, organisms, parent materials (usually rocks), and time. Any particular combination of these factors can produce a distinctive soil type. For example, the vastly different climates of western and eastern Washington can produce very different soil types.

To say that soils are alive—living ecosystems—is to bear witness not only to the living roots that penetrate the soil mantle. All soils harbor a microcosm of miniature life: bacteria, fungi, protozoa, and small invertebrates, in addition to the occasional fossorial rodent or even burrowing owl.

The unique chemical constituent of soil is its clay fraction. Clays are colloidal, minute minerals chemically distinct from the minerals of the rocks from whence they weathered. Put a teaspoon of soil in a glass of water, shake well, and observe: The coarse particles settle out—silt, sand and gravel—while the cloudy suspension remains turbid—the fine silt and clay fraction. Far from inert, the clay particles are electrically charged to retain, and eventually release, nutrient elements—ammonium, calcium, magnesium, potassium, sodium, and minor elements. This nutrient exchange capability can vary from low to high values; it is expressed numerically as the cation (or base) exchange capacity of a soil. The clay particles, with their nutrient surface layer, are in turn in continuity with the soil solution (water with dissolved nutrients) and the tiny rootlets of plants. It is this clay particle–soil solution–root complex that gives soil its life-sustaining qualities. The chemical elements necessary for life enter the ecosystem at this vital interface. Puget Sound soils are so young that little clay has formed; fine organic particles can also effect nutrient exchange.

Soils, like plants and animals, are classified by their unique attributes. In Puget Sound country, most soils have been formed only since the retreat of the continental ice sheet. Yet over the ten to twelve thousand years of soil formation, respectable soil profiles have developed, given the slow rate for soils formation (approximately two to four centimeters per 1,000 years). The quality of the region's soils is defined mostly by the coniferous forests they support. Forest soils have a vertical sequence (profile) of organic and leached layers (the A horizon), a lower leached mineral horizon underlain by a deposit of accumulated mineral (the B horizon), and the C horizon of parent rock (bedrock or glacial till) at the bottom. Forest soils have an acid reaction (pH values of four to six) and are relatively poor in nutrient quality. Yet such soils have supported magnificent forest for thousands of years. Low fertility and luxuriance of vegetation hardly would seem to go hand in hand. Yet the inconsistency can be explained by the crucial recycling ability of the living soil mantle; the "trash-burners" of the soil (bacteria, fungi, etc.) continuously consume organic matter from the forest canopy to make available simple elemental nutrients. In the tropics, such recycling is the only source of nutrition for the luxuriant vegetation and can take place in one year; in temperate forests it may take several years to recycle the bulkier organic debris of the litter (Anon. 1957; Franklin and Dyrness 1988).

A common soil of Puget lowland forests is called the Alderwood Series. Alderwood soils, developed on gently undulating terrain, have good surface drainage, but display restricted subsurface drainage because of a hardpan layer in the C horizon. These soils have a rather coarse texture: gravelly to sandy loams, with depths of twenty-eight to thirty-two inches to the hardpan or glacial till layer at the bottom, C horizon. (The typical loam is a soil that has roughly equal percentages of sand and silt and a small amount of clay.) Similar forest soils are identified by soil scientists as the Everett, Indianola, Kitsap, and Lynden series. All originally supported coniferous forests, before agriculture or urbanization. These acidic and rather infertile soil types are mostly primary or residual, having been formed in place from parent rock or glacial till. Several other soil series in Puget basin are secondary (or alluvial), having been transported mostly by water (less often by wind or ice). Such alluvial soils are fine-textured, with more silt and clay than primary, forest soils; they usually support vegetation of shrubs and herbs (wetland habitats, for example). Alluvial soils can be quite fertile and their best versions provide the richest agricultural land in the basin. The Skagit River delta is one such fertile alluvial plain (Gessel and Cole 1969).

The urbanization that has swept over lowland Puget country has badly mistreated soils in its juggernaut path. Bulldozed, carted away to landfills, or covered over by asphalt and concrete, the soils so mistreated reflect a universal ignorance about their slow genesis, their potential for supporting natural and cultivated vegetation, and their living fabric. Yes, we have treated soils like dirt! It is time to reverse this maltreatment of a precious resource.

Bibliography

References Cited

Adams, D. "The paleoecology of two lakes in Western Washington." Master's thesis, Univ. of Washington, 1973.

Agee, J. K. "Fire effects on Pacific Northwest forests: Flora, fuel, and fauna." Northwest Fire Council Conference Proceedings, pp. 54–66, 1981.

Anon. "An Introduction to the Forest Soils of the Douglas Fir Region of the Pacific Northwest." Forest Soils Committee of the Douglas Fir Region. College of Forest Resources, Univ. of Washington, Seattle.

Angell, T., and K. C. Balcomb III. *Marine Birds and Mammals of Puget Sound.* Washington Sea Grant and Univ. of Washington Press, Seattle, 1982.

Audubon, J. "The Ohio." In *America the Vanishing,* ed. S. R. Ogden, pp. 24–28. Stephen Greene Press, Brattleboro, VT, 1969.

Avery, Mary W. *Washington: A History of the Evergreen State.* Univ. of Washington Press, Seattle, 1961.

Barash, D. P. "Evolution of marmot societies: A general theory," *Science* 185:415–20, 1974.

Berg, A. W. "Formation of Mima mounds: A seismic hypothesis," *Geology* 18:281–84, 1990.

Berg, R. Y. "Adaptation and evolution in *Dicentra* (Fumariaceae), with special reference to seed, fruit, and dispersal mechanism," *Nytt. Magasin for Botanik* 16:49–75, 1969.

Bigg, M. A., G. Ellis, J. Ford, and K. Balcomb. *Killer Whales: A Study of Their Identification, Genealogy, and Natural History in British Columbia and Washington State.* Phantom Press, Nanaimo, B.C., 1987.

Billings, W. D., and H. A. Mooney. "The ecology of arctic and alpine plants," *Biological Reviews* 43:481–529, 1968.

Bodhaine, G. L., and W. H. Robinson. "Floods in western Washington: Frequency and magnitude in relation to drainage basin characteristics," U.S. Geol. Survey Circ. 191, 1952.

Bormann, F. H., and G. E. Likens. "Nutrient cycling," *Science* 155:424–29, 1967.

Bowles, J. B. "Ornithology of changing forest stands on the western slope of the Cascade Mountains in Central Washington." Master's thesis, Univ. of Washington, 1963.

Bretz, J. Harlen. *Glaciation of the Puget Sound Region,* Washington Geol. Survey Bull. 8, 1913.

Brooke, R. C., E. B. Peterson, and V. J. Krajina. "The subalpine mountain hemlock zone," *Ecology of Western North America* 2:147–349, 1970.

Buechner, H. K. "Some biotic changes in the state of Washington, particularly during the century 1853–1953." In *Washington Territorial Centennial*

Number, pp. 154–92. Research Studies of the State College of Washington, 1953.

Burns, R. E. *The Shape and Form of Puget Sound.* Washington Sea Grant and Univ. of Washington Press, Seattle, 1985.

Cahalane, V. H. *Mammals of North America.* Macmillan Co., New York and London, 1961.

Cates, R. G. "The interface between slugs and wild ginger: Some evolutionary aspects," *Ecology* 56:391–400, 1975.

Caughley, G. "Eruption of ungulate populations, with emphasis on Himalayan thar in New Zealand," *Ecology* 51:53–72, 1970.

Church, P. E. "Seattle—a spectacular and clean air city," *Weatherwise* 15:50–56, 1962.

Church, P. E., and L. J. Fritschen. "The climates and microclimates of western Washington." In *Working with Environmental Factors.* Institute of Forest Products, Univ. of Washington, Seattle, 1968.

Clemens, W. A., and G. V. Wilby. *Fishes of the Pacific Coast of Canada.* Bulletin 68, 2d ed. Fisheries Research Board of Canada, Ottawa, 1961. (Revised 1973, *Pacific Fishes of Canada* by J. L. Hart.)

Cox, G. W. "Mounds of mystery," *Natural History* 93(6):36–45, 1984.

Cushman, M. J. "The influence of recurrent snow avalanches on vegetation patterns in the Washington Cascades." Ph.D. diss., Univ. of Washington, 1981.

Dahlquest, W. W., and V. B. Scheffer. "The origin of the Mima mounds of western Washington," *J. of Geol.* 50:68–84, 1942.

DeLacy, A. C., B. S. Miller, and S. F. Borton. "Checklist of Puget Sound Fishes." Washington Sea Grant Pub., Div. of Marine Resources, Univ. of Washington, Seattle, 1972.

del Moral, R. "The vegetation of Findley Lake basin," *Amer. Midland Naturalist* 89:26–40, 1973.

del Moral, R. "The impact of the Olympic marmot on subalpine vegetation structure," *Amer. J. of Botany* 7:1228–36.

Dice, L. R. "Ecologic and genetic variability within species of *Peromyscus,*" *Amer. Naturalist* 74:212–21, 1940.

Douglas, D. "Sketch of a journey to the Northwestern parts of the continent of North America during the years 1824–25–26–27," *Oregon Hist. Soc. Quarterly* 5:230–71, 325–69, 1904.

Downing, J. *The Coast of Puget Sound: Its Processes and Development.* Washington Sea Grant, Seattle, 1983.

Dunnell, R. C., and J. W. Fuller. "An archeological survey of Everett Harbor and the Lower Snohomish estuary-delta." U.S. National Park Service CS-9000-4-0101 (mimeo.), 1975.

Dyrness, C. T., J. F. Franklin, C. Maser, A. Cook, J. D. Hall, and G. Faxon. *Research Natural Area Needs in the Pacific Northwest: A Contribution to Land-Use Planning.* Pac. Northwest Forest and Range Experiment Station, Portland, Ore., U.S. Dept. of Agriculture, 1975.

Edmonds, R. L., ed. *Analysis of Coniferous Forest Ecosystems in the Western United States.* US/IBP Synthesis Ser. No. 14. Hutchinson Ross Publishing Co., Stroudsburg, PA, 1982.

Edmondson, W. T. "Nutrients and phytoplankton in Lake Washington." In *Nutrients and Eutrophication Special Symposia*, vol. 1, pp. 172–93. Amer. Soc. of Limnology and Oceanography, 1975.

Egan, T. *The Good Rain: Across Time and Terrain in the Pacific Northwest*. A. A. Knopf, New York, 1990.

Ehrlich, A. H., and P. R. Ehrlich. *Earth*. Franklin Watts, New York, 1987.

Ficken, R. E., and C. P. LeWarne. *Washington: A Centennial History*. Univ. of Washington Press, Seattle, 1988.

Fitzgerald, B. J. "The microenvironment in a Pacific Northwest bog and its implications for establishment of conifer seedlings." Master's thesis, Univ. of Washington, 1966.

Fladmark, K. R. *British Columbia Prehistory*. National Museums of Canada, Ottawa, 1986.

Franklin, J. F., and N. A. Bishop. "Notes on the natural history of Mount Rainier National Park." Mount Rainier Nat. Hist. Assoc., Longmire, WA (pamphlet), no date.

Franklin, J. F., L. J. Dempster, and R. H. Waring, eds. *Proceedings—Research on Coniferous Forest Ecosystems: A Symposium*. Pac. Northwest Forest and Range Experiment Station, Portland, Ore., U.S. Dept. of Agriculture, 1972.

Franklin, J. F., and C. T. Dyrness. *Natural Vegetation of Oregon and Washington*. Forest Service Gen. Tech. Report PNW-8, U.S. Dept. of Agriculture, 1973. (Reprinted with bibliography supplement, Oregon State Univ., Corvallis, 1988).

Franklin, J. F., F. C. Hall, C. T. Dyrness, and C. Maser. *Federal Research Natural Areas in Oregon and Washington: A Guidebook for Scientists and Educators*. Pac. Northwest Forest and Range Experiment Station, Portland, Ore., U.S. Dept. of Agriculture, 1972.

Fritschen, L. J. "The lysimeter installation on the Cedar River watershed." In *Proceedings: Research on Coniferous Forest Ecosystems: A Symposium*, pp. 255–60. Pac. Northwest Forest and Range Experiment Station, Portland, Ore., U.S. Dept. of Agriculture, 1972.

Gessel, S. P., and D. W. Cole. "The Soils of Western Washington: Description and Properties." In *Working with Environmental Factors*, Inst. of Forest Products, Univ. of Washington, Seattle, 1969.

Giles, L. J. "The ecology of the mounds on Mima Prairie with special reference to Douglas fir invasion." Master's thesis, Univ. of Washington, 1970.

Grant, K. "A hypothesis concerning the prevalence of red coloration in California hummingbird flowers," *Amer. Naturalist* 100:85–97, 1966.

Gunther, E. *Ethnobotany of Western Washington*. University of Washington Pub. in Anthropology 10:1–62, 1945. (Revised 1973, Univ. of Washington Press, Seattle.)

Habeck, J. R., and E. Hartley. *A Glossary of Alpine Terminology*. 2d ed. Dept. of Botany, Univ. of Montana, Missoula, 1968.

Hanley, T. A., and R. D. Taber. "Selective plant species inhibition by elk and deer in three conifer communities in western Washington," *Forest Sci.* 26:97–107, 1980.

Hardin, G. "Tragedy of the commons," *Science* 162:1243–48, 1968.

Harris, L. D. *The Fragmented Forest: Island Biogeography Theory and the Preservation of Biotic Diversity.* Univ. of Chicago Press, Chicago, 1984.

Hart, J. L. *Pacific Fishes of Canada.* Fisheries Research Board of Canada, Ottawa, 1973. (Revision of *Fishes of the Pacific Coast of Canada,* Clemens and Wilby, 1961).

Hoham, R. "Laboratory and field studies on snow algae of the Pacific Northwest." Ph.D. diss., Univ. of Washington, 1971.

IBP Coniferous Forest Biome Project. "Ecosystem analysis," unpub. proposal, Internat'l Biological Program, Univ. of Washington, 1972.

Johnson, D. "Air pollution and the distribution of corticolous lichens in Seattle, Washington," *Northwest Science* 53:257–63, 1979.

Jones, G. N. *A Botanical Survey of the Olympic Peninsula, Washington.* Univ. of Washington Publ. in Biology 5, 1936.

Kane, P. "Wanderings of an artist." In *Masterworks of Canadian Authors,* vol. 71. Radisson Society of Canada, Toronto, 1925.

Keen, F. P. *Insect Enemies of Western Forests.* U.S. Dept. of Agriculture Misc. Publ. 273, 1952.

Kozloff, E. N. *Seashore Life of the North Pacific Coast: An Illustrated Guide to Northern California, Oregon, Washington, and British Columbia.* Univ. of Washington Press, Seattle, 1983.

Kruckeberg, A. R. "Plant life on serpentine and other ferromagnesian rocks in northwestern North America," *Syesis* 2:15–114, 1969.

Kruckeberg, A. R. *Gardening with Native Plants of the Pacific Northwest: An Illustrated Guide.* Univ. of Washington Press, Seattle, 1982.

La Chappelle, E. *The ABC of Avalanche Safety.* Colorado Outdoor Sports Co., 1970.

Larrison, E. J. *Washington Mammals: Their Habits, Identification, and Distribution.* Seattle Audubon Society, 1970.

Larrison, E. J., and K. G. Sonnenberg. *Washington Birds: Their Location and Identification.* Seattle Audubon Society, 1968.

Lawton, E. *Moss Flora of the Pacific Northwest.* Hattori Botanical Laboratory, Nichinan, Japan, 1971.

Leopold, A. *A Sand County Almanac.* Oxford Univ. Press, New York, 1987.

LeWarne, C. P. *Washington State.* Univ. of Washington Press, Seattle, 1986.

MacArthur, R. H. "Population ecology of some warblers of north-eastern coniferous forests," *Ecology* 39:599–619, 1958.

McKee, B. *Cascadia: The Geologic Evolution of the Pacific Northwest.* McGraw-Hill Book Co., New York, 1972.

Macior, L. W. "The pollination ecology of *Pedicularis* on Mount Rainier," *Amer. J. of Botany* 60:863–71, 1973.

Mackin, J. H. "Glacial geology of the Snoqualmie-Cedar area, Washington," *J. of Geology* 49:449–81, 1941.

Mackin, J. H., and A. S. Cary. *Origin of Cascade Landscapes.* Information Circ. 41, Div. of Mines and Geology, State Dept. of Conservation, Olympia, WA, 1965.

Markham, J. W. "Vertical distribution of epiphytes on the stipe of *Nereocystis luetkeana* (Mertens) Postels and Ruprecht," *Syesis* 2:227–40, 1969.

Martin, P. S., and H. E. Wright. *Pleistocene Extinctions: A Search for a Cause.* Yale Univ. Press, New Haven, 1967.

Maser, C. "Black bear damage to Douglas Fir in Oregon," *Murrelet* 48:34, 1967.

Mathews, D. *Cascade-Olympic Natural History: A Trailside Reference.* Raven Editions (Audubon Soc.), Portland, OR, 1988.

Menzies, A. *Menzies' Journal of Vancouver's Voyage: April to October 1792.* Archives of British Columbia, Memoir No. 5, 1923.

Meeuse, B. J. D. *The Story of Pollination.* Ronald Press, New York, 1961.

Morwood, W. *Traveller in a Vanished Landscape.* Clarkson H. Potter, New York, 1973.

Moziño, J. *Noticias de Nutka.* Ed. by Iris H. Wilson. Univ. of Washington Press, Seattle, 1970.

Nadkarni, N. "Biomass and mineral capital of epiphytes in an *Acer macrophyllum* community of a temperate moist coniferous forest, Olympic Peninsula, Washington," *Canadian J. of Botany* 62:2223–28, 1984.

Newcomb, R. C. "Hypothesis for the periglacial 'fissure polygon' origin of the Tenino Mounds, Thurston County, Washington," *Newsletter*, Geological Society of Oregon County (abst.) 4:182, 1940.

Noson, L. L., A. Quamar, and G. W. Thorsen. "Washington State earthquake hazards." Washington Div. of Geology and Earth Resources Info. Circ. 85, State Dept. of Natural Resources, Olympia, 1988.

Pacific Northwest River Basins Commission. *Puget Sound and Adjacent Waters.* Appendix III: "Hydrology and Natural Environment"; Appendix XII: "Flood Control." Water Quality Control, Puget Sound Task Force, 1970.

Peattie, D. C. *A Natural History of Western Trees.* Houghton Mifflin, Boston, 1953.

Pellmyr, O., and J. M. Patt. "Function of olfactory and visual stimuli in pollination of *Lysichiton americanum* (Araceae) by a staphylinid beetle," *Madrono* 33:47–54, 1986.

Penman, H. L. "The water cycle." In *The Biosphere*, pp. 39–45. A Scientific American Book. W. H. Freeman and Co., San Francisco, 1970.

Phillips, E. L. "Weather highlights in the Pacific Northwest," *Weatherwise* 15:75–81, 1962.

Phillips, E. L. "Climate of Washington." In *Climates of the States.* Government Printing Office, Washington, D.C., 1965.

Phillips, E. L. "Washington climate" [King, Kitsap, Mason, Pierce Counties]. College of Agriculture, Cooperative Ext. Ser., Pullman, WA, 1968.

Phillips, R. C. "Ecological life history of *Zostera marina* L. (eelgrass) in Puget Sound." Ph.D. diss., Univ. of Washington, Seattle, 1972.

Porter, S., ed. *Guidebook for Field Conference. J. Pacific Northwest*, pp. 1–108. International Assoc. for Quaternary Research, Seventh Cong. Nebraska Academy of Science, Lincoln, 1965.

Post, A., and E. La Chappelle. *Glacier Ice.* The Mountaineers, Seattle, 1971.

Raven, P. "Why are bird-visited flowers predominantly red?" *Evolution* 26:674, 1972.

Ricketts, E. F., and J. Calvin. *Between Pacific Tides.* 4th ed. (Revised by J. W. Hedgpeth). Stanford Univ. Press, Stanford, 1968.

Rigg, G. B. *The Peat Resources of Washington.* Bull. No. 44, Div. of Mines and Geology, State Dept. of Conservation, Olympia, WA, 1958.

Ritchie, A. M. "The erosional origin of the Mima mounds of southwest Washington," *J. of Geology* 61:41–50, 1953.

Rothacher, J., C. T. Dyrness, and R. L. Fredriksen. *Hydrologic and Related Characteristics of Three Small Watersheds in the Oregon Cascades.* Pac. Northwest Forest and Range Experiment Station, U.S. Forest Service, Corvallis, OR, 1967.

Scheffer, T. H. "Mountain beavers in the Pacific Northwest: Their habits, economic status and control." U.S. Dept. of Agriculture Farmer's Bull. 1598, Washington, D.C., 1929.

Scheffer, T. H. "Spring incidence of damage to forest trees by certain mammals," *Murrelet* 33:38–41, 1952.

Scheffer, Victor B. "The mystery of the Mima mounds," *Scientific Monthly* 65:283–94, 1947.

Scheffer, V. B. "The killer whale." Pacific Search Leaflet No. 67–8, 1967.

Scheffer, V. B. "Marine mammals." In *Washington Environmental Atlas,* p. 52. U.S. Army Corps of Engineers, 1975.

Scheffer, V. B., and R. Robinson. "A limnological study of Lake Washington," *Ecological Monographs* 9:95–143, 1939.

Scheffer, V. B., and J. W. Slipp. "The whales and dolphins of Washington State with a key to the cetaceans of the west coast of North America," *Amer. Midland Naturalist* 39:257–337, 1948.

Schultz, L. P. "Treasures of the Pacific." In *The Book of Fishes,* ed. J. O. LaGorce, pp. 219–62. National Geographic Society, 1939.

Schultz, L. P. "Fishing in Pacific Coast Streams." In *The Book of Fishes,* ed. J. O. LaGorce, pp. 263–94. National Geographic Society, 1939.

Smith, C. C. "Interspecific competition in the genus of tree squirrels *Tamiasciurus.*" Ph.D. diss., Univ. of Washington, Seattle, 1965.

Smith, L. S. "The Pacific salmon's long voyage." Pacific Search Leaflet No. 67-22, 1967.

Snaveley, P. D., Jr., and H. C. Wagner. "Tertiary geologic history of western Oregon and Washington." Report of Investigation No. 22, State Dept. of Conservation, Olympia, WA, 1963.

Stewart, H. *Cedar: Tree of Life to the Northwest Coast Indians.* Douglas & McIntyre, Vancouver, B.C.; Univ. of Washington Press, Seattle, 1984.

Stiles, E. W. "Bird community structure in alder forests." Ph.D. diss., Univ. of Washington, Seattle, 1973.

Strickland, R. M. *The Fertile Fjord: Plankton in Puget Sound.* Washington Sea Grant and Univ. of Washington Press, Seattle, 1983.

Sturman, W. A. "Description and analysis of breeding habits of the chickadees, *Parus atricapillus* and *P. rufescens,*" *Ecology* 49:418–31, 1968.

Sudworth, G. B. *Forest Trees of the Pacific Slope.* U.S. Dept. of Agriculture, 1908.

Sumner, F. B. "Genetic, distributional and evolutionary studies of the subspecies of deer mice (*Peromyscus*)," *Biblio. Genetica* 9:1–106, 1932.

Swan, J. G. *The Northwest Coast, or, Three Years' Residence in Washington Territory.* Univ. of Washington Press, Seattle, 1972. (Originally pub. in 1857.)

Thorson, G. W., ed. "The Puget lowland earthquakes of 1949 and 1965." Div. of Geology and Earth Resources Info. Circ. 81, State Dept. of Natural Resources, Olympia, WA, 1986.

Thorson, R. "Ice-sheet glaciation of the Puget Lowland, Washington, during the Vashon Stade (Late Pleistocene)," *Quaternary Research* 13: 303–21, 1980.

Waggoner, P. E., and I. Zelitch. "Transpiration and the stomata of leaves," *Science* 150:1413–20, 1965.

Washburn, A. L. "Mima mounds: An evaluation of proposed origins with special reference to the Puget lowland." Div. of Geology and Earth Resources Report 29, State Dept. of Natural Resources, Olympia, WA, 1988.

Went, F. "Air pollution," *Scientific American* 192:63–71.

White, L., Jr. "The historical roots of our ecologic crisis," *Science* 155:1203–07, 1967.

Whittaker, R. H. *Communities and Ecosystems.* 2d ed. Macmillan, New York, 1975.

Wilkes, Charles. *Narrative of the United States Exploring Expedition During the Years 1838, 1839, 1840, 1841, 1842.* Vol. 4. Lea and Blanchard, Philadelphia, 1845.

For Further Reading

Geology

Alt, D. D., and D. W. Hyndman. *Roadside Geology of Washington.* Mountain Press Publishing Co., Missoula, MT, 1984.

Anon. *The Alpine Lakes: Environmental Geology.* Dept. of Geological Sciences, Univ. of Washington, Seattle, 1972.

Anon. *The Nisqually Delta.* Dept. of Geological Sciences, Univ. of Washington, Seattle, 1971.

Campbell, C. D. "Introduction to Washington geology and resources." Circ. No. 22R. Washington Geological Survey, Olympia, WA, 1962.

Clark, T. H., and C. W. Stern. *Geological Evolution of North America.* Ronald Press, New York, 1968.

Cornwall, I. *Ice Ages: Their Nature and Effects.* Humanities Press, New York, 1970.

Easterbrook, D. J. *Geology and Geomorphology of Western Whatcom County.* Western Washington State College, Bellingham, 1970.

Easterbrook, D. J., and D. A. Rahm. *Landforms of Washington: The Geologic Environment.* Western Washington State College, Bellingham, 1970.

Galster, R. W. *Engineering Geology in Washington.* Washington Div. of Geology and Earth Resources Bulletin 78, vols. 1 and 2. Dept. of Natural Resources, Olympia, 1989.

Harris, S. L. *Fire and Ice: The Cascade Volcanoes.* Rev. ed. The Mountaineers, Seattle, 1980.

Livingston, V. E., Jr. "Fossils in Washington." Information Circ. No. 33, State Dept. of Conservation (Nat. Resources), Olympia, WA, 1959.

Livingston, V. E., Jr. "Geological history and rocks and minerals of Washington." Information Circ. No. 45, State Dept. of Natural Resources, Olympia, WA, 1969.

Porter, S. C. *Pleistocene Geology of the East-Central Cascade Range, Washington.* Guidebook for Third Pacific Coast Friends of the Pleistocene Field Conference, Seattle, 1969.

Climate and Weather

Anderson, B. R. *Weather in the West from the Midcontinent to the Pacific.* Amer. West Publishing Co., Palo Alto, CA, 1975.

Anon. *Climates of the States.* Government Printing Office, Washington, D.C., 1941.

Phillips, E. L. "Washington climate for these counties: King, Kitsap, Mason, Pierce." College of Agriculture, Cooperative Extension Service, Pullman, WA, 1968.

Schroeder, M. J., and C. C. Buck. *Fire Weather: A Guide for Application of Meteorological Information to Forest Fire Control Operations.* U.S. Forest Service Agricultural Hndbk. 360, 1970.

Natural History

General

British Columbia Provincial Museum. Handbook Series Nos. 1–24. Dept. of Education, B.C. Provincial Museum, Victoria.

Pyle, Robert M. *Wintergreen: Rambles in a Ravaged Landscape.* Scribners, New York, 1986. A sadly beautiful account of a battered western Washington ecosystem.

Schwartz, S. *Cascade Companion.* Pacific Search Books, Seattle, WA, 1976.

Schwartz, S. *Nature in the Northwest: An Introduction to the Natural History and Ecology of the Northwestern United States from the Rockies to the Pacific.* Photographs by Robert and Ira Spring. Prentice-Hall, Englewood Cliffs, NJ, 1983. A Spectrum Book.

Plants

Arno, S. F., and R. P. Hammerly. *Northwest Trees.* The Mountaineers, Seattle, 1977.

Arno, S. F., and R. P. Hammerly. *Timberline: Mountain and Arctic Forest Frontiers.* The Mountaineers, Seattle, 1984.

Barbour, M., and D. W. Billings, eds. *North American Terrestrial Vegetation.* Cambridge Univ. Press, New York and Cambridge, 1988. Chapter 4, by Jerry Franklin, "Pacific Northwest Forests," is must reading for understanding Northwest forest ecology.

Benoliel, D. *Northwest Foraging: A Guide to Edible Plants of the Pacific Northwest.* Signpost Publications, Seattle, WA, 1974.

Brockman, C. Frank. *Trees of North America: A Guide to Field Identification.* New York: Golden Press, 1979.

Clark, L. J. *Lewis Clark's Field Guides to Wildflowers of the Pacific Northwest.* Nos. 1–6. Gray's Publishers, Sidney, B.C.

Corner, E. J. H. *The Life of Plants.* Mentor Books, The New American Library, New York, 1968 (1964).

Crawford, V. "Wetland plants of King County and the Puget Sound lowlands." King County Planning Division, Seattle, WA, 1981.

Ervin, Keith. *Fragile Majesty: The Battle for North America's Last Great Forest.* The Mountaineers, Seattle, 1989.

Franklin, J. F., K. Cromack, W. Denison, A. McKee, C. Maser, J. Sedell, F. Swanson, and G. Juday. *Ecological Characteristics of Old Growth Douglas-Fir Forests.* U.S. Forest Service Gen. Tech. Report PNW-118, Corvallis, WA, 1981.

Franklin, J. F., W. H. Moir, M. A. Hemstrom, S. E. Green, and B. G. Smith. *The Forest Communities of Mount Rainier National Park.* Scientific Monograph Series No. 19. U.S. National Park Service, Washington, D.C., 1988.

Gleason, H. A., and A. Cronquist. *The Natural Geography of Plants.* Columbia Univ. Press, N.Y., 1964.

Griffiths, A. J. F., and F. R. Ganders. *Wildflower Genetics: A Field Guide for British Columbia and the Pacific Northwest.* Flight Press, Vancouver, B.C., 1983.

Hitchcock, C. L., and A. Cronquist. *Flora of the Pacific Northwest.* Univ. of Washington Press, Seattle, 1973.

Kozloff, E. N. *Plants and Animals of the Pacific Northwest: An Illustrated Guide to the Natural History of Western Oregon, Washington, and British Columbia.* Unvi. of Washington Press, Seattle and London, 1976.

Lyons, C. P. *Trees, Shrubs, and Flowers to Know in Washington.* J. M. Dent & Sons, Ltd., Vancouver, B.C., 1956.

McKenny, M., and D. E. Stuntz. *The Savory Wild Mushroom.* Univ. of Washington Press, Seattle, 1971. (Revised and enlarged by Joseph Ammirati, 1987.)

Meeuse, B. J. D., and S. Morris. *The Sex Life of Flowers.* Facts on File, New York, 1984.

Phillips, R. C., and C. P. McCoy, eds. *Handbook of Seagrass Biology: An Ecosystem Perspective.* Garland STPM Press, New York, 1980.

Proctor, M., and P. Yeo. *The Pollination of Flowers.* Taplinger Publishing Co., New York, 1972.

Raven, P. H., F. R. Evert, and S. E. Eickhorn. *The Biology of Plants.* Fourth ed. Worth Publishers, Inc., New York.

Taylor, R. J. *Northwest Weeds.* Mountain Press Pub. Co., Missoula, 1990.

Taylor, R. J., and G. W. Douglas. *Mountain Wild Flowers of the Pacific Northwest.* Binfords & Mort, Portland, OR, 1975.

Taylor, T. M. C. *The Ferns and Fern-Allies of British Columbia.* Handbook No. 12, Dept. of Education, British Columbia Provincial Museum, Victoria, 1956.

Taylor, T. M. C. *Pacific Northwest Ferns and Their Allies.* Univ. of Toronto Press, Toronto, 1970.

Vitt, D., J. Marsh, and R. Bovey. *Mosses, Lichens, and Ferns of Northwest North America: A Photographic Field Guide.* Univ. of Washington Press, Seattle, 1988.

Waaland, J. R. *Common Seaweeds of the Pacific Coast.* Pacific Search Press, Seattle, 1977.

Weinmann, F., M. Boule, K. Brunner, J. Malek, V. Yoshino. *Wetland Plants of the Pacific Northwest.* U.S. Army Corps of Engineers (Seattle District), No. 595-045. U.S. Government Printing Office, Washington, D.C., 1985.

Zwinger, A., and B. E. Willard. *Land Above the Trees: A Guide to the American Alpine Tundra.* Harper and Row, New York, 1972.

Animals

Anon. *Washington State Shellfish.* Washington Dept. of Fisheries, Olympia, WA, 1971.

Anon. *Pacific Northwest Marine Fishes.* Washington Dept. of Fisheries, Olympia, WA, 1970.

Black, H. C., ed. *Wildlife and Forest Management in the Pacific Northwest.* Forest Research Lab., Corvallis, OR, 1974.

Brown, F. R., ed. *Management of Wildlife and Fish Habitats in Forests of Western Oregon and Washington.* Pt. 1. Pac. Northwest Region, U.S. Forest Service, Portland, 1985.

Chauvin, R. *The World of an Insect.* McGraw-Hill (World Univ. Library), New York, 1967.

Childerhose, R. J., and M. Trim. *Pacific Salmon and Steelhead Trout.* Douglas & McIntyre, Vancouver, B.C.; Univ. of Washington Press, Seattle, 1979.

Ford, A., ed. *Audubon's Animals: The Quadrupeds of North America.* Studio Pubs, T. Y. Crowell, New York, 1951.

Furniss, R. L., and V. M. Carolin. *Western Forest Insects.* U.S. Forest Service Misc. Pub. 273, 1952.

Harper, A. B. *The Banana Slug: A Close Look at a Giant Forest Slug of Western North America.* Bay Leaves Press, Aptos, CA, 1988.

Hunn, E. N. *Birding in Seattle and King County.* Trailside Series. Seattle Audubon Society, 1982.

Ingles, L. G. *Mammals of the Pacific States.* Stanford Univ. Press, Stanford, 1965.

Kozloff, E. N. *Plants and Animals of the Pacific Northwest: An Illustrated Guide to the Natural History of Western Oregon, Washington, and British Columbia.* Univ. of Washington Press, Seattle and London, 1976.

Kritzman, E. B. *Little Mammals of the Pacific Northwest.* Pacific Search Press, Seattle, 1977.

Larrison, E. J. *Washington Mammals: Their Habits, Identification, and Distribution.* Seattle Audubon Society, 1970.

Maser, C., B. R. Mate, J. F. Franklin, and C. T. Dyrness. *Natural History of Oregon Coast Mammals.* U.S. Forest Service Gen. Tech. Report PNW-133, Corvallis, 1981.

Meslow, E. C., C. Maser, and J. Verner. "Old-growth Forests as Wildlife Habitat," *Transactions,* North American Wildlife Natural Resources Conference, 46:329–44, 1981.

Poelker, R. J., and H. D. Hartwell. "Black bear of Washington." *Biological Bull.* No. 14, Washington State Game Dept., Olympia, 1973.

Potts, M. K., and R. K. Grater. *Mammals of Mount Rainier National Park.* Mount Rainier Natural History Assoc., Longmire, WA, 1949.

Pyle, R. M. *Watching Washington Butterflies.* Seattle Audubon Society, 1974.

Runham, N. W., and P. J. Hunter. *Terrestrial Slugs.* Hutchinson, London, 1970.

Somerton, D., and C. Murray. *Field Guide to the Fish of Puget Sound and the Northwest Coast.* Washington Sea Grant and Univ. of Washington Press, Seattle, 1976.

Swan, L. A., and C. S. Papp. *The Common Insects of North America.* Harper and Row, New York, 1972.

Wright, S. G. *The Origin and Migration of Washington's Chinook and Coho Salmon.* Information Booklet No. 1. Washington State Dept. of Fisheries, Olympia, 1968.

Yocum, C. F. *Waterfowl and Their Food Plants in Washington.* Univ. of Washington Press, Seattle, 1951.

Ecology and Natural History

Carson, R. L. *The Edge of the Sea.* Houghton Mifflin, Boston, 1955.

Edmondson, W. T. *The Uses of Ecology: Lake Washington and Beyond.* Univ. of Washington Press, Seattle, 1991.

Franklin, J. F., K. Cromack, W. Denison, A. McKee, C. Maser, J. Sedell, F. Swanson, and G. Juday. "Ecological characteristics of old growth Douglas-fir forests." U.S. Forest Service Gen. Tech. Report PNW-118, Corvallis, OR, 1981.

Goldman, C., and A. J. Horne. *Limnology.* McGraw-Hill Book Co., New York, 1983.

Maser, C., and J. M. Trappe, eds. "The seen and unseen world of the fallen tree." U.S. Forest Service Gen. Tech. Report PNW-164, Corvallis, OR, 1984.

Trappe, J. M., J. F. Franklin, R. F. Tarrant, and G. M. Hansen. "Biology of alder." Pacific Northwest Forest and Range Experiment Station, Forest Service, Portland, OR, 1968.

Watts, M. T. *Reading the Landscape: An Adventure in Ecology.* Macmillan, New York, 1957.

Whitney, S. *A Sierra Club Naturalist's Guide: The Pacific Northwest.* Sierra Book Clubs, San Francisco, 1989.

Indians

Claiborne, R. *The First Americans.* Time-Life Books, New York, 1973.

Cole, D. *Captured Heritage: The Scramble for Northwest Coast Artifacts.* Univ. of Washington Press, Seattle, 1985.

Collins, J. M. *Valley of the Spirits: The Upper Skagit Indians of Western Washington.* Univ. of Washington Press, Seattle, 1974.

Daugherty, R. D. "Early man in Washington." Information Circ. No. 32. Dept. of Conservation (Natural Resources), Olympia, WA, 1959.

Drucker, P. *Cultures of the North Pacific Coast.* Chandler, San Francisco, 1965.

Gunther, E. *Indian Life on the Northwest Coast of North America as Seen by the Early Explorers and Fur Traders during the Last Decade of the Eighteenth Century.* Univ. of Chicago Press, Chicago, 1972.

Haeberlin, H. K., and E. Gunther. *Indians of Puget Sound.* Publ. in Anthropology 4, Univ. of Washington Press, Seattle, 1930.

Jennings, J. D. *Prehistory of North America.* 3rd ed. Mayfield Pub., Mountain View, CA, 1989.

Kirk, Ruth. *Exploring Washington Archaeology.* Univ. of Washington Press, Seattle, 1978.

Kirk, R. *Tradition and Change on the Northwest Coast.* Univ. of Washington Press, Seattle; Douglas & McIntyre, Vancouver and Toronto, 1986.

McFeat, T. F. S. *Indians of the North Pacific Coast.* McClelland and Stewart, Toronto, 1966. (Reprinted 1971, Univ. of Washington Press, Seattle.)

Ruby, R. H., and J. A. Brown. *Indians of the Pacific Northwest: A History.* Univ. of Oklahoma Press, Norman, 1981.

Smith, A. H. "The Indians of Washington." In *Washington Territorial Centennial Number.* Research Studies of the State College of Washington 121:85–113, 1953.

Taylor, H. C., Jr., and G. F. Grabert. *Western Washington Indian Socio-economics: Papers in Honor of Angelo Anastasio.* Western Washington Univ., Bellingham, 1984.

Underhill, R. *Indians of the Pacific Northwest.* Indian Life and Customs No. 5, Educational Div., U.S. Office of Indian Affairs, Washington, D.C., 1944.

Waterman, T. T. *Notes on the Ethnology of the Indians of Puget Sound.* Indian Notes and Monographs No. 59, Museum of the American Indian, Heye Foundation, New York, 1973.

Early Western Exploration and Settlement

Anderson, B. *Surveyor of the Sea: The Life and Voyages of Captain George Vancouver.* Univ. of Washington Press, Seattle, 1960.

Binns, A. *Sea in the Forest.* Doubleday, Garden City, N.Y., 1953.

Chasan, D. J. *The Water Link: A History of Puget Sound as a Resource.* Washington Sea Grant and Univ. of Washington Press, Seattle, 1981.

Henry, J. F. *Early Maritime Artists of the Pacific Northwest.* Univ. of Washington Press, Seattle, 1984.

McCurdy, J. G. *By Juan de Fuca Strait: Pioneers Along the Northwest Edge of the Continent.* Binfords and Mort, Portland, OR, 1937.

Manning, H. *Walking the Beach to Bellingham.* The Mountaineers, Seattle, 1987.

Meany, E. S. *Vancouver's Discovery of Puget Sound.* Macmillan, New York, 1907.

Meany, E. S. *History of the State of Washington.* Macmillan, New York, 1924.

Morgan, M. *Puget's Sound: A Narrative of Early Tacoma and the Southern Sound.* Univ. of Washington Press, Seattle, 1981.

Newcombe, C. F., ed. "Menzies' Journal of Vancouver's Voyage: April to October 1792." Archives of British Columbia Museum, Memoir No. 5. Provincial Library, Victoria, B.C., 1923.

Winthrop, T. *The Canoe and the Saddle, or Klallam and Klickitat.* John H. Williams, Tacoma, 1913.

Marine Environments

Carefoot, T. *Pacific Seashores: A Guide to Intertidal Ecology.* Univ. of Washington Press, Seattle; Douglas & McIntyre, Vancouver, 1977.

Carson, R. L. *The Edge of the Sea.* Houghton Mifflin, Boston, 1955.

Chasan, D. J. *The Water Link: A History of Puget Sound as a Resource.* Washington Sea Grant and Univ. of Washington Press, Seattle, 1981.

Collias, E. E., and A. C. Duxbury. *Bibliography of Literature on Puget Sound Marine Environment.* Washington Sea Grant Book WSG 71-6. Div. of Marine Resources, Univ. of Washington, Seattle, 1971.

Cousteau, J. Y. *The Living Sea.* Harper and Row, New York, 1963.

Gotshall, D. W. *Pacific Coast Inshore Fishes.* Sea Challengers, Los Osos, CA, 1981.

Hart, J. L. *Pacific Fishes of Canada.* Fisheries Research Board of Canada, Ottawa, 1973. (Revision of the 1961 book by Clemens and Wilby, *Fishes of the Pacific Coast of Canada.*)

Hewlett, S., and K. G. Hewlett. *Sea Life of the Pacific Northwest.* McGraw-Hill/Ryerson, Canada, 1976.

Phillips, R. C., and C. P. McRoy, eds. *Handbook of Seagrass Biology: An Ecosystem Perspective.* Garland STPM Press, New York and London, 1980.

Richter, Joanne. *State of the Sound, 1988 Report.* Puget Sound Water Quality Authority, Seattle, 1988.

Smith, L. S. *Living Shores of the Pacific Northwest.* Pacific Search Press, Seattle, 1976.

Somerton, D., and C. Murray. *Field Guide to the Fish of Puget Sound and the Northwest Coast.* Washington Sea Grant Publication, Seattle, 1976.

Wydoski, R. S., and R. R. Whitney. *Inland Fishes of Washington.* Univ. of Washington Press, Seattle, 1979.

Yates, S. *Marine Wildlife of Puget Sound, the San Juans, and the Strait of Georgia.* Globe Pequot Press, Chester, CN, 1988.

Freshwater Environment

Coal, G. A. *Textbook of Limnology.* Mosby, St. Louis, 1975.

Goldman, C., and A. J. Horne. *Limnology.* McGraw-Hill Book Co., New York, 1983.

Hynes, H. B. N. *The Ecology of Running Waters.* Univ. of Toronto Press, Toronto, 1970.

Wolcott, E. E. *Lakes of Washington.* Vol. 1: *Western Washington.* Water Supply Bulletin 14, Division of Water Resources, Olympia, WA, 1961.

Conservation

Calder, N. *Eden Was No Garden: An Enquiry into the Environment of Man.* Holt, Rinehart, Winston, New York, 1967.

Caldwell, L. K. *In Defense of Earth.* Indiana Univ. Press, Bloomington, 1972.

Darling, F. F., and J. P. Milton, eds. *Future Environments of North America.* Natural History Press, Garden City, NY, 1966.

Dasman, R. F. *The Last Horizon*. Macmillan Co., New York, 1963.

Dasman, R. F. *Environmental Conservation*. Wiley, New York, 1968.

Hardin, G. *Exploring New Ethics for Survival: The Voyage of the Spaceship Beagle*. Viking, New York, 1972.

Lawrence, R. D. *The Place in the Forest*. M. Joseph, London, 1967.

Rolston, H., III. *Philosophy Gone Wild: Essays in Environmental Ethics*. Prometheus Books, Buffalo, NY, 1986.

Sears, P. B. *Land Beyond the Forest*. Prentice-Hall, Englewood Cliffs, NJ, 1969.

Shepard, P., and D. McKinley, eds. *The Subversive Science: Essays Toward an Ecology of Man*. Houghton Mifflin, Boston, 1969.

Periodicals

Audubon. National Audubon Society, New York.

Douglasia. Newsletter of Washington Native Plant Society. Dept. of Botany, Univ. of Washington, Seattle, 1976–.

Natural History. Journal of the American Museum of Natural History, New York.

Pacific Northwest. (Formerly Pacific Search Magazine.) Nature and Man in the Pacific Northwest. Pacific Search Press, Seattle.

Trip Guides

Alt, D. D., and D. W. Hyndman. *Roadside Geology of Washington*. Mountain Press Publishing Co., Missoula, MT, 1984.

Darvill, F. T., Jr. *North Cascades Highway Guide*. Pacific Northwest National Parks and Forests Assn., Mount Vernon, WA, 1986.

The Dittmar Family. *Visitors' Guide to Ancient Forests of Western Washington*. The Wilderness Society. The Mountaineers, Seattle, 1989.

Kirk, R. *Exploring Mount Rainier*. Univ. of Washington Press, Seattle, 1968.

Livingston, V. E. "A geologic trip along Snoqualmie, Swauk, and Stevens Pass highways." Information Circ. 38. Division of Mines and Geology, Dept. of Natural Resources, Olympia, WA, 1963.

McKee, B. "Washington trip guides." Appen. C in *Cascadia: The Geologic Evolution of the Pacific Northwest*. McGraw-Hill, New York, 1972.

Manning, H. *Footsore 1. Walks and Hikes around Puget Sound*. 3rd ed. The Mountaineers, Seattle, 1988.

Morgan, M. *Puget's Sound: A Narrative of Early Tacoma and the Southern Sound*. Univ. of Washington Press, Seattle, 1979.

Porter, S. C., ed. *Guidebook for Field Conference J. Pacific Northwest*. Nebraska Academy of Sciences, Lincoln, 1965.

Scott, J. W., M. A. Reuling, and D. Bales. *Washington Public Shore Guide: Marine Waters*. Univ. of Washington Press, Seattle and London, 1986.

Shane, S. *Discovering Mount St. Helens: A Guide to the National Volcanic Monument*. Univ. of Washington Press, Seattle, 1985.

Whitney, S. R. *A Field Guide to the Cascades and Olympics*. The Mountaineers, Seattle, 1983.

Whitney, S. R. *Nature Walks in and around Seattle.* The Mountaineers, Seattle, 1987. (See also other hiking guides from the The Mountaineers.)

Wood, R. L. *Olympic Mountains Trail Guide: National Park and National Forest.* The Mountaineers, Seattle, 1984.

Maps and Atlases

Kimerling, A. J., and P. L. Jackson, eds. *Atlas of the Pacific Northwest.* 7th ed. Oregon State Univ. Press, Corvallis, 1985.

Lake Washington Ship Canal and Lake Washington, Washington. Nautical Chart 18447. National Oceanic and Atmospheric Admin., U.S. Dept. of Commerce, Washington, D.C., 1984.

Puget Sound Environmental Atlas. Vols. 1 and 2. U.S. Army Corps of Engineers, Seattle Dist.

Scott, J. W., and R. L. DeLorme. *Historical Atlas of Washington.* Univ. of Oklahoma Press, Norman, 1988.

Washington Atlas and Gazetteer. DeLorme Mapping Company, Freeport, ME, 1988.

Directories

Nature Guide. 1989. P.O. Box 1015, Tacoma, Washington 98401. (Lists natural history contacts for Puget Sound and worldwide.)

Institute for Environmental Studies, University of Washington, Seattle, Washington 98195. (206) 543-1812 (Contact for names of conservation groups.)

Washington Environmental Council, 4516 University Way, NE, Seattle, Washington 98105. (Contact for names of conservation groups.)

Credits

The author and the publisher give special thanks to the contributing photographers and artists for their efforts on behalf of the book and their sustained interest in the project.

Also gratefully acknowledged are the photographs, charts, maps, and diagrams courtesy of the following:

Preface and Introduction

p. x: Screens prepared by Robert Hutchins.

p. xiv: Washington State Dept. of Natural Resources.

p. xvi: LANDSAT photo from EROS Data Center, U.S. Geological Survey; mosaic prepared by Instructional Media Services, Univ. of Washington.

p. xxii, *right*: Special Collections Division, Univ. of Washington Libraries.

Chapter 1

p. 5: Washington State Dept. of Ecology oblique aerial, June 6, 1977.

pp. 10–11: Maps from Snavely and Wagner, "Tertiary geologic history of western Oregon and Washington," Report of Investigation, No. 22, 1963, State Dept. of Conservation, Olympia.

p. 14, *left*: From Roland Tabor, *Guide to the Geology of the Olympic National Park*, Univ. of Washington Press, Seattle, 1975, fig. 58; *above right*: Delano Horizons, Inc., Portland.

p. 16, *bottom*: Delano Horizons, Inc., photo no. 57669.

p. 17, *bottom*: From Franklin and Dyrness, *Natural Vegetation of Oregon and Washington*, USFS PNW-8, 1973.

p. 18: Washington State Dept. of Natural Resources, Olympia.

p. 19, *top right*: *The Seattle Times*, April 13, 1949.

p. 25, *top right*: After C. Barnowsky in E. Leopold, "An ecological history of old prairie areas in southwestern Washington." *Arboretum Bulletin* (Univ. of Washington) 50, p.15, 1987.

p. 31: From A. L. Washburn, "Mima mounds," Division of Geology and Earth Resources Report 29, Washington State Dept. of Natural Resources, Olympia, 1988.

Chapter 2

p. 38, *bottom*: *The Seattle Times*, January 3, 1988.

p. 39: From *Arboretum Bulletin* (Univ. of Washington) 49(2), pp. 17, 18, 20, 1986.

p. 40: From *An Introduction to the Forest Soils of the Douglas Fir Region of the*

Pacific Northwest. College of Forest Resources, Univ. of Washington, 1957, fig. IV-2.

p. 44: *The Seattle Post-Intelligencer*, March 5, 1989.

p. 47, *top*: *The Seattle Times*, January 5, 1989.

p. 49, *top right*: Washington State Game Dept., photo no. 807; *bottom*: Special Collection Division, Univ. of Washington Libraries, neg. no. 97.

p. 50, *top*: Washington State Historical Society, Tacoma, photo no. 21229; *bottom left*: *Seattle Post-Intelligencer* Collection, Museum of History and Industry, Seattle.

p. 51: *Seattle Post Intelligencer* Collection, March 5, 1961, Museum of History and Industry, Seattle.

p. 53: *The Seattle Post-Intelligencer*, January 13, 1988.

p. 55: *The Seattle Times*, December 13, 1985.

p. 56, *top*: Washington State Dept. of Wildlife, Olympia, photo no. 3390; *bottom*: from A. C. Warner Collection, Special Collections Division, Univ. of Washington Libraries, neg. no. 349.

p. 57: Photo of northwest Everett, *The Seattle Times*, December 26, 1966.

p. 58: Type prepared by Robert Hutchins.

Chapter 3

p. 64: From R. Burns, *The Shape and Form of Puget Sound*, Univ. of Washington Press, 1985, p. 58.

p. 65: Office of Information Services, Univ. of Washington, Dept. of Oceanography photo no. S-16324-5A.

pp. 66–67, *center top*: Washington State Dept. of Parks and Recreation; *middle*: Washington State Dept. of Natural Resources.

pp. 68–69, *center*: Washington State Department of Parks and Recreation.

p. 71: From 1985 Tide Tables, West Coast of North and South America, National Oceanic and Atmospheric Admin., 1985.

pp. 72–73: *The Seattle Times*, February 2, 1960.

Chapter 4

p. 76, *top*: Washington Sea Grant Program, Univ. of Washington.

p. 78: Washington Sea Grant Program, Univ. of Washington.

p. 86: Drawing from R. Dahlgren et al., *The Families of the Monocotyledons: Structure, Evolution, and Taxonomy*, Springer-Verlag, Berlin, 1985, p. 317.

p. 92: Washington Sea Grant Program, Univ. of Washington.

pp. 95, 96–97: From Somerton and Murray, *Field Guide to Fishes of Puget Sound*, Univ. of Washington Press, 1976.

p. 103, *top and bottom*: Historical Society of Seattle and King County, Museum of History and Industry Photographic Archives, Seattle, neg. nos. 10593 and 23046.

p. 111, *bottom*: Washington State Dept. of Wildlife. .

p. 112: From M. Bigg, G. Ellis, J. Ford, and K. Balcomb, *Killer Whales*, Phantom Press & Publishers Inc., Nanaimo, B.C., 1987, p. 15.

p. 113: Courtesy Victor B. Scheffer.

Chapter 5

p. 116: From Franklin and Dyrness, *Natural Vegetation of Oregon and Washington*, USFS PNW-8, 1973, p. 80.

p. 120: From R. Platt, *Bioscience*, Van Nostrand Reinhold, New York, 1967.

p. 122: From Franklin and Dyrness, *Natural Vegetation of Oregon and Washington*, USFS PNW-8, 1973; prepared by Instructional Media Services, Univ. of Washington.

p. 124: From Nathaniel Portlock, *Voyage Round the World, 1789*, p. 226, Special Collections Division, Univ. of Washington Libraries.

pp. 128–29, *left*: From Franklin and Dyrness, *Natural Vegetation of Oregon and Washington*, USFS PNW-8, 1973, p. 52; *center and right*: Special Collections Division, Univ. of Washington Libraries, neg. nos. 8-K and 24E.

p. 133: Historical Society of Seattle and King County, McCurdy Collection no. 1644.

p. 139, *top*: U.S. Forest Service photo no. 00596; left: From Stephen Arno and Ramona Hammerly, *Northwest Trees*, 1977, reproduced with permission of The Mountaineers, Seattle, WA.

p. 146: Washington State Department of Wildlife.

p. 148: U.S. Forest Service photo.

pp. 151, 153: From Arno and Hammerly, *Northwest Trees*, with permission of The Mountaineers, Seattle.

p. 155: Washington State Dept. of Wildlife.

p. 160: From Arno and Hammerly, *Northwest Trees*, with permission of The Mountaineers, Seattle.

p. 165: Washington State Historical Society, Tacoma, photo no. 58204.

p. 184, *far left, bottom*: Washington State Historical Society, Tacoma, photo no. 27771.

p. 186: Historical Society of Seattle and King County, Museum of History and Industry Photographic Archives, neg. no. 23019.

p. 187: Brubaker Aerial Survey photo, 1927, Delano Horizons, Inc. Portland.

p. 188: From E. Reade Brown, ed., *Management of Wildlife and Fish Habitats in Forests of Western Oregon and Washington*, USFS PNW 6-F&WL-192, 1985, p. 174.

Chapter 6

p. 194: Washington State Dept. of Wildlife, photo no. 305.

p. 200: From *IBP Coniferous Forest Biome*, "Ecosystem analysis," Univ. of Washington, 1972, fig. 3.2.

p. 203: "Fort Vancouver" by Sir Henry Ware, ca. 1845; Special Collections Division, Univ. of Washington Libraries.

p. 206: Washington State Dept. of Wildlife.

p. 207: From Franklin and Dyrness, *Natural Vegetation of Oregon and Washington*, USFS PNW-8, 1973, p. 66.

p. 208: Weyerhaeuser Company Corporate Photograph.

p. 209: Washington State Dept. of Wildlife.

p. 212: Washington State Dept. of Wildlife.

pp. 214–15, *top*: Weyerhaeuser Company Corporate photograph.

p. 217: Washington State Dept. of Wildlife.

p. 222: Courtesy of Ingreth Deyrup-Olsen.

p. 225: Type prepared by Robert Hutchins.

pp. 226, 227, and 228, *top*: From Pest Leaflet, nos. 9, 21, and 31, Pacific Forest Research Center, Victoria, B.C.; prepared by Robert Hutchins.

p. 238: From E. Reade Brown, ed., *Management of Wildlife and Fish Habitats in Forests of Western Oregon and Washington*, USFS PNW 6 F&WL-192, 1985.

p. 241: From J. B. Bowles, "Ornithology of changing forest stands on the western slope of the Cascade Mountains in Central Washington," Master's thesis, Univ. of Washington, 1963.

p. 243, *left*: From *The Bremerton Sun*, Bremerton, WA.

Chapter 7

p. 249: From *The Alpine Lakes Environmental Geology*, Dept. of Geological Sciences, Univ. of Washington, 1972.

p. 250: From P. Dansereau, *Biogeography: An Ecological Perspective*, Ronald Press, New York, 1957, p. 162.

p. 251: From C. R. Goldman and A. J. Horne, *Limnology*, McGraw-Hill, New York, 1983, p. 16.

p. 253: Aerolist Photographers Inc., photo no. 75674–11

p. 254: Metro Library, Seattle.

p. 255: Washington State Dept. of Natural Resources.

p. 257, *top*: *The Seattle Times*, 1985; far right: From W. T. Edmondson and J. T. Lehman," The effects of change in the nutrient income on the condition of Lake Washington," *Limnology and Oceanography* 26(1), 1981, pp. 1–29; *bottom*: *The Seattle Times*, Nov. 15, 1981.

p. 258: Special Collections Division, Univ. of Washington Libraries, neg. nos. 10003 and 10004.

pp. 262–63: From Dave Beauchamp, unpublished data; type prepared by Robert Hutchins.

p. 263, *bottom*: Metro Library, Seattle.

p. 264, *top*: Aerolist Photographers Inc., photo no. 75319–12.

p. 265, *bottom left*: Special Collections Division, Univ. of Washington Libraries.

p. 266, *left*: Washington State Dept. of Wildlife, "Lakes of Washington," vol. 1; *right*: *IBP Coniferous Forest Biome*, "Ecosystem analysis," Univ. of Washington, 1972.

pp. 268–69: From Daniel Adams, "The paleoecology of two lakes in Western Washington," Master's thesis, Univ. of Washington, 1973.

pp. 274–75: From G. B. Rigg, *The Peat Resources of Washington*, Bull. 44, Div. of Mines and Geology, State Dept. of Conservation, Olympia, 1958.

p. 278, *bottom*: From E. Reade Brown, ed., *Management of Wildlife and*

Fish Habitats in Forests of Western Oregon and Washington, USFS PNW 6-F&WL-192, 1985, p. 59.

p. 279, *below left and right*: Washington State Dept. of Natural Resources/Heritage, neg. nos. 14, 9A.

pp. 280–81: From E. Reade Brown, ed., *Management of Wildlife and Fish Habitats in Forests of Western Washington and Oregon*, USFS PNW 6-F&WL-192, 1985, p. 83.

p. 283: Washington State Dept. of Wildlife.

p. 284: Washington State Dept. of Natural Resources, aerial photo no. 10-38-250, T17N R1E, sec. 32.

p. 287, maps: From Frank Lang, "A study of vegetation change on the gravelly prairies of Pierce and Thurston counties, Western Washington," Master's thesis, Univ. of Washington, 1961.

p. 289, *bottom*: From R. Thorson, "Ice sheet glaciation of the Puget Lowland, Washington, during the Vashon Stade (late Pleistocene)," *Quaternary Research*, vol. 13.

p. 293, *top and bottom*: From A. L. Washburn, "Mima mounds: An evaluation of proposed origins with special reference to the Puget lowland," Div. of Geology and Earth Resources Report 29, Washington State Dept. of Natural Resources, Olympia, 1988.

p. 294: Royal Ontario Museum, Museums of Canada, Ottawa.

p. 298: Profile by M. Tsukada and S. Sugita, p. 8, from A. L. Washburn, "Mima mounds," Div. of Geology and Earth Resources Report 29, Washington State Dept. of Natural Resources, Olympia, 1988.

Chapter 8

p. 310: Prepared by Instructional Media Services,, Univ. of Washington.

p. 311: From original drafts by the author.

p. 316, *top*: From Arno and Hammerly, *Northwest Trees*, with permission of The Mountaineers, Seattle; left and bottom right: U.S. Forest Service.

p. 319, *right*: U.S. Forest Service, photo no. 000608.

p. 320: From *Douglasia Occasional Papers* no. 3, 1988.

p. 321: U.S. Forest Service.

p. 324: From Arno and Hammerly, *Northwest Trees*, with permission of The Mountaineers, Seattle.

p. 329: Washington State Historical Society, photo no. 21635.

p. 331, *top, far right*: Washington State Dept. of Wildlife.

p. 336, *bottom*: Washington State Historical Society, photo no. 56694.

p. 345, *bottom*: From Franklin and Dyrness, *Natural Vegetation of Oregon and Washington*, USFS PNW-8, 1973, p. 289.

Chapter 9

pp. 350, 353: Type prepared by Robert Hutchins.

p. 354: *The Seattle Times*, photo no. 2327, 1990.

p. 355: *Seattle Post-Intelligencer* Collection, photo no. 23094, February 30, 1934, Museum of History and Industry, Seattle.

p. 357: Appendix 12 of "Flood Control," *Comprehensive Study of Water and Related Land Resources*, Pacific Northwest River Basins Commission, 1970.

p. 358: From G. L. Bodhaine and W. H. Robinson, *Floods in Western Washington: Frequency and Magnitude in Relation to Drainage Basin Characteristics*, U.S. Geological Survey Circ. 191, 1952.

p. 360: *Seattle Post-Intelligencer* Collection, Jan. 25, 1956, Museum of History and Industry, Seattle.

p. 361: Special Collections Division, Univ. of Washington Libraries.

p. 367: From Franklin and Dyrness, *Natural Vegetation of Oregon and Washington*, USFS PNW-8, 1973, p. 100

p. 368: From *The Alpine Lakes Environmental Geology*, Dept. of Geological Sciences, Univ. of Washington, 1972.

p. 371: Adapted from F. Went, *The Plants*, Life Nature Library, 1963, p. 83; type prepared by Robert Hutchins.

pp. 374–75, *right*: U.S. Forest Service photo no. 460552, August 2, 1950; *center*: Water Pollution Control Admin., Dept. of the Interior, Washington, D.C.

p. 376: From J. Rothacher, C. T.Dyrness, and R. L. Fredrikson, *Hydrologic and Related Characteristics of Three Small Watersheds in the Oregon Cascades*. USFS Forest and Range Experiment Station, 1967.

p. 377: Washington State Dept. of Wildlife.

Chapter 10

pp. 382, 385, 386: Special Collections Division, Univ. of Washington Libraries, neg. nos. NA289, NA253, NA284.

p. 388: From H. C. Taylor, Jr., and G. F. Grabert, *Western Washington Indian Socio-Economics*, Western Washington Univ., 1984; cartography by R. O. Taylor and P. P. Erlandson, compiled by Herbert C. Taylor.

p. 390: Special Collections Division, Univ. of Washington Libraries, neg. no. NA342.

p. 391: Thomas Burke Memorial Washington State Museum, Seattle, neg. no. 2.5A489.

p. 392: Special Collections Division, Univ. of Washington Libraries.

pp. 394–95: Special Collections Division, Univ. of Washington Libraries.

pp. 396–97: Special Collections Division, Univ. of Washington Libraries.

p. 399: Thomas Burke Memorial Washington State Museum, Seattle.

p. 491: Special Collections Division, Univ. of Washington Libraries, neg. no. NA231.

p. 403: Special Collections Division, Univ. of Washington Libraries, neg. no. NA486.

Chapter 11

p. 405: *The Seattle Times*, July 8, 1983.

p. 409: Hunt Institute for Botanical Documentation, Carnegie Mellon Univ., Pittsburgh.

p. 410: U.S. National Archives Record Group 76.

p. 412, *top*: Special Collections Division, Univ. of Washington Libraries; bottom: Weyerhaeuser Company Corporate Photograph.

p. 415, *top*: Historical Society of Seattle and King County, neg. no. 9498; *bottom*: Washington Sea Grant Program, Univ. of Washington.

p. 417: Delano Horizons, Inc., Portland.

p. 418, *top*: Washington State Dept. of Ecology oblique aerial, June 25, 1977; *bottom*: Delano Horizons, Inc., Portland.

pp. 420–21: Walker and Associates, Seattle.

Index

Boldface numerals indicate illustrations. Common names of organisms are listed in the index.

About the author

Arthur R. Kruckeberg, a Northwest ecology specialist for forty years, is professor emeritus of botany at the University of Washington. He is the author of *Gardening with Native Plants of the Pacific Northwest* (Univ. of Washington Press, 1982), among other regional titles.